Missing the Meaning

Missing the Meaning

The Development and Use of Print and Nonprint Text Materials in Diverse School Settings

Edited by Alan Peacock and Ailie Cleghorn

MISSING THE MEANING

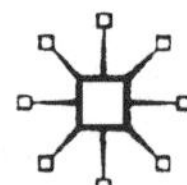

© Alan Peacock and Ailie Cleghorn, 2004

First published 2004 by
PALGRAVE MACMILLAN™
175 Fifth Avenue, New York, N.Y. 10010 and
Houndmills, Basingstoke, Hampshire, England RG21 6XS
Companies and representatives throughout the world

PALGRAVE MACMILLAN is the global academic imprint of the Palgrave Macmillan division of St. Martin's Press, LLC and of Palgrave Macmillan Ltd. Macmillan® is a registered trademark in the United States, United Kingdom and other countries. Palgrave is a registered trademark in the European Union and other countries.

ISBN 1–4039–6090–9 hardback
ISBN 1–4039–6091–7 paperback

Library of Congress Cataloging-in-Publication Data
    Missing the meaning : the development and use of print and non-print text materials in diverse school settings / edited by Alan Peacock and Ailie Cleghorn.
        p. cm.
    Includes bibliographical references and index.
    ISBN 1–4039–6090–9—ISBN 1–4039–6091–7 (pbk)
      1. Teaching—Aids and devices—Cross-cultural studies. 2. Science-Study and teaching (Elementary)—Cross-cultural studies. 3. Science—Textbooks—Cross-cultural studies. 4. Science—Computer-assisted instruction—Cross-cultural studies. I. Peacock, Alan, 1942– II. Cleghorn, Ailie, 1940–

LB1044.88.M57 2004
371.33—dc21   2003053597

A catalogue record for this book is available from the British Library.

Design by Newgen Imaging Systems (P) Ltd., Chennai, India.

First edition: February, 2004
10 9 8 7 6 5 4 3 2 1

Printed in the United States of America.

Contents

SECTION ONE
WHAT DO WE BELIEVE WE ARE DOING WITH TEXT-BASED AND
OTHER LEARNING MATERIALS?

SECTION TWO
WHY DO LEARNERS HAVE PROBLEMS WITH TEXT MATERIALS?

SECTION THREE
HOW CAN TEXT AND OTHER LEARNING MATERIALS BE BETTER MATCHED TO THE PRECONCEPTIONS, EXPECTATIONS, AND INCLINATIONS OF LEARNERS AND TEACHERS?

List of Figures

List of Tables

List of Contributors

Robertta H. Barba is Associate Professor at San Jose State University where she teaches graduate coursework in Instructional Technology, including: Introduction to Instructional Media, Advanced Computer Graphics, Interactive Instructional Video, Educational uses of HyperCard/Hyper Studio, Distance Education: Web-based Learning, Emerging Technologies, and Digital Photography for Educators. Dr. Barba received her B.S. and M.S. degrees at the University of Delaware and her Ph.D. degree at the Pennsylvania State University. She has previously held faculty positions at San Diego State University and the University of New Mexico. rbarba@email.sjsu.edu.

Ailie Cleghorn is Associate Professor in the Department of Education at Concordia University in Montreal. She teaches mainly graduate courses in the Educational Studies masters program. Her Ph.D. from McGill University is in Comparative Sociology of Education. She has carried out more than 15 years of qualitative studies in Kenya and in Zimbabwe primary schools, the focus of which is on the use of language for teaching science and mathematics in rural as well as urban classrooms. The results of these studies appear in several African and North American academic journals including the *Southern African Journal of Applied Language Studies, Comparative Education Review*, and *Qualitative Studies in Education*. ailie@education.concordia.ca.

Graham Cooper completed a Ph.D. in 1988 at the University of New South Wales (UNSW) in the areas of cognitive processes and instructional design. From 1989 to 1995 Graham worked within industry as an instructional designer for computer-based training projects involving the operation of complex equipment and systems (including submarines, underground mining, and heavy industry). Since 1996 Graham has been active in teaching and research associated with the application of cognitive processes to the design of educational multimedia and computer based training. He is currently a lecturer at Southern Cross University in instructional design for multimedia. gcooper@scu.edu.au.

Janet Donin is Associate Professor in the Department of Educational & Counselling Psychology and the Department of Integrated Studies in Education at McGill University, Montreal, Canada. She has published in the areas of discourse processing, text comprehension and production, and bilingual text processing. Currently she is studying scientific writing in both first and second languages. She is also involved in the development of computer tutoring environments that are based on the analysis of discourse within natural learning environments. janet.donin@mcgill.ca.

Simon Gates has a B.Sc. in Zoology from Liverpool University, United Kingdom, and subsequently gained an M.Sc. in Landscape Ecology Design and Management at Wye College, London University. He is currently completing his Ph.D. at the University of Exeter based on a study of teachers' understanding of diagrams in school Biology textbooks and national test papers. He has been Head of Science and Head of Biology in various secondary and further education colleges in the United Kingdom, including as a Lecturer at Yeovil College, Somerset, United Kingdom. Simon has written on the teaching of Biology as well as contributing to textbooks, and has carried out prior research into primary school teachers' use of science textbooks. S.M.G.Gates@exeter.ac.uk.

Thomas Hardy graduated from Cambridge University in 1971, and began teaching maths and science first in Nigeria and then in Jamaica. Returning to the United Kingdom in 1980 he joined Cambridge University Press as an editor, and has worked in educational publishing since then, producing Maths and Science courses for the U.K. market with CUP, Macmillan, and Thomas Nelson. He recently rejoined Macmillan as publisher for their international section, producing educational books for Africa and the Caribbean. He is interested in the tension between the commercial nature of publishing, and the public service of provision for education, which is embodied in educational publishing. t.hardy@macmillan.com.

Theresa A. Holleran is currently Associate Professor in the Division of Mathematics and Information Sciences at Ohio Dominican University. She is a Ph.D. candidate in Studies in Technologies of Instruction and Media at The Ohio State University. Her dissertation, expected to be completed in 2003 is on the use of strategies for the comprehension and retention of nonfiction text in computer environments. She holds an M.S. in Computer Science from Bowling Green State University and a B.S. in Mathematics from Ohio Dominican University. Her teaching and research interests include: computer languages, the effects of computer environments on the process of learning, and the effects of learning on computer environments. hollerat@ohiodominican.edu.

Wayne Leahy is a research fellow and tutor in the School of Education at the University of New South Wales, Sydney, Australia where he completed a Ph.D. in 2000. He also holds a Bachelor of Education from the University of South Australia and a Master's degree from Deakin University, Victoria. He taught for 16 years in Primary schools before moving into tertiary education. His research area is in cognitive processes and instruction with a main focus on "cognitive load theory." wmleahy@ bigpond.com.

Catherine C. Lewis is currently a senior research scientist at Mills College, principal investigator of the NSF-funded project, "Lesson Study: Case Studies of an Emerging Reform," and author of two studies of Japanese science textbooks published in *National Standards and School Reform* (Teachers College Press, 2002). Fluent in Japanese, she has conducted research in Japanese schools since 1979, and her writings and videotapes, including "Lesson Study: A Handbook of Teacher-Led Instructional Change" and "Can You Lift 100 Kilograms?" have introduced many U.S. educators to lesson study, the core form of professional development in Japan. A graduate of Harvard University (B.A.) and Stanford University (Ph.D.), she has authored more than 40 publications on elementary education and child development, including the award-winning book *Educating Hearts and Minds: Reflections on Japanese Preschool and Elementary Education* (Cambridge University Press, 1995). clewis@mills.edu.

Elizabeth H. McEneaney is Lecturer in the Department of Curriculum, Teaching, and Learning at the Ontario Institute of Studies in Education. She has a Ph.D. in sociology from Stanford University. Current research and teaching interests include globalization, the sociology of science and science education, and research methods. In addition, she is developing ways to assess urban reforms involving school choice from a geographical perspective. emcenean@csulb.edu.

Mirjamaija Mikkilä-Erdmann earned her doctorate in Educational Sciences from the University of Turku, Finland, in 2002. In addition to her Masters degree in Education, she also holds a postgraduate teaching certificate in German language. She is a member of the European Association for Research on Learning and Instruction. Her professional field of interest is learning from text and pictures, conceptual change, and the development of learning materials. While she is now living in Germany, she is also working as a researcher in the Department of Education in the University of Turku. mirmik@utu.fi.

Katrina Miller is Principal Lecturer in the School of Education, University of Brighton, United Kingdom. Having coordinated and taught Science Education across the School's initial teacher education programs for the past 10 years, she is now Course Leader for the School's M.A. Education progams. She tries to relate her science education experience and interest in history and philosophy of science to her teaching of research methodology. She is undertaking a Ph.D. project exploring the paradoxes for women becoming teachers of science in primary education from a feminist perspective. k.miller@bton.ac.uk.

Beatrice Murila is Lecturer at Kenyatta University, Kenya, in the department of communication skills in the School of Education and Human Resource Development. She holds a Bachelor of Education (hons) from the University of Nairobi, an M.Ed (TESOL) from the University of Manchester and an M.Phil. in education from the University of Exeter. Her research has focused on second-language issues in the areas of reading, writing, and teaching of science. She has also carried out evaluations of teaching materials in Kenyan public universities. susie@africaonline.co.ke.

P. Karen Murphy is Associate Professor at The Pennsylvania State University. Her teaching and research interests focus on the processes underpinning students' learning, and how cognition and motivation impact these processes. Her current research projects pertain to the impact of students' and teachers' knowledge, beliefs, and interest on learning, the impact of technology in text-based comprehension, and the role of group discussion in reading comprehension. Dr. Murphy serves on several editorial boards and has authored or coauthored numerous publications in outlets like the *Journal of Educational Psychology*, *Contemporary Educational Psychology*, and the *Educational Researcher*. pkm15@psu.edu.

Mitch O'Toole has long been involved in the preparation of resources for science teachers who have become conscious of the language component of their expectations of students at various levels of education. He is currently employed by the University of Newcastle, Australia, with responsibility for secondary science teacher preparation and postgraduate retraining, as well as the overall program of professional experience for secondary student teachers. Mitch's major research interests are in the impact of language style on science teaching and in the interaction between student and teacher understandings of the history and nature of science. He has published many articles in both national and international journals as well as textbooks and research-based teacher resource books for secondary science. Mitch.O'Toole@newcastle.edu.au.

Alan Peacock is Reader in Science Education at the School of Education and Lifelong Learning, University of Exeter, United Kingdom. His career spans teaching, training, research, and consultancy in African and South Asian countries as well as England, Scotland, and Northern Ireland and currently involves a study of science education in francophone Africa. He has researched and published widely on children's use of science text materials in developed and developing countries, and has written pupils' and teachers' primary science books for various countries in Africa, the Caribbean, and United Kingdom. He has recently completed the Tanzania Primary Science series, and a teachers' guide (*Teaching Primary Science*) for African states. a.peacock@exeter.ac.uk.

Jrene Rahm is Assistant Professor in Educational Psychology at the Université de Montréal. She is interested in the study of math and science learning in informal educational contexts such as after-school and youth programs pursued through in-depth qualitative case studies and discourse analysis. Her work also centers on how notions of subject matter contribute to or constrain learning and development. She teaches courses such as adolescent development and learning in the secondary teacher education program as well as graduate courses on sociocultural theory, discourse and learning, and learning outside of school. jrene.rahm@umontreal.ca.

Marissa Rollnick is the Director of an access program at the University of the Witwatersrand (Wits), where she teaches chemistry at the access level and science education at the postgraduate level. Her research interests include second-language learning of science and issues around access in science. Prior to teaching at Wits, she spent 15 years in Swaziland, both at a teachers' college and at the University of Swaziland. She holds a masters degree in chemical education from the University of East Anglia, United Kingdom and a Ph.D. in science education from Wits. marissa@aurum.chem.wits.ac.za.

Wolff-Michael Roth is Lansdowne Professor of Applied Cognitive Science at the University of Victoria. Having completed a M.Sc. in physics, he taught middle and high school science in several Canadian provinces. He received his Ph.D. for a study of learning to reason with ratios and proportions among adult students. Over the past decade, he studied how individuals know and learn science in a variety of settings, including formal educational settings (from elementary school to university) and everyday out-of-school settings (ecological fieldwork, experimental biology, hatchery operations, environmentalists). He also studied the processes of being and becoming a teacher. His publications include 10 books and over 210 journal articles and book chapters. mroth@uvic.ca.

Laura Smolkin is Associate Professor of Elementary Education in the University of Virginia's Curry School of Education. With an undergraduate degree in English and Linguistics and a doctorate in Language, Literature, and Reading, she has focused her research on text features and text use in various sociocultural contexts. Her published papers appear in journals such as Reading Research Quarterly and Research in the Teaching of English; her current research addresses comprehension of science trade books in primary grade classrooms. Professor Smolkin teaches courses in language and literacy education, including children's literature. lbs5z@virginia.edu.

John Sweller is a cognitive psychologist who is Professor of Education at the School of Education, University of New South Wales, Sydney, Australia. His major research and teaching interests are cognitive processes and instructional procedures. He and colleagues from around the globe have developed cognitive load theory, a theory designed to use relations between working and long-term memory to provide instructional design principles. Many such principles have been identified and tested using controlled experimental procedures. j.sweller@unsw.edu.au.

Sharon Walpole is Assistant Professor in the Department of Education at the University of Delaware. She earned her doctorate in Reading Education at the University of Virginia in 2000 with a focus on the characteristics of effective comprehension instruction across the elementary school years. She learned that teachers in effective schools teach comprehension in the context of interactive read-alouds, especially with information trade books. She is particularly interested in helping direct instructional change efforts by using school-level achievement data. swalpole@ udel.edu.

Preface

This book is about the problems and prospects relating to print and nonprint learning materials as they are developed and used primarily, but not only, in today's primary classrooms. Whilst the problems that we are concerned with may be found in the texts and other learning materials of most subject areas, the difficulties have been shown by studies carried out in the United Kingdom, United States, Canada, Japan, anglophone Africa and elsewhere, to be particularly acute in science, for teachers as well as for learners. Thus both the theoretical premises of this book as well as the practical examples will come from our own and our international group of contributors' experience, much of which is within the domain of science education. In this way we intend that this book will have wide appeal, both geographically and conceptually, with each section resonating with readers from all parts of the globe.

By texts and other learning materials we are referring first to school textbooks. Second we are referring to the learning materials that teachers often develop or adapt from the textbooks that are available, adaptations that are intended to meet the particular needs of students or simply to make sections of a textbook available due to general shortage of textbooks for all. Third, we include the new array of computer and Internet-generated materials such as CD-ROMs and web-based programs; these are making their way into regular classrooms as well as distance and open learning settings, even in rural communities where homes still lack electricity.

The reader will find in these chapters some common threads relating to the features of the various kinds of learning materials just mentioned as well as to the manner they are used in a wide range of school settings. The purposes of this book are thus not only to lay out a theoretical position and to describe a relatively well-known problem, but also to throw new light on that problem in ways that educators, policy makers, and publishers will sit up and pay attention to. The particular aims of this book are therefore:

> ➢ to highlight for educators the well-researched problems within print–based learning materials, the effects of these on the teaching–learning process and on learning in a wide range of school settings throughout the world;

> ➤ to alert educators to the nature of the changes in the Teacher–Learner–Text (TLT) relationship when shifts in types of learning materials take place and as educational systems move increasingly to the use of nonprint learning materials;
> ➤ to suggest ways in which both print and nonprint learning materials can be better matched to the preconceptions, worldviews and inclinations of diverse groups of learners and teachers in varied learning settings.

Several of the chapters in this book will refer to and elaborate on the ample evidence that learning materials pose many different kinds of problems. Briefly however, it is of note that a number of faulty assumptions underlie the development of learning materials: about learners, about learning, and about the ways in which text materials will be used by teachers and learners. With school systems everywhere looking to web-based sources of learning as a way to improve learning and to assist teachers, we feel it is critical to try to capture the essence of the mistakes that have become so embedded in the way print materials are developed, in order to avoid the same sorts of mistakes in the development of nonprint materials. Whilst we acknowledge that there are already significant differences in the two forms of learning materials, others who have carried out research on this topic confirm that many of the same kinds of faulty assumptions underlie both.

As co-editors of this book, we have asked ourselves if this book is really necessary and if it can have an impact. Will new text materials always look much like those of the past? Will publishers continue to publish only that which has been proven to sell? Will parents continue to demand that their children learn certain types of things in particular ways, from familiar looking texts? Will glossy materials, whether print or nonprint, always be assumed to teach better?

In the light of these questions, it may be risky and expensive (or less so!) to change the status quo, but developments in technology and communications are forcing the issue. Technological developments provide an opportunity to make changes that are not only technically feasible but also take account of the research evidence about the way knowledge is effectively structured and presented. In the end, we hope that this book will increase the potential for integration of the various dimensions of materials development, that is, those carried out by writers, curriculum specialists, illustrators, designers, product and marketing managers, all of which ideally should be informed by those who are most experienced in their use—the educators.

With the proliferation of nonprint text materials in schools, in distance learning and nonformal learning situations throughout the world, it has become urgent that we understand better what the problems are and have been with print-based materials. There is a high risk that the same mistakes will be repeated in simply more eye-catching ways; the promise that nonprint, web-based learning materials are going to make teaching and learning easier sounds like the start of a new myth. Therefore at the core of this book is a reexamination of the traditional Teacher–Learner–Text (TLT) relationship to see in what ways we can inform the evolving TLT relationship as a means to more effective design and use of text material. It is well to remember for example, that one does not have to go to open or distance learning situations to see the TLT relationship take a sharp turn when the use of materials in a classroom shifts from print to nonprint, yet there has been little research as yet on this very topic.

This book is written for teachers, teacher educators, student teachers, curriculum developers, education policy makers, and publishers of educational learning materials. It could serve as a main or supplementary text in teacher preparation courses and in the study of curriculum theory, science education, learning theory, and classroom processes. Its critical perspective also makes it suitable for interdisciplinary courses in Educational Studies programs.

The reader will find the three main sections of the book to be thematically connected rather than a selection of loosely related chapters. Each section will be introduced by the coeditors, Alan Peacock and/or Ailie Cleghorn. Within each section there are four or five chapters written by different experts in the field. Each section then ends with a summary overview, written by a notable academic with wide-ranging experience of the topic.

The three sections of the book address past development, current problems and future directions. The first section begins with the question: *What do we believe we are doing with both print and nonprint texts?* This section presents three theoretical perspectives, sociological, psychological, and sociocultural, to review how the textbook industry evolved worldwide and how we came to hold the assumptions that we do. The authors of these three chapters, Betsy McEneaney, Janet Donin, and Jrene Rahm, examine the dominant thinking about how children learn from text materials and how this is reflected in existing forms of materials, both print and nonprint. Catherine Lewis (Mills College, California) provides the overview of this section, referring as she does so to her research on Japanese texts and classrooms.

Following from this analysis, the second section asks *why learners have problems with text materials.* It outlines the nature of those problems particularly as they are nested within the TLT relationship. The authors of this section are Tom Hardy, Wayne Leahy with Graham Cooper and John Sweller, Marissa Rollnick, Beatric Murila, Karen Murphy with Theresa Holleran, and Tom Hardy. They describe the many sources of constraint on the effective development and use of text materials, including globalization of the textbook industry, and other constraints stemming from publishers, traditions of design and the resurgence of concern with standards and testing regimes. The overview of this section is by Mitch O'Toole (University of Newcastle, Australia).

The third section looks at future prospects. That is, we ask *how the intentions of text materials can be better matched with the preconceptions, expectations, and inclinations of learners and teachers.* In this, the overall concern of the authors—Sharon Walpole, Katrina Miller with Alan Peacock, Simon Gates, and Robertta Barba—is with making the lives of teachers easier and with increasing learners' access to the content of both print and nonprint materials. To this end, one avenue of discussion centers on how the TLT relationship operates in varied ways in traditional as well as nontraditional teaching–learning situations. The section ends with an overview by Wolff-Michael Roth (University of Victoria, Canada).

Acknowledgments

Busy academics do not assemble such complex compilations as this one without a great deal of cooperation, and we therefore owe our thanks to many people. The list of acknowledgments goes back many years; in a way, they tell the story of how this book came about.

In the mid-1980s, Ailie carried out an ethnographic study of language use in rural and urban primary classrooms in Kenya, funded by the Social Sciences and Humanities Research Council of Canada (SSHRC). This study eventually focused on language use in the teaching of science. A later study carried out in the 1990s in Zimbabwe was also funded by SSHRC and built in a research component to a link between Concordia University and the University of Zimbabwe that was funded by the Canadian International Development Agency (CIDA). In addition to these grants, generous internal support was received from Concordia University as well as from Concordia's Dean of Arts and Science International Initiatives Fund. Without these grants the research would not have been done, coauthored articles would not have been written and this book would not have happened.

Meanwhile in the early 1980s, Alan was training teachers in Kenya and developing science materials for their primary schools at the invitation of John Aldridge of Macmillan publishers, inspired by the "Beginning Science" books of Alex Berluti. Alan went on in the 1990s to work closely with the Handspring Trust in South Africa, evaluating the implementation of their innovative and unique "Spider's Place" science comics and videos for children. The South African links were probably crucial in what followed. There were, first, the insights and encouragement of Handspring's Michael Kahn, Basil Jones, and Peter Esterhuizen; then the contacts with Carol Macdonald and her colleagues within the Threshold Project, often aided by Peter Glover, Director of the Primary Science Programme, who helped with funds to oil the wheels of collaboration. The inspiration and enthusiasm of our South African colleagues were perhaps the biggest stimulus to our research in this field, which came together when Alan came across an article of Ailie's that appeared in *The Comparative Education Review*.

Following initial contact by e-mail, which helped us ascertain that we were both on the same track, it seemed fitting that we should produce jointly written articles and presentations in South Africa for conferences of the Southern African Association for

Research on Mathematics, Science and Technology Education (SAARMTSE). These led eventually to a formal link being established between the University of Exeter and Concordia University under the British Council U.K./Canada Collaborative Links Programme. Without the grants from British Council this book would not have been written: the grant provided travel funds to allow for two face-to-face meetings a year for three years, and it was early during these meetings that talk of a book emerged. So a very special thank you goes to Sarah Dawbarn, British Council Director Montreal, who went out of her way several years in a row to help us secure continuing funds.

We need above all to thank our contributors, busy as they are, for delivering their chapters quickly and for being ready and willing to follow suggestions regarding amendments that would help the book cohere. At Concordia, doctoral students Annie Potter and Mariam Kakkar helped to format the chapters consistently and in conformity with APA style. Finally, we are grateful to both Tom Hardy at Macmillan United Kingdom, and Amanda Johnson at Palgrave, for their own encouragement and enthusiasm about the book. To plagiarize T.S. Eliot, from whom our title derives, we hope you will have the experience but *not* miss the meaning.

Section One

What Do We Believe We are Doing
with Text-Based and Other
Learning Materials?

1

Introduction

Ailie Cleghorn and Alan Peacock

This first section of *Missing the Meaning* sets out three theoretical perspectives—sociological, psychological, and sociocultural—that may be used to address the question, "What do we believe we are doing with text-based and other learning materials?" While there are some strong hints of answers coming from a number of studies, we do not expect to arrive at any definitive answers in a single book. The aim therefore of this section is to prod the reader into thinking more about this question so that little by little a fuller understanding for teachers, educators, policy makers, and publishers may be achieved.

Most of the existing research takes *either* a psychological (and cognitive) approach *or* a social (sociological or sociocultural) approach to questions relating to textbooks and other learning materials; few studies span or integrate the cognitive with the social. Thus with the cognitive approach we see text materials and/or the individual learner as the unit of analysis. With the social approaches, the analysis of text materials and their use normally flows from a large- to mid-scale societal, cultural, or classroom context. The methodological stance in the former tends to be experimental and de-contextualized while the methodological stance in the latter is more often qualitative, interpretive and thus contextualized, having been carried out in naturalistic settings. Each of these perspectives will be elaborated in the three chapters of this section of the book, however, they will also be found at the basis of most of the subsequent chapters. First, however, some definitions are in order. In the following pages we outline the sociological, psychological and sociocultural perspectives, in particular as they are used in studies relating to textbooks and other learning materials. Then we discuss the need for more studies that integrate these perspectives.

SOCIOLOGICAL PERSPECTIVE

Educational sociologists are interested in a wide range of issues, all of which touch directly or indirectly on what it is we think we are doing in classrooms with texts and other learning materials. The sociological perspective thus nests learning materials and their use within the complex of interrelated variables that are involved in the processes of schooling.

At the level of the relationship between schooling and society at large, sociologists of education explore questions relating to the manifest and latent functions of schooling. They ask about the nature of contradictions between the stated aims of an education system and actual practice and how this relates to maintenance or change within the existing social structure. They ask who decides what is and what is not to be included in the curriculum and whose interests are served by the school system and its established curriculum. (Aronowitz & Giroux, 1993; Bourdieu & Passeron, 1977; Hawes, 1979; Mifflen & Mifflen, 1982).

At the level of the school, educational sociologists ask questions about the form and climate of social control, and about the relations between the groups within the school. For example, issues relating to gender, ethnicity, race, religion, social class are seen as possible sources of marginalization in the teaching–learning process and are at the basis of many studies in multicultural and other diverse school settings. Studies that focus on teachers and teacher groups form another line of research (Cleghorn & Genesee, 1984; Jackson, 1968; Lortie, 2002; Martin & MacDonnell, 1978).

At the micro-level of the classroom sociologists ask the following types of questions. How are classes organized for learning, for example, ability groups, cooperative learning, direct instruction? What is the pedagogical emphasis, for example, oral, reading, writing, rote question-answer routines? What is the official language of instruction and does that differ from the learners' home language (L1)? Does the teacher share the same L1 as some or all of the learners? If so, is that language used at all during instruction, informally or otherwise? Do the textbooks and other learning materials appear in the learners' L1? How do teachers use textbook and other materials when working with the whole class, with small groups, with individuals? That is, what is the nature of the teacher–learner–text (TLT) relationship within the classroom and which side of the triangle sees the most interaction? (Apple & Christian-Smith, 1991; see several chapters in this book).

Betsy McEneaney (chapter 2) takes a sociological approach to examine the construction of school science. In this she talks about how every school program has to present itself as global (and thus "modern") while attending to local and national needs, pressures that are reflected in print and nonprint curricular materials. Her discussion includes an historical analysis of textbooks and other print materials used in Ontario since World War II, showing how school science is portrayed as Canadian within a global context. In doing so she highlights the current role of international organizations and publishing houses in applying pressure to "internationalize" curricula, thereby supporting the now global textbook industry.

Psychological Perspective

When questions such as the one we pose at the start of this section are addressed by psychologists, a cognitive and experimental approach is most likely to be used. Cognitive psychology looks at textbooks and other learning materials and their use in terms of the ways that information is represented in written, graphic, or pictorial form, and the correlation of that representation to learning. The focus is on how text materials do or do not promote comprehension in the individual learner. In this, the social context of instruction may be peripheral with attention being noted of students' social class, gender, race, and language as background variables. In our opinion it may be the dominance of this theoretical position in education that is responsible for the unitary but generalized and deficit view of the learner that seems to govern the minds of many textbook publishers.

Cognitive psychologists are mainly concerned with the nature of learning and its components. For example, they ask what are the stages in human cognitive development, that is, what is the human capable of learning at different stages of life? To this they add what are the roles of seeing, listening, speaking, reading, writing in the learning process? With specific regard to text materials they are interested in the range of types of text material available for teaching and learning and in this they include oral text, written text, diagrams, and other visual representations of everyday life and of ideas. Psychologists are also interested in the conceptions of knowledge that are embedded in print and nonprint text materials, and in the kinds of text materials that best promote learning at different stages of development. They want to know what learners perceive when they confront different types of text and what the role is of short-term and long-term memory in the processing of information from different kinds of text, for example, print and nonprint. Within the classroom they are most concerned with identifying the kinds of learning conditions in which text materials best promote learning, for instance, open-structured classrooms, closed classrooms, whole group, cooperative learning groups, individual instruction.

Recent work by cognitive psychologists has centered on how humans link prior knowledge to new understandings. In this, several studies have sought to classify and categorize text materials as having the purpose and capacity to inform, to argue or to explain (Kintsch, 1998). Others have built upon the work of Tufte (1990) to display in graphic form such relationships as cause–effect, sequence, compare and contrast, addressing a central concern of this book, which is to identify problems that are common to word-based and visual text learning materials. For example, a series of studies carried out in Finland (Mikkilä & Olkinuora, 1994) explored two questions: whether conceptions of knowledge now held by cognitive psychologists are reflected in current textbooks, and how students of varying abilities process standard textbooks. Underlying these questions is a critical look at the actual role of textbooks in the learning process, their importance being a taken-for-granted assumption by many educators and researchers alike. The research by Mikkilä and Olkinuora points to the limitations of textbooks and other learning materials in both individual and classroom learning contexts.

Janet Donin (chapter 3) complements and builds further on the just-mentioned studies by using a cognitive-psychological approach to present a multilayered model of text processing, drawing on the implications of this model for the use of text materials in classroom contexts. She discusses learning from oral and written text to show comprehension not as a receptive process but as an active one in which meaning is the representation of the text that the reader or listener constructs. In this way her chapter makes an important link to the social context of instruction.

Sociocultural Perspective

The sociocultural perspective finds its roots in the field of social anthropology and the study of culture. For our purposes here culture is defined as all those ways of thinking, speaking, seeing, believing and doing that characterize the members of a social group (Geertz, 1975). This definition thus includes the ways in which the members of a social group arrive at shared meanings of events. A social group can be an entire society, a group of students within a classroom, a subgroup within that classroom, or a group of students learning in an alternative, nonformal context with alternative texts. This perspective therefore allows for a direct observational focus on the culture of teaching and learning, for the creation of fine-grained, thick descriptions of events as they take place in formal and nonformal teaching–learning settings (LeCompte & Preissle, 1993).

In response to the question that this section of the book poses, "What do we think we are doing with text-based and other learning materials," a sociocultural perspective allows for phenomenological insight, that is, for obtaining teachers' and learners' perceptions of the meaning of text materials and their use. This kind of insight is critical for explaining patterns of achievement that vary by such variables as race or religion, as well as for throwing light on the learning-limiting effects of an imposed curriculum in a still-developing country, for instance.

The kinds of questions that are asked by researchers who hold to a sociocultural perspective are many. As in the case of the sociological perspective described earlier, studies that are carried out from this perspective ask questions that tend to move from the large in scale (macro) to the smaller in scale (micro) as a study progresses. Such studies are generally qualitative, interpretive and theory building, rather than theory testing. Drawing from the work of Gee (1990), Lave and Wenger (1991), Hawkins and Pea (1987), and others, the following typify the kinds of questions asked from the sociocultural point of view.

Again, starting at a general level and with questions that are particularly relevant in diverse school settings, we ask what are the characteristics of the culture of the community in which a school is located? Does the culture of the school reflect that of the surrounding community? Are the particular norms for talking, thinking and behaving within a community at odds in any way with those that prevail within the school or in the classroom? More specifically for example, to what extent do school-based norms promote individualism and competition rather than communal norms and a social construction of knowledge that is in accord with local ways of knowing?

Next, it may be asked if the classroom community is the predominant community of practice in which students participate, can the culture of specific subject domains be created in a classroom while teaching that subject, for example history, science? To elaborate, when the professional norms of a particular discipline such as science need to be taught as part of what students need to know about doing science, to what extent do those norms contradict, say, the spiritual beliefs of the student group? (Clark & Ramahlape, 1999; Shumba, 1999b). And with specific attention to teachers and students, it is important to ask what is the significance of written materials and books within the teachers' and learners' home culture and what strategies teachers use to interpret second language (L2) text materials to learners? Finally, what might students have to give up in terms of experience, values, status, and power in relation to their peers in order to attend to the knowledge that is being offered them? Stated differently, what risks to identity—ethnic, family, peer group, personal—are involved in doing well in school?

The sociocultural/anthropological approach allows for many different kinds of insights. For example, people's beliefs about text use may be understood in terms of the community's norms governing thinking, talking, acting, and reading. Understanding can be gained of mis-communications as well as the misinterpretation of text materials when those materials contain visual symbols and ideas that are foreign and unfamiliar, not only to the students but sometimes to the teacher as well. And, insight into the norms governing the particular community of text use practice that students are being socialized into can help us further understand how the use of learning materials links to the social and collective construction of knowledge.

Jrene Rahm (chapter 4) provides a sociocultural view of the role that alternatives to textbooks and other learning materials may play in the teaching–learning process, especially in nonformal teaching–learning situations. The chapter illustrates the close connection between the TLT and the notion of border crossing, illuminating how "other culture" students require explicit help in crossing the cultural, conceptual, and/ or linguistic borders that they encounter through text materials and in other ways, in school (Jegede & Aikenhead, 1996). Thus this chapter expands on the ideas stemming from the work of Vygotsky and others to show how, in order to make the necessary cognitive connections, the teacher needs to play the role of culture broker, helping the learner to cross from the culture of the home community to the culture and language of schooling.

The Need for an Integrated Theoretical Approach

However valuable the above perspectives might be, none of them in isolation can provide a full understanding of the complexity of text use and learning from text in authentic classroom contexts. Yet relatively few studies stand as examples of a systematically integrated theoretical approach to the question that this section asks, *What do we believe we are doing with text-based and other learning materials?*

Much of our own thinking about text materials and their use comes from our research on primary science education in second language, developing country school settings (Cleghorn, 1992; Cleghorn, Merritt, & Abagi, 1989; Cleghorn, Mtetwa, Dube, & Munetsi, 1998; Cleghorn & Shumba, 2001; Peacock, 1995; Peacock, Cleghorn, & Mikkila, 2002;). Science education (including environmental education) in such settings provides a window for observing the manner in which the use of text materials, culturally unfamiliar concepts, and language use, interact within the teacher–learner–text relationship. While mainly social in perspective (sociological or sociocultural), the ultimate concern of these studies is cognitive—that is, to find ways to promote learning. To this end these studies are a start at integrating the theoretical approaches discussed earlier.

Language of Text Materials, Language and Culture of Learners

Peacock, Cleghorn and Mikkilä (2002) (see also chapter 13) identified some of the attitudes that appear to underlie the production of text materials. An analysis of text materials used in second-language school settings showed that they are often written *as if* the readers are first-language speakers of the language that the text is written in. The fact that the vast majority of the world's children are learning via a language they do not use at home appears irrelevant. This observation suggests the presence of a widespread deficit view toward learners as a-cultural, empty vessels. This unitary view of the learner reinforces the tendency for text materials to be developed as if "one size fits all", and thus to be mass produced.

Peacock et al. further observe how frequently classroom-based research makes little mention of the content of the text materials in use, nor of how they are used, yet textbooks and other materials are considered central to the teaching–learning process. This is evidenced by the fact that when textbooks and other materials are in short supply, as in many still-developing countries, the education system is quickly regarded by the international community as impoverished, if not inadequate (Heyneman & Jamison, 1980; Lockheed & Verspoor, 1991). When text materials are in short supply, inappropriate materials may be considered to be better than none.

If it is the case that such attitudes do tend to underlie the production and dissemination of text materials, then it is critically important to find out what teachers believe about text materials and their use. If the content is culturally unfamiliar, then those materials need a different kind of use with learners than otherwise is the case. And under these circumstances teachers need a different kind of training. These were some of the issues explored in Zimbabwe by Shumba (2000) and Shumba and Cleghorn (2002).

Beginning in 1994, substantial changes were incorporated into preservice courses in order to help Zimbabwe's teachers to reorient themselves from the Science Education curriculum to Environmental Science (Shumba, 2000). Implicit within the new curriculum was the need for teachers to adopt different attitudes toward the curriculum material, and to use textbooks and other materials in new ways, in effect changing their methods of teaching. The question arose as to the extent that teachers were aware of these new demands on their teaching skills. A study was thus carried out to determine if preservice teachers who were near the end of their training held attitudes toward Environmental Science and the use of science text materials that were dovetailed to the new curriculum. The findings were mixed, showing that teachers were operating in the face of conflicting societal and professional norms. On the one hand they expressed very open attitudes toward the value of hands-on activity for learning Environmental Science, on the other hand they did not think it was important for children to ask questions. In many traditional African cultures observation and imitation are most valued for learning while questions from young people to adults in authority are often discouraged since they may be seen as a challenge to that authority. The findings seemed to confirm those of others, which indicate that teachers who hold rigid beliefs about science, for example that it is culture free or value free, are likely not to engage in much cultural interpretation of text materials to learners, but rather accept the U.S. or U.K. values that the texts portray (Haney, Czerniak, & Lumpe, 1996; Lumpe, Haney, & Czerniak, 1998; Lynch, 1997).

As the last section of this book will elaborate further, findings such as those just mentioned underline the need for teachers to mediate students' cultural expectations, their prior knowledge and their beliefs about the nature of phenomena whilst taking cognizance of the practices of the science community. In order to take on the added role as bridges between academic content and students' home cultures, teachers need to be aware of the ways in which their own culture and language backgrounds intersect with their beliefs about teaching and about the use of textbooks and other learning materials (Aikenhead & Huntley, 1999; Aikenhead & Jegede, 1999; Cobern, 1993, 1996; Fradd & Lee, 1999).

Cross-cultural, crosslinguistic problems relating to the use of text materials are not particular to developing country school settings. In diversely populated classrooms of North America and Europe, text materials may also be used in ways that are not helpful to second-language learners; recommendations for their use tend to be exported along with the texts, in the form of teachers' guides that are often also developed from the unitary kind of perspective mentioned above. Peacock (1995) found that the expository nature of science text made it inaccessible to young second-language learners and that illustrations did not help since their conventions were so rooted in an assumed understanding of Western symbols. This tendency may be increasing with the globalization of the text book industry, with an increase in Internet-like visual formats and an assumed culturally free subjectivity of the reader (McEneaney, 2000).

While the visual aspects of text materials will be discussed in section three, Clark's (1997) studies in South Africa and Shumba's (1999a,b) in Zimbabwe demonstrate the interaction between visual symbols, culture, and teachers' use of language during instruction. Clark found that it was not just the technical terms that posed difficulty for students but, like Peacock (1995), found that everyday words such as *describe* and *observe* caused confusion. In this vein, Shumba observed teachers' difficulty in explaining the concept *transparent* of which there is no direct translation in Shona, the local language. In an effort to get the idea across teachers used the Shona word for *white*. While sometimes resulting in factual inaccuracies, other studies have suggested that code switching has the potential of making sense of the cultural non-sense that text materials sometimes present to learners (Clark, 1997; Cleghorn & Rollnick, 2002; Dube & Cleghorn, 1999; Scott, 1998).

Schooling and learning can be seen not only in terms of acquisition of knowledge (whose knowledge?) but also as a form of assimilation into a global culture—a new way of thinking, believing, seeing, and doing. Similarly, if the language of the home community for so many in the Majority world differs from the language of schooling, then schooling can be seen as a process of crossing linguistic borders, from the L1 to what is in many cases a dominant use of the L2. At the risk of being simplistic, it may be that an integrated approach to our question requires that researchers not only think in terms of linking new knowledge with students' prior knowledge but also with their "prior" language and "prior" culture.

References

Aikenhead, G.S. & Huntley
(1999). Teachers' views on Aboriginal students learning western and Aboriginal science. *Canadian Journal of Native Education, 23* (2), 159–175.

Aikenhead, G.S. & Jegede, O.J.
(1999). Cross-cultural science education: A cognitive explanation of a cultural phenomenon. *Journal of Research in Science Teaching, 36* (3), 269–288.

Apple, M.W. & Christian-Smith, L.K. (Eds.)
(1991). *The politics of the textbook*. New York: Routledge.

Aronowitz, S. & Giroux, H.
(1993). *Education still under siege*. New York: Bergin & Garvey.

Bourdieu, P. & Passeron, J.C.
(1977). *Reproduction in education: Society and culture*. California: Sage.

Clark, J.
(1997). Beyond the turgid soil of science prose: STAP's attempt to write more accessible science text materials in general science. *Proceedings of the 5th annual Meeting of the Southern African Association for Research in Science and Mathematics Education*, Johannesburg, 390–396.

Clark, J. & Ramahlape, K.
(1999). Crackles and sparks: Stepping out of the world of lightning with the 'Science Through Applications Project' (STAP). In J. Kuiper (Ed.), *Proceedings of the 7th annual conference, Southern African Association for Research in Mathematics and Science Education*, January, Harare, 110–120.

Cleghorn, A.
(1992). Primary level science in Kenya: Constructing meaning through English and indigenous languages. *International Journal of Qualitative Studies in Education, 5*(4), 311–323.

Cleghorn, A. & Genesee, F.
(1984). Languages in contact: an ethnographic study of interaction in an immersion school. *TESOL Quarterly, 18* (4), 595–625.

Cleghorn, A. & Rollnick, M.
(2002). The role of English in individual and societal development: A view from African classrooms. *TESOL Quarterly, 36*(3), 347–372.

Cleghorn, A. & Shumba, O.
(2001). Prospective teachers' views of science and science education for children: Cross-national comparisons. Paper presented at the Comparative and International Education Society Conference, Washington, D.C.

Cleghorn, A., Merritt, M., & Abagi, J.O.
(1989). Language policy and science instruction in Kenya. *Comparative Education Review, 33* (1), 21–39.

Cleghorn, A., Mtetwa, D., Dube, R., & Munetsi, C.
(1998). Classroom language use in multilingual settings: mathematics lessons from Quebec and Zimbabwe. *International Journal of Qualitative Studies in Education, 11* (3), 463–477.

Cobern, W.W.
(1993). A co-operative research group for the study of culture and science education. Paper presented at the UNESCO International Conference on Science Education in Developing Countries, January, Jerusalem, Israel.

Cobern, W.W.
(1996). Constructivism and non-western science education research. *International Journal of Science Education, 18* (3), 295–310.

Dube, R. & Cleghorn, A.
(1999). Code switching in mathematics lessons in Zimbabwe. *Zimbabwe Journal of Educational Research, 11* (1), 1–12.

Fradd, S. & Lee, O.
(1999). Teachers' roles in promoting science inquiry with students from diverse language backgrounds. *Educational Researcher, August–September,* 14–20.

Gee, J.P.
(1990). *Social linguistics and literacies: Ideology in discourses.* London: Falmer.

Geertz, C. (Ed.)
(1975) *The interpretation of cultures.* New York: Basic Books.

Haney, J.J., Czerniak , C.M., & Lumpe, A.T.
(1996). Teacher beliefs and intentions regarding the implementation of science education reform strands. *Journal of Research in Science Teaching, 33* (9), 971–993.

Hawes, H.
(1979). *Curriculum and reality in African primary schools.* Essex, UK: Longman.

Hawkins, J. & Pea, R.D.
(1987). Tools for bridging the cultures of everyday and scientific thinking. *Journal of Research in Science Teaching, 24,* 291–308.

Heyneman, S. & Jamison, D.
(1980). Student learning in Uganda: Textbook availability and other factors. *Comparative Education Review, 20* (2), 206–220.

Jackson, P.
(1968). *Life in classrooms.* New York: Holt, Rinehart & Winston.

Jegede, O. & Aikenhead, G.
(1996). Transcending cultural borders: Implications for science teaching. Proceedings of the STS conference, Tokyo, 64–73.

Kintsch, W.
(1998). *Comprehension: A paradigm for cognition.* Cambridge: Cambridge University Press.

Lave, J. & Wenger, E.
(1991). *Situated learning: legitimate peripheral participation.* New York: Cambridge University Press.

LeCompte, M.D. & Preissle, J.
(1993). *Ethnography and qualitative design in educational research.* New York: Academic Press.

Lockheed, M. & Verspoor, A.
(1991). *Improving primary education in developing countries.* New York: Oxford University Press.

Lortie, D.
(2002). Schoolteacher: A sociological study. Chicago: Chicago University Press.

Lumpe, A.T., Haney, J.J. & Czerniak, C.M.
(1998). Science teacher beliefs and intentions to implement Science-Technology-Society (STS) in the classroom. *Journal of Science Teacher Education, 9* (1), 1–24.

Lynch, S.
(1997). Novice teachers' encounter with national science education reform: Entanglements or intelligent interconnections? *Journal of Research in Science Teaching, 34* (9), 3–17.

McEneaney, E.H.
(2000). Models of science, experts, and nature: A view from primary school textbooks. Paper presented at the Comparative and International Education Society conference, San Antonio, March.

Martin, W.B.W. & MacDonnell, A.
(1978). *Canadian education.* Toronto: Prentice Hall.

Mifflen, F.S. & Mifflen, S.C.
(1982). *The sociology of education: Canada and beyond.* Calgary: Detselig.

Mikkilä, M. & Olkinuora, E.
(1994). Problems of current textbooks and workbooks: Do they promote high-quality learning? In DeJong and Van Hout-Wolters (Eds.), *Process oriented instruction and learning from text.* Amsterdam, VU University Press.

Peacock, A.
(1995). An agenda for research on text material in primary science for second-language learners of English in developing countries. *Journal of Multilingual and Multicultural Development, 16* (5), 389–402.

Peacock, A., Cleghorn, A. & Mikkilä, M.
(2002). Multiple perspectives on the teacher–learner–text relationship in primary school science. *Curriculum and Teaching, 17* (2), 55–72.

Scott, P.
(1998). Teacher talk and meaning making in science classrooms: A Vygotskian analysis and review. *Studies in Science Education, 32*, 45–80.

Shumba, O.
(1999a). Relationship between secondary science teachers' orientation to traditional culture and beliefs concerning science instructional ideology. *Journal of Research in Science Teaching, 36* (3), 333–355.

Shumba, O.
(1999b). Critically interrogating the rationality of western science vis a vis scientific literacy in non-western developing countries. *Zambezia, XXVI, 1*, 55–75.

Shumba, O.
(2000). *Monitoring and evaluation findings on the Better Environmental Science Teaching Programme (BEST) in primary schools and teacher training colleges in Zimbabwe.* Curriculum Development Unit (CDU) and Technical Co-operation of Germany (GTZ): Harare.

Shumba, O. & Cleghorn, A.
(2002). Prospective teachers' views about science education for children: Some insights from Zimbabwe. Under review.

Tufte, E.R.
(1990). *Envisioning information.* Cheshire, CT: Graphics Press.

2

The Global and the Local in the Construction of School Science: The Case of Canada

Elizabeth H. McEneaney

In this chapter, I examine both the global and local influences in the construction of the elementary school subject of science, focusing on the case of Canada since the 1950s. Using a neo-institutionalist theoretical framework, I argue that legitimate science curricula must be both global and local, and these pressures are manifested in curricular materials such as school textbooks. In the first section, I give a brief overview, sociological in perspective, of the various functions of official learning materials such as textbooks. I then turn to a discussion of neo-institutional theory, specifically as it applies to science and education as global cultural frames. The role of international organizations and international testing regimes to promote global standards and expectations about elementary school science is explained. I then describe ways in which science has been constructed to reflect local culture. For the purpose of this essay, local is taken to mean "national" as opposed to global or transnational influence.

Building on this general discussion, I will present an empirical analysis of how these processes play out (or fail to play out) in a historical sample of elementary textbooks published in Canada for use in Canadian schools since the 1950s. How is school science presented as both in line with global norms but also, somehow, distinctively Canadian? How does this change over time? The historical patterns seen in the development of Canadian school science may be instructive as we consider the impact of globalization not only economically, but also culturally in the form of mass education.

THEORETICAL BACKGROUND

The Functions of Official Learning Materials

Officially sanctioned learning materials serve the varied purposes of schooling in several ways. In general, we educationists hope that such print and nonprint materials effectively convey to students the subject knowledge that has been deemed as core and essential. Historically, learning materials may be intended to serve as the authoritative and central source of expertise in a classroom (as in the "teacher-proof" curriculum), or they may be intended as a complement to expertise that already resides in the classroom—in the teacher or in the students or both. In either case one function of these materials is that they help students learn the subject matter. Understandably, researchers in all corners of the world exert quite some effort to evaluate and improve the effectiveness of learning materials along this dimension, often using sophisticated mathematical techniques to estimate the degree of improvement on mean test scores that the use of one type of textbook or website produces relative to another. Some of the work in this book attends to this important issue.

In addition to this manifest function of learning materials, however, are latent functions that are subject to careful consideration only in isolated pockets of the world of educational research. From a critical theory perspective, the learning materials widely used in schools much more often than not have served to socialize children into starkly unequal social hierarchies, usually mirroring discriminatory practices and structures in the classroom and school. For most of the twentieth century in European and North American mass education systems, for example, students quite plausibly learned from approved curricular materials that people of color as well as white women had no serious place in the world of science. Too often, there was nothing in the usual classroom dynamics to counteract the conclusion any student might reach through their exposure to these learning materials.

Another latent function of official learning materials, related to the maintenance of social hierarchies, has to do with commemoration. Official learning materials enshrine not only what knowledge is deemed to be of most worth (Apple, 1988) but also idealized visions of children as learners as well as the role of the subject area and discipline. This is particularly true for media that are both long-lasting and portable enough to be easily displayed for public review (e.g., textbooks). In their symbolic role, textbooks are "the visible manifestation of the school's beliefs and intentions, an open script that can be scrutinized by different segments of society" (Venezky, 1992, p. 436). In this way, textbooks are like museums. Like museums, they are public displays of knowledge, with similar manifest educational functions. While museums have shifted from "glass-cased," curatorial organizations of knowledge (Macdonald, 1998) toward much more "interactive" styles of presentation (Barry, 1998), so too have textbooks been transformed historically. In science, for example, school textbooks have shifted from Audobon-style collections of specimens (e.g., of flora, fauna, minerals, or machines) to often lush fusions of text and image designed to entice the student reader into a kind of dialogue with the material in which students are prompted for their opinions and feelings (McEneaney, 1998). Barry describes the contemporary highly interactive museum as enabling visitors to "make choices and to experience [the exhibits] 'in their own way.'" New and recent textbooks from many countries also have this quality.

The idealized nature of the content in official learning materials is reflected in the notion of the "textbook case." The phrase describes a rare instance of reality approaching a pure vision, without complications. In other words, the textbook case is like Max Weber's concept of the ideal type. Furthermore, it is much easier culturally to commemorate than to discredit, and so textbooks and core materials have tended to become longer and more elaborate over time.[1] Localized conflicts about particular aspects of textbooks and other learning materials (such as the battle over evolution in a few areas of the United States) are fueled with an emotion that goes beyond concern for student learning and into the legacy of commemoration, much like conflicts over museum exhibits or public memorials. The usual solution to such conflicts in contemporary liberal democracies is to relent to some type of commemoration and official inclusion rather than to exclude, and it is easy to see this development in textbooks as well.

A powerful symbolic function of textbooks—common to virtually all educational systems, the wealthy and the impoverished—is that they signal to the rest of the world that a nation has a "state of the art" approach to mass education. This process of signaling is especially important in terms of attracting foreign investment, crucially so in less developed countries but also in small, relatively wealthier nations like Canada. Much more than ministerial curricular guidelines that are often quite vague, textbooks and other core print materials model in much finer detail what is supposed to happen in a classroom. As international comparison and scrutiny of educational systems grows, the importance of the signaling function of printed learning materials like textbooks will grow as well. A recent example of this kind of detailed scrutiny of textbooks was part of the Third International Mathematics and Science Study (TIMSS) (Schmidt, 1996). Official adoption of printed learning materials that are in keeping with the latest global pedagogical thinking therefore commemorates in a very essential way that a nation is committed to progress in a modern sense.

Neo-institutional Perspectives on Globalization and Education

The notion of institutionalization is central to the theoretical framework I use here. Scott (1992, p. 117) defines it as "[t]he process by which actions are repeated and given similar meaning by self and others." Institutional theorists premise their views with the idea that reality is socially constructed; that is, our sense of reality is built up on the basis of pervasive and dense webs of social interaction (Berger & Luckman, 1967).

Institutionalization processes are most likely to come into play when the links between means and ends are unclear, when the technologies about how to reach particular goals are uncertain. In organizational arenas such as schools and churches, where the means for creating the "educated" and the "saved" are less clear on a technical basis than the means for manufacturing widgets, ideas about how to proceed develop mostly through social interaction. Notions of the "best" form of education (or more modestly, "appropriate" forms of education), and who is best or appropriately educated by whom develop through social interactions in which the categories and routines of schooling are infused with meaning.[2]

Mostly, the interactions that matter most in the institutionalization process occur between credentialed experts: academics, policymakers, and lobbyists. Occasionally, an uncredentialed but highly charismatic politician may sway the prevailing discourse with a few media-savvy pronouncements, but the institutionalization process in education (and other fields) relies mostly on the steady, quiet drumbeat of written and oral interactions among the credentialed experts. The power of the "rationalized myths" about education that develop in this way lies not in their reflection of objective truth (though there may be some of that), but rather in their status as *collective* belief systems (Meyer & Rowan, 1977).

Although neo-institutionalism has been applied to processes within organizations (Brunsson & Olsen, 1993; Powell & Dimaggio, 1991), one strain of it also offers a distinctive perspective on globalization. Meyer, Boli, Thomas, and Ramirez (1997), Watson (1992), and Thomas, Meyer, Ramirez, and Boli (1987) draw attention to the formation of a world society and culture, which transcends nation-states. From this viewpoint, globalization is the rise and structuring of a world society with a shared culture, that is, shared cognitive frames and understandings built through entrenchment in institutions. Like any "society" at the national or subnational levels, the emerging world society (sometimes known as "world polity") described by neo-institutionalists has tensions, conflicts, and contradictions. Yet, neo-institutional theory emphasizes the social forces that lead to massive and quiet compliance with norms, and the relatively high degree of cohesiveness within the world system.

The idea that a unitary "world culture" exists, even in nascent form, is highly controversial. It is helpful to keep in mind that at the national and subnational levels (i.e., at levels for which the idea that culture exists is less controversial), cultures apply variably to subsets of people and activities. Moreover, cultures from different levels can readily coexist and overlap (e.g., Southern culture within American culture, Parisian culture within French culture). This mixture of the global and the local corresponds to Robertson's 1994 notion of "glocalization." Likewise, according to neo-institutionalist theorists, world culture holds variable sway in different parts of the world and over different types of activities. In places where world culture penetrates a bit more, it is not necessarily the case that national or subnational cultures are weakened.

What is the content of this emerging world culture? Boli and Thomas (1997, 1999) suggest that the culture pervading the world polity evolved out of the West and reflects dominant Western values. They claim that the many thousands of international organizations such as Greenpeace, the International Union of Biological Sciences, and UNESCO help to construct but also to carry world culture. That is, world cultural principles are institutionalized within international organizations, often through the social interaction and discourse produced by credentialed experts. In an impressive historical analysis of the changing aims of international nongovernmental organizations, they found several major themes that constitute the emerging world culture. The first is an emphasis on *universalism*. Human beings around the world are understood to have the same basic needs and goals. Moreover, all human beings are endowed with agency: that is, they have the capacity (and in fact a responsibility) to act toward achieving those goals. The universalism inherent in world culture makes explicit and formal denunciation of the "other" somewhat more difficult. This has implications for curricula and curricular materials in mass education systems, which are increasingly premised, at least formally, on notions such as "All children can learn."

A second theme identified by Boli and Thomas is *individualism*. Individual persons are understood to be the most fundamental "actors" in any social system. Collectivities come to be seen essentially as aggregates of individuals. As such, various kinds of group membership are secondary in that they serve as instruments to attain individual goals. As world culture becomes entrenched in mass educational systems around the world, curricula and curricular materials such as textbooks are likely to focus more on demonstrating to students that understanding the content is in their own, individual interest. In other words, it becomes important to show that the content is personally relevant.

Another element of world culture is *rationalism*, both as a procedure for collective action and, writ large, as a blueprint for societal progress and development. The cultural tenet is that establishment and fine-tuning of cultural rules and procedures leads to just, equitable, and efficient societies, in short to "progress"—not only economic development, but social and political development and individual fulfillment as well. Science is one particular and vitally important form of rationalism, and is therefore subject to much attention in global discourse, whether at the level of mass education or elite research and development activity. However, the cultural espousal of rationalism[3] can take many forms: formal accounting; ranking systems in the arts, education, and entertainment and so on.

Nations often adopt particular policies or models of governance supported by the world culture. This produces great worldwide similarity (isomorphism) of policies and behaviors despite the widely varying local circumstances that nations face. Activities that are closely related to nation-statehood are most susceptible to the impact of this emerging global culture. For this reason, researchers in this theoretical tradition sought to apply it to the development of mass education, one of the central activities of modern nation-states.[4] Educational policy, organizational structure, curricula, and even the physical infrastructure of schools are similar throughout the world, even though national economies and the skills and knowledge required of the labor force vary from subsistence agriculture to postindustrial societies (Meyer, Ramirez, & Soysal, 1992; McEneaney & Meyer, 2000; McEneaney, 2003; Rauner, 1998; Bradley & Ramirez, 1996). In short, the neo-institutional perspective predicts a long-term global homogenization of core state activities such as mass education, as nation-states adopt approaches that for the most part resonate with world cultural principles.

Neo-institutional views contrast sharply with economic globalization perspectives such as world-systems theory that emphasize the *divergent* consequences of the different levels of material circumstances of countries around the world (Chase-Dunn, 1989; Wallerstein, 1974, 1979, 1991). Neo-institutional theorists do not deny that economic globalization impacts on the provision of mass education *in practice*, but rather they aim to draw attention to the potential for a homogenizing transnational influence shaping schooling in its *idealized form*, such as portrayed in curricular statements and textbooks.

Global Culture and Science Education

How does the existence of a global culture relate to science and science education? The world cultural value of rationalism is key. Modern societies are characterized by a high degree of both structural and cultural rationalization. The emergence of an expanded science is a major component of the more general process of cultural rationalization of society (Frank, Meyer, & Miyahara, 1995). Science, as a set of abstract principles, becomes one of the major conceptual yardsticks of progress. Drori (1997) describes the process as the "scientization of society," suggesting that its cultural potency comes primarily from a rationalist image of science as contributing to national development (particularly economic development) through the building of a skilful and more efficient labor force. In countries everywhere (with the possible exception of the fundamentalist Islamic world), science is seen as the most legitimate source of solutions for social and economic problems. Thus, science constitutes a powerful cultural framework that strongly influences political, social, and economic, as well as educational structures. As science becomes an all-encompassing *Weltanshauung*, we would expect changes in all aspects of the curriculum: general curricular frameworks, instruction, and materials, particularly in the areas of science and mathematics.

As discussed earlier, international organizations play a key role in constituting and consolidating world culture. Norms regarding legitimate policies and practices are communicated through these organizational ties to the world polity. Much empirical research has demonstrated that extensive organizational linkages catalyze social change. The typical argument is that all kinds of international organizations carry and perpetuate global norms such as rationalism, individualism, and universalism. That is, it is not membership in any particular organization or program that generates the isomorphism. Instead, it is a nation-state's broad and ongoing participation in international governmental and non-governmental organizations that plays a role in "inscribing rules of reason" (Popkewitz, 2000) about legitimate approaches to state activity, especially mass education.

International Organizations and the Globalization of Ideas about Science Education

One can see the influence of international organizations on normative educational practices. This is clearly the case in the developing world, where donor countries, the World Bank, and UNESCO not only have the more overt "power of the purse string" over textbook development, they also offer extensive consultative expertise that serves to institutionalize standard curricular approaches, particularly in areas such as science and mathematics that are so closely linked to economic development (Altbach & Kelly, 1988; Farrell & Heyneman, 1989).

In science, the International Council of Associations for Science Educators (ICASE) is quite active in this area, with 150 member organizations from over 60 countries (ICASE, n.d.). The norm-setting influence of UNESCO's Education for All initiative has been described in detail by Chabbott (2003). As a follow-up, UNESCO collaborated with ICASE and other international organizations on Project 2000+, which sought to advance "scientific and technological literacy for all." The world cultural theme of universalism is clear in these initiatives, and the emphasis on building literacy skills subtly resonates with the theme of individualism. ICASE (n.d.) publishes a journal, *Science Education International*, that aims to "provide a means for [all those] concerned with science education to share perspectives, concerns, ideas and information which will foster cooperative efforts to improve science education."

International testing programs such as those conducted by the International Association for the Evaluation of Educational Achievement (IEA) and the Organization for Economic Co-operation and Development (OECD) also help institutionalize approaches to science education on a global scale. Building on the First International Mathematics Study (FIMS) in 1964, the IEA conducted the First International Science Study (FISS) in 1971. Follow-up studies with a new set of participating countries were conducted in 1982 and 1984, the Second International Mathematics Study (SIMS) and the Second International Science Study (SISS) respectively. Finally, assessments of both subject areas were combined in the 1994 IEA study, the Third International Mathematics and Science Study (TIMSS) and TIMSS-Repeat in 1998. OECD's PISA program has emerged to challenge IEA's dominance of international testing. Importantly, it is no longer sufficient in either of these programs to only assess achievement—all kinds of data on students, teachers, schools, and curricular materials are also collected and analyzed. Both the IEA and OECD programs therefore construct a comprehensive "global yardstick" by which national education systems are judged. Nieswandt (2002), for example, documents Germany's "PISA panic" when its students fared poorly relative to other countries in PISA's mathematics and science components. Systemic performance is gauged through comparison with other educational systems, and the international testing regime serves as a mirror for this purpose. Germany, like the United States in the early 1980s,[5] doesn't like what it sees.

Role of Multinational Firms
Finally, this discussion of the role of international organizations in the shaping of science education would not be complete without acknowledging the powerful, though not well-documented role of multinational textbook publishing companies. Although some nations use textbooks written and published by their ministries of education, most nations rely at least in part on commercial publishers to produce texts in accord with curricular guidelines. Altbach and Kelly (1988) and Farrell and Heyneman (1989) discuss the towering influence of multinational and educational publishers on textbook production and distribution in developing countries. Luke (1988) makes a similar economically based argument about the impact of U.S. policies and corporations in shaping the development of Canadian basal readers.

In addition, however, multinational publishing firms have found a strategy of tweaking existing texts to make them acceptable for use in other countries to be the most viable means to profitability. For example, in the mid-1970s, Heinemann published textbooks for integrated science for use in intermediate grades in England, Scotland, Hong Kong, and Nigeria. Activities, topics, and themes were remarkably similar across the set of books, although the race of individuals depicted, their clothing, as well as many geographical place names were changed (McEneaney, 1998). Deeper adaptations, such as translation into local, indigenous languages are typically not seen as commercially viable (Association of Namibian Publishers, 1995, pp. 80–89). Since that time, the global consolidation of the educational publishing industry has surged, dramatically intensifying the institutionalized homogenization of curricular approaches. For example, although Heinemann was operating in quite a few countries in the 1970s, it is now part of Harcourt Education, which also owns Ginn and Holt, Rinehart and Winston. Harcourt and its subsidiaries now sell their products in southern Africa, the Caribbean, Ireland, the United States, Canada, and the United Kingdom (Harcourt General, n.d.).

The British giant Longman Publishing merged with U.S. textbook industry leader Addison-Wesley in 1995. Several years later, this merged entity was acquired by Pearson plc, a multinational media firm. At around the same time, Viacom, another global media conglomerate, sold Simon & Schuster (which has had a long-term presence in educational publishing) to Pearson plc. Today, Pearson Education claims to be the world's largest educational publisher, with 10,000 employees in 40 countries (Pearson Education, n.d.). Pearson's "family" of imprints includes such well-known firms as Silver Burdett, Scott Foresman, Prentice Hall, Macmillan and Allyn and Bacon. These acquisitions give Pearson a dominant position in Anglophone regions of the world, but it is also active in France, French-speaking Canada, Spain, Italy, North and South Asia, and South America (Pearson Education, n.d.). In contrast, Oxford University Press has resisted the merger mania, but it produces schoolbooks for markets in Australasia, Singapore, Mexico, Pakistan, South Africa, Botswana, and Namibia in addition to North America and Great Britain (Oxford University Press, n.d.).

It is fairly straightforward to imagine all of the local influences on curricula and curricular materials such as textbooks. The global influence is equally multifaceted but mostly beyond everyday experience. Taking science textbooks as an example, I have outlined ways in which multinational publishing firms and international organizations may have a homogenizing influence. International testing programs such as TIMSS and OECD's PISA studies prompt low-scoring educational systems to consider adopting policies and practices broadly accepted by other systems. Most important, however, are the foundational values that help constitute acceptable or appropriate policy and practice. World culture provides the global frame (individualized, universal, and rationalized) within which curricular materials such as textbooks are developed and used.

The Case of Canada

With this theoretical backdrop in place, Canada is an interesting case to consider for several reasons. It clearly is among the world's economically developed "core," with a per capita gross national income of US$21,340 (World Bank, 2002). Canada's per capita gross national income is substantially below that of the United States ($34,870), but is at about the same level of Ireland, France, the Netherlands, and Italy. Canada thus has enough material wealth to employ professionals to develop curricular standards thought to be roughly appropriate to the needs of the populations in each of its provinces and territories. It has enough material wealth to make teachers aware that these standards exist and to monitor curricular materials such as textbooks to ensure that they meet the standards. In short, Canada is wealthy enough to create its "own" school science.

In terms of connections to the world polity, Canada has a long-standing and broadly complex relationship to the rest of the world. As a former British colony and a continuing member of the British Commonwealth, it shares elements of an educational tradition with many other countries.[6] Since confederation in 1867, however, the development of Canada's identity as an independent nation-state has struggled with the cultural, political, and economic domination of the United States, as that country began its rise to global prominence. Finally, Canada's place in the international community more recently has also been characterized by active and consistent participation in a full array of international organizations and conferences.

Canada is well connected to the web of international organizations that help create and support the world polity, as discussed in the previous section. In 1992, for example, Canada belonged to 1,920 international nongovernmental organizations. On a per capita basis, Canada's number of organizational memberships clearly outranks that of many European countries and the United States and Japan, which belonged to 2,127 and 1,749 international nongovernmental organizations respectively (Union of International Associations, 1993). More specific to mathematics and science education, Canada has participated extensively in studies sponsored by the International Association for the Evaluation of Educational Achievement (IEA) and the Organization for Economic Cooperation and Development (OECD). Although Canada sat out the first, limited set of studies sponsored by IEA in the 1960s, it has participated in the Second International Mathematics Study (1982), the Second International Science Study (1984), the Third International Mathematics and Science Study (TIMSS) (1994–95) and the 1998 TIMSS Repeat (TIMSS-R) study. Canada has a long-term commitment to the OECD's Programme for International Student Assessment (PISA), which is an ongoing data collection and analysis effort focused on math, science, and reading literacy (OECD, 2000).

Canadian Educational Publishing

Despite Canada's material wealth, economic globalization processes have greatly weakened the Canadian educational publishing industry. In 1991–92, the last year that Statistics Canada reported these breakdowns, foreign publishers controlled 85 percent of the postsecondary textbook market (Canadian College Publishing, n.d.). Branch plant operations held by non-Canadian conglomerates such as Pearson PLC (Addison Wesley Longman, Prentice Hall Ginn), McGraw-Hill (McGraw-Hill Ryerson), and Harcourt (Holt, Rinehart and Winston) dominate the list of approved and recommended learning resources for elementary and secondary mathematics and science in provinces across the country. Canadian-owned publishers Gage, Irwin, and ITP Nelson are modestly represented (Ontario Ministry of Education, n.d.; Bureau d'approbation du material didactique, n.d.a; Alberta Learning, n.d.; British Columbia Ministry of Education, n.d.).[7] Historically, foreign publishers commonly produced "Canadian editions" of science textbooks previously published elsewhere such as John C. Winston, Ltd.'s *Discovering Why* series (1951), and Macmillan's *Journeys in Science* (1990). These texts were previously published in the United States under the same title.

Given the globalization of the industry, it is difficult to insist that textbooks and other learning resources have purely Canadian origins. If Canadian firms are not publishing the majority of textbooks used, how can local, Canadian perspectives be preserved? In Ontario, the Ministry of Education mandates that authorized learning materials must be "Canadian product," manufactured in Canada and "wherever possible . . . written, adapted or translated by a Canadian citizen . . . or by a permanent resident." Furthermore, authorized materials must reflect "Canadian orientation" through "acknowledgement of Canadian contributions and achievements," use of Canadian spelling, and "wherever possible, use Canadian examples and references"

(Ontario Ministry of Education, 2002, p. 8). Quebec does not require Canadian authorship or manufacture, but requires that materials are "consonant with moral and religious values," though it does not offer any details about the nature of those values (Bureau d'approbation du material didactique, n.d.b, "Criteria"). In Ontario, Quebec, and other provinces, ministries assert Canadian identity through insistence on the use of the metric system. Elsewhere in the world, this requirement would clearly not be an affirmation of local preferences, but in the context of the full-scale retreat of the United States from metric system usage, it is a straightforward means of signaling distinctiveness. Thus, policy about textbooks at the provincial level can help construct a local Canadian character in a formal sense. Within these formal strictures, though, how is the local element enacted in the actual content of the textbooks? And in what ways does the content reflect the values of world culture? In the next section, I address these questions with a focus on school science in Ontario.

Canadian School Science: The Global and the Local

If world polity theory is correct, all of these kinds of international linkages should lead Canada toward adopting a school science that reflects global culture. At the same time, we should also see signs of a distinctly Canadian school science. To investigate these different influences, I have systematically coded 25 science textbooks published in Canada between 1950 and the present. To assure that the textbooks were aligned with contemporary mainstream thinking about science education, I restricted the sample to textbooks listed on the Ontario Ministry of Education's *Circular 14* (recently renamed the *Trillium List*). The Ministry authorizes use of provincial funds to purchase curricular materials listed in the annual *Circular 14*. All of the sample textbooks were intended for use in grades 4 through 7.[8]

To assess the degree to which Canadian textbooks resonate with global trends and emphasize distinctly Canadian perspectives, data from the Canadian sample were compared with a much larger set of primary and intermediate level science textbooks ($N = 265$). I have documented elsewhere (McEneaney, 1998, 2003) the broader historical and cross-national trends found in this larger set of textbooks, which included materials published since 1900 from 60 countries.[9] This "comparison set" helps to clarify and contextualize trends seen in Canadian texts. I developed a textbook coding form with open- and closed-ended questions. Open-ended questions were analyzed using a constant comparative approach (Strauss & Corbin, 1990).

Canadian Distinctiveness

How are science textbooks recognizably Canadian in nature? That is, we have seen that Ontario's Ministry of Education insists that authorized textbooks are "formally" Canadian, but looking at textbooks as cultural products, what constitutes Canadian content in practice? There are four major forms in which textbook content reveals itself as distinctively Canadian: (1) specific references to local features, (2) multiculturalism, (3) portrayals of Canada as part of North America, and (4) portrayals of Canada as part of the international community. Throughout the time period covered in this study, textbooks can demonstrate their Canadian identity, as the latest Ontario ministerial requirements dictate, through specific references to local flora, fauna, and geography. Other books highlight Canadian research capacity or the residence and educational backgrounds of ordinary Canadian scientists. A text by Longfield, Wells, and Richter shows the influence of the local by picturing a boy wearing a Toronto Blue Jays baseball cap and a former member of the Canadian Olympic team driving a zamboni in a hockey rink (1986, pp. 9 and 145). Other texts refer to the range of minerals mined in Canada (Gough & Flanagan, 1980, pp. 220–233) and its universal health care system (Asseltine & Peturson, 1999, p. 121).

More recent textbooks emphasize multiculturalism. This is a core element in the contemporary conceptualization of the Canadian identity. Canadians often contend that their society is a cultural "mosaic," often in contrast to the historical notion of U.S. society as a cultural "melting pot." As a concrete manifestation of this multiculturalism, Canadian science textbooks published in the 1980s and 1990s universally picture people of apparently different races and ethnicities. Although this is a worldwide trend (McEneaney, 1998), Canadian texts portray a more broadly diverse range of people at earlier time points than most other countries. The book by Flanagan, Teliatnik, and Christopher (1983) is a relatively early example of a text that clearly highlights diverse representations of race and ethnicity. In the 1990s, textbooks begin to incorporate elements of aboriginal culture. Asseltine and Peturson's textbook is equitable in terms of gender representations, and includes portrayals of blacks, East and South Asians, as well as aboriginal people. After describing a scientist's interpretation of how a large boulder came to rest near Calgary, the text offers an alternative explanation: "According to Aboriginal people of the Blackfoot Nation, a mighty warrior named Napi chased the big rock to its present location" (Asseltine & Peturson, 1999, p. 223).

Canadian science textbooks also tend to manifest local character through portrayals of Canada as part of North America. In practice, this means depictions of the shared impact in Canada and the United States of both natural phenomena and scientific research. In contrast, none of the 24 U.S. textbooks examined as part of an earlier study made reference in this way to Canada (McEneaney, 1998). Some of these portrayals of Canada included descriptions of the impact of weather and sharing weather data (Asseltine & Peturson, 1999, pp. 214; Gough & Flanagan, 1980, pp. 347–348; Ingram, Herridge, & Moore, 1993, pp. 40–41).

In much Canadian political discourse, descriptions of the bilateral relationship are tempered by the reality of U.S. dominance. The analogy of a mouse sleeping with an elephant is often invoked in the Canadian popular media to describe the country's tenuous position. This is reflected in one book's sanguine description of acid rain:

> Sometimes pollution that causes acid rain gets into the air in one place. The movement of air and weather carries the pollutants to other places. Acid rain can then form in these other places . . . In North America most of the acid rain occurs in the large industrial cities or downwind from those cities. Some scientists think that the rain in those places may have 40 times more acid than normal. (Beugger & Yore, 1990, p. 81)

Despite quite clear scientific evidence that acid rain originates in the United States and drifts northward, this textbook exemplifies a Canadian identity as it avoids placing blame on its neighbor to the south.

Finally, recent science texts increasingly highlight Canada and Canadian science as part of an international community. The earliest traces of this trend are seen in the late 1970s as textbooks adopt the metric system. More recent texts manifest this internationalism more directly in terms of content. Text by Ingram et al. describes how the International Air Transport Association's Live Animals Board developed guidelines so that animals might be transported safely to zoos around the world (1993, p. 65). Another text raises the issue of adaptation to environment with the following activity: "In a small group, choose a country that you think is very different than Canada. Imagine that you and your family moved there. What parts of life might be easier? More difficult? Why?" (Asseltine & Peturson, 1999, p. 55). Not only does this activity enhance awareness of life in other countries, it is also premised on a common notion about what life in Canada is like. Although one finds these kind of international references in some European science textbooks, they remain rare in U.S. textbooks.

RESONANCE WITH WORLD CULTURE

Hence, there are some common, identifiable devices in which Canadian school science textbooks reveal their local identity. But what about transnational influences? In what ways do Canadian science textbooks resonate with world culture? As I noted earlier, the core value of rationalism is manifested directly in the heightened emphasis on science education over time. More specifically in textbooks, the other core values of individualism and universalism are evident, as clearly in Canadian textbooks as in texts from other countries.

The primacy of the individual is shown historically, even since the 1950s, in dramatically more frequent depictions of individual people doing science. The textbook written by Bruce and Carter (1953) depicts people only a few times, focusing instead solely on the natural phenomena or scientific equipment. The notion that science is conducted by and for humans is not a central point of the textbook. Another relatively early text in the Canadian sample downplays individuals in science by depicting only adult hands and fingers examining objects and holding tools (Gough & Flanagan, 1980). In contrast, in more recent texts, people (especially children) are pictured nearly every page or two (in textbooks by Longfield et al., 1986; Beugger & Yore, 1990; and many others). This trend is clearly in keeping with broader global trends in school science (McEneaney, 1998).

The individualism heralded in world culture is also embodied in the insistence on hands-on activities. Asseltine and Peturson's recent textbook (1999) invites broad participation from each student with frequent "Let's Experiment," Let's Observe," "Let's Investigate" features. The imperative to participate is also conveyed well in supplementary resources entitled *Science is an Action Word* (Perdue, 1991), *Daily Science Workout* (Nelson Canada, 1994), and *Sciencing: An Involvement Approach* (Cain, 1990). Historically too there has been a shift away from the importance of science in a collective sense toward an emphasis on personal utility. While Bruce and Carter's 1953 text emphasized collective government efforts to improve research, a later book poses the question "What is science?" and then responds "Science is—for you" (Longfield et al., 1986, p. 6).

Individualism is embodied in the newest textbooks on another level. In textbooks around the world, and in Canada in particular, recent textbooks are much more likely to frame the academic material within a broad range of emotions. This contrasts with earlier constructions, which centered on the cognitive appeal of science, with only a limited range of emotional content. Writers of more recent textbooks invoke emotions that are motivating from a child-centered point of view. The cover of the text written by Ingram et al. is a vivid color picture of a small marsupial climbing a tree at night. Looking directly into the camera, the animal's eyes are bulging, pupils huge. Vaguely human in its facial features, it seems to exude wonderment and surprise, but it also evokes mild disgust. The book seems to draw energy from both a sense of wonder and slightly naughty tricksterism. There is a kind of white magic of wonderment in its description of egg whites as "amazing," but a touch of black magic in the invitation to students to "get the lowdown on ooze" (1993, pp. 6–7).

Asseltine and Peturson's textbook (1999, pp. 228–232) devotes an entire concluding chapter to this kind of emotion work. The chapter "Celebrating Science" has a section called "Science on Parade" that outlines a small group activity in which students build parade floats to "celebrate [their] learning" in science. Other Canadian books convey the intended emotional message more subtly. The pictures of people that fill the pages of the textbooks depict adults and children who, by and large, are smiling and having fun. This contrasts with earlier textbooks, such as Bruce and Carter (1953), in which focus and deep concentration are depicted—science as serious business. This trend toward linking school science to emotional content is therefore evident specifically in Canadian textbooks from the last decade or so, which is consistent with the global trend I have documented elsewhere (McEneaney, 2003).[10]

Finally, the global cultural element of universalism plays out quite dramatically in science texts with a reconfiguration of the concept of expertise. This development is global in scope (McEneaney, 2003), but Canadian texts in particular seem to follow the trend closely. Children and ordinary adults become experts, with much less emphasis on portraits of the "greats" such as Newton and Galileo. Children's lives become suitable objects of study. In the textbook by Winkler, Bernstein, Schachter, and Wolfe (1980, p. 55) students are asked to make a table of "Foods I Ate Today" as a starting point for analysis. Another book pictures a group of ordinary adults (a housepainter, a veterinarian, a baker, a pilot, etc.) in a feature called "Scientists in Action" with the explanation: "All of them have to know about science. They use science everyday in the work they do" (Asseltine & Peturson, 1999, p. 11).

Earlier texts from Canada and other industrialized countries remove science from an everyday world, with science depicted as occurring in specialized areas such as labs and using specialized language (e.g., textbooks by Bruce & Carter, 1953; Gough & Flanagan, 1980). Later texts are more likely to extend the range of places in which scientists work, and to de-emphasize scientific terms. The textbook by Winkler et al. (1980) is an early example, with a regular activity feature entitled "Do This at Home." Bruegger and Yore's textbook (1990) employs noticeably everyday materials and equipment (e.g., wheelbarrows, water slides, plastic buckets) to demonstrate science concepts. This move toward everyday science (including so-called kitchen chemistry) is a prominent trend in recent textbooks around the world.

Conclusion

Educational researchers and policy makers routinely read and publish internationally, subject education systems to international measurement and scrutiny, and crisscross the world traveling to conferences. We educationists often imagine however that mass education in our individual countries remains solely under the sway of local influences. I have argued here that in Canadian elementary science, one can find both local and global influences. Even in science, a subject area that would seem to rise above national or subnational cultures, a seemingly completely abstracted body of knowledge, one that is timeless and placeless, is no longer viable. Science textbooks published in Canada are discernibly Canadian in a variety of ways. The rather straightforward incorporation of specific references to Canadian places, natural phenomena, and people has been a feature of Canadian textbooks since 1950, although the ratio of Canadian references to American and British references has increased in recent decades, partly due to mandates such as those of the Ontario Ministry of Education. The other ways in which local Canadian flavor are incorporated include a strong and early emphasis on multiculturalism, and a self-consciousness about Canada as part of North America and as part of the international community.

This localism is matched with equal force by the impact of globalization on the construction of school science. Canadian textbooks embody some trends that are seen in textbooks from a wide variety of countries. Fundamentally, science moves from a set of abstract principles to something that ordinary people can understand and do. It is no longer reserved solely for a high priesthood of university-trained practitioners. The classical questions are replaced in centrality by a kid's everyday questions about their own lives: how bicycles work, whether it will rain tomorrow, why spread salt on an icy road. This global change in the way in which science is conceptualized sweeps through Canadian materials as surely as it does those from many other countries. Thus, there are both clearly local as well as transnational influences on the construction of school science, not only in the broadly abstract curricular outlines, but also in the densely detailed portrayals of school science contained in elementary level textbooks. The local elements do not baldly contradict the transnational elements, so that they may coexist in Canadian textbooks of the future. However, in the absence of ministerial mandates about Canadian "orientation" and authorship such as Ontario's, it is difficult to imagine why the handful of multinational publishing conglomerates that increasingly dominate the industry would bother to sustain these nuanced local aspects of school science in Canada. Furthermore, the homogeneity inherent in emerging world culture could prove to be very good for business.

Notes

1. John Meyer and I have argued that curricula are becoming more expansive, inclusive of topics, and eclectic over time (2000, pp. 200–201). That is, the normative curriculum is no longer marked by Bourdieu's (1984) cultural "distinction," in which elite individuals learn to narrow their cultural preferences, but by what Peterson and Kern refer to as cultural "omnivorousness," in which high status taste is "an openness to appreciate everything" (1996, p. 904).

2. Some scholars claim that this meaning-laden set of social categories and routines entirely constitutes "educational knowledge" (Popkewitz, 2000).

3. I will refer to the espousal of rationalism and individualism in cultural forms as rationalization and individualization respectively. This espousal, which is usually at the official policy level, isn't necessarily reflected in a tightly coupled way to actual practice.

4. Other activities that are closely related to the essence of nation-statehood include the military and economic development. That is, a national government cannot claim to be fully legitimate if it does not take action in these realms. Areas such as culture are less central to nation-statehood, and matters pertaining to the family or religion are often seen as outside the responsibility of nation-states.

5. Shrill accusations of the ineptitude of U.S. schools subsequently appeared in the well-known report *A Nation at Risk*.

6. The British tradition is of course much weaker in Quebec, which was a French colony for centuries prior to British rule.

7. Canadian publishers seem to have more success gaining a foothold in other subject areas, where niche markets such as French immersion, aboriginal education, and Canadian literature and history, are not served by the large multinational firms.

8. The textbooks in the Canadian sample are housed at the Ontario Institute for Studies in Education in both the regular and historical collections.

9. The textbooks in the larger sample were found in the following collections: Stanford University, Teachers College Special Collections, Michigan State, Institute for Science Education (Kiel, Germany), University of Bielefeld, the Library for Historical Education Research (Berlin), German Foundation for Development (Bonn), Textbook Repository Library (Tokyo).

10. The emotional content of science can be seen in the *Grossology* books and museum exhibits that are very popular around the English-speaking world or in the popular children's television show in Germany "Sach und Lach" [Science and Smiles]. Hence this global trend goes well beyond official textbooks.

References

Alberta Learning.
(N.d.). The authorized resources database. Retrieved October 2, 2002 from http:// ednet.edc.gov. ab.ca/lrdb.

Altbach, P. & Kelly, G.
(1988). Textbooks and the third world: An overview. In P. Altbach and G. Kelly (Eds.), *Textbooks in the third world: Policy, content and context* (pp. 3–18). New York: Garland Publishing.

Apple, M
(1988). *Ideology and curriculum*. Boston: Routledge and Kegan Paul.

Asseltine, L. and Peturson, R.
(1999). *Science everywhere 4*. Toronto: Harcourt Brace, Canada.

Association of Namibian Publishers.
(1995). Publishing in Namibian Languages. In K. Legère (Ed.), *African languages in basic education* (pp. 80–89). Windhoek: Gamsberg Macmillan.

Barry, A.
(1998). On Interactivity: Consumers, Citizens, and Culture. In S. Macdonald (Ed). *The politics of display: museums, science, culture* (pp. 98–117). New York: Routledge.

Berger, P. & Luckmann, T.
(1967). *The social construction of reality.* New York: Doubleday.

Beugger, P. & Yore, L.
(1990). *Journeys in science.* Toronto: Collier Macmillan Canada.

Boli, J. & Thomas, G.
(1997). World culture in the world polity. *American Sociological Review, 62,* 171–190.

Boli, J. & Thomas, G. (Eds.)
(1999). *Constructing world culture: International Nongovernmental Organizations Since 1875.* Stanford, CA: Stanford University Press.

Bourdieu, P.
(1984). Distinction: a social critique of the judgment of taste. Translated by Richard Nece. Cambridge, Mass.: Harvard University Press.

Bradley, K. & Ramirez, F.
(1996). World polity promotion of gender parity: Women's share of higher education, 1965–85. *Research in Sociology of Education and Socialization, 11,* 63–91.

Bruce V. & Carter, A.
(1953). *Intermediate science, book 1.* Toronto: Sir Isaac Pitman and Sons.

Brunsson, N. & Olsen, J.P.
(1993). *The reforming organization.* London: Routledge.

Bureau d'approbation du material didactique.
(N.d.). Instructional materials approved for preschool and elementary levels. Retrieved October 1, 2002, from http://www.meq.gouv.qc.ca/bamd/pedagogi/p0085a.htm.

Bureau d'approbation du material didactique.
(N.d.). General information. Retrieved October 1, 2002, from http://www.meq.gouv.qc.ca/bamd/pedagogi/intro_a.htm.

Cain, S.
(1990). *Sciencing: An Involvement approach to elementary science methods* (3rd ed.). Toronto: Collier Macmillan.

Canadian College Publishing: Who owns whom?
(N.d.). Retrieved October 22, 2002, from http://www.garamond.ca/wow2.htm.

Chabbott, C.
(2003). *Constructing education for development: International organizations and Education for All.* New York: Routledge Falmer.

Chase-Dunn, C.
(1989). *Global formation: Structures of the world economy.* Cambridge: Harvard University Press.

Discovering Why Series.
(1951). Toronto: John C. Winston.

Drori, G.
(1997). The national science agenda as a ritual of modern nation-statehood: The consequences of national 'science for development' projects. Unpublished Ph.D. dissertation, Department of Sociology, Stanford University, Stanford, CA.

Farrell, J. & Heyneman, S. (Eds.)
(1989). *Textbooks in the developing world: economic and educational choices.* Washington, DC: The
World Bank.

Flanagan, F., Teliatnik, A., & Christopher J.
(1983). *Focus on science 4.* Toronto: DC Heath Canada.

Frank, D., Meyer, J., & Miyahara, D.
(1995). The individualist polity. *American Sociological Review, 60,* 360–377.

Gough, D. & Flanagan, F.
(1980). *Focus on science: Exploring the natural world.* Toronto: DC Heath Canada.

Harcourt General.
(N.d.). Retrieved October 17, 2002 from http://www.harcourteducation.co.uk.

Ingram, J., Herridge, D., & Moore, N.
(1993). *Explore! A book of science, 5.* Don Mills, ON: Addison Wesley Publishers.

International Council of Associations for Science Education [ICASE]
(N.d.). Retrieved October 2, 2002, from http://sunsite.anu.edu.au/icase.

Journeys in Science
(1990). Toronto: Macmillan.

Longfield, A. Wells, J., & Richter, K.
(1986). *Science: The nature of things* (rev. ed.). Toronto: Oxford University Press (Canada).

Luke, A.
(1988). *Literacy, textbooks and ideology: Postwar literacy instruction and the mythology of Dick and Jane.*
London: Falmer Press.

Macdonald, S.
(1998). Exhibitions of power and powers of exhibition: an introduction to the politics of display.
In *The politics of display: museums, science, culture* (pp. 1–24). New York: Routledge.

McEneaney, E.
(1998). The transformation of primary school science and mathematics: a cross-national
analysis, 1900–1995. Unpublished Ph.D. dissertation, Department of Sociology, Stanford
University, Stanford, CA.

McEneaney, E.
(2003). Elements of a contemporary school science. In G. Drori, J. Meyer, F. Ramirez, &
E. Schofer (Eds.), *Science in the modern world polity: Institutionalization and globalization*
(pp. 136–154). Stanford, CA: Stanford University Press.

McEneaney, E. & Meyer, J.W.
(2000). The content of the curriculum: An institutionalist perspective. In M.T. Hallinan (Ed.),
Handbook of sociology of education (pp. 189–211). New York: Kluwer Academic/Plenum
Publishers.

Meyer, J., Boli, J., Thomas, G., & Ramirez, F.
(1997). World society and the nation state. *American Journal of Sociology, 103,* 144–181.

Meyer, J.W., Ramirez, F., & Soysal, Y.
(1992). World expansion of mass education 1870–1980. *Sociology of Education, 50,* 242–258.

Meyer, J. W. & Rowan, B.
(1977). Institutionalized organizations: Formal structure as myth and ceremony. *American Journal of Sociology, 83*, 340–363.

Nelson Canada.
(1994). *Daily science workout.* Toronto: Author.

Nieswandt, M.
(2002). Germany's PISA Shock. Paper presented at the National Association for Research on Science Teaching, April 2002.

Ontario Ministry of Education.
(N.d.). Trillium list. Downloaded October 2, 2002, from http:mettowas21.edu.gov.on.ca:80/trilliumlist/k8textbooklog.pdf.

Ontario Ministry of Education.
(2002). Guidelines for approval of textbooks. Downloaded October 2, 2002 from http://www.edu.gov.on.ca.

Organization for Economic Co-operation and Development [OECD].
(2000). *Measuring student knowledge and skills: The PISA 2000 assessment of reading, mathematical, and scientific literacy.* Paris: Author.

Oxford University Press.
(N.d.). Teaching and Learning Resources. Retrieved October 13, 2002, from http://www.oup.com/teach.

Pearson Education.
(N.d.). About Pearson Ed. Retrieved October 17, 2002, from www.pearsoned-ema.com/history.htm.

Perdue, P.
(1991). *Science is an action word.* Scarborough, ON: Gage Educational Publishing.

Peterson, R.A. & Kern, R.M.
(1996). Changing highbrow taste: From snob to omnivore. *American Sociological Review, 61*, 900–907.

Popkewitz, T.
(2000). Globalization/regionalization, knowledge and the educational practices: Some notes on comparative strategies for educational research. In *Educational knowledge* (pp. 3–27). Albany, NY: State University of New York Press.

Powell, W. & DiMaggio, P.
(1991). *The new institutionalism in organizational analysis.* Chicago: University of Chicago Press.

Rauner, M.
(1998). The worldwide globalization of civics education topics from 1955–1995. Unpublished Ph.D. dissertation, School of Education, Stanford University, Stanford, CA.

Schmidt, W. (Ed.)
(1996). *Characterizing pedagogical flow: An investigation of mathematics and science teaching in six countries.* Boston: Kluwer.

Scott, W.R.
(1992). *Organizations: Rational, natural and open systems* (3rd ed.). Englewood Cliffs, NJ: Prentice-Hall.

Strauss, A. & Corbin, J.
(1990). *Basics of qualitative research: Grounded theory procedures and techniques.* Newbury Park, CA: Sage.

Thomas, G., Meyer, J., Ramirez, F., & Boli. J.
(1987). *Institutional structure: Constituting state, society, and the individual.* Beverly Hills, CA: Sage.

Union of International Associations.
(1993). *Yearbook of international organizations.* Munich, Germany: K.G. Saur.

Venezky, R.
(1992). Textbooks in school and society. In P.W. Jackson (Ed.), *Handbook of research on curriculum* (pp. 436–464). New York: Macmillan.

Wallerstein, I.
(1974). *The modern world-system: Capitalist agriculture and the origin of the European world-economy in the sixteenth century.* New York: Academic Press.

Wallerstein, I.
(1979). *The capitalist world-economy.* New York: Cambridge University Press.

Wallerstein, I.
(1991). *Geopolitics and geoculture: Essays on the changing world system.* Cambridge: Cambridge University Press.

Watson, A.
(1992). *The evolution of international society: A comparative historical analysis.* London: Routledge.

Winkler, A., Bernstein, L., Schachter, M., & Wolfe, S.
(1980). *Concepts and challenges in science 1.* Toronto: Gage Publishing.

World Bank.
(2002). World Development Indicators. Washington, DC.

3

Text Processing Within Classroom Contexts

Janet Donin

It is now almost thirty years since there was a radical shift within the research literature on text comprehension. Until the 1970s, with few exceptions, the psychological literature was dominated by a "bottom-up" model of reading. The reader moved from letter–sound decoding through word recognition and sentence processing to the acquisition of meaning from the text. Once a text was decoded comprehension was assumed to be relatively automatic. This view of reading was consistent with the behaviorist orientation that had dominated psychology in the preceding decades and had moved psychologists to study not text comprehension but its assumed component processes and to do this within laboratory settings.

With the "cognitive revolution" of the 1970s a new emphasis was placed on the role of the reader. At the same time researchers were recognizing that adding components together did not necessarily produce the whole and researchers moved to new methods and models to study text comprehension (e.g., text recall, text summary, semantic analyses of texts). This change of emphasis led some initially to propose completely "top-down" models in which readers or listeners[1] slot information into their already existing frameworks. However, it soon became apparent that these models also have serious problems.

Current approaches to text processing view the comprehension process as one in which the individual constructs the meaning of a text based on both aspects of the text and previous knowledge that the comprehender has stored and is able to relate to the particular text and situation (e.g., Frederiksen & Donin, 1991; Kintsch, 1998; Sanford & Garrod, 1998). Thus, comprehension is not a receptive process in which the meaning of a written or oral text is perceived by the reader or listener, but an active process in which "meaning" is the representation of the text that the reader or listener constructs. In addition, the process is not a serial process (i.e., either top-down or bottom–up) but rather one in which processing at multiple levels is proceeding concurrently. This chapter will discuss this model, some of the data on which it is based and its implications for the use of textual materials in classroom settings.

Interaction of Reader with Text

From a cognitive perspective, the meaning of a text for a reader is the representation of the text that the reader constructs during and after reading. This representation is a function of features of the text but it is highly dependent on the knowledge that the reader brings to the text and the reading situation. Early research showed that text characteristics such as propositional density (the amount of semantic information contained in a syntactic unit) (e.g., Kintsch & Keenan, 1973) and the sequencing of information within a text (e.g., Marshall & Glock, 1978; Rothkopf & Koether, 1978) affect comprehension. However, of equal if not greater importance is the relationship of the text material to the knowledge that the reader already possesses and the way that features of the text might signal that knowledge. In a now classic series of studies, Bransford and Johnson (1972, 1973) showed that placing a text in context (by using titles or pictures), through which readers could relate an ambiguous text to their prior knowledge, enabled those readers to recall the text. Richard Anderson and his colleagues conducted a number of studies in which they showed that text interpretation depended on the background knowledge of the readers. In one study, for example, Anderson, Reynolds, Schallert, and Goetz (1977) constructed texts that could be given more than one interpretation. Most of the participants in their study, however, saw only one meaning in each text and that was dependent on their own backgrounds (whether they were music students or physical education students). In another study that manipulated cultural contexts of texts and cultural backgrounds of their readers, Steffenson, Joag-Dev, and Anderson (1979) found that Indian and American students read texts faster, recalled more material, and displayed fewer distortions when reading texts that were consistent with their own cultures. They also found that the two groups rated very different information as being important in the two texts.

These were among the studies that were taken as support for "schema theory." In this general model of text comprehension, readers or listeners are seen as approaching a situation with well-established sets of expectations that are based on their previous experience (e.g., Rumelhart, 1975, 1980). These expectations take the form of schemata, abstract representations that contain variables that may be "instantiated" by the particular information contained in a given text. The process of comprehension is seen as a top-down process in which the variable slots are filled to satisfy the constraints of both the schemata and the text (Anderson et al., 1977). Since schemata are seen as connected networks their activation would make other information connected to them more readily available to the comprehender. Schema theory is able to explain a variety of research results, some of which will be discussed later. It does not, however, present a complete model of text processing. It does not account for how the schemata themselves are constructed nor for what individuals do when they find themselves in situations in which they recognize that they do not have the appropriate schemata. It also leaves unanswered the question of how a reader or listener learns from a text that does not conform to a preexisting framework.

Multilevel Compensatory Models of Text Processing

Current cognitive models of text processing view both bottom-up and top-down sequential processing models as too simple. Instead processing is seen as proceeding at multiple levels at the same time. As the reader or listener perceives visual or aural information from a text, he or she uses whatever sources of knowledge are available. "The sources interact to help the reader compile information about the textual input, attribute meaning to it, and integrate it with what has come before" (Beck, 1993, p. 66). Current models differ with respect to the weight that they place on different types of processing. For example, Kintsch (1998) while discussing both "text" and "situation" models seems to give priority to the text; Sanford and Garrod (1998), on the other hand, give primary importance to world knowledge.

As an example of such a multilevel model, I would like to present an expansion of the model of text comprehension elaborated by Frederiksen and Donin (1991). In this model it is recognized that reading or listening, involves multiple levels, or strata, of processing and that the outcome of processing at one level affects processing at another level. Processing at the different levels does not require processing at any other level to be complete. Rather, the model assumes that processes may operate in parallel "with individual processes operating whenever they have data" (Frederiksen & Donin, p. 41). The levels may be grouped into three broad categories: morpho-lexical and syntactic (linguistic) structures of natural-language expressions; semantic structures, that is, the propositional meanings expressed in linguistic structures; and conceptual or frame-level (knowledge) structures used or constructed in the particular text comprehension situation (Frederiksen, 1986). In comprehending a discourse in a particular situation, a reader or listener is seen as constructing a conceptual representation from propositions derived from lexical and syntactic information. At the same time, knowledge representations that the reader or listener already possesses may be used both in the construction of a text representation and in processing at lower levels. Figure 3.1 illustrates

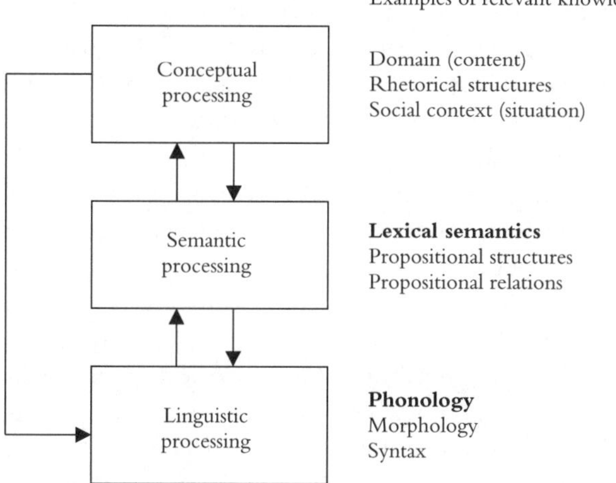

Figure 3.1.   Multilevel model of text processing

these general levels and their interaction as well as some of the types of knowledge that may be associated with each level.

At the linguistic level, relevant knowledge includes knowledge of the phonology, morphology, and syntax of the language of the text. If the text is a written text, this would include knowledge of the features that are specific to written language. Oral situations might require the ability to decode particular accents. Thus, a reader's or listener's linguistic knowledge will affect the way that the text is processed.

Semantic processing involves the mapping of linguistic forms to their underlying meaning. This requires not only knowledge of the word meanings but also how those words can be put together to form a coherent network or "propositional structure" (Frederiksen, 1975, 1986). This includes, for example, knowledge of whether particular actions require, or may have, an agent, an object, and so on. If I were to say the word "hit," a native speaker would assume that there was an agent of the action as well as an object (The boy hit the ball). A fluent speaker would also know that the action could have an instrument (The boy hit the ball with the bat), a recipient (The boy hit the ball to the girl), and so on. Someone who is either not familiar with the language or with the action referred to by that language would not make the same assumptions. Semantic processing also involves knowledge of the relationships that may link propositional structures together; such as, causal and conditional relations, temporal relations, and the embedding of one propositional structure within another. Differences in these types of knowledge will produce differences in the way that the same text is processed by different individuals.

While it may be impossible to specify all the types of knowledge involved in conceptual processing, some types of knowledge that can affect text processing have been well-documented. Consider students reading a science text in a classroom: each one has many types of "world knowledge" that may affect how he or she comprehends the text. These include the knowledge of the topic or domain of the text. How much relevant content knowledge does the student have? Does the student know how texts in this domain are typically organized; that is, the rhetorical structures that writers in this domain use? What does the student know about the situation in which the text is being read? This may be his first science class or he may have a long history of using science texts within classes in general and/or within this particular classroom. All of these types of knowledge will affect the strategies that are employed in reading the text and the reader's ultimate representation of the text material.

As the arrows in figure 3.1 illustrate, processing at each level can affect processing at each other level. One can construct semantic and conceptual representations based on linguistic representations; however, conceptual representations can affect both the semantic and linguistic representations that one constructs. One possible result of this latter situation is that individuals can use high-level conceptual processing to overcome limitations imposed by lack of automaticity in sentence-level syntactic and semantic processing. This has been suggested by compensatory processing models of reading such as those of Perfetti (1985, 1990) and Stanovich (1986). Such compensatory processing is, of course, a function of the availability of both the requisite conceptual information, and of sufficient information based on lexical and syntactic processing to allow for its use (Stanovich, 1986).

IMPLICATIONS OF A MULTILEVEL COMPENSATORY MODEL FOR TEXT PROCESSING IN CLASSROOM CONTEXTS

There are a number of implications of this model for the processing of textual materials within classroom contexts. In order to begin to use textual materials one must be able to decode those materials. However, decoding is necessary but not sufficient. Stanovich (1986) has argued eloquently for the existence of a "Matthew's effect" in reading. The consequences of a child not being able to decode text efficiently at an early age increase as that child advances in schooling. Perfetti (1985, 1990) has also discussed the consequences of inefficient processing at the lexical level and below. If a reader or listener is expending all her effort on letter-sound correspondences or on trying to recognize words, then how can she construct meaning from that text, or use it as a basis for acquiring information? Thus, it is important to assure oneself that students who are using textual materials are able to decode them and access the required lexical information. One cannot necessarily assume efficient lower-level processing of text.

On the other hand, the current emphasis, particularly within the North American reading literature on lower-level processing (i.e., letter-sound correspondences) (e.g., Rayner Foorman, Perfetti, Pesetsky, & Seidenberg, 2002), has the potential of making individuals forget that decoding does not equal comprehension or the ability to use the text as a source of information. One needs to be reminded of the early work of Sticht et al. (1974) who found that individuals who had difficulty using written text materials had similar difficulties "auding"; that is, listening to spoken language. Decoding a text may be an essential first step but it is only that. To construct meaning from a text requires that one be able to build a conceptual representation for that text. Whether this is done by slotting information from the text into schemata that one already possesses or by constructing new conceptual structures, one thing that the last 30 years of research has clearly shown is that comprehension does not automatically follow from decoding the text.

Determiners of Comprehension: Reader's or Listener's Knowledge and Expectations and Characteristics of the Texts

This model makes explicit the importance of all levels of knowledge that the reader or listener brings into a situation for text comprehension and how that knowledge generates expectations that can, in turn, affect text processing. The reader or listener must recognize the lexical and syntactic forms of the language and be able to map these efficiently into their underlying semantic structures. Thus the reader's or listener's already existing semantic structures are of primary importance. What structures will be accessed will be affected not only by how they are connected into larger conceptual structures but also by the expectations that these structures engender in the reader or listener. These knowledge structures and expectations may affect how the text is perceived and how particular parts of it are processed.

However, the model does not assume that the reader or listener is simply slotting text information into already existing structures. While there are circumstances where this might be the case, there are other situations in which the reader or listener will be building new structures or modifying previous structures based on information from the text itself. Thus, text characteristics are also important in determining how a text is understood.

Multiple Types of Knowledge Affect Text Processing

The knowledge structures that affect text processing go well beyond the "background knowledge" suggested by the early studies discussed earlier. Research has demonstrated that the expectations that the reader or listener brings into a situation may reflect such things as: (a) content knowledge; that is, knowledge, such as that which may be specific to a particular domain, that allows the reader or listener to assess the semantic content of the text; (b) knowledge of rhetorical structures; that is, knowledge of how a particular type of text or a text in a particular domain is organized; and (c) situation-specific knowledge, for example, knowledge of how the text material is to be used and so on.

Content Knowledge

Most of the research on the effects of content knowledge on text comprehension has focussed on narratives and emphasized culture-specific knowledge, as illustrated by the studies mentioned earlier. This has been particularly true of research dealing with non-native speakers. Researchers have repeatedly illustrated that second-language speakers' text comprehension difficulties are often due not to language problems but to unfamiliarity with culture-specific materials that reflect the host culture (e.g., Carrell, 1983; Johnson, 1981). It is to be expected that even if these texts were in these readers' first language they would have difficulty with them. Unfortunately these studies have not looked at both first- and second-language text comprehension.

In our own research we have looked directly at first- and second-language text processing *within individuals* by using semantically equivalent texts related to the work or academic environments of the participants. The first set of studies looked at nursing students' comprehension and sentence reading times of matched medical case files in both their first and second languages (Donin & Silva, 1993; Goyette & Donin, 1993). In general, the results of these studies are consistent with the interpretation that individuals at an intermediate level of second-language proficiency use their content knowledge to overcome limitations imposed by lack of automaticity in sentence-level syntactic and semantic processing.

Chen and Donin (1997) looked at domain-specific content knowledge when they investigated, at an English language university, Chinese first-language graduate engineering and biology students' recall of biology texts in English and Chinese. They found that whether or not readers had specific domain-relevant knowledge affected multiple aspects of text comprehension while second-language proficiency did not. Second-language proficiency did affect reading time. Interestingly, reading time for the English texts was also affected by content knowledge with the engineering students reading the English (biology) texts more slowly than the biology students. A similar effect was *not* found in Chinese. This suggests that lack of the appropriate content knowledge for these students not only affected their comprehension but also affected the efficiency with which they could complete the lower-level processing of these materials in their weaker language. Thus, these data are consistent with the part of the model that states that conceptual processing can affect linguistic processing.

Knowledge of Genre and Text Types

There has been increasing recognition of the fact that oral and written texts of different types and within different domains are structured differently. Both within and across content areas, specific types of texts have different features and organizations. For example, a procedural text (one that tells the reader or listener how to do something) reflects the fact that procedures are goal-oriented, sequenced in time, and are hierarchical (a general goal or procedure is made up of parts that often may also be divided into subparts) (Frederiksen, 1986; Longacre, 1996; Meyer & Freedle, 1984). In contrast, narrative text is made up of sequences of events or actions that are linked in time and space (Frederiksen, 1986) and by agency (Longacre, 1996). Consistent developmental differences have been found in the text comprehension literature with young children showing better comprehension of narrative texts than of procedural or explanatory texts within the same content domain (Donin, Doehring, & Browns, 1991; Frederiksen, 1989; Langer, 1986).

While "text types" may be thought of as distinct from particular content domains, a construct that is more closely tied to academic disciplines is that of "genre." This term has been extended from its traditional categorization roots within literary studies, to "a class of communicative events, the members of which share some set of communicative purposes. These purposes are recognized by the expert members of the parent discourse community, and thereby constitute the rationale for the genre" (Swales, 1990, p. 58). This definition rests on the sociological and sociolinguistic research into what constitutes a speech and discourse community (see Hymes, 1972 and Kress, 1989 for discussion of these concepts). One group that would constitute such a community would be the practitioners of a particular scientific field. Within that field rules would have evolved as to how texts should be written or even spoken; for instance, what constitutes a laboratory report or a scientific explanation. This would include formal properties of the texts as well as what conceptual information should be expressed. A number of researchers have been studying textual materials within disciplines from a genre perspective (e.g., Bazerman, 1988; Halliday and Martin, 1993), some with the purpose of teaching second-language apprentices of the discipline how to communicate within that discipline (e.g., Swales, 1990). For many researchers interest has been on how the rules are established within a community; however, from a cognitive perspective these rules are another type of knowledge that an expert in the field would have and that a novice student would have to acquire.

Those who are functioning in a second-language situation need to be aware not only of culture-specific content but also of the fact that texts are organized differently across cultures. Recent research in "contrastive rhetoric" (Connor, 1996; Hinds, 1990; Grabe & Kaplan, 1996) have documented cross-cultural differences in the structures of arguments, newspaper articles, and so on. Kintsch and Greene (1978) demonstrated that narrative texts that were organized in a manner consistent with readers' cultural expectations (Native American folktale structure versus European folktale structure) were more readily recalled. Thus, it is to be expected that students would have difficulty not only writing texts that violate their first-language cultural norms with respect to text structures but also comprehending such texts.

Knowledge of Situational Contexts

Recent years have seen a growing awareness within the text processing literature that all texts occur and are processed within contexts (e.g., Van Dijk, 1997) and that any complete model of text processing must be social as well as cognitive. The knowledge representations that the individual possesses include representations specific to, and developing within, the embedded contexts in which the particular texts and discourse activities are occurring (Duranti & Goodwin, 1992). For example, a teacher enters a science classroom with a model of the scientific domain that includes both a global organizing structure and specific knowledge structures that are a function of her particular background. The teacher also possesses a pedagogical model; that is, a model of how and what to teach. Added to this is the history of interaction that the teacher has had both with this class and with previous classes. On the basis of these models the teacher plans the classroom activities.

The students also possess models of the domain that they may, or may not, share with the teacher and with each other. They also possess models of what is expected from them in classes in general and in this class in particular. Interactive roles have also been established and knowledge of these roles form part of both the students' and the teacher's models of the situation. These provide the multiple-layered context into which the particular activities and the texts and discourse linked to those activities are embedded. How any given text is processed will depend not only on the activities to which it is linked but also to the students' perceptions of the functions of the text and its related activities. These student perceptions may or may not coincide with the teacher's models of what is happening in the situation. Also, if students are functioning in relatively new situations, they might not have sufficient knowledge of the relevant contextual information to be able to form an adequate or useful representation of the presented texts or discourse. Thus, it is important to recognize that the student's context may be different from the teacher's, and as a consequence so might be the "text."

There is a need for well-designed texts that are appropriate to their readers while "meaning" may be the representation of the text that the reader or listener constructs, that construction is a function of the text itself. As stated earlier, readers or listeners may use their conceptual knowledge to compensate for difficulties in lower-level processing; however, the reverse of this is that for readers or listeners who are lacking in conceptual knowledge the text is all that they have. Therefore, text characteristics are especially important when readers or listeners lack requisite background knowledge. One explanation for the fact that the engineering students in the Chen and Donin study read the texts more slowly than did the biology students was that the engineers required the texts to obtain all the needed information. The biology students, on the other hand, could read the texts more quickly because they could use them as a means to trigger information that they already possessed to some degree. For the student who must place greater reliance on the text, the text, in turn, must present that information in such a way that it can be readily accessed by the student.

Analyses of both classroom discourse (Frederiksen & Donin, 1996) and science textbooks (Unsworth, 2001) suggest that in many situations information is not explicitly stated by either the teacher or the textbook and that students in these situations must infer much of the necessary information. This may not be a problem but rather an effective teaching tool in a situation such as that studied by Frederiksen and Donin in which the teacher was referring to information previously covered in class, provided that the students are able to make the necessary connection. Chi, Bassok, Lewis, Reiman, and Glaser (1989) presented evidence that in learning from examples the students who generated self-explanations of the steps in the procedure were highly successful. However, they also state that the usefulness of the self-explanations is dependent on the student's initial understanding of the presented text or problem (Chi & Bassok, 1989). Thus, while it may be that for students who possess considerable background knowledge in an area, texts that require them to generate inferences might be useful tools for learning. For students who do not have that degree of knowledge, highly coherent texts that do not require the students to infer information that they do not possess would be necessary. This would also seem to be the case for students who do not possess a high degree of knowledge about the particular genres being used. Beck and McKeown (1989) analyzed expository texts that had been included in basal readers for the purpose of introducing young readers to expository genres. They found that these texts tended to be poorly organized and to violate many of the requirements of text coherence such as that all parts be relevant to the central topic.

Both spoken and written texts are used to promote conceptual change particularly within science classrooms. Researchers have repeatedly demonstrated the difficulty of changing students' erroneous models of physical phenomena (e.g., Carey, 1985; Chinn & Brewer, 1993). Guzzetti, Snyder, Glass, and Gamas (1993) did a meta-analysis of texts designed to promote conceptual change and found that unless the text content specifically refuted misconceptions, the texts were unlikely to promote change. This further demonstrates that texts used in such situations need to be carefully constructed.

The issue still exists, however, as to what criteria need to be used in constructing school texts. Criticism of the use of "readability" formulas, based primarily on sentence length and limited vocabulary, to adapt texts for school use have been raised for some time now (Anderson & Davison, 1988; Kintsch & Vipond, 1979) because of the lack of both theoretical and empirical support for their use. We need, however, a greater understanding of what constitutes "reader friendly" texts both within particular content domains and for students with different backgrounds.

Texts and Contexts

In this chapter, I have attempted to describe some of the processing requirements for texts (i.e., written texts and extended classroom discourse) to promote learning for students with different background experiences and acquired knowledge. The model presented in figure 3.1 represents the interaction of the reader or listener with the text from the perspective of an individual functioning within a given situation. The entire model should be placed schematically within a series of boxes labeled "contexts." In order to truly reflect any authentic instance of text processing, the model must be located within a specified situational context; for example, at a point in time within a particular classroom with a given history. Whether a text is oral or written, its value within a learning situation depends on both the local and global social situations in which it is functioning (cf., Bloome, 1989; Kelly & Green, 1998), as well as the structure of the activity within the situation in which the discourse is embedded (cf., Cole & Engestrom, 1995). The meaning of an oral or written text to a student might depend on the utterance that preceded it. How that utterance is interpreted would be a function of the classroom norms that had developed over the course of the school year or possibly longer and the students' knowledge (explicit or implicit) of those norms.

"Situated cognition" has come to represent a perspective in which skills and knowledge are viewed as dependent on the situations in which they are developed and used (e.g., Greeno, 1997). While written texts or transcriptions of oral texts might exist outside of a particular context, how they are processed is definitely situation-dependent. The more we know about the specifics of the situations in which texts are used, the more we will be able to predict how they will be understood and used as sources of learning. However, defining the social situation still does not allow us to know how a *particular* individual will understand a *particular* text. To predict that would require that we know precisely what that individual knows and is likely to access at that point in time. Current interactive models of text processing elucidate the complex nature of such processing within classroom contexts. The socio-cognitive character of discourse processing means that texts, both oral and written, can play various roles within a classroom setting. It also means that texts do not stand by themselves but rather form part of different classroom activities and environments. Whether or not a text is meaningful or deficient will depend on the nature of the activities in which it is embedded and on the characteristics of the actors in the situation. Knowing more about the characteristics of both the actors and the situations will enable us to construct and use potentially meaningful texts for those contexts.

Note

1. I am adopting a definition of "text" that is consistent with the text linguistic and text comprehension literature in which text is viewed as "an instance of language in use, either spoken or written: a piece of language behaviour which has occurred naturally . . ." (Stubbs, 1996, p. 4) (cf., Halliday & Martin, 1993; Sanford & Garrod, 1998).

References

Anderson, R.C., Reynolds, R.R., Schallert, D.L., & Goetz, E.T.
(1977). Frameworks for comprehending discourse. *American Educational Research Journal, 14* (4), 367–381.

Anderson, R.C. & Davison, A.
(1988). Conceptual and empirical bases of readability formulas. In A. Davison & G.M. Green (Eds.), *Linguistic complexity and text comprehension: Readability issues reconsidered* (pp. 22–53). Hillsdale, NJ: Erlbaum.

Bazerman, C.
(1988). *Shaping written knowledge: The genre and activity of the experimental article in science.* Madison: University of Wisconsin Press.

Beck, I.L.
(1993). On reading: A survey of recent research and proposals for the future. In A.P. Sweet & J.I. Anderson (Eds.), *Reading research into the year 2000* (pp. 65–87). Hillsdale, NJ: Erlbaum.

Beck, I.L. & McKeown, M.G.
(1989). Expository text for young readers: The issue of coherence. In L. Resnick (Ed.), *Knowing, learning and instruction: Essays in honor of Robert Glaser* (pp. 47–65). Hillsdale, NJ: Erlbaum.

Bloome, D. (Ed.)
(1989) *Classrooms and literacy*. Norwood, NJ: Ablex.

Bransford, J.D. & Johnson, M.K.
(1972). Contextual prerequisites for understanding: Some investigations of comprehension and recall. *Journal of Verbal Learning and Verbal Behavior, 11*, 717–726.

Bransford, J.D. & Johnson, M.K.
(1973). Consideration of problems of comprehension. In W.G. Chase (Ed.), *Visual information processing*. New York: Academic Press.

Carey, S.
(1985). *Conceptual change in childhood*. Cambridge, MA: MIT Press.

Carrell, P.
(1983). Three components of background knowledge in reading comprehension. *Language Learning, 33*, 183–207.

Chen, Q. & Donin, J.
(1997). Discourse processing of first- and second-language biology texts: Effects of domain-specific knowledge and language proficiency. *Modern Language Journal, 81* (2), 209–227.

Chi, M.T.H. Bassok, M., Lewis, M.W., Reimann, P., & Glaser, R.
(1989). Self-explanations: How students study and use examples in learning to solve problems. *Cognitive Science, 13*, 145–182.

Chi, M.T.H., Bassok, M.
(1989). Learning from examples via self-explanations. In L. Resnick (Ed.), *Knowing, learning and instruction: Essays in honor of Robert Glaser* (pp. 251–282). Hillsdale NJ: Erlbaum.

Chinn, C.A. & Brewer, W.F.
(1993). The role of anomalous data in knowledge acquisition: A theoretical framework and implications for science instruction. *Review of Educational Research, 63*, 1–49.

Cole, M. & Engestrom, Y.
(1995). Commentary. *Human Development, 38* (1), 19–24.

Connor, U.
(1996). *Contrastive rhetoric: Cross-cultural aspects of second-language writing*. Cambridge: Cambridge University Press.

Donin, J., Doehring, D.G., & Browns, F.
(1991). Text comprehension and reading achievement in orally-educated hearing-impaired children. *Discourse Processes, 14*, 307–337.

Donin, J. & Silva, M.

(1993). The relationship between first- and second-language reading comprehension of occupation-specific texts. *Language Learning, 43* (3), 377–343.

Duranti, A. & Goodwin, C. (Eds.).

(1992). *Rethinking context: Language as an interactive phenomenon.* Cambridge: Cambridge University Press.

Frederiksen, C.H.

(1975). Representing logical and semantic structure of knowledge acquired from discourse. *Cognitive Psychology, 7,* 371–458.

Frederiksen, C.H.

(1986). Cognitive models and discourse analysis. In C.R. Cooper & S. Greenbaum (Eds.), *Studying writing: Linguistic approaches* (pp. 227–267). Beverly Hills, CA: Sage.

Frederiksen, C.H.

(1989). Text comprehension in functional task domains. In D. Bloome (Ed.), *Classrooms and literacy* (pp. 189–222). Norwood, NJ: Ablex.

Frederiksen, C.H. & Donin, J.

(1991). Constructing multiple semantic representations in comprehending and producing discourse. In G. Denhière & J.P. Rossi (Eds.), *Texts and text processing* (pp. 19–44). Amsterdam: North-Holland.

Frederiksen, C.H. & Donin, J.

(August 1996). *Conceptual processing in text comprehension and learning through discourse.* Paper presented at invited symposium at XXVI International Congress of Psychology, Montréal.

Goyette, E. & Donin, J.

(April 1993). *Second-language text comprehension: Knowledge and text types.* Paper presented at the annual meeting of the American Educational Research Association, Atlanta, GA.

Grabe, W. & Kaplan, R.B.

(1996). *Theory and practice of writing.* London: Longman.

Greeno, J.G.

(1997). On claims that answer the wrong questions. *Educational Researcher, 26,* 5–17.

Guzzetti, B.J., Snyder, T.E., Glass, G.V., & Gamas, W.S.

(1993). Promoting conceptual change in science: A comparative meta-analysis of instructional interventions from reading education and science education. *Reading Research Quarterly, 28* (2), 116–155.

Halliday, M.A.K. & Martin, J.R.

(1993). *Writing science: Literacy and discursive power.* Pittsburgh, PA: University of Pittsburgh Press.

Hinds, J.

(1990). Inductive, deductive, quasi-inductive: Expository writing in Japanese, Korean, and Thai. In U. Connor & A.M. Johns (Eds.), *Coherence in writing: Research and pedagogical perspectives.* Alexandria, VA: TESOL.

Hymes, D.

(1972). On communicative competence. In J.B. Pride & J. Holmes (Eds.), *Sociolinguistics* (pp. 269–293). Harmondsworth: Penguin.

Johnson, P.
(1981). Effects on reading comprehension of language complexity and cultural background of a text. *TESOL Quarterly, 15*, 169–181.

Kelly, G.J. & Green, J.
(1998). The social nature of knowing. In B. Guzzetti & C. Hynd (Eds.), *Perspectives on conceptual change: Toward a sociocultural perspective on conceptual change and knowledge construction* (pp. 145–182). Mahwah, NJ: Erlbaum.

Kintsch, W.
(1998). *Comprehension: A paradigm for cognition.* Cambridge: Cambridge University Press.

Kintsch, W. & Greene, E.
(1978). The role of culture-specific schemata in the comprehension and recall of stories. *Discourse Processes, 1*, 1–13.

Kintsch, W. & Keenan, J.M.
(1973). Reading rate and retention as a function of the number of propositions in the base structure of sentences. *Cognitive Psychology, 5*, 257–279.

Kintsch, W. & Vipond, D.
(1979). Reading comprehension and readabillity in educational practice and psychological theory. In L.G. Nilson (Ed.), *Perspectives on memory research* (pp. 325–365). Hillsdale, NJ: Erlbaum.

Kress, G.
(1989). *Linguistic processes in sociocultural practice.* Oxford: Oxford University Press.

Langer, J.A.
(1986). *Children reading and writing: Structures and strategies.* Norwood, NJ: Ablex.

Longacre, R.E.
(1996). *The grammar of discourse.* New York: Plenum Press.

Marshall, N. & Glock, M.D.
(1978). Comprehension of connected discourse: A study of the relationship between the structure of text and information recalled. *Reading Research Quarterly, 14*, 10–56.

Meyer, B.J.F. & Freedle, R.
(1984). Effects of discourse type on recall. *American Educational Research Journal, 21*, 121–143.

Perfetti, C.A.
(1985). *Reading ability.* New York: Oxford University Press.

Perfetti, C.A.
(1990). The cooperative language processors: Semantic influences in an autonomous syntax. In D.A. Balota, G.B. Flores d'Arcais, & K. Rayner (Eds.), *Comprehension processes in reading* (pp. 205–230). Hillsdale, NJ: Erlbaum.

Rayner, K., Foorman, B., Perfetti, C., Pesetsky, D., & Seidenberg, M.
(2002). How should reading be taught? *Scientific American, 286* (3), 85–91.

Rothkopf, E.Z. & Koether, M.E.
(1978). Instructional effects of discrepancies in content and organization between study goals and information sources. *Journal of Educational Psychology, 70* (1), 67–71.

Rumelhart, D.E.
(1975). Notes on a schema for stories. In D.G. Bobrow and A. Collins (Eds.), *Representation and understanding* (pp. 211–236). New York: Academic Press.

Rumelhart, D.E.
(1980). Schemata: The building blocks of cognition. In Spiro, R., Bruce, B.C., & Brewer, W.F. (Eds.), *Theoretical issues in reading comprehension* (pp. 33–58). Hillsdale, NJ: Erlbaum.

Sanford, A.J. & Garrod, S.C.
(1998). The role of scenario mapping in text comprehension. *Discourse Process, 26* (2), 159–190.

Stanovich, K.E.
(1986). Matthew effects in reading: Some consequences of individual differences in the acquisition of literacy. *Reading Research Quarterly, 21,* 360–406.

Steffenson, M.S., Joag-Dev, C., & Anderson, R.C.
(1979). A cross-cultural perspective on reading comprehension. *Reading Research Quarterly, 15,* 10–29.

Sticht, T., Beck, L.B., Hauke, R.N., Kleiman, G.M., & James, J.H.
(1974). *Auding and reading.* Alexandria, VA: Human Resources Research Organization.

Stubbs, M.
(1996). *Text and corpus analysis.* Oxford: Blackwell.

Swales, J.W.
(1990). *Genre analysis: English in academic and research settings.* Cambridge: Cambridge University Press.

Unsworth, L.
(2001). Evaluating the language of explanation in different types of explanations in junior high school science texts. *International Journal of Science Education, 23* (6), 585–609.

Van Dijk, T.A.
(1997). *Discourse as structure and process.* London: Sage.

4
Community-Gardens and Science Laboratories as Texts for Science Literacy Development

Irene Rahm

In this chapter, I examine symbolic systems not usually thought of as textual—a community garden and a science laboratory. Most important, I focus on how such texts mediate science literacy development. In doing so, I rely on sociocultural theory within which text is understood as a tool for meaning-making and literacy development (Vygotsky, 1978; Wertsch, 1991). Accordingly, a text is not seen as simply transmitting information and having a monologic function (Lotman, 1988), but also as promoting dialogue resulting in the generation of new meaning(s). Put differently, texts can be thought of as objects and participants (Bernhardt, 1987). The former underlines that texts are often understood as the primary dispensers of the curriculum in that they present science knowledge as well as a worldview of science, something that many critical language projects have made evident and problematized (Kress, 1996). In contrast, the notion of texts as participants underlines the texts' dynamic nature in that they mediate sense-making and can change and grow in concert with their users. It is this latter perspective that informs my analysis of environments as texts.

I therefore examine how students made meaning of science through texts such as a garden and a laboratory. I approach such an examination with the assumptions that texts are agents with which students interact and that the students themselves are active meaning builders. Lemke (1989) describes such a process as "making text talk." That is, to make sense of a written text students need to do more than simply put a text into spoken language. They have to contribute to its thematic content by elaborating and commenting on it and by connecting it to prior ways of knowing and other contexts of knowing. Similarly, to make sense of the science embedded in a garden and a laboratory, students have to interact with and engage in a dialogue with such texts. Accordingly, I focus on science in the making and on how science is interactionally established and made by youth and adults. Put differently, I am interested in "how science is invoked, appropriated, positioned, understood and taken up by participants" (Kelly & Chen, 1999, p. 886) as they interact with and make meaning of two different texts, a garden and a laboratory.

The two cases chosen for this chapter show the manner whereby an environment can become a text for meaning-making of science, a text that defines outdoor education but not necessarily science education per se. For example, see the move toward community science that exposes students to a variety of texts by pushing the boundaries of science beyond the school walls (e.g., Roth & Désautels, 2002; see also Cleghorn, 2003). The first case illustrates how a garden becomes a resource and text for science literacy development of youth who have few opportunities to interact with nature otherwise. The second case illustrates how a scientists' laboratory can be thought of as a text that makes visible to youth some dimensions of the world of scientists. In presenting these two different yet complementary cases, this chapter attempts to reassess what we mean by text and to address whether contexts such as the ones described here can be taken as having embedded in them texts that come to constitute our students' science literacy development. It appears as if these kinds of texts have remained underexamined and their value underestimated given our focus on written text materials in the past. Yet, I hope to show that such contexts are pertinent to students' sense-making of the complex worlds of science.

Methodology

The two cases are taken from a larger ethnographic case study of an inner-city youth gardening program (first case from data collected in 1996; second case from data collected in 2000; Rahm, 2001, 2002). Sponsored through 4-H,[1] the City Farmers program is an eight-week community program that offers inner-city youth opportunities to grow, harvest, and market herbs and vegetables during their summer school-break. The program is intended to teach participants team and life skills while science is seen as a secondary goal. The program is often portrayed as a prevention program by the 4-H community, in that it is tailored toward middle-school inner-city students who are at risk of dropping out of school and have few opportunities to engage in other extracurricular activities or summer programs. The study was conducted in the third year of the program's existence.

The garden plot hosting the City Farmers program is set in an ethnically diverse neighborhood in a low-income inner-city area in the midwest. The eight weeks in the garden are structured around four activity settings among which teams rotate in a two-week cycle: (1) nurturing, (2) harvesting, (3) marketing, and (4) special projects. In nurturing, participants prepare the soil, plant different vegetable seeds, transplant seedlings of herbs, and ensure proper growth by watering and weeding. The students learn about the use of different gardening tools, the needs of different plants, and how to identify plants. In harvesting, crops are harvested and processed for the marketing team. Students learn to identify marketable crops, to harvest them correctly and to prepare them for the market. In marketing, the produce is sold to neighborhood businesses and at local markets. The students also contact businesses by phone or through visits, fill out order and delivery sheets, and develop marketing skills as they sell produce at local markets. Activities such as to beautify the garden through artwork (e.g. murals), to plant trees, and to set a sandstone path are central to special projects. That group is also in charge of community outreach and provides tours of the garden to visitors. Since one of the program goals is for students to develop team skills, they stay within the same team for the duration of the program. Prior to the gardening work, a three-week training session helps familiarize students with the kind of garden science, work, and life skills of value in the program. Typically, about twenty (primarily African American) participate in the program and are guided in their work by four team leaders, two Master Gardeners, and the program director.

CASE 1. COMMUNITY-GARDENS AS TEXTS FOR SCIENCE LITERACY DEVELOPMENT

The first case was constructed from data collected in 1996. At the time, I followed one group of six middle-school aged students (five African American and one European American; four male and two female) with the video camera, as they began with the planting of seeds (nurturing), then moved on to harvesting, marketing, and eventually completed the eight-week program with special activities. My aim was to understand what it means to do science in a garden. Clearly, the camera served as a note-taking tool, with the same purpose and subjectivity as the ethnographer's pencil and note-book (Jordan & Henderson, 1995). Decisions had to be made "in situ" about which activities to record when the team pursued more than one project at a time in smaller groups. However, by supplementing my recordings with fieldnotes, I could keep track of all the activities that I observed on a given day even if not everything could be captured on video.

I transcribed verbatim all segments of the videos that pertained to gardening activities and integrated those transcriptions with the fieldnotes. To infer what it meant to do science in the City Farmers community, I conducted a domain analysis of these extensive fieldnotes and developed taxonomies of the kinds of activities the program supported (Spradley, 1980). Based on that analysis, I could then identify the program activities entailing science. To arrive at such inferences, I also used school activities in plant science as an interpretive template. That analysis led to a thick description of garden science consisting of vignettes and excerpts (VanMaanen, 1988; for further details see Rahm, 1998). For the purpose of this paper, I identified dialogue excerpts that make apparent the manner whereby the garden became a text for science literacy development. I also relied on interview data from students to underline their perception of garden science in relation to school science.

Garden as a Text for Science Learning

To understand the science embedded in gardening, it is important to examine the manner whereby meanings were constituted by the students' and adults' interactions with each other and the garden. On the one hand, adults made explicit some of the science in the garden by pointing and explaining while at the same time, students themselves demistified garden science through their own actions and interactions with the environment and through questions. For instance, in the following excerpt, Marie, a volunteer Master Gardener, introduced the use of row covers as she also identified the "red giant mustard" and in turn, alluded to the fact that they were engaged in organic gardening and briefly explained what that means.

Excerpt 1

MARIE: Here we have what's called row covers. I'll uncover this for you and show you what we have here. We have some red giant mustard here. This plant right here [points it out to youth] and it grows about that tall [indicates with hand gesture about 20 inches in height]. And these are just wires that are crossed and then put into the ground. And the reason we put this cover on it is because of the giant mustard because of flee-bees, it keeps them away. It also protects them from the wind. But the water can go right through. But it keeps out the bugs. And since we do not use any bug-killers, everything out here is organic which means, we don't put any chemicals on it.

Note how many concepts Marie introduced in this rather brief statement. She identified one of the plants in the garden as the "red giant mustard" and explained the practice of row covers as pest control in organic gardening. In essence, by pointing and talking, Maria made visible to the students the kind of knowledge essential to successful gardening and hidden in practices such as the set-up of row covers.

Continuous questions and comments by the students make evident their own sense-making of garden science. For instance, as they were planting seeds, one boy wondered whether they would use a chemical to help the plant grow.

Excerpt 2

Will: Are we gonna use Miracle-Gro?
MARIE: No, it's organic out here. No chemicals.
Buddy: But Miracle-Gro is not a chemical?
MARIE: Sure, it's a growth chemical. It's like vitamins.
Tamara: You said this used to be a waste dump?
MARIE: [nods]
Tamara: There is still chemicals down here in the ground, then this is not . . .
MARIE: No, there were no chemicals dumped on here. It's not like some of the dumps in the recycle places that we have now.

Obviously, Will struggled with the concept of organic gardening that Marie had explained previously. Note also that Marie referred to Miracle-Gro as a "growth chemical" and invoked an analogy to further clarify its meaning "it's like vitamins" (something that may be more confusing than not, however). In turn, Tamara joined the conversation and brought up the issue that the garden used to be a "waste dump" and hence may contain chemicals for this reason. Marie discounts such an inference since "no chemicals were dumped on here." Yet, the garden was clearly filled with glass splinters and other remains of garbage (metal, cans, plastic) and youth were encouraged to use gloves for gardening to protect themselves. This brief episode of sense-making shows how implicated youth were in the gardening practice.

Take another example of the students' sense-making of garden science. In this case, a students had prepared the soil for the planting of zucchini seeds under the guidance of one of the Master Gardeners. They were told to plant at least three seeds in each hole on their mound (a pile of dirt that facilitates growth of zucchini in that it prevents the development of mildew, a plant mushroom). One of the boys wondered why they needed to put three seeds. He figured that one should be enough.

Excerpt 3

MARIE:	You do not get growth from each one.
Will:	I want to know what would happen if two seeds sprout?
MARIE:	That's fine, the stronger one wins.
Will:	So it's some kind of survival of the fittest?
MARIE:	Yeah.
Will:	Oh, that's neat.

When asked for a reason for the practice of planting at least three seeds per hole, Marie explained that typically "one does not get growth from each one." Will then wondered "what would happen if two seeds sprout." Marie simply responded that the "stronger one wins," which helped Will make a link to the principle of the "survival of the fittest." Even though the principle underlying the survival of the fittest is more complex than the competition between seeds, it did help Will make sense of the planting practice he was exposed to here. His comment "that's neat" suggests that he was now able to understand the practice and understand its embedded meaning.

As these examples make apparent, the science in gardening is hidden rather than marked, as may be the case of science in the classroom. Only through students' actions and questions and adults' spontaneous explanations did the science behind gardening surface. At the same time, the students valued such ways of learning. In fact, by physically interacting with the environment by planting herbs, by watering them, and by observing and ensuring their growth, these young people and the garden became almost inseparable. That is, the two together came to constitute the kind of science that emerged. In the excerpt that follows the students were engaged in the harvesting of salad leaves. In this activity, they had to handle plants they themselves had grown, yet plants, they only knew as the "green stuff" on the shelves in grocery stores. Most important, through this activity, they were able to notice components of a salad leaf— the milky sap—that were new and intriguing to them.

Excerpt 4

Tamara:	There is some lotion on these things!
	[she comments on the juice coming out of the stem of the salad leaves that they are harvesting]
MARC:	Lotion on it? [appears confused about Tamara's comment]
Matthew:	It's not lotion. It's milk.
Will:	Not milk!

Figure 4.1. Inspection of salad leaves

Matthew: Yes, it is. Well, it's not milk but plants . . .
Will: That stuff is poisonous hey?
MARC: No . . . [others mumble] . . . some of the plants, like lettuce is one of them,
                  have a kind of milky sap to them . . .
Matthew: That's what I was trying to . . .
MARC: . . . so that is the sap of the plant, OK.
Matthew: Is it edible?
MARC: It is in there when we eat it! [giggles] It is in the lettuce you buy from the
                  grocery store too!
Tamara: Me and my Mama don't eat lettuce, we don't even eat red meat!

As this dialogue and figure 4.1 show, students were actively seeking out ways to make meaning of what they were doing and observing. In this case, the lotion Tamara noticed created much anxiety in that Will wondered whether it is poisonous. It was clearly a novelty to this group of learners. Marc, the Master Gardener attempted to clarify its meaning by referring to the lotion as a "milky sap." Matthew then wondered to what extent such a milky sap is really "edible" while Tamara still appeared concerned. She made sure to share with the group that she had never eaten such a substance since her family "don't eat lettuce." This example reveals the extent to which meaning-making in the garden was also a social endeavor. By exchanging ideas and explanations of what they observed, the students used each other, in addition to the environment to construct new ways of knowing science.

As noted by Pugh (1988), a garden's fluid and transient nature means that "it can never be pinned down, fixed, it can never be a definitive text" (p. ix). What meaning is constructed depends on the actors, the knowledge they bring to a garden, and their interest in exploring new phenomena. More specifically, another group of learners might not ever have noticed the milky sap in salad leaves, and as such would never have become a topic of discussion. Accordingly, meaning-making of gardening can take many forms. There is no one single text to be comprehended. Instead, the text emerges from students' interactions with each other, with the experts, and with the garden itself. The science content is in essence invisible and to be constructed rather than absorbed, as is often the case in written texts (even though we now understand that texts portray multiple layers of meaning; see chapter 3 by Donin in this book). In essence, the practice of gardening can only be understood by taking an active part in it, which in turn appears to make it also intriguing and interesting to learners who are otherwise used to rather traditional models of science education. As Tamara put it, "here they put you through it and at school, they just put it on paper." Later she added, in school "they just teach us, they don't show us," a statement made by many others too. Benita put it her way, "[Here] you get to do the whole package!" Similarly, Tarr and others noted, "Out in the garden [we are] like doing it ourselves and then like in school . . . we just talk about it." And because of that, Stephen added, "I think I learn more in this program than I'll ever learn in school." Hence, these young people highly valued learning by doing and the hands-on approach of the program that led to purposeful and meaningful activities in which science content was embedded and details could be learned. They were aware of the fact that the garden promoted a different text of science than their classroom, and highly valued the former.

With this case, I hope to have illustrated the richness and dynamic nature of an environment as text. In the second case, I illustrate the manner whereby a physical environment can make science accessible to impoverished students.

CASE 2. SCIENTISTS' LABORATORY AS A TEXT FOR SCIENCE LEARNING

The second example is taken from an activity I pursued with a group of youth from the gardening program in summer 2000 (see Rahm & Downey, 2001, 2002). I worked with a group of seven fourteen-year-old second-year students one morning a week during the eight-week program (six African American, one European American). The goal was to conduct oral histories of scientists and thereby learn more about the world of scientists. The actual visits to scientists' workplaces were followed by reflections about the scientists' and their science, leading to a poster that was then presented to the whole gardening program. Our reflections in the garden and visits to scientists were captured on video and supplemented by fieldnotes and journals, allowing for a variety of detailed qualitative analysis. Here I draw from a visit to an atmospheric chemist in a research institution (Susan). I show how physical items of a scientist's laboratory, in this case a liquid nitrogen bottle, can be thought of as a physical text that made evident to the students the kind of science this particular scientist engaged in.

Susan's office was in the basement of a big building and cluttered with tools of her trade. While the meanings of these tools were transparent to her, the obscurity of them in the eyes of youth made them important means to learn about atmospheric chemistry. In fact, a huge bottle ejecting steam got the attention of all of us right away and became the focus of our talk in a manner that Susan herself might not have anticipated. That is, the bottle became a text for science literacy development. Somebody wanted to know "what's that" pointing to the big metal bottle that Susan was leaning on, leading to the following exchange (see figure 4.2):

Excerpt 5

    Susan: Well, that's a good question. This is a big tank that has liquid nitrogen in it, and mmh, we had just taken some out of here. And liquid nitrogen is EXTREMELY cold, it's the coldest liquid you can find. And so, it's minus 195 centigrade. I am not sure what that is in Fahrenheit, but really cold. [searches for a funnel and bucket to let the liquid nitrogen flow into for demonstration]

    Michael: What's all the ice on the pipe up there?

    Susan: Well, what this is, this is normally, mmh, a brass pipe, mmh, but what happens here is because this is so cold, the moisture that's in the air condenses on this right away. It's like, if you have a glass and you put ice in it and you put water in it and it's real humid outside, after a while you get water on the glass, on the outside of the glass, the same process is happening here, it's just really cold and the water just condenses on it because it is so cold. So that's why it's white like that. Normally, the pipe, I don't wanna touch it because it is really cold, but normally it would be like this pipe [points to another one]. It's just water that's condensed outside.

    Troy: . . . If you would stick your finger in it, can it kill you?

    Susan: [giggles] If you would stick your finger in it, you would probably freeze yourself. It's extremely cold.

Interesting here is the manner whereby Susan attempted to explain the coldness of liquid nitrogen, relying both on oral (explanation of concept; responding to ice on pipe) and physical demonstrations (pouring of liquid on floor without touching it). This interaction offered the students a means to learn about the kind of chemicals Susan deals with. Susan took advantage of their interest in her environment and then explained the use of nitrogen to "freeze" air samples that they collect in metal bottles in the outer stratosphere. That is, she explained how liquid nitrogen is used to "freeze" air-samples on slides that can then be examined under the microscope for analysis. She also took us to a backroom to show the "bath-tub" they had constructed in which bottles were cleaned and prepared for the next data collection session (see figure 4.3). Again, student-initiated questions were supported and led to learning opportunities about the science pertinent to atmospheric chemistry.

Excerpt 6

    Susan: . . . and all it is is actually a big bathtub. [stands in front of bottle cleaning area] OK, you look underneath here, you see these lights they seem like heat lights. You see them here. OK. And the reason that we have this set up here is . . . this is one of the cans that we use to collect our air samples with, so this is mainly steel.

    Troy: This is empty?

    Susan: Yeah, but steel isn't very heavy so they aren't very heavy. So after we are done with the sample we need to clean these things out before we use them again. And that's what this is for. All those cans will fit right down here. So we put all the cans on here, we lower this thing down and we heat them up. And basically just flush them out over and over again. To clean them out until they are ready to go for the next time around. So that's what all this is for.

Kevin: How long does that take?

Susan: Mmmh, it actually takes about twenty-four hours, but we do the flushing and then the heating over-night and then we flush them again, the next day. And then, we send them, we send them out in the field with air, with just blank air in them. And then we pump them out when we get up.

Note how the student's questions helped make more science content accessible. It helped clarify the instruments (kind of metal of bottle), the duration of the cleaning process, and the methods of data collection (see figure 4.3). Interesting is Susan's note

Figure 4.2. Learning about liquid nitrogen with Susan

Figure 4.3. Explanation of cleaning process

that the bottles are steel, something that explained the light weight of the bottles to her, yet not necessarily so to Troy, who wondered whether the bottle was empty or not. It attests to a difference in the level of expertise in science between the two speakers. To illustrate how the bottles are used for data collection, Susan then took us to another room filled with racks of metal bottles. She showed us how the bottles are mounted onto racks and explained how racks get attached to the outside of an airplane for data collection. She pointed to the valve that lets air accumulate in the bottles and makes it possible to retrieve air-samples from the stratosphere.

This case shows how these learners were given an opportunity to understand the scientists' work in context, in that they got to see the tools Susan uses, the steps of data gathering she engages in, and the kind of maintenance work—such as cleaning the bottles—Susan is responsible for. By actually holding the metal bottles and seeing the giant bathtub, students could interact with scientific objects in ways that made the science less mystical to them. In essence, youth learned about "how people do science" (Lee & Roth, 2002, p. 38), a kind of scientific literacy not easily translated into the kind of scientific facts valued in science classrooms, yet certainly more representative of what the doing of "real" science is about. How such ways of knowing influenced these students' management of school science was beyond the focus of this study but would be worth considering in the future. Judging from student interviews, however, exposure to such texts of science were perceived as interesting and new. As Marti noted, "We got to look at things that we haven't even known existed." Adam said, "I thought science was dumb until I learned I was doing it." Clearly, these students learned about science by doing it (understanding in practice) rather than simply by talking about it (culture of acquisition; Lave, 1990), a differentiation they became aware of and valued.

The excerpts also illustrate how all participants were engaged in inquiry, attesting to their level of interest in the scientific work of an atmospheric chemist. By posing questions, students made the science of Susan's work more transparent and accessible for themselves and the quiet participants of this group. They highly valued such interactions, as is apparent in Michael's statement:

> I liked how we got to have people tell us, instead of us having to look at a textbook . . . and I enjoyed the fact that we got to meet them, that we got to visit them and look at things that we haven't even known existed.

Again, youth appear to have realized that such an interaction offered them a different text for science education than the one they experienced daily in their classrooms. Most important, for this group of students, the garden and the laboratory became settings and texts of science they could relate to and became interested in, unlike the kinds of texts of science they knew from school. These texts did not convey science to them as a muddle of facts and as a domain only accessible to the elite—the scientists' science. Instead, science was something embedded in everyday activities in their community and presented as an area of study that can be intriguing and worth exploring.

Note also that in the cases presented here, the environment constituted the science the students constructed. In contrast, written texts are often peripheral or subsidiary to meaning-making in the classroom (Peacock, Cleghorn, & Mikkila, 2002). Hence, written, oral, and physical texts also take on different positions within different communities (Gee, 1986; Kelly & Chen, 1999). It suggests that we have to move beyond privileging one text over another and instead focus on the kind of text that is culturally meaningful within a community.

Conclusion

The two cases underline the value of thinking of texts in broader terms and in particular, to begin to examine the role of physical texts in students' meaning-making of science. Interestingly, physical texts do play an important role in current science reform movements that attempt to break down the barriers between classrooms and the community. Take for example activities surrounding a watershed as studied by Lee and Roth (see also Roth & Lee, 2002). In this case, middle school students, members of an environmental activist group, farmers, and local residents worked together to protect and enhance a creek stream system through the construction of riffles. Through this project, students learned to use science as a means to make their community a better place to live. The science was developed in the classroom through discussions as well as in situ through interactions with members of other communities (farmers, activists) and the environment (exploration of the ecological state of the creek along with experts such as environmental activists and water technicians). Steps could then be identified and undertaken to make the creek a more ecologically viable place. Such a model of science education made it possible for these students to participate in everyday activities in which scientific knowledge is a resource for action. The students also had the opportunity to draw upon multiple texts. In fact, the creek became a physical text for science education in a similar manner as the garden and the laboratory described here. And it was the richness of such a physical text and the kind of science it made available to its students (a science that can be used for action rather than a science that consists of meaningless memorized facts) that made the community project a success.

Similarly, the physical texts described in this chapter became tools to make a world of science accessible to youth that was new to them, yet a world of science they valued and could relate to. It was a more powerful text of science than the traditional science text these youth were exposed to in their schools. It was a text they could relate to, position themselves within, and see as intriguing and relevant. Unlike textbooks, such physical texts made the people, tools, and social contexts involved in the construction of science visible. It was also no longer the teacher or the textbook controlling the kind of knowledge that counted (Brickhouse, 1994). In fact, through the students' questioning and active sense-making, they came to play an active part in defining the kind of science they were exposed to. Accordingly, the environment as text can be understood as a participant in these students' meaning-making of science (Bernhardt, 1987).

Furthermore, as emphasized by the sociocultural perspective (Wertsch, 1991), mediational means such as tools and language also shape action. That is, if we think of the garden and the laboratory as texts for science literacy development and hence as tools that mediate meaning-making of science, such tools can also be understood as having shaped students' actions and interactions with science. Namely, through students' manipulation of the environment, their observations and inquiry of the environment, they came to talk and learn about the science embedded in the garden and laboratory setting and *understand in practice* (Lave, 1990). It is for these reasons that the notion of physical environments as texts for science literacy development is worth further consideration.

Unfortunately, most inner-city youth in impoverished neighborhoods lack access to such texts of science (Barton, 2001). The culture of acquisition of scientific facts still dominates (Lave, 1990). In addition, they have to contend with schools with few resources, outdated textbooks, and few science-related extracurricular activities (Oakes, 1990). They also lack access to certified math and science teachers that support high-quality science teaching (Ingersoll, 1999), have access to fewer high-level math and science courses (Oakes, 1990) and if tracked, often do no science at all. Physical texts as the ones described here may become particularly important resources for changing such a state and for making science education more inclusive and tied to the lives and needs of our students.

Note

1. The 4-H program is one of the oldest extracurricular educational programs in the United States, originally targeting youth in rural farm communities. The four H's in its name refer to the head, heart, hands, and health. It is a program of the Cooperative Extension Service, jointly supported by the U.S. Department of Agriculture, land-grant universities, and local county governments.

References

Barton, A.C.
(2001). Science education in urban settings: Seeking new ways of praxis through critical ethnography. *Journal of Research for Science Teaching, 38* (8), 899–917.

Bernhardt, E.B.
(1987). The text as a participant in instruction. *Theory Into Practice, 26* (1), 32–37.

Brickhouse, N.
(1994). Bringing in the outsiders: Reshaping the sciences of the future. *Curriculum Studies, 26* (4), 401–416.

Cleghorn, A.
(2003). An ethnographic eye on text talk and teacher talk in developing country classrooms. *Ways of Knowing.* In press.

Gee, J.P.
(1986). Orality and literacy: From the savage mind to ways with words. *TESOL Quarterly, 20* (4), 719–746.

Ingersoll, R.
(1999). The problem of underqualified teachers in American secondary schools. *Educational Researcher, 28* (2), 26–31.

Jordan, B. & Henderson, A.
(1995). Interaction analysis: Foundations and practice. *The Journal of the Learning Sciences, 4* (1), 39–103.

Kelly G. & Chen, C.
(1999). The sound of music: Constructing science as sociocultural practices through oral and written discourse. *Journal of Research in Science Teaching, 36* (8), 883–915.

Kress, G.
(1996). Representational resources and the production of subjectivity. In C.R. Caldas-coulthard & M. Coulthard (Eds.), *Texts and practices* (pp. 15–31). New York: Routledge.

Lave, J.
(1990). The culture of acquisition and the practice of understanding. In J.W. Stigler, R.A. Shweder, & G. Herdt (Eds.), *Cultural psychology: Essays On comparative human development* (pp. 309–328). New York: Cambridge University Press.

Lee, S. & Roth, W.M.
(2002). Learning science in the community. In W.M. Roth & J. DéSautels (Eds.), *Science education as/for sociopolitical action* (pp. 37–66). New York: Lang.

Lemke, J.L.
(1989). Making text talk. *Theory Into Practice, 18* (2), 136–141.

Lotman, Y.M.
(1988). Text within text. *Soviet Psychology, 26* (3), 32–51.

Oakes, J.
(1990). *Multiplying inequalities: The effects of race, social class, and tracking On opportunities to learn mathematics and science.* Santa Monica, Ca: RAND.

Peacock, A., Cleghorn, A., & Mikkila, M.
(2002). Multiple perspectives on the teacher-learner-text relationship in primary school science. *Curriculum and Teaching, 17* (2), 55–72.

Pugh, S.
(1988). *Garden, nature, language.* Manchester: Manchester University Press.

Rahm, J.
(1998). *Growing, harvesting, and marketing herbs: Ways of talking and thinking about science in a garden.* Unpublished Dissertation. University of Colorado at Boulder.

Rahm, J.
(2001). Science literacy in the making in an inner-city youth program: "They take the time to show us how a plant grows." In M. Hedegaard (Ed.), *Learning in classrooms* (pp. 144–165). Aarhus, Denmark: Aarhus University Press.

Rahm, J.
(2002). Emergent learning opportunities in an inner-city youth gardening program. *Journal of Research in Science Teaching, 39* (2), 164–184.

Rahm, J. & Downey, J.
(2001). *Oral Histories of Scientists as a Tool to Make Meaning of Science: Stories from An Inner-City Youth Gardening Program.* Paper Presented at the Annual Meeting of the American Educational Research Association, Seattle.

Rahm, J. & Downey, J.
(2002). "A scientist can be anyone!" Oral histories of scientists can make real science accessible to youth. *The Clearing House, 75* (5), 253–257.

Roth, W.M & DéSautels, J.
(2002). *Science education as/for sociopolitical action.* New York: Lang.

Roth, W.M. & Lee, S.
(2002). Breaking the spell: Science education for a free society. In W.M. Roth & J. DéSautels (Eds.), *Science education as/for sociopolitical action* (pp. 67–95). New York: Lang.

Spradley, J.P.
(1980). *Participant observation.* New York: Harcourt Brace Jovanovich.

VanMaanen, J.
(1988). *Tales from the field: On writing ethnography.* Chicago, Il: University of Chicago Press.

Vygotsky, L.S.
(1978). *Mind in society.* Cambridge, Ma: Harvard University Press.

Wertsch, J.
(1991). *Voices of the mind.* Cambridge: Harvard University Press.

5

What is a Science Text?: An Overview of Section One

Catherine C. Lewis

In 1993, I was sitting in Japanese elementary classrooms for months on end, gathering data for a book focused on the social and civic aspects of Japanese elementary education (Lewis, 1995). My observational focus had nothing to do with science. Yet all at once I began to notice pendulums and levers everywhere. (These were two of the topics under study by the students during my months of observation.) For example, while walking to the train one day, I suddenly noticed that where I attached my heavy briefcase to my long-handled rolling suitcase was a problem in levers. I noticed that I couldn't swing my arms at the same rate when I tried to speed-walk with a short umbrella hanging down from one arm: a problem in pendulums! Pendulums and levers had surrounded me for a long while, but I had never noticed them until I started learning science with Japanese elementary students. These daily-life objects had suddenly become "text" for me, as the community gardens and scientist's laboratory described by Rahm (chapter 4) became text for the students she studied.[1]

Consider the impact when the objects in one's daily life—from can-openers to clocks—suddenly become educative text. The potential of this resource can be imagined by comparing the number of hours per week I studied science with the Japanese students in class—two hours—and the number of waking hours—perhaps 100 per week—during which daily-life levers and pendulums were suddenly available to me to study. To make a bad pun, something about the way science was taught in those Japanese elementary classrooms had leveraged my formal science instruction in a way that increased my capacity to learn from daily life.

The three chapters of this section explore in very different ways what it means to learn science from a text. In chapter 2, McEneaney traces the changes in Canadian elementary science textbooks since the 1950s, comparing a sample of Canadian textbooks (used in grades 4 through 7) with a larger sample of texts from 60 countries. A number of interesting points emerge. First, McEneaney points out that textbooks have an official national function:

> textbooks are like museums . . . localized conflicts about particular aspects of textbooks
> and other learning materials . . . are fueled with an emotion that goes beyond concern
> for student learning and into the legacy of commemoration, much like conflicts over
> museum exhibits or public memorials. (p. 22)

Second, McEneaney explores the controversial idea that an ideology characterized by rationalism, universalism, and individualism is beginning to gain dominance around the world, resulting in an increasing homogeneity in world culture. In this spreading ideology, rationalism is a key value and "science is seen as the most legitimate source of solutions for social and economic problems." McEneaney argues that nations seek to align their textbooks with the latest global pedagogical thinking in order to commemorate "in a very essential way that a nation is committed to progress in a modern sense" (p. 3). International science testing (e.g., TIMSS, PISA) and multinational textbook publishing companies are suggested as mechanisms that accelerate global homogenization of science textbooks. A second ascending value is universalism: the idea that human beings around the world have the same basic needs. The third is individualism: the idea that individuals are the most fundamental actors in the social system, and that science can appeal to individuals through creation of textbooks with personally relevant content. Finally, McEneaney argues that, at the same time that there may be pressures toward globalization of textbooks, there are also manifestations of "local" (i.e., national) influences on Canadian textbooks, such as use of Canada-specific flora and fauna, Canadian places and people, and the metric system (often an explicit departure from parent texts written for the U.S. market).

In summary, McEneaney helps us think about the "commemorative" function of textbooks; recognize the ways in which "global" values of universalism, individualism, and rationality may shape science textbooks around the world; to identify some of the means (e.g., multinational textbook companies and international tests) through which such international uniformity may be built; and also to recognize the distinctively Canadian features that are simultaneously being emphasized (the colorful term "glocalization," from Robertson, 1994, is used).

In chapter 3, Donin presents a multilevel model of text processing, making the case that comprehension of text is "not a serial process (i.e., either top-down or bottom-up), but rather one in which processing at multiple levels is proceeding concurrently" (p. 56). Donin's definition of text rests on language: "an instance of language in use, either spoken or written" (p. 1). In the model proposed in chapter 3, a reader or listener uses lexical and syntactic information to construct a conceptual representation and at the same time uses existing knowledge to aid in lower-level processing of text. Implications for text use in classrooms are drawn out, including: (1) that decoding is a necessary but not sufficient condition for comprehension of text; (2) that both text characteristics and reader/listener characteristics affect comprehension; and (3) that multiple types of knowledge affect processing, including content knowledge, knowledge of genre and text type, and knowledge of situational context in which the text is to be used.

In contrast to the language-based definition of "text" laid out in chapter 3, chapter 4 provides case studies of a community-garden and a scientific laboratory used as "texts" for science learning by urban middle-school students; both cases are taken from a larger ethnographic study of an urban youth gardening program in midwestern United States. Excerpts of discourse from the two cases document how the students notice features of interest in each place, ask questions about them, bring their own ideas to bear, and reflect on science and their own learning of it. As one student aptly contrasts school science with the science experienced in the garden: "Out in the garden [we are] like doing it ourselves and then like in school . . . we just talk about it." Rahm (p. 98) summarizes the potential of this approach:

> It was a more powerful text of science than the traditional science text these youth were exposed to in their schools. It was a text they could relate to, position themselves within, and see as intriguing and relevant. Unlike textbooks, such physical texts made the people, tools and social contexts involved in the construction of science visible. It was also no longer the teacher or the textbook controlling the kind of knowledge that counted (Brickhouse, 1994). In fact, through youths' questioning and active sense-making, they came to play an active part in defining the kind of science they were exposed to.

Each of the three chapters raises fundamental issues about how students learn science from texts—issues that speak directly to the challenges faced by many North American students in learning science. What is a good science text? How do we hope students will be changed by interaction with a good text? I will return to these issues after we examine science education from a contrasting vantage point: the case of Japanese elementary science textbooks.

The Nature of Japanese Elementary Science Textbooks

Japanese elementary science textbooks are remarkably different from their North American counterparts (Okamoto et al., 1992; Tsuchida & Lewis, 2002). Figure 5.1 summarizes some of the differences that make the slim, half-letter-size, sparsely worded textbooks used by Japanese elementary students hard to recognize as part of the same category as the thick, discursive, reference-like textbooks used by many North American elementary students. When my son attended elementary school in Japan, all six of his textbooks together weighed less than any one of his U.S. textbooks.

Several characteristics of Japanese textbooks provide an interesting vantage point to think about the chapters of this section. First, Japanese textbooks are sparsely worded: as shown in table 5.1, the Japanese textbooks devote an average of 18 sentences to electricity (compared with an average of 165 in the U.S. textbooks). This does not necessarily mean, however, that they introduce fewer ideas about a particular topic. Elementary science textbooks in the two countries are roughly similar in the number of scientific terms defined in each unit, and in the number of photographs, illustrations, and experiments they provide (table 5.1; Tsuchida & Lewis, 2002). Japanese textbooks cover a much smaller number of topics, each one in depth. So the Japanese elementary curriculum allows a dozen or so periods (of 45 minutes each) to learn

Lessons 1 & 2

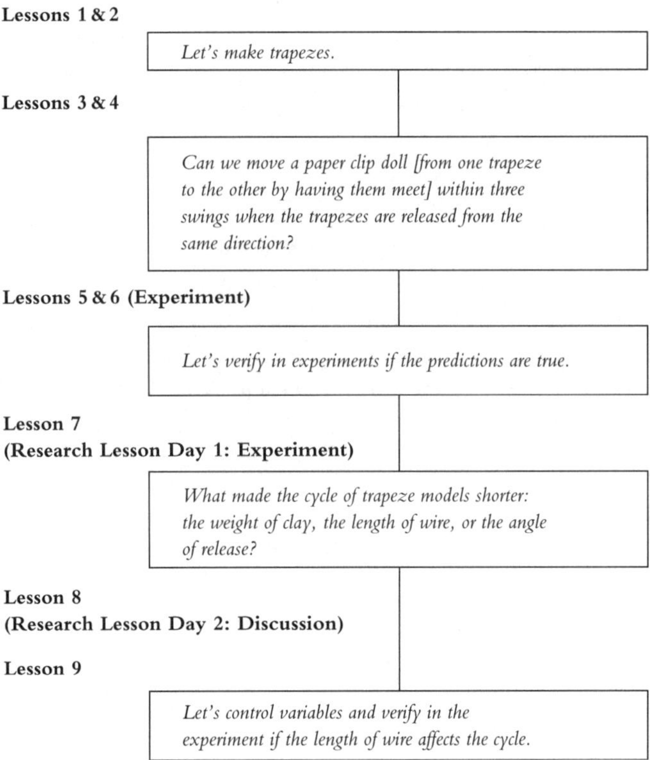

Lessons 3 & 4

Lessons 5 & 6 (Experiment)

Lesson 7
(Research Lesson Day 1: Experiment)

Lesson 8
(Research Lesson Day 2: Discussion)

Lesson 9

Figure 5.1. Unit organization: description of planned teacher instruction

Note: The pendulum unit was planned to be nine lessons, with the seventh and eighth lessons to be research lessons with observers. The instructional plan for the nine lessons is written in italics inside the rectangles.

Table 5.1. Elementary science textbooks

	U.S.	Japan
Size	5 pounds, 500 pages	1 pound, 100 pages
Content	Wide-ranging content	10 studied topics only
Electricity Unit		
Pages	18	14
Sentences	205	17
Experiments and activities	4	4
Photos	23	24
Illustrations	7	20

Source: Data for this table taken from Tsuchida & Lewis, 2002, where study details may be found. Two U.S. and two Japanese textbooks were analyzed; numbers are averages for the two texts from each country.

about levers, enabling teachers to plan a coherent sequence of lessons like those laid out in figure 5.1.

The smaller amount of language in Japanese texts is further understood by looking at the role of visual material. Although U.S. and Japanese texts devote a comparable amount of space to visual images, the Japanese images generally provide information to guide students' activities and experiments, whereas the U.S. images may be "extraneous or eye-catching" illustrations, such as a girl blowing dry her long hair to illustrate the chapter on electricity (Tsuchida & Lewis, p. 39). Although the photograph of the long-haired girl takes up 40 square inches of space,

> each of the three photographs of a boy making an electric motor occupy only 4 square inches. Thus the details of the step-by-step photographs of the motor building process are hard to see. As if to compensate for the inadequacy of the photographs, the accompanying written explanation for building the motor is long with one to five sentences for each step. Although U.S. textbooks often showed the step-by-step procedures for experiments, the illustrations did not clearly show the details. (Tsuchida & Lewis, p. 39)

Further analyses of Japanese and U.S. elementary science textbooks conducted by Tsuchida and Lewis (2002) suggest that the activities and experiments included in the Japanese textbook are closely connected to one another and to the prose in the unit, forming a coherent whole, whereas U.S. textbooks provide a wide range of information that is not closely integrated with the suggested activities.

> The U.S. texts rely heavily on written explanation that is often weakly connected to suggested student activities or experiments. While the U.S. texts emphasize reading about science, the Japanese texts emphasize doing science, through a series of tightly connected activities and experiments, supported with spare, simple prose. (Tsuchida & Lewis, p. 39)

In summary, the Japanese texts focus on *doing* science (often using objects familiar to students from their daily life) rather than *reading* about science as "the accumulation of facts that someone else has actually gathered" (Okamoto et al., 1992, p. 26). The word "mijika na" (close-at-hand or familiar) to describe what is studied in science is a favorite term in the Japanese Elementary Course of Study for Science (Monbusho, 1999) and in research lessons developed by Japanese teachers as a way to collectively improve teaching (Lewis & Tsuchida, 1997, 1998; Linn, Lewis, Tsuchida & Songer, 2000).

Why Do Japanese and U.S. Textbooks Differ?

The overall contours of textbook development are very similar in the United States and Japan (Lewis, Tsuchida, & Coleman, 2002). Independent commercial publishers develop texts and local school boards select among competing textbook series what will be adopted in their jurisdiction; often teachers are involved in the selection process. In both Japan and in many U.S. states, school boards may select only from texts that have been approved by a government-designated textbook approval committee. Then why do the two countries end up with such different textbooks?

In both countries, precedent—or maybe one should say inertia—is powerful: each successive version of the textbook looks a great deal like the prior textbook, which is to say a slim, spare guide to "do" science in the Japanese case, and an inclusive reference book to read about science in the U.S. case (Lewis & Tsuchida, 2002). Second, approval processes push the textbooks in opposite directions; to be approved in as many U.S. states as possible, U.S. textbook publishers include at every grade level content that is required by any large state. In contrast, the committee designated by the Ministry of Education, Science, Sports and Technology to approve Japanese textbooks requires publishers to cut out any content not explicitly included in the *Course of Study* (Lewis & Tsuchida, 2002). In response to grade 3–6 elementary science textbooks submitted by one Japanese publisher in 1994, the Ministry of Education's Textbook Authorization and Research Council requested 99 changes, and nearly one in five pertained to material the Council regarded as beyond the scope of the *Course of Study*. For example, the textbook publishers were asked to cut material related to soil, development of internal organs, and the relationship between animal life and food source, because these topics are not included in the *Course of Study* (Lewis, Tsuchida, & Coleman, 2002, p. 52).

A third major influence on Japanese elementary textbooks is the agreement among textbook publishers to keep texts within a certain page limit and certain number of color and black-and-white photographs; this agreement effectively enables publishers to limit costs (without setting a price, which would violate antimonopoly laws) and keeps any publisher from offering an expanded textbook as a loss-leader in order to wrest market share from others (Lewis & Tsuchida, 2002).

A fourth important influence is that Japanese elementary science texts are written by elementary teachers rather than by professional writers, and are based in actual lessons taught to students that are extensively and collaboratively studied through the system of "research lessons" (Lewis & Tsuchida, 1997, 1998; Lewis, 2002). The writing of elementary textbooks is highly collaborative, involving a group of about ten elementary educators who are actively involved in the development and study of research lessons in a particular topical area within science, whose writing is reviewed by each other and then by an additional group of about 10 people (including many university professors) who review the work for errors and so forth. While U.S. textbook author-educators describe working in isolation as "consulting authors" who individually respond to express-mailed manuscripts written by the "real authors," Japanese textbook author-educators report that classroom teachers are the ultimate authorities:

> I think the voice of classroom teachers is decisive in the textbooks. No matter how much professors say "Let's do X" or "Let's do Y," it's the classroom teachers who are actually central. Whether it makes a good lesson or not is the deciding factor. (Lewis et al., 2002)

Because the Japanese texts focus on doing science, rather than reading about it, the Japanese textbook author-educators reported many textbook revisions that had been made based upon their own use of the textbook: for example, a unit on balance and weight that had originally begun with children constructing a mobile was rearranged to begin with a simple balance scale and include the mobile-making activity (which proved to be quite difficult for students) at the end of the unit, after students had had considerable experience with weight and balance (Lewis, Tsuchida & Coleman, 2002). In addition, textbook companies systematically surveyed teachers about the parts of the textbook that were difficult to use, and gave this information to the textbook author-educators. For example, one author, quoted here, designed an activity that was included in the textbook but eliminated from the subsequent version (about four years later) because teachers found it too difficult to use.

> There are things of mine that have been not well received. For example, I designed one experiment where the air from a ball goes into a balloon and the ball shrinks and the balloon becomes larger than the ball. It became part of the textbook, but . . . It was hard because when they attached the hose between the ball and the balloon, air leaked from somewhere. That was the feedback that the textbook company got on that section of the textbook. So, in the next textbook we changed the experiment . . . . The idea behind the ball and balloon was that air is not just air. A child has a hard time grasping the idea that air shrinks or expands. So the fact that the balloon would get bigger than the ball was interesting to them. But air leaked out and so it was too hard to do. The textbook company gathered feedback from around the country, and they identified that unit as being one that was hard to teach. Also I think the things needed to do that particular experiment—the pump and so forth—took some trouble to gather. The textbook companies regularly bring together teachers to get their impressions of the textbooks. So they hear what units are difficult to do or to understand and they tell us that. You might call it a kind of market research that we learn from. The textbook has to be something that anyone can use (Lewis, Tsuchida, & Coleman, 2002).

In contrast, U.S. author-educators did not mention systematic data collection on the *current* textbook in order to find which parts were difficult to use; U.S. market research seemed to remain within the textbook companies and to focus on field-testing upcoming versions, as far as the U.S. author-educators were aware. Japanese textbooks may lend themselves to this type of market research more easily because the whole textbook is covered in class and it is used to guide lessons, not as a reference or reading book (Lewis, Tsuchida, & Coleman, 2002).

Despite enormous competition among Japanese textbook publishers and secrecy about some aspects of textbook contents, the lessons that form the basis of the Japanese textbooks are taught and studied publicly as research lessons before their incorporation into textbooks. (See Lewis, 2002, for discussion of the research lessons that are central to the process of "lesson study.") Japanese textbook author-educators affirm that "if you have a really good idea you want it to be seen by as many people as possible because otherwise the upper echelons within the textbook company might not see it as good and they might refuse it" and the "the more people who have seen your idea and reacted to it the more data you have to argue that this might be a good change" (Lewis et al., 2002, p. 56). In other words, textbooks make widely available lessons that have already been tested and improved as research lessons. Research lessons mix two spheres that are often kept separate in the United States: instructional policy and its implementation. So ideas from policy documents—for example, that science should be taught in ways that build students' "initiative" and capacity to "pursue problems . . . in their immediate environment with interest and concern" (Ministry of Education,

1993, p. 3; 1998, p. 58)—are brought to life in actual research lessons by teachers, in public venues where teachers and policymakers can collectively make sense of the worth of these approaches (Lewis & Tsuchida, 1997; Lewis, 2002).

After our brief tour of Japanese science textbooks, let us revisit three interesting issues raised by the chapters of this section.

What are the Constraints on Global Homogenization of Textbooks?

The first issue relates to the constraints on global homogenization of textbooks. McEneaney, for example, explores the forces pushing toward increasing global uniformity in science textbooks, as well as the ways in which local (Canadian) values assert themselves (or fail to do so). Japanese science textbooks provide an interesting case in which to examine the competing trends she documents. Japanese textbooks are published by Japanese publishers, and have remained slim volumes devoted to the doing of science, rather than becoming large reference books. Perhaps because Japanese score at or near the top in international assessments of science, the need to make Japanese science textbooks "commemorate" a particular international vision of science has not been remarked upon. This silence is especially noteworthy in comparison to the vocal public discussions of the contents of Japanese social studies textbooks (DeCoker, 2002). Why don't Japanese science textbooks look more like their North American counterparts, and what does this say about globalization of science textbooks? And, on the other hand, why haven't the international tests such as TIMMS and PISA resulted in the translation and wide availability of the textbooks of Japan (which are available only in Japanese) and other high-scoring countries? A Japanese educational researcher recently commented at an international conference on mathematics and science education: "Many Japanese think our textbooks need to be much bigger, but I don't hear a single American who thinks that bigger textbooks are better." He put his finger on an interesting problem: what exactly are the international and national pressures shaping textbook development, and how do these vary across subject areas?

How does Language-Based Text Compare with Other Text Forms for Learning Science?

The second issue centers on language-based text versus other forms of text. Here we see that Japanese fifth-graders read 22 sentences and engage in a series of hands-on experiments closely related to each other and to the print text in order to learn about levers; U.S. students read 130 sentences about levers and are offered several activities that may or may not be hands-on and may or may not be related to levers—such as figuring out how to use simple machines to move a piano into a truck and to move a roll of tape from floor to desktop (Tsuchida & Lewis, 2002). In the United States, we often treat reading as a prerequisite to science learning, and we devote enormous attention to studying comprehension processes, documenting readability of texts, and boosting reading skills of second-language learners and slow readers (rather than strengthening alternative access routes to science). But as Donin argues, knowledge builds decoding as well as vice versa. Yet in practice we often assume that reading is the key to science learning, and we know relatively little about the role of visual material, activities, discussion, and other nonwritten elements in students' understanding of science. In Japan and in other settings where science learning is not as heavily dependent on written language, how do learners use various forms of information to build comprehension? How do poor readers and second-language learners fare in these settings? What is the optimal role of written text in science learning, and how does this vary for different subgroups of students?

How can Textbooks Leverage Other Texts?

It has been a decade since my experiences in a Japanese elementary school led me to notice levers and pendulums all around me. I now realize that my connection of formal science learning to daily life did not happen by chance; helping students notice science in daily life is an explicit goal of the Japanese elementary curriculum, and one that is often talked about by teachers as they plan and evaluate research lessons. For example, when a group of Japanese elementary teachers conducted lesson study during a unit on levers, the art teacher commented, "Students [who studied levers last year] may not understand levers even though they studied them. When they were digging clay to make pottery, the earth was very hard, and I noticed that some of the students moved their hands closer to the shovel head, rather than farther out along the handle." Later on in the same lesson study cycle, another teacher shared her disappointment that students lifting a 30-kilogram sack using a counterweight did not talk about "the weight used to lift it. Since they studied weight last year, I would have hoped they would think about it quantitatively" (Can You Lift, 2000). Observations like these, which attend to whether students are spontaneously applying to daily life information learned in science class, are often central to the evaluation and redesign of science units in Japan.

Linn and Muilenberg (1996) have noted that formal science instruction gains power by leveraging daily life as a text for further science learning. The extent to which students see scientific principles as applicable outside the rarefied environment of the laboratory is a powerful predictor of their eventual science achievement (Linn & Songer, 1991). Since the 1990s Japanese educators have steadily increased the opportunities for informal, student-initiated science learning. During the 1990s, science and social studies were eliminated for students in grades 1 and 2, and a new subject area, life environment studies, was instituted, in which students take the lead in investigating both the natural and socially created features of their local environment (Lewis & Tsuchida, 1997). In the new millenium, even more time has been freed up within the Japanese curriculum for sougoutekina gakushu (comprehensive learning) in which students are expected to take the lead in investigation of issues that interest them (Monbushou, 1999). How do such experiences with "texts" outside the classroom fit in with formal learning from texts? Rahm (this volume, chapter 4, pp. 48–49) writes

> As noted by Pugh (1988), a garden's fluid and transient nature means that "it can never be pinned down, fixed, it can never be a definitive text" (p. ix). What meaning is constructed depends on the actors, the knowledge they bring to a garden, and their interest in exploring new phenomena. More specifically, another group of youth might not ever

have noticed the milky sap in salad leaves, and such would never have become a topic of discussion. Accordingly, meaning-making of gardening can take many forms. There is no one single text to be comprehended. Instead, the text emerges from youths' interactions with each other, with the experts, and with the garden itself.

Students' experiences with a garden will differ. Yet it makes sense to think in advance about what we would like students to gain from the garden experience, and to research what they do gain, and to understand the elements of the experience that make it successful—or unsuccessful—for various groups of students. Such systematic study of the features that lead to learning in real-world settings, and development of theory that predicts learning across various settings, is a central feature of the design experiments (and design research) that is increasingly in use in North America (Cobb, Confrey, diSessa, Lehrer, & Schauble, 2003; Design-Based Research Collective, 2003; Lobato, 2003).

When Japanese teachers investigate student learning during research lessons (as part of the larger process of lesson study), they think in advance about their long-term goals (both for science learning and for students' development more broadly) and they accumulate evidence related to these goals. For example, in the research lessons documented in "The Secret of Trapezes," teachers studied whether students developed an understanding of the influence of length, weight, and release point on a pendulum's cycle time; whether the students developed scientific habits of mind (e.g., whether they spontaneously controlled variables when conducting experiments); and students' initiative and desire as learners. These goals were studied in various ways, including work done by the students, narrative records of several students' speech and activities and recording of student behavior that might indicate interest and self-motivation such as under-breath mutterings and "shining eyes" (Lewis, 2002). Students were selected to represent different types of challenges, including a very quiet student, one who tended to provide answers without thinking carefully about subject matter, and one who already "knew" what was to be learned about levers from reading outside of school. The teachers traced the students' learning and development over the course of several lessons, studying how they applied the material studied in class to novel situations, how often and under what circumstances the quiet student spoke up, how the knowledgeable student connected prior book learning to the hands-on experiments, and so on. Rahm (this volume, chapter 4) notes print text does not constitute a single text. Yet we often act as if it does, studying textbooks in isolation from other experiences. Studying the interplay of students' prior knowledge, personal qualities, classroom community, hands-on activities, discussion, and use of print text is the heart of lesson study in Japan, and the learning about student learning that teachers accrue during lesson study is passed on through research lessons (attended about 10 times a year by the Japanese elementary teachers studied by Yoshida, 1999), in daily interactions with colleagues, and through written records of research lessons (Lewis, 2002; Yoshida, 1999). The three chapters of this section represent very different approaches to studying science texts, and very different perspectives on the question of how and what students learn from texts. Yet another layer of complexity is added by looking at Japanese science texts—which are remarkably different from the North American counterparts, and which are studied in vivo during lesson study—as one influence on student learning, and progressively refined based on evidence about students' development of knowledge and scientific habits of mind.

Note

1. This material is based upon work supported by the National Science Foundation under grant no. 0207259. Any opinions, findings, and conclusions or recommendations are those of the author and do not necessarily reflect the views of the National Science Foundation.

References

Brickhouse, N.
(1994). Bringing in the outsiders: Reshaping the sciences of the future. *Curriculum Studies, 26* (4), 401–416.

Can you lift 100 kilograms?: Excerpts of the Japanese lesson study cycle.
(2000). (Video, 18 minutes). Available from lessonresearch.net.

Cobb, P., Confrey, J., diSessa, A., Lehrer, R., & Schauble, L.
(2003). Design experiments in educational research. *Educational Researcher, 32* (1), 9–13.

DeCoker, G.
(2002). What do national standards really mean? In G. DeCoker (Ed.), *National standards and school reform in Japan and the United States.* Teachers College: Columbia University. (pp. xi–xx).

Design-Based Research Collective.
(2003). Design experiments: An emerging paradigm for educational inquiry. *Educational Researcher, 32* (1), 5–8.

Lewis, C.
(1995). *Educating hearts and minds: Reflections on Japanese preschool and elementary education.* New York: Cambridge University Press.

Lewis, C.
(2002). *Lesson study: A handbook of teacher-led instructional improvement.* Philadelphia: Research for Better Schools.

Lewis, C. & Tsuchida, I.
(2002). How do Japanese and U.S. elementary science textbooks differ? Depth, breadth, and organization of selected physical science units. In G. DeCoker (Ed.), *National standards and school reform in Japan and the United States* (chapter 3, pp. 35–45). Teachers College: Columbia University.

Lewis, C., & Tsuchida, I.
(1998). A lesson is like a swiftly flowing river: Research lessons and the improvement of Japanese education. *American Educator,* Winter, 14–17 and 50–52.

Lewis, C. & Tsuchida, I.
(1997). Planned educational change in Japan: The shift to student-centered elementary science. *Journal of Education Policy, 12* (5), 313–331.

Lewis, C., Tsuchida, I., & Coleman, S.
(2002). The creation of Japanese and U.S. elementary science textbooks: Different processes, different outcomes. In G. DeCoker (Ed.), *National standards and school reform in Japan and the United States* (chapter 4, pp. 46–66). Teachers College: Columbia University.

Linn, M., Lewis, C., Tsuchida, I., & Songer, N.B.
(2000). Science lessons and beyond: Why do US and Japanese students diverge in science achievement?, *Educational Researcher, 29* (3), 4–14.

Linn, M. & Muilenberg, L.
(1996). Creating lifelong science learners: What models form a firm foundation? *Educational Researcher, 25* (5), 18–24.

Linn, M. & Songer, N.
(1991). How do students' views of science influence knowledge integration? *Journal of Research in Science Teaching, 28* (9), 761–784.

Lobato, N.
(2003). How design experiments can inform a rethinking of transfer and vice versa. *Educational Researcher, 32* (1), 17–20.

Monbushou (Ministry of Education).
(May 1999). Shougakkou Gakushu Shidou Youryou Keisetsu: Rikahen (Elementary Course of Study Explanation: Science). Tokyo: Touyoukan Shuppansha.

Okamoto, Y., Calfee, R.C., Varghese, S., and Chambliss, M.
(1992). A Cross-Cultural Comparison of Textbook Designs. Paper presented at the meeting of the American Educational Research Association, Washington, D.C.

The secret of trapezes: Excerpts of two science research lessons.
(1999). (Video, 16 minutes). Available at lessonresearch.net.

Yoshida, M.
(1999). Lesson Study: A Case Study of a Japanese Approach to Improving Instruction through Actual-Based Teacher Development. Doctoral dissertation, University of Chicago.

Section Two

Why do Learners have Problems with Text Materials?

6

Introduction

Alan Peacock and Ailie Cleghorn

The paradox relating to the use of nonfiction text materials in primary schools is that on the one hand they are seen as central to the process of teaching and learning, whilst on the other hand there is little evidence of their effective use by *learners themselves*. This is true not only in second-language and developing country contexts but also in countries such as the United States and United Kingdom where publication and use of such text material in primary schools has been fostered for several decades, and where a wide range of material is available. In the United States, for example, Shulman (1987) concluded that most teaching is initiated by some form of text; yet Ball and Feiman-Nemser (1988) demonstrated that teachers in training were discouraged from using the set texts, and instead were encouraged to develop their own materials. In U.K. teacher education institutions, most trainees are not taught or encouraged to use existing text material in science (Peacock & Gates, 2000); instead we stress the importance of differentiation and therefore as in the United States, we encourage trainees to develop and use materials (often worksheets) of their own construction.

Why should we have all this professionally produced and expensive material and not really use it? The answer is complex, as the various chapters in this section show. It relates partly to the nature of the materials themselves, partly to our ideas about good teaching, and partly to the context in which books are used. Children in most cultures tend to learn to read and use text material largely through the use of linear "storybooks," which are narrative in structure. Nonfiction books, such as those used in math, geography, and science on the other hand, are expository: they do not simply tell a story, but set out information, ask questions and give instructions, often by the use of diagrams and illustrations as well as words, and often using all kinds of design and format conventions (icons, symbols, boxes, highlights, variable columns). The language of expository text uses vocabulary and connectives that children have often not encountered in storybooks. This new kind of text material can pose problems for many children, particularly those learning in a second language: the text can become a source of difficulty, rather than a source of help, for teachers as well as children.

The most extensive evidence relating to science texts and second-language learners comes from the research of the Threshold Project in Southern Africa (Langhan, 1993; Macdonald 1990a,b; van Rooyen, 1990). Again, text materials are here shown to be available but ineffectively used: and the paradox is partly explained in terms of the quality of the materials themselves. The Threshold team exposed difficulties of various kinds with science text material, including: (1) *Linguistic Problems* relating to children's comprehension, the demands of the text being too great for the levels of language development of the children using them; (2) *Pedagogical Problems* of mismatch between teaching styles implied in the text and those normally adopted by teachers in the contexts studied; (3) *Perceptual Problems* arising from teachers' own understanding of the phenomena of science and the subject matter content of the text.

The project found that teachers did not follow the demands of the text material, but rather interpreted the materials in their own way, maintaining their traditional teaching styles and the forms of interaction that their pupils were used to, such as teacher-talk, closed questions, and pupil copying of notes. When project staff redesigned materials and subsequently retested children in the light of their previous difficulties, modest learning gains were noted. However, the project also reported that teacher adaptation of materials often meant that they no longer provided the pupils with any published text resources to use themselves. Pupils were thus not participating in the kind of discourse that makes the text accessible and its value apparent, an issue discussed in detail by Rollnick in chapter 8.

The same situation has been observed in Peacock's research in London and Murila's research in Kenya, described in chapter 9. In London, teachers in classes where a high proportion of children were EAL speakers justified not using text material with the children. They explained that such materials did not meet children's needs, demanded language abilities beyond the children's levels of development, didn't foster group discussion, demanded too much teacher mediation and were not written by authors with an understanding of the specific mother-tongue context (Peacock, 1995a). Simplified worksheets were often adapted from sections of the schemes, and teachers often suggested ways in which texts could be improved, in terms of vocabulary, use of graphics and of different cultural expressions and meanings. However, teachers rarely if ever referred to the importance of children needing to be able to deal with published expository text, for example in order that they would be better able to cope with text-based discourse on entry into secondary school, where use of such textbooks was and is more widely prescribed.

In Kenya, Murila's study in primary schools in urban Nairobi and rural Western Kenya suggests that provision of mandatory texts varies in quantity from school to school, but that the text is still used widely in classrooms. However, the main use of the pupils' text by teachers is to require pupils to copy material from textbook to notebook (Murila, 2002). Kenyan teachers were reluctant to explain new words from the text, what Rollnick refers to as "learning to talk the language of science" partly because of pressure to complete the overloaded syllabus and partly as a consequence of their own lack of understanding of the text and of the subject matter represented in it. A further factor is commonly their limited command of English, the language of instruction and of the text itself (Cleghorn, 1992; Cleghorn & Rollnick, 2002). These observations echo the findings of most other research in Africa on primary teachers' science misconceptions (e.g., Rollnick & Rutherford, 1990) and their implications are discussed in chapter 8.

It is also important for primary teacher trainers to understand and teach not only the subject matter content of science but also, and crucially, those reading, writing, and visual literacy skills appropriate to the use of expository text, with particular emphasis on children learning in a second language. Several other strands of research exist in relation to the analysis of text material, all of which shed some light on the paradox of their underuse in classrooms.

LINGUISTIC PROBLEMS

Linguistic analysis of science texts has been largely focused on the secondary phase of schooling and on first-language contexts. Evidence relating to primary schools and second-language contexts is summarized in Peacock (1995b). Briefly, the research that exists suggests: (i) readability measures are too crude an indicator of pupils' potential difficulties; (ii) texts used during the stage of transition from mother-tongue to English as a medium of instruction are crucial. Yet they are often not written with progression in mind, for example in terms of the different demands made by nonfiction subject-based texts on the one hand, and language teaching schemes on the other; (iii) texts are usually written *by* first-language speakers *as if* for first language speakers, and take no account of bilingual learning or the languages and cultures of minorities. For example, some children in the United Kingdom (such as Sylheti-speaking children of Bangladesh) speak a language at home that is not written down and therefore does not have any books.

VISUAL LITERACY: GRAPHICS, STRUCTURE, AND FORMAT

The literature on visual literacy suggests that the actual function of graphic material (illustrations, icons, symbols, diagrams, photographs, tables) in nonfiction texts is much more complex than imagined and that these are often therefore ineffective. Illustrations do not always motivate and arouse interest, as assumed, but sometimes distract attention: being able to read the language of the text and having previous experience of graphics is an essential precursor to visual literacy. In developing countries, rural children have much greater difficulty interpreting diagrams and pictures than do urban children (Peacock, 1995b).

Science books can also be analyzed in terms of their structure and format. They tend to use graphics and text for a complex range of functions, and so are also "more literate" in terms of the "deep structure" demands made (Cummins, 1983; Gilbert 1989; Hyltenstam & Stroud, 1993; Vachon & Heaney, 1991). Biber (1991) has stressed the dangers of simplification by teachers: trying to make the text easier can impoverish the concepts being taught, and does not necessarily improve comprehension of science content. But there is very little research on pupils' comprehension of science ideas when learning from "teacher-made" text material, and as yet, very little research relating to pupils' learning on-line, either using linear text or hypertext, as pointed out by Murphy and Holleran in chapter 10.

Message and Voice

Dowling (1995) has analyzed texts from a sociological standpoint, in terms of how they "reproduce" activities. His study of primary school textbooks in mathematics introduces concepts such as Textual Strategies, Setting, Message, and Voice to discuss how texts work, and concludes that such texts create a "myth of participation." What this means is that since the teaching method is not usually made explicit in the textbook, "knowing what to do" with the text has to come from either the learner or the classroom setting. For example when the "voice" of the text says *collect some different materials . . ."* the pupil has to decide whether to *actually* follow this message (is this what my teacher wants me to do?) or simply to read on to where the text provides answers or information. Yet learning the science that the text intends is often dependent on collecting the materials and observing them, so that if the classroom setting prevents the pupil from doing this, participation is illusory and therefore the intended learning doesn't take place. This "myth of participation" or virtual rather than real experience, is increasingly common amongst pupils using on-line media, and is as yet very under-researched. As chapter 10 points out, computers are here to stay, yet huge levels of investment in ICT may lead us to assume a higher impact on learners than is apparent. The vastness of the web may be its own downfall: the more information there is, the more it tends to become difficult for a learner to find the specific information that may be of particular relevance to a particular activity or problem situation. Navigation skills thus become crucial.

Virtual activity through text seems to happen in many classrooms, in both developed and developing countries, and particularly in science lessons. For example, evaluations of the innovatory "Spider's Place" materials in comic-book and video form in South Africa (Perold & Bahr, 1993) showed that, where the teachers and trainers implementing the new materials possessed a limited repertoire of teaching strategies, the materials were not used as intended, and the participation implied by the messages in the text did not take place. Trials of new primary science texts for learners that puts materials directly into children's hands is also suggesting that, without the presence of a mediating teacher, pupils do not follow the "message" of the text, and therefore do not learn what the text intended (Francis, 1996). Instead, whilst the text implies one set of teaching methods, pupils often make sense of it by reference to another and very different idea of how to use it, determined by their own culturally determined knowledge of what is expected in the classroom (Kouladis & Tsatsaroni, 1996).

Teaching the Reading of Nonfiction Text

This problem is often made worse by the fact that formal teaching of reading tends to stop when pupils can decode narrative text effectively, that is at the stage when pupils are beginning to meet and use expository texts for the first time. This, crucially, is also the "threshold" stage when most pupils in developing-country schools are switching from being taught in their mother-tongue to learning from texts in English or some other lingua franca. Macdonald and van Rooyen observed that many such children were never taught the new strategies needed for reading and making sense of expository text material. Roth (1985) has gone further, suggesting that good as well as poor readers have difficulty learning from science texts for this reason. Rollnick in chapter 8 addresses the issue of how teachers can help pupils access text by using and translating the academic language of the text into the life-world language of pupils, and encouraging them to use this language in their discourse about the topic.

Texts rarely talk to their pupil-audience about the meta-cognitive ("how to learn from this book") aspects of what they are trying to achieve; exceptions are the "Spider's Place" series already referred to, which has a section at the beginning of the pupil's comic (the text) that addresses issues of both content and appropriate learning strategies, and the Nuffield Primary Science (1993, 1998) materials from the United Kingdom, which overtly draw attention to constructivist ideas of concept development throughout each text.

Nonfiction texts can thus make big demands on pupils. They not only present learners with new concepts but also require learners to process the structure and format in which ideas are presented. The demand introduced by abstract concepts is itself high; a "Considerate" text therefore attempts to minimize the demands made by the language, structure, and format. "Inconsiderate" text is that which makes no such attempt. The interactivity between these two demands, described by Sweller (1994) as the "Cognitive Load" of the text material, is dealt with by Leahy, Cooper, and Sweller in chapter 7.

What Does this Mean for Teachers?

In relation to pupils' comprehension, where teachers are aware of the problems inherent in commercially produced texts, they tend to respond to these difficulties in different ways. In some contexts they respond by not using such text material, choosing instead to develop their own materials, even though these materials may impoverish content and not improve comprehension, and even though their pupils will sooner or later need text-processing skills. In other contexts, particularly bilingual classrooms, teachers tend to mediate conceptual messages by switching between languages as and when appropriate. The impact of this code-switching on the use of science text is discussed by Rollnick in chapter 8.

Texts for pupils have within them implicit messages about teaching which, whilst they may be made explicit elsewhere (e.g., in Teachers' Guides) are only rarely made explicit to pupils. These implicit messages are often at odds with the methods adopted by teachers in their classrooms. Left to themselves, learners do not appear to follow the task messages in a text, even when these are explicit, and require the individual help of a teacher to make sense of what the text demands. Murphy and Holleran in chapter 10 suggest that pupils are even less likely to "follow" the text and make relevant links when using on-line hypertext formats. The need for mediation is especially important in developing-country contexts, where historically, approaches to learning have not encouraged learner-text engagement except of a limited, mechanical kind such as reading aloud or copying. Yet most teachers stick to their familiar ways of teaching, rather than those implicit in the text, so that a "myth of participation" perpetrated by the text is often reinforced by the teacher.

Though considerable research has often gone into *science content* at the text development stage (e.g., the SPACE research project in the United Kingdom and the subsequent Nuffield Primary Science materials, 1993), the role of text seems to be seen by many authors, designers, and publishers as "simply" to re-present this knowledge in an attractive format. Even at the proof-reading stage, whilst careful attention is given to the written text, major misconceptions are often introduced into the final published materials through the illustrations and format (see example later). Thomas Hardy discusses the constraints under which commercial publishing has to operate in chapter 11, and provides insights into the existence of such problems.

TEACHER TRAINING

Primary teachers, as noted earlier, do not seem to be given much in-service training on the use of expository text in science with children. Rather, there is evidence that training programs for a variety of reasons discourage pupils' use of text, and encourage the development of personal contextualized materials by trainees. However, teachers must themselves be able to teach text-processing skills to children. Therefore a crucial question is: what do teachers need to know about using nonfiction textbooks with children, and in particular with second-language learners? To try to answer this, it is helpful to look at specific examples of published science materials. Merely approaching such questions in general terms from a literacy perspective is inadequate, since as we have seen, many teachers themselves need help to fully understand the way a science text is intended to be used.

ANALYSIS OF TEXT MATERIAL

Extracts from two texts will be analyzed in terms of what they attempt to represent, how they work, and how children respond to them, leading to suggestions about how to help teachers to use text more effectively.

Example A (see figure 6.1) is the trial version of a lesson on Evaporation from a commercially published South African text. The trial version was given to a class of children in the absence of their teacher; they were then observed using it and interviewed afterward. The title on page 1 does not indicate what the substantive science focus is. The first instruction is in three stages ("make a puddle . . ." "draw . . . a line . . ." and "go back later . . .") and incorporates illustrations to represent the activities visually. The page ends with a question requiring the children to suggest an explanation of how the water disappeared. Adjacent is a box containing an illustration and a question relating to their general knowledge about drying washing on a line.

Linguistically, a crucial problem on this page was the word "puddle," which most children did not know. Only when they were given a bottle of water and questioned about the first illustration were they able to understand what the first step required of them. Two-thirds of the children did not *see* the three "starred" steps as being related in a logical progression. Hence most of them stopped for further instruction after step 1.

The visuals presented several problems. Most children thought that the boy was drawing a picture; the dots in the illustration were thought of as sand; the two arrows

Going Up?

Watch some water disappear

☆ Make a puddle outside on some tar or cement.
☆ Draw or scratch a line where the edge of the
  water is.
☆ Go back later and see what happened.

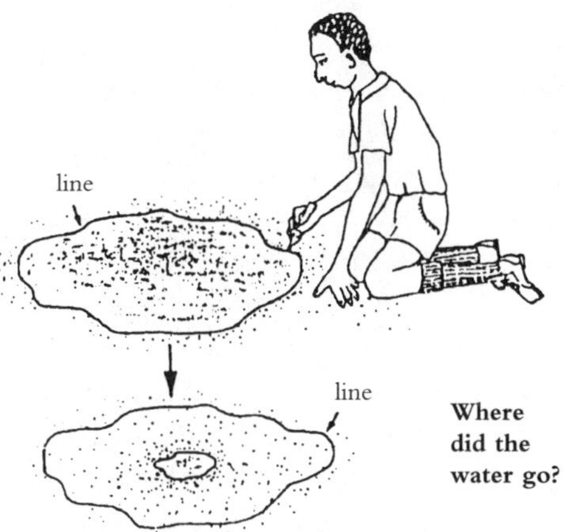

Do it again in a saucer

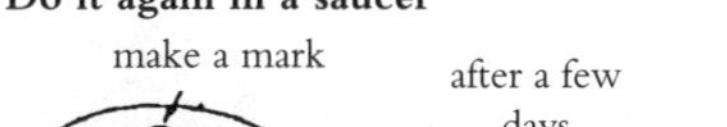
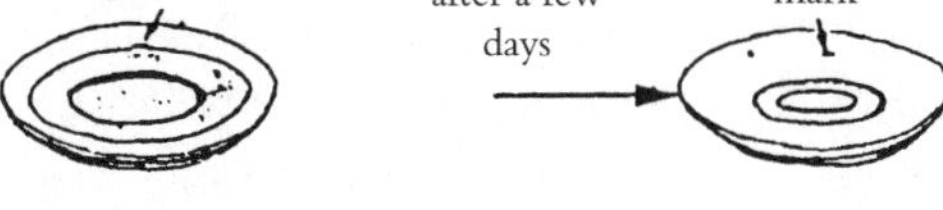

Where did the water go?

Maybe some of the puddle-water soaked into the
ground. This can't happen in a saucer or a bowl. It
must have got out another way.

Figure 6.1. Textbook illustration of evaporation
Source: Peacock, 1997

indicating "line" were correctly interpreted, but the function of the central arrow (indicating progression to the later stage of the activity) was not understood by anyone. And in the second illustration, presumably by analogy with the first, pupils interpreted the arrows as requiting them to write "make a mark" on the saucer. Some wrote "make a mark after a few days," underlining the two separate instructions in the illustration. Most children also ignored the boxed question (bottom left).

On page 2, pupils were presented with information about evaporation in written form. Only a minority understood the title before they started reading. Pupils were unable to link "tiny bits" with "particles," and "you can no longer see them" with "invisible"; a minority could point to the "surface" of a puddle. Some could identify names of liquids but could not explain what a liquid was, even though the definition is implicit in the last sentence of the first paragraph. Unlike the box on page 1, children's attention was drawn to the cartoon on page 2 even before they read the preceding text, perhaps suggesting that they were happy with this "comic" format, reinforcing the evidence of the "Spider's Place" evaluation (Peacock & Perold, 1995).

The children's responses illustrate the "myth of participation," quite clearly. They had to be prompted to act at each stage, even though the instructions are clearly practical and in the imperative, However, there is a practical *illogicality* in step 3 ("go back later …") since they cannot actually do this during the same lesson; so they have to decide; should they carry on with the rest of the page or not? Here, it is a question of whose "voice" they are hearing: pupils did not act until the "teacher" directly reinforced the message of the text. The voice in the text is not the teacher's voice. Yet the researcher reported their enthusiasm to try it out at home and observe what would happen (Francis, 1996).

This example was modified for inclusion in the final version of the text, to iron out some of these difficulties for pupils. By contrast, Example B is taken from the published version of a Pupils' Book on "Electricity and Magnetism," part of the Nuffield Primary Science materials (figure 6.2). It has not been evaluated with children as part of this research program but has been analyzed by trainee teachers in terms of the role it is intended to play in presenting subject matter to children and the potential problems it might create.

The Teachers' Handbook accompanying the scheme stresses that pupils' books are supplementary and not intended as a substitute for practical work and discussion: they can be used to "start small-group activity," to "arouse curiosity or provoke questions for discussion," as "links to work in other subject areas" or "to revise or consolidate classroom teaching." It is recommended that they are "used flexibly as an aid for learning" in "organisation of work that children can do on their own or in small groups" (Nuffield Primary Science, 1993).

In relation to the example spread on "Currents," the Teachers' Guide to the Electricity and Magnetism unit mentions the concept of current in several places; for example, as new vocabulary to be introduced; as a concept with which children have difficulty; and under "Background Science," the Guide provides a technical explanation of its meaning in terms of movement of electrical charge, direct and alternating current, mains electricity and so on. Children may also do the activities on constructing circuits described in the Teachers' Guide, and their attainment will be assessed through observation and questioning.

In order to decide how and when to use the section on "Currents" in the pupils' book, therefore, what does a teacher need to decide? Our earlier review of research suggests that a teacher must first assess the language level of the text and compare it to that of his/her pupils. Next the teacher needs to consider the illustrations, assess the difficulties and demands they might make on pupils, identify possible ambiguities. Third, the "message" of the text needs to be considered as well as the transparency of task demand (if pupils are to use the text independently) and the extent to which active participation is required by the "voice" speaking in the text. Fourth, the teacher should identify the concepts covered and the implied conceptual development, and match this to the level of development of the pupils, and finally, consider the overall

Figure 6.2. Textbook illustration of electrical current

cognitive load or "text demand" arising from interaction of these expectations—is it a "considerate" text?

Even a superficial analysis in these terms reveals that in each case the text is likely to present ambiguities that will demand teacher mediation, particularly with second-language learners. For example, the abstract concept "Energy" appears four times in four different parts of the page, but is not explained, nor does it appear in either index or glossary at the end of the book. The diagrams of the mixer and of the bulb connected to the battery are both intended to illustrate *flow* of current—"*through a lightbulb*" as the text says at one point—yet unfortunately, the illustrations could be taken to show wires actually entering through the glass of the mixer bowl and the *bulb in each case.* Questions are posed ("Can you think of some other ways in which the energy of an electrical current is used?") but the message about how to answer is not transparent: does this expect an oral or written response, or neither? Clearly, the teacher would need to anticipate these difficulties and assist the reader to get over them in order to use the page effectively and independently, as intended by such pupil books.

In terms of the format of the double-page spread, there are alternative sequences in which the written text and illustrations could be addressed, yet no signage or guidance (such as, "now go to …") is provided. The reader, whilst dealing with the cognitive demand of abstract concepts and visual images, also has to process the nonnarrative complexity of the format, as discussed by Leahy, Cooper and Sweller in chapter 7; hence the cognitive load is high.

Implications of the Evidence about the Role of Text and Difficulties of Text Use

These examples—and they are more typical than exceptional—show that there are many potential obstacles to the effective use of expository text by pupils. The role of the textbook is diverse in terms of the intentions of authors, designers, and publishers. Yet the messages about role and use embedded in these texts are often not transparent. In some cases, even where the message is clear, it is overridden in use by the pressures of the syllabus and examinations perceived by teachers, and the expectations of pupils. It is also clear from some of the examples analyzed that the subject matter knowledge "covered" by the text can only be learned if pupils participate in the activity demanded by the text; yet such participation is rare, sometimes because it is not logistically possible, sometimes through not being demanded by the teacher. The introduction of the National Literacy Strategy (NLS) in the United Kingdom in 1998 held out hope that text-processing strategies would be taught more effectively to pupils. Evidence from guidance to teachers and our experience, however, is that explicit teaching focuses on processing of written text, largely ignoring the difficulties of visuals, format, and message (Peacock, 2001). In addition, a more recent study (Peacock & Weedon, 2002) suggests that retrieval strategies learned in literacy lessons are not transferred to text use in other subjects. Pupil use of text is thus likely to need teacher mediation most of the time; and teachers are likely to need help not only with their understanding of the content of text, but also with the analysis of the specific text material they are likely to need to use. Teacher mediation is also frequently dependent on shared understanding of the language of the text: where this cannot be assumed, as in second-language classrooms, strategies for interpreting into life-world language have to be acquired by teachers and pupils alike, as described later by Rollnick. This means there must be collaboration, in the training of primary teachers, between trainers responsible for curriculum science programs and other programs, such as those in language and literacy; and it suggests that teachers, particularly during initial training, may need more help than they currently receive with how to make best use of existing text. It is likely that such help will also need to be text-specific, because the difficulties will differ from one scheme or book to another. Help will also need to be context-specific, depending on the age and language background of the children being taught and the teaching styles preferred in schools. Section three of this book presents a variety of approaches to tackling these problems.

Yet further research and development is urgently needed. It might usefully focus on aspects such as,

> progress made by studies of how children can be helped to interrogate nonfiction text, such as that of the EXEL Project (Wray & Lewis, 1995);
> training strategies and how to support the use of nonfiction text by trainees during their period of internship, such as by use of the Index of Text Demand (ITD) and strategies such as "Teaching the Page" (see chapter 15);
> detailed studies on the way pupils actually "navigate" a page or chapter of text, whether it be on the printed page or on screen as a CD-ROM or website, along the lines of the studies by Mikkilä and colleagues in Finland, mentioned in chapter 1.

IMPLICATIONS FOR TEACHERS

Given the difficulties described earlier, the final question is, should a teacher focus on using existing material in the school, on obtaining better materials, or on producing customized materials? Work to develop better texts is going on, but it is widely accepted that there will never be a "perfect" textbook that will be appropriate in all the different contexts likely to be encountered. There are many reasons for this, some of which relate to the constraints of commercial publishing as described by Hardy in chapter 11, the main one being is that publishers remain commercially viable. Current worldwide financial constraints mean that fewer books are being purchased for schools (in a well-resourced London borough, the most commonly owned schemes were around 20 years old!). As with so many aspects of teaching, producing, and acquiring better texts is something that we may know how to do, but don't have the resources with which to do it.

Similarly, there will always be room for teachers' "hand-made" worksheets and handouts, but most pupils are wary of "death by worksheet," and it is clear that writing your own can be a minefield leading to difficulties as great or greater for pupils than the ones found in published materials. Web-based material is increasingly used, but questions have to be asked, and research initiated, concerning the extent to which web-page designers take account of learners' requirements as described earlier, and discussed in detail in chapter 10.

All children will, sooner or later (certainly on entering secondary school), need to be able to use a wide range of text effectively, whether it is considerate or not. Teaching them to use it must be preferable to having them torment teachers with their endless "what am I *supposed* to do?" or "I don't get it, miss!" It is therefore essential to look closely at the text all primary-age children will use in school, and to analyze it as above, to see if and where they are taught the skills needed to use it.

References

Ball, D.L. & Feiman-Nemser, S.
(1988). Using textbooks and teachers' guides: a dilemma for beginning teachers and teacher educators. *Curriculum Inquiry, 18* (4), 401–423.

Biber, D.
(1991). Oral and literate characteristics of selected primary schools texts. *Text, 11*, 12–25.

Cleghorn, A.
(1992). Primary level science in Kenya: Constructing meaning through English and indigenous languages. *Qualitative Studies in Education, 5* (4), 311–323.

Cleghorn, A. & Rollnick, M.
(2002). The role of English in individual and societal development: A view from African classrooms. *TESOL Quarterly, 36* (3), 347–372.

Cummins, J.
(1983). Language proficiency and academic achievement, in J.W. Oller (Ed.), *Issues in language testing research*. Rowley, MA: Newbury House.

Dowling, P.
(1995). A sociological analysis of school texts. *Proceedings of the Annual Conference of the Southern African Association for Research in Mathematics and Science Education*, Cape Town.

Francis, V.
(1996). *Personal communication*, December 20.

Gilbert, S.W.
(1989). An evaluation of the use of analogy, simile and metaphor in science texts. *Journal of Research in Science Teaching, 30* (2), 187–207.

Hyltenstam, K. & Stroud, C.
(1993). *Final Report and Recommendations from the Evaluation of Teaching Materials for Lower Primary in Mozambique: (II) Language Issues*. Stockholm: Stockholm Institute of Education.

Koulaidis, V. & Tsatsaroni, A.
(1996). A pedagogical analysis of Science textbooks: How we can proceed? *Research in Science Education, 26* (1).

Langhan, D.
(1993). *The Textbook as a Source of Difficulty in Teaching and Learning: Final Report of the Threshold 2 Project*. Pretoria: Human Sciences Research Council.

Macdonald, C.A.
(1990a). *School-based learning experiences: A final report of the Threshold Project*. Pretoria: Human Sciences research Council.

Macdonald, C.A.
(1990b). *Standard 3 General Science Research 1987–88: A Final Report of the Threshold Project*. Pretoria: Human Sciences Research Council.

Murila, B.
(2002). An investigation into the use of science textbooks in selected primary schools in Kenya Unpublished Masters thesis. University of Exeter, UK.

Nuffield Primary Science.
(1993). *Teachers' guides*. London: Nuffield Foundation/Collins Educational.

Nuffield Foundation.
(1998). *Science and literacy: A guide for primary teachers*. London: Nuffield Foundation/Collins Educational.

Peacock, A.
(1995a). Access to science learning for children in rural Africa. *International Journal of Science Education, 17* (2), 149–166.

Peacock, A.
(1995b). An agenda for research on text material in primary science for second language learners of English in developing countries. *Journal of Multilingual and Multicultural Development, 16* (5), 389–401.

Peacock, A.
(2001). The potential impact of the Literacy Hour on the teaching of science from text material. *Journal of Curriculum Studies, 33* (1), 25–42.

Peacock, A. & Gates, S.M.G.
(2000). *Newly-qualified teachers' perceptions of the role of text material in teaching science.* Paper presented at the Comparative and International Education Society Annual Conference, Toronto, April 1999.

Peacock, A. & Perold, H.
(1995). Helping primary teachers develop new approaches to science teaching: A strategy for the evaluation of 'Spider's Place.' *Proceedings of Annual Meeting of the Southern African Association for Research in Mathematics and Science (SAARMSE)*, Cape Town, January 1995.

Peacock, A. & Weedon, H.
(2002). Children working with text in science: disparities with 'Literacy Hour' practice. *Research in Science and Technology Education, 20* (2), 185–197.

Perold, H. & Bahr, M.A.
(1993). *National science education project dealing with primary science: Report on the evaluation of the materials comprising the pilot programme.* Johannesburg: Handspring Trust.

Rollnick, M.S. & Rutherford, M.
(1990). African primary school teachers what ideas do they hold on air and air pressure? *International Journal of Science Education, 12* (1).

Roth, K.J.
(1985). *Conceptual change learning and student processing of science texts.* Michigan: Michigan State University Institute for Research on Teaching.

Shulman, J.
(1987). Knowledge and teaching; foundations of the new reform. *Harvard Educational Review, 57* (1), 1–22.

Sweller, J.
(1994). Cognitive Load theory, learning difficulty and instructional design. *Learning and Instruction, 4,* 295–312.

Vachon, M.K & Haney, R.E.
(1991). A procedure for determining the level of abstraction of Science reading material. *Journal of Research in Science Teaching, 28* (4), 343–352.

van Rooyen, H.
(1990). *The disparity between English as a subject and English as the medium of learning: A final report of the Threshold Project.* Pretoria: Human Sciences Research Council.

Walpole, S.
(1999). Changing texts, changing thinking: Comprehension demands of new science textbooks. *The Reading Teacher, 52* (4), 358–369.

Wray, D. & Lewis, M.
(1995). Extending interactions with non-fiction texts: An exit into understanding. *Reading, 29* (1), 20–35.

7

Interactivity and the Constraints of Cognitive Load Theory

Wayne Leahy, Graham Cooper, and John Sweller

THE MIND AS AN INFORMATION PROCESSING SYSTEM

Over the last 30 years there has been considerable interest in the functions and processes of the human mind. This interest has stemmed particularly from the field of cognitive psychology that explores human thought, consciousness, memory and problem-solving abilities. Figure 7.1 illustrates the characteristic way contemporary cognitive psychology views the human mind as an information-processing system. This figure conceptualizes the model developed by Atkinson and Shiffrin (1968) and provides the foundations for human cognitive architecture. Very broadly speaking, processing of information advances from left to right and is composed of three interdependent components; sensory memory, working memory, and long-term memory.

Sensory and Working Memory

Input enters sensory memory from the human senses. Information is retained in sensory memory for only a very short period varying from 0.5 to 1.0 seconds for visual information (Sperling, 1960), and 3.0 to 4.0 seconds for audio information (Darwin, Turvey, & Crowder, 1972). Material in working memory is composed of: (a) new sensory information and (b) previously learned information retrieved from long-term memory. The working memory store, for new and unfamiliar information, is very limited in both capacity (only able to hold about 7 items of information; Miller, 1956) and duration (only able to hold information for around 15–30 seconds unless the information is subject to mental manipulation such as rehearsal, reordering or comparison) (Leahey & Harris, 1989).

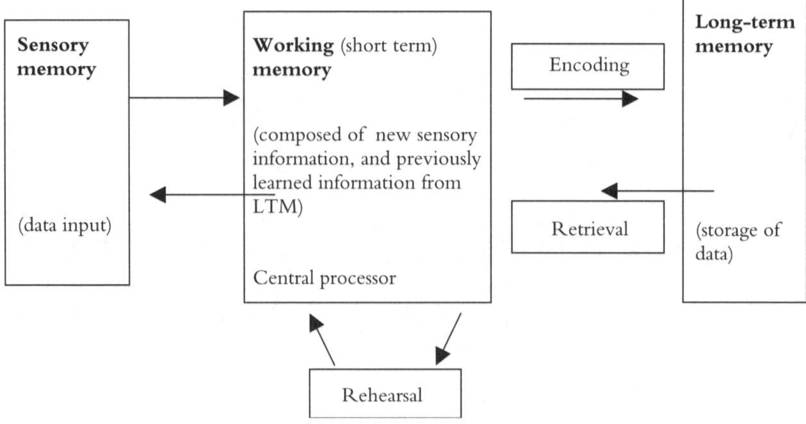

Figure 7.1. One model of the human processing system as analogy to computer

Long-Term Memory and Schemas

In contrast to the extreme limitations of working memory, long-term memory is capable of storing an extensive amount of information (all of our knowledge) for long periods of time (often a lifetime). Information is encoded, located, recovered and deciphered from long-term memory using schemas. According to Sweller (1994), "A schema is a cognitive construct that organizes elements of information according to the manner with which they will be dealt." The term "schema" entered into psychology most directly from Bartlett (1932) and also is related to the work of Head (1920). Bartlett (1932) demonstrated that what is remembered is only partly reliant on the presented information itself. It is the prior knowledge and experience of a person (manifested as schemas) that determines how new information is recognized, interpreted, categorized, encoded and recalled. Schemas provide the basic building blocks of knowledge and can account for a considerable degree of our learning-mediated intellectual performance (Sweller, 1999).

Bartlett's (1932) summation of schemas' role in learning and memory is as follows: when reading a complex text, or acquiring any new information, humans must assimilate the new material to their current concepts or schemas. The result is that learning does not copy exactly what was presented, but rather depends on both what was presented and the schema to which it is assimilated. New information is modified to fit the existing concepts, already held as schemas. In this process, some details are lost and the knowledge becomes more coherent to the individual. Thus, schemas are vigorously and constantly modified as new information is added to them. For example, when reading, different typographical versions are instantly recognizable because of previously acquired schemas. For a reasonably fluent reader, a word in many fonts is readily identifiable.

Automation

Developing schemas is an important part of our cognitive architecture because as they become more comprehensive they reduce the burden placed upon our finite working memory resources. Shiffrin and Schneider (1977), Kotovsky, Hayes, and Simon (1985) and others have made a distinction between automatic and controlled (or deliberate) processes. Automatic processes do not involve allocation of attention and can be performed in parallel with other cognitive processes or activities. In contrast, controlled processes must be performed serially because they require a higher degree of attention (Leahey & Harris, 1989), whereas automatized behaviors require minimal or no attention (Naslund, 1990).

For instance, an "expert" driving an automobile while carrying out a conversation is one example of an automatic process. The finer details of operating the vehicle are performed without deliberate allocation of attention to operating the clutch, accelerator, gears and so on. The research on expert/novice differences unearths one general finding; that of the experts' ability to automatize a range of skills and procedures when problem-solving within their specific domain of expertise (Shiffrin, 1985). This automation releases working memory resources to consider other aspects of any problem or task at hand.

Theoretical and Empirical Background of Cognitive Load Theory

Cognitive load theory rests on several fundamental principles. The first is that excessively high levels of cognitive load may directly result from the instructional materials given to students. Second, if the instructions place an unnecessary burden on limited working memory resources, then learning (in terms of schema acquisition and automation) may be impaired. Third, redesigning instructional materials to reduce the level of extraneous cognitive load may enhance understanding. Cognitive load theory, using these principles, has been used successfully to develop instructional techniques that facilitate learning (Chandler & Sweller, 1991, 1996; Sweller, 1988, 1989, 1993, 1994, 1999, in press; Sweller & Chandler, 1994; Sweller, van Merrienboer, & Paas, 1998).

The theory specifically emphasizes:

(1) humans possess an extremely small working memory in contrast to an extensive long-term memory.
(2) this limited working memory is compensated by the very large long-term memory and the learning mechanisms of schema acquisition and automation.

These two premises have marked implications for the design of effective instructional materials. Traditional methods of instructional design based upon visual elegance, common sense and convenience, are rendered ineffectual (Chandler & Sweller, 1991).

Cognitive load theory is concerned with the manner in which cognitive resources are focused and used during problem-solving and learning. Many problem-solving and learning procedures encouraged by instructional formats result in students engaging in cognitive activities far-removed from the ostensible goals of the task. The cognitive load generated by these irrelevant activities can impede skill acquisition (Chandler & Sweller, 1991).

Relations Between Intrinsic and Extraneous Cognitive Load

Two broad sources of cognitive load exist: intrinsic and extraneous. Intrinsic cognitive load is strictly dictated by the intellectual complexity of the content. This complexity cannot be altered because it is a property of the to-be-learnt information. Extraneous cognitive load is produced by the format of the instructional materials (e.g., textual or diagrammatical) and the instructional activities (e.g., watching or doing) in which learners are engaged. Extraneous cognitive load is open to manipulation because it is a property of the *way* in which to-be-learnt information is presented, say in a text.

Intrinsic and extraneous cognitive load combined constitute total cognitive load. If the total cognitive load experienced by a learner is more than their limited working memory capacity then learning will be inhibited. In such situations the total cognitive load needs to be reduced if meaningful learning is to be accomplished. Since intrinsic cognitive load is immutable, the only way to achieve a reduction in total cognitive load is to modify the instructional techniques in such a way that the extraneous cognitive load is sufficiently reduced.

Consider an example where school students are to learn how to correctly link two batteries, a bulb, a switch and numerous clamps and wires for a science experiment on basic electrical principles. The instructions can embody an array of formats. They may be presented as a diagram with written instructions, a practical demonstration, a video or audiotape. Therefore, the extraneous cognitive load can differ in accordance with these different presentational formats.

Intrinsic Cognitive Load and its Relations to High- and Low-Element Interactivity

All learning material imposes a level of intrinsic cognitive load, which is subject to two factors: the features of the to-be-learned content and the ability (or more correctly, the currently held schemas) of the learner. To determine why some material is more diffi-cult to understand, it is helpful to examine the notion of element interactivity, that is, how the items to-be-learned relate to each other. Some relations between elements will be "null" in so far as there is no relation at all. However, other relations between elements will be meaningful in that they may be definable in terms of mathematical formulae, grammar, syntax, procedures, or concepts. Each of these meaningful relations thus becomes a component of information that in itself must be learnt.

We are now in a position to consider why we perceive some instructional material to be "complicated," yet other material to be easy to understand. Cognitive load theory suggests that the element interactivity, that is, the degree of interrelatedness between each element to be learned, determines the level of difficulty. For example, learning the syntax and semantics of a language is difficult because it is high in element inter-activity. Each word must be understood in relation to the other words. Consider the phrase, "three loaves of sliced bread." Most other combinations such as "three bread of sliced loaves" would be unacceptable in English, although the *meaning* may still be present because the vocabulary is identical. For learners of English as a second language, not only does the vocabulary need to be acquired, but the relation of each word to every other word with respect to syntax must also be learned. This example demonstrates the burden placed upon cognitive resources when dealing with material that consists of elements that have a high level of interrelatedness.

Interactivity and Interpretation of Diagrams

Many science concepts are high in element interactivity. For example, consider students who must learn to interpret temperature diagrams in the form of single and double-line, bar and column graphs. These graph types, and indeed many diagrams, involve high element interactivity. Consider the following example from interpreting a two-day temperature graph denoting the degrees Celsius for an hourly time (see figure 7.2).

The complete reading and interpreting of this form of line graph involves a high level of intrinsic cognitive load. The high load occurs because several learning elements interact and need to be processed simultaneously: in this case, a vertical temperature line with 11 points from 16 degrees Celsius to 36 degrees Celsius, and a horizontal time line with eight points from 9 a.m. to 4 p.m. Additionally, there are unbroken and broken lines indicating time and temperature for a Monday and a Tuesday. To answer a question such as, *which day has the lower temperature at 3p.m.?*, the learner has to attend to all of these various elements simultaneously, the steps involved being:

1. Locate one day.
2. Locate time.
3. Locate temperature.
4, 5 and 6.   Follow same steps for the other day.
7. Compare the result of Step 3 with the result of Step 6 to determine which is the lower value, while simultaneously remembering which day was associated with each of these two steps.

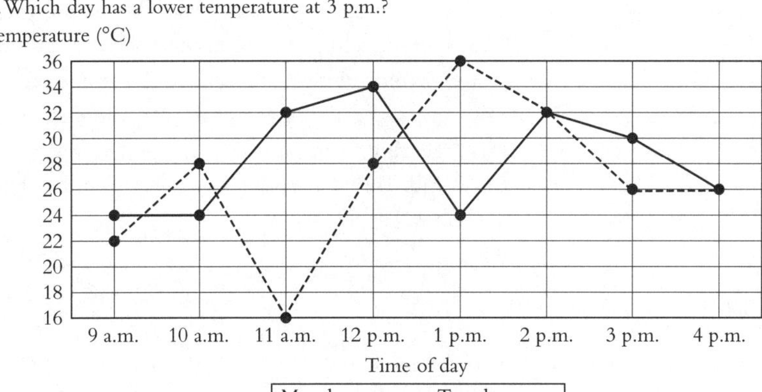

Figure 7.2. Graph involving element interactivity

Here, the level of element interactivity is high and consequently, intrinsic cognitive load is likely to also be high. Intrinsic cognitive load cannot be manipulated by instructional design without affecting intelligibility. In contrast, extraneous cognitive load is determined by the format of the instructional materials and the instructional activities. The extraneous cognitive load can be altered by changing the manner in which the information is presented and/or the activities required of the learner.

To summarize, instructional content that is high in element interactivity contributes significantly to total cognitive load and may result in processing requirements exceeding working memory capacity. This cognitive overload will inhibit schema acquisition and automation. It is for this reason that, in complex conceptual areas such as exist within science, the extraneous cognitive load that a text may impose is critical to learning.

Learner Expertise

Another critical component is learner expertise. Consider the example of a child learning to read the word "water." He or she is involved in controlled processing whereby the letters are attended to as a series of separate schemas. Gradually, however, the schema for recognizing the word "water" will be acquired. Attendance to separate letters will no longer be necessary and the child will consciously recognize the word as a single element. This reduces the burden placed upon cognitive resources. With further experience the single schema for reading "water" will become automated, further reducing the burden placed upon cognitive resources.

If a learner is a novice and the to-be-learnt material is high in element interactivity, structuring learning material may be crucial to enable learning. In contrast, experienced learners, who have therefore developed schemas, may have little difficulty dealing with high-element interactivity material because the interacting elements are subsumed within their schemas.

Cognitive Load Research

Cognitive load theory has been used to develop effective instructional procedures and to identify a number of "effects," in a variety of educational fields. These procedures and effects have proved beneficial when dealing with complex material because they recognize the limited capacity of working memory, the effectively unlimited capacity of long-term memory and the dynamics of schema acquisition and automation within the learning process. The "effects" relevant to text processing involve *worked examples, split attention, modality, redundancy,* and *levels of element interactivity*. These, along with other effects are discussed in the following sections.

The Worked Example Effect

One technique that may increase schema acquisition is to make a far greater than normal use of worked examples. Often, only a few worked examples of a problem-type are given, followed by many examples of the problem to solve. More emphasis is put on the problem-solving process rather than the worked examples. Such an emphasis may be misdirected because for novices, studying worked examples may be superior to solving the equivalent problems. Worked examples direct problem-solving. They operate as a replacement for a novice's lack of schemas and as a form of direct instruction. When studying worked examples, learners concentrate on each problem-state and the move that can be used to transform it into the next problem-state. Many studies strongly support the suggestion that students learn more from studying worked examples rather than solving the equivalent problems (Carrol, 1994; Cooper & Sweller, 1987; Paas, 1992; Paas & van Merrienboer, 1994; Pillay, 1994; Quilici & Mayer, 1996; Sweller & Cooper, 1985; Trafton & Reiser, 1993).

The Split-Attention Effect

The split-attention effect occurs when learners must focus on multiple sources of mutually referring information that must be mentally integrated before meaning can be derived from the material. Cognitive load theory states that formats for instruction that place a heavy burden on working memory will constrain learning. It cannot be assumed that all worked examples under all circumstances will be of benefit. Consider the conventional worked example version of the temperature graph in figure 7.3. In this second version, it consists of a diagram located above the text, a given question, and outlines the solution steps.

The diagram alone does not indicate a solution and the solution steps 1–3 below the diagram are meaningless in isolation. For this worked example to be comprehended by a novice, the diagram and the solution steps must be mentally integrated. The act of mental integration makes heavy demands on working memory. Yet only when the text is mentally integrated in the appropriate places, will the learner comprehend the information.

This constant search and match process may involve a considerable cognitive load. At the same time, attention may be directed to an exercise that is unconnected to schema acquisition and rule automation. The learner must mentally search and match

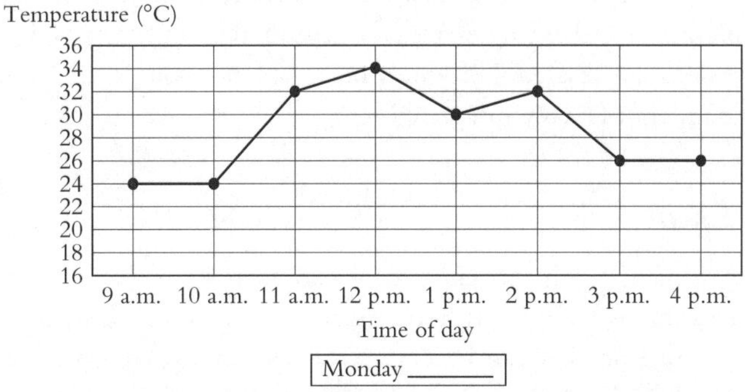

Q. What is the temperature at 1 p.m.?
Find time: On the time line find 1p.m. and move up to the thick black line.
Find temperature: Follow across to the temperature line that shows 30°C.
So at 1 p.m. it is 30°C.

Figure 7.3. A conventional worked example in a split-attention format

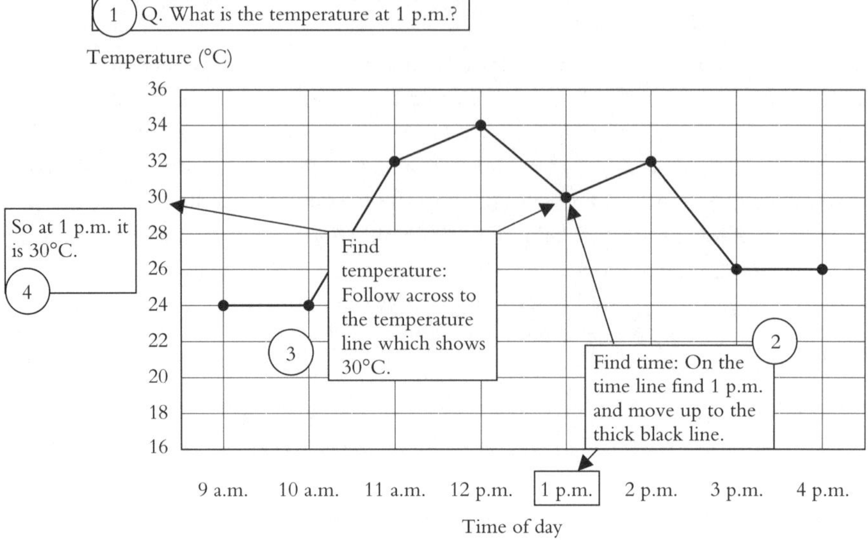

Figure 7.4. An integrated diagram format of figure 7.3

written statements with different parts of the diagram. Therefore, a heavy cognitive load is imposed that may constrict learning.

In a more considerate format, the cognitive effort required to mentally integrate this "split source" information can be lowered or eliminated by physically integrating the various entities. Rather than placing the text statements below or next to the diagram as normally occurs, the relevant statements can be incorporated within the diagram (see figure 7.4). In this way a search and match procedure is unnecessary.

The integration of text and diagram removes the need to search for connections between the text and diagram, reducing working memory load and freeing cognitive resources for learning. If conventionally structured worked examples are compared with physically integrated examples, results normally demonstrate an advantage for the integrated versions. The material may only be comprehensible to the learner when the text and diagram are mentally integrated.

The Modality Effect

An alternative strategy is to introduce information in a partly auditory, partly visual format. Because the use of a partly auditory and partly visual format can increase the amount of information that can be effectively held in working memory (Baddeley, 1992; Baddeley & Hitch, 1974; Penney, 1989), there are pertinent instructional design concerns. Rather than attempting to reduce extraneous cognitive load, this alternative strategy should expand effective working memory capacity.

Figure 7.5 is a simple mapping exercise for middle to upper primary school students. It is composed of statements and a corresponding map. Conventionally, both

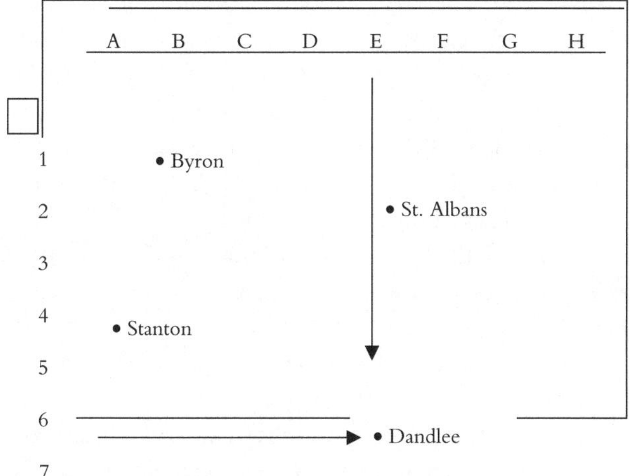

You can use a map to find out what is located at a particular grid reference.
Let us find out what is located at grid reference E6.
Starting at the letter E at the top of the page, slowly follow the line down the page.
At the same time, starting at number 6, follow the line across the page.
Where the lines meet is the grid reference E6.
As you can see, located at grid reference E6 is Dandlee.

Figure 7.5.   Visually split-attention text instructions that may be replaced by audio instructions

the statement and map are presented visually in this split-attention format. An option for this conventional instructional technique is to present the diagram on paper or a computer screen while the statement component is presented in an auditory form from a computer or cassette recorder. By presenting some of the material in auditory form rather than all in visual form (as occurs in figure 7.5), effective working memory should be expanded resulting in enhanced learning.

This effect has been verified in a number of cognitive load studies (see Jeung, Chandler, & Sweller, 1997; Leahy, Chandler, & Sweller, in press; Mayer, 2001; Mayer & Moreno, 1998, Moreno & Mayer, 1999; Mayer, Heiser, & Lonn, 2001; Mousavi, Low, & Sweller, 1995; Tindall-Ford, Chandler, & Sweller, 1997). An additional benefit with computer-presented multimedia formats is that the audio presentations may be coordinated in synchronicity with screen highlights and/or animations to guide attention to the associated visual elements. Such techniques aid in reducing cognitive load that would otherwise be imposed by screen search (Jeung et al., 1997).

The Redundancy Effect

If a source of instruction is fully intelligible by itself and other sources of information merely redescribe the original source then only one source of instruction should be used. The other source, which is redundant, should be omitted completely from the instructional materials. For example, the diagram in figure 7.5 is understandable by itself and the addition of identical text below or above, which merely repeats the information, is unnecessary. Furthermore, integrating the diagram and text renders the instruction even less effective because the redundant text is difficult to ignore under integrated conditions. Experiments have shown that by simply deleting an unnecessary source of information, instruction time is minimized and learning is enhanced.

The redundancy effect has been demonstrated in different contexts over many decades (Chandler & Sweller, 1991; Leahy, et al., in press; Miller, 1937; Reder & Anderson, 1980, 1982). In all cases, the inclusion of redundant material interfered with, rather than enhanced, learning. Although differing explanations have been offered for these findings, they nonetheless have one commonality in that additional, redundant information interferes with core information. It is commonly assumed, and is seemingly intuitive, that additional explanatory information is at least neutral and probably advantageous. Nonetheless, it has been shown that the inclusion of redundant information (in a text) can have very strong detrimental effects.

The effect can be explained within a cognitive load framework. If one form of instruction is comprehensible and sufficient, offering equivalent information in another form will impose an extraneous cognitive load. It is likely to be only after learners have processed the additional information that they will be conscious that the procedure was needless.

The Element Interactivity Effect

The effects mentioned here all have a connecting relationship in regard to the instructional materials used in the experimental studies. These instructional materials required knowledge and skills that were demanding from a cognitive perspective. In other words, the material given to the learners was difficult to learn regardless of the instructional format. On the other hand, if the material is composed of many elements but they can be assimilated autonomously or serially, element interactivity is considered to be low and therefore the material is low in intrinsic cognitive load. These effects produced by cognitive load theory may only develop in an environment of high-element interactivity (Sweller, 1994).

The Imagination Effect

Using some form of mental rehearsal or imagining as an aide to learning can be useful (Ericsson & Charness, 1994; Ericsson, Krampe, & Tesch-Romer, 1993). The benefits of mentally "running through" a process in working memory has been well documented within contexts such as sports psychology (Driskell, Copper, & Moran, 1994). More recently the activity of imagining has been applied to purely cognitive tasks (Cooper, Tindall-Ford, Chandler, & Sweller, 2001). In a series of experiments Cooper et al. (2001) found that learners given instructions to "imagine" a set of text-based procedures that needed to be learned, performed better than learners given conventional instructions. Cooper et al. (2001) found that such instructions were only effective if learners had a degree of experience in the relevant field. It was suggested that in order to imagine some procedures, learners had to be able to manipulate the relevant material in working memory. Experience in the content area was argued to be a prerequisite because it provided the necessary schemas.

The Expertise Reversal Effect

It has been shown repeatedly that the effects discussed earlier tend to reverse once learners have attained some domain expertise. Most, perhaps all of the cognitive load effects described in the previous sections, depend on the use of novices. For example, groups of novices given diagrams only performed the worst on tests because the text was essential for understanding (Kalyuga, Chandler, & Sweller, 1998).

However, with additional practice, schemas were obtained to replace the text and the previously essential guidance provided by the text became increasingly unnecessary. In due course, with further instruction, the text became redundant and the diagram alone was sufficient for the learners to understand and learn from. For these now more experienced learners, a redundancy effect was attained, with the optimum-learning environment provided by the diagram alone format.

Kalyuga, Chandler, and Sweller (1999, 2000) found that other cognitive load effects, such as the modality effect, also vanish and then reverse with improved expertise. The text was better given in spoken rather than written form, indicating the modality effect. As the learner's knowledge increased, the modality effect disappeared. In due course, presenting only the visual material was better than an audio-visual presentation or any presentation that incorporated the text, because with increases in expertise, the text became redundant. Kalyuga, Chandler, Tuovinen, and Sweller (2001) in the same way, established that the worked-example effect reversed as expertise was increased. Worked examples become redundant once schemas have been obtained.

For instructional designers, these outcomes suggest that as learners progress from inexperience to fluency in a domain, direction or guidance is provided more by schemas rather than instruction. Therefore, the direction made available by instruction (e.g., through the medium of the text) should be incrementally lowered. Direction that is not required has a negative, not a neutral effect.

Conclusion

Our knowledge of research into concepts such as cognitive load, working memory and interactivity have been used to directly generate the instructional designs discussed in this chapter. Those designs vary from most instructional designs in reducing extrinsic load, and their success offers substantial evidence supporting the cognitive theories outlined. The implications for the design of text material, particularly in areas containing many abstracts concepts to be learned, are powerful, for they are sometimes counterintuitive and yet demonstrate the need to integrate the demands of written text, visual imagery and format, as represented in the increasingly design-dominated world of textbooks.

References

Atkinson, R.C. & Shiffrin, R.M.
(1968). Human memory: A proposed system and its processes. In K.W. Spence & J.T. Spence (Eds.), *Advances in the psychology of learned and motivation research theory. Vol. 2.* New York: Academic Press.

Baddeley, A.
(1992). Working memory. *Science, 255,* 556–559.

Baddeley, A. & Hitch, G.
(1974). Working memory. In G.A. Bower (Ed.), *Recent advances in learning and motivation* (Vol. 8, pp. 47–90). New York: Academic Press.

Bartlett, F.C.
(1932). *Remembering: A study in experimental and social psychology.* London: Cambridge University Press.

Carrol, W.
(1994). Using worked examples as an instructional support in the algebra classroom. *Journal of Educational Psychology, 86,* 360–367.

Chandler, P. & Sweller, J.
(1991). Cognitive load theory and the format of instruction. *Cognition and Instruction, 8,* 293–332.

Chandler, P. & Sweller, J.
(1996). Cognitive load while learning to use a computer program. *Applied Cognitive Psychology, 10,* 1–20.

Cooper, G.A. & Sweller, J.
(1987). Effects of schema acquisition and rule automation on mathematical problem solving transfer. *Journal of Educational Psychology, 79,* 347–362.

Cooper, G., Tindall-Ford, S., Chandler, P., & Sweller, J.
(2001). Learning by imagining. *Journal of Experimental Psychology: Applied, 7,* 68–82.

Darwin, G.J., Turvey, M.T., & Crowder, R.G.
(1972). An auditory analogue of the Sperling partial report procedure: Evidence for brief auditory storage. *Cognitive Psychology, 3,* 255–267.

Driskell, J.E., Copper, C. & Moran, A.
(1994). Does mental practice enhance performance? *Journal of Applied Psychology, 79,* 481–492.

Ericsson, K.A. & Charness, N.
(1994). Expert performance; its structure and acquisition. *American Psychologist, 49,* 725–747.

Ericsson, K.A., Krampe, R.T., & Tesch-Romer, C.
(1993). The role of deliberate practice in the acquisition of expert performance. *Psychological Review, 100,* 363–406.

Head, H.
(1920). *Studies in neurology.* London: Frowde.

Jeung, H., Chandler, P., & Sweller, J.
(1997). The role of visual indicators in dual sensory mode instruction. *Educational Psychology, 17,* 329–343.

Kalyuga, S., Chandler, P., & Sweller, J.
(1998). Levels of varying expertise and instructional design. *Human Factors, 40,* 1–17.

Kalyuga, S., Chandler, P., & Sweller, J.
(1999). Managing split-attention and redundancy in multi-media instruction. *Applied Cognitive Psychology, 13,* 351–371.

Kalyuga, S., Chandler, P., & Sweller, J.
(2000). Incorporating learner experience into the design of multimedia instruction. *Journal of Educational Psychology, 92,* 126–136.

Kalyuga, S., Chandler, P., Tuovinen, J., & Sweller, J.
(2001). When problem solving is superior to studying worked examples. *Journal of Educational Psychology, 93,* 579–588.

Kotovsky, K., Hayes, J.R., & Simon, H.A.
(1985). Why are some problems hard? Evidence from Tower of Hanoi. *Cognitive Psychology, 17,* 248–294.

Leahey, T.H. & Harris, R.J.
(1989). *Human learning.* New Jersey: Prentice Hall.

Leahy, W.M., Chandler, P., & Sweller, J.
(in press). When auditory presentations should and should not be a component of multimedia instructions. *Applied Cognitive Psychology.*

Mayer, R.E.
(2001). *Multimedia learning.* New York: Cambridge University Press.

Mayer, R., Heiser, J., & Lonn, S.
(2001). Cognitive constraints on multimedia learning: When presenting more material results in less understanding. *Journal of Educational Psychology, 93,* 187–198.

Mayer, R.E. & Moreno R.
(1998). A split-attention effect in multimedia learning: Evidence for dual-processing systems in working memory. *Journal of Educational Psychology, 20,* 312–320.

Miller, G.A.
(1937). The picture crutch in reading. *Elementary English Review, 14,* 263–264.

Mousavi, S.Y., Low, R., & Sweller, J.
(1995). Reducing cognitive load by mixing auditory and visual presentation modes. *Journal of Educational Psychology, 87,* 319–334.

Moreno, R. & Mayer, R.E.
(1999). Cognitive principles of multimedia learning: The role of modality and contiguity effects. *Journal of Educational Psychology, 91,* 358–368.

Naslund, R.
(1990). Advanced educational psychology for educators, researchers and policymakers. New York: HarperCollins.

Pass, F. & Van Merrienboer, J.
(1994). The efficiency of instructional conditions: An approach to combine mental-effort and performance measures. *Human Factors, 35,* 737–743.

Penney, C.G.
(1989). Modality effects and the structure of short-term verbal memory. *Memory and Cognition, 17,* 398–442.

Pillay, H.
(1994). Cognitive load and mental rotation: structuring orthographic projection for learning and problem solving. *Instructional Science, 22,* 91–113.

Quilici, J.L. & Mayer, R.E.
(1996). Role of examples in how students learn to categorize statistics word problems. *Journal of Educational Psychology, 88*, 144–161.

Reder, L. & Anderson, J.
(1980). A comparison of texts and their summaries: Memorial consequences. *Journal of Verbal Learning and Verbal Behavior, 19*, 121–134.

Reder, L.M. & Anderson, J.
(1982). Effects of spacing and embellishment on memory for main points of text. *Memory and Cognition, 10*, 97–102.

Shiffrin, R.M.
(1985). Attention. In R.C. Atkinson, R.J. Herrstein, & R.D. Luce (Eds.), *Steven's handbbook of experimental psychology*. New York: John Wiley & Sons.

Shiffrin, R. & Schneider, W.
(1977). Controlled and automatic human information processing: II. Perceptual learning, automatic attending, and a general theory. *Psychological Review, 84*, 127–190.

Sperling, G.
(1960). The information available in brief visual presentations [Special issue]. *Psychological Monographs, 74* (498).

Sweller, J.
(1988). Cognitive load during problem solving: Effects on learning. *Cognitive Science, 12*, 257–285.

Sweller, J.
(1989). Cognitive technology: Some procedures for facilitating learning and problem solving in mathematics and science. *Journal of Educational Psychology, 81*, 457–466.

Sweller, J.
(1993). Some cognitive processes and their consequences for the organisation and presentation of information. *Australian Journal of Psychology, 45*, 1–8.

Sweller, J.
(1994). Cognitive load theory, learning difficulty and instructional design. *Learning and Instruction, 4*, 295–312.

Sweller, J.
(1999). *Instructional design in technical areas*. Melbourne, Australia: ACER Press.

Sweller, J.
(in press). Evolution of human cognitive architecture. In B. Ross (Ed.), *The psychology of learning and motivation*. San Diego: Academic Press

Sweller, J. & Chandler, P.
(1994). Why some material is difficult to learn. *Cognition and Instruction, 12*, 185–233.

Sweller, J. & Cooper, G.A.
(1985). The use of worked examples as a substitute for problem solving in learning algebra. *Cognition and Instruction, 2*, 59–89.

Sweller, J., van Merrienboer, J., & Paas, F.
(1998). Cognitive architecture and instructional design. *Educational Psychology Review, 10*, 251–296.

Tindall-Ford, S., Chandler, P., & Sweller, J.
(1997). When two sensory modes are better than one. *Journal of Experimental Psychology: Applied, 3* (4), 257–287.

Trafton, J.G. & Reiser, B.J.
(1993). The contribution of studying examples and solving problems to skill acquisition. Proceedings of the 15th Annual Conference of the Cognitive Science Society (pp. 1017–1022). Hillsdale: Erlbaum.

8

Finding the Meaning: Sociolinguistic Issues in Text Access

Marissa Rollnick

This chapter will examine the tensions that exist between those who advocate simplification of science texts to ensure accessibility to young or second-language English readers and the situated cognitionists, such as Gee (1996, 1997, 2001), who emphasize the importance of participating in the discourse of science if one is to access science texts. The key question to be answered is, does oversimplification of science texts exclude learners from further participation in the study of science or does it open doors? This debate will be analyzed and will be a way forward for writers of the text examined.

Students are seated in a first-year geography lecture at a historically disadvantaged South African institution. All present use English as an additional language and speak a variety of other South African languages as their main language. Their lecturer, an enthusiastic honors graduate of the same university, proudly clutches his copy of the manual held by all the students in the lecture and reads from the manual,

> . . . cold temperatures may result in death due to cell destruction by freezing or complete desiccation of plant tissue.

He continues:

> Now, what does desiccation mean? What does desiccation mean? Any response? What does desiccation mean? . . . (silence). They're saying cold temperature may result in death due to freezing or complete desiccation of plant tissue . . . . So what I am saying is, what does desiccation mean? Any idea? (Silence) What does desiccation mean? Cold temperatures may result in death due to the cell destruction by freezing or complete desiccation of plant tissue, that is, complete desiccation of plant tissue, complete destroyal of plant tissue.

The phrases from the manual are repeated like a mantra, apart from the slightly inaccurate paraphrase in the last sentence. But no response is forthcoming from the students. Is a response expected? Is it reasonable to expect a class of second-language speakers to access this text without mediation? Does what the lecturer is doing constitute mediation? How would the students respond to a simpler text or do we insult students by "dumbing down" the text and defeat the purposes of teaching them science by doing so?

This chapter explores the different perspectives that allow us to determine what it is about text that makes it accessible to various types of learners, particularly those who are learning through the medium of an additional language. The focus is particularly on those who come from a background where there has been little support for the learning of disciplines like science due to lack of background on the part of the families of these learners.

I draw particularly from the discipline of science and the South African situation where issues around accessing of text become particularly exposed when most learners are operating in a language that is not their main language. The perspective of this chapter is that of a science educationist who is interested in the role played by language in the learning of science, rather than that of a linguist. Thus the aim of the chapter is to explore learners' use of text for learning, (1) where the text is the primary source or teacher, such as in distance learning contexts, and (2) where the text is mediated by a teacher in a formal learning context.

Theoretical Frameworks on Accessing Text

Most readers trying to access a text will be able to report whether they are finding a text accessible or not. Commonsense will tell us that various reader factors such as knowledge of the subject area and competence in the language of the text will play a role in their ability to understand the text. Some research has also found that interest in the subject of a text will allow readers to read far above their normal reading level. For example, Bracken (1982) found that fourth grade learners, identified as poor readers increased their comprehension when the stories they read were personalized rather than standardized.

During the 1970s and 1980s there was great interest in the idea of readability and several formulae and tests were in use, both purely text-based and reader/text-based, for example, Rush (1985). This was accompanied by a series of validations of the various formulae and tests (e.g., Crook, 1977) and followed by a series of studies questioning their validity (e.g., Gordon, 1980) as well as the superficiality of the formulae and tests. The studies also point to the underlying structure of text as opposed to surface structure. Interestingly studies of readability have become more rare in the last two decades, possibly due to an increasing distrust of the validity of the tests used. However, some researchers for example, Doidge (1997) while acknowledging the limitations of readability formulae, decided by other means that the readability of most South African biology textbooks made them inaccessible to the majority of South African learners. At best they could be read with extensive mediation from the teacher.

The theoretical perspective of the researcher is what underpins most studies of the accessibility and use of texts. Some research examines text from a cognitivist perspective, while other researchers emerge from a sociolinguistic point of view. The sociolinguists have more recently been enriched by contributions from those operating from a situated cognition perspective and it is from this viewpoint that most of the analysis in this essay will be conducted.

Both the cognitivist and situated cognition perspectives arise from a constructivist theoretical framework. The cognitivists focus more on the learning of the individual, while sociocultural theory stresses the importance of the community. Hence the view of situated cognition claims that knowing and understanding is fundamentally tied to the context in which it is produced. Cobb and Bowers (1998) provide some insight into the difference between the two perspectives. These two different perspectives lead to completely different approaches to the study of access to text.

Inevitably, the focus of cognitive psychology is on words and concepts in the text, while the focus of the sociocultural perspective is on the discourse employed and its relationship to the social situation of the reader. Within some proponents of the cognitivist approach is a view of reading as information processing (e.g., Rumelhart, 1980). Using this perspective, the challenge of improving learners' ability to access text becomes a case of helping with difficult words, improving readability of the text, lessening extraneous "noise" (Johnstone & Wham, 1982) and above all, simplifying language. Learners are assisted in achieving this objective through overt teaching.

Gee (1996) on the other hand talks of acquiring Discourse that embodies much more than just language and words. Use of language is embodied in contexts that carry with them social mores and ways in which language is used. So it is possible to speak grammatically perfect sentences yet make utterances that are totally inappropriate to the situation. The implication for a learner accessing text is that if the text is simplified to an extent that it no longer belongs to the Discourse of the discipline being learnt, then the learner will not be able to function as a participant in the social practice of the discipline: he or she will not become a scientist for example. Gee distinguishes acquisition and learning as two different activities. He maintains that to enter the Discourse of the discipline a learner has to *acquire* the language, social practice and functioning of the group by participation involving trial and error in natural settings. Alongside acquisition, learning can occur, but learning is primarily a process of gaining meta-knowledge, primarily about the difference between the Discourse to be acquired (Gee refers to this as a secondary Discourse) and the learner's primary Discourse (the language the learner already has in relation to the community he/she comes from).

In the context of the Discourse of science, Gee identifies various characteristics of scientific Discourse that distinguish it from everyday discourse. In many cases the object of interest in scientific Discourse changes from being a person to an abstract entity. For example the sentence that opens this chapter, ". . . cold temperatures may result in death due to cell destruction by freezing or complete desiccation of plant tissue," may be translated into what Gee calls life-world language as follows:

plants will freeze to death in cold weather because their cells will dry out.

Much of the "scientific message" is lost and the focus has changed from the effect of the low temperatures on plant cells to the fate of the plants. Thus in terms of this perspective, for learners to acquire scientific discourse, texts need to use the language of scientists.

This view is echoed by Lemke (2001) in the context of scientific knowledge who states,

> The most sophisticated view of knowledge available to us today says that it is a falsification of the nature of science to teach concepts outside of their social, economic, historical and technological contexts. Concepts taught in this way are relatively useless in life, however well they may be understood in a test.

Both Lemke and Gee go on to attest to the personal cost to the individual of acquiring a new discourse. Lemke (2001) claims that any conceptual change can involve a difficult change in identity while Gee (2001) maintains that in order to acquire an academic social language learners must be willing to accept certain losses and see the acquisition of the academic language as a gain.

An important part of acquisition of scientific discourse is learning to use the discourse and both Moje (1995) and Lemke (1990) mention "learning to talk the language of science." The challenge of acquisition of discourse is far greater for those whose primary language is not English. Moje, Collazo, Carrillo, and Marx (2001, p. 473) agree with this position in their discussion of instructional and interactional discourses in which they argue that

> If the discourses of science and of secondary classrooms represent a challenge to understanding, the language of instruction and text for students whose first language is English . . . we must acknowledge the even greater cognitive demands on students for whom English is not a first language.

Research on Learners Accessing Text

Some cognitivist studies have pointed to difficulties learners have in accessing texts due to conceptual or verbal problems in the texts themselves. In South Africa, a set of South African biology textbooks studied by Linkonyane and Sanders (1997) revealed errors in the books on the topic of respiration in biology. In another study, Clark (1997) describes an attempt to write accessible materials for Grade 9 learners in South Africa. He makes the point that the most difficult words for the learners were the nontechnical words. At the secondary school level similar findings were reported by Prophet and Towse (1999) who found that familiar words used in a science context provided great difficulty to second-language learners in both Botswana and Britain. The concern was most of all for the second-language learners in Britain whose learning was further hampered by socioeconomic disadvantage. Difficulties in vocabulary are supported by Tendencia (1999) who looked at words in textbooks found difficult by Grades 4 and 5 Bruneian children. The words *describe* and *observe* were universally mentioned.

Also in the cognitivist vein are studies by Musheno and Lawson (1999) and Glyn and Takahashi (1998). Using an information processing perspective, Musheno and Lawson found that producing a text that starts with examples and lower-order concepts first, led to improved comprehension as tested by posttests. Glyn and Takahashi found that analogy-enhanced texts have better immediate and two-week recall than those that do not use analogies.

At the secondary level, Kearsey and Turner (1999) show how subjecting texts to genre analysis can assist in deciding how accessible textbooks are. The expository nature of scientific texts makes them inaccessible to school pupils, forcing teachers to mediate what Lemke (1982, p. 263) refers to as "the ponderous style of text book science." O'Toole (1996) explains that it is no accident that scientific prose is so compact. Scientists consider it necessary in order to communicate accurately with their peers.

At the tertiary level, Chen and Donin (1997) studied how Chinese speaking postgraduates processed biology texts in their home language and in English. They found that domain-specific knowledge was a far more important factor in their comprehension of text than language proficiency. There was no difference in the recall ability of the subjects when recalling the text in English or Chinese and more language proficient students could read faster than those who were less proficient. The authors do caution that the general English proficiency of all subjects in the study was not particularly low, though some were better than others. Nevertheless, the findings of this study can be supported by Gee (1997, p. 255) who states,

> Learning to read situated texts of certain types is like learning the meanings of words. It is a matter of having lots of experiences that allow one to become familiar with patterns and sub patterns, that is, what I have called situated meanings . . . guided by cultural models that explicate and evaluate these situated meanings, and are, in turn, ultimately formed by them.

The subjects in Chen and Donin's study can generally be assumed to have a reasonable schooling background in general, unlike many of the second-language learners in developing countries.

Resolving the Dilemma

The findings reviewed earlier and common sense both suggest that for learners to access text, it must be within their zone of proximal development (Vygotsky, 1978). Gee also convincingly argues that learners will not become part of the community they are trying to access if they are not initiated into the discourse of that community. Writers of educational texts are in a dilemma. By writing in the target discourse they are risking losing learners; by writing in the life-world language they risk leaving learners outside the scientific community. Below I attempt to map a way forward for two particular contexts, the first being the learner in a face-to-face situation who benefits from the mediation of a teacher and the other being the learner in a distance setting where all they have to help them is the written materials.

In the case of face-to-face learning situations there are numerous opportunities other than using text to introduce the learner to the discourse and practice of the community, yet studies with second-language learners in underresourced contexts show that this is rarely the case (Cleghorn & Rollnick, 2002; Peacock, 1995; Rollnick, Manyatsi, Lubben, & Bradley, 1998) MacDonald (1990) found that there was a marked disparity in the demands of the English language reading books and the English appearing in science texts for the year of transition from home-language instruction to English medium. The science texts were more difficult in terms of vocabulary, sentence structure and style. A similar finding was reported by Ryf and Cleghorn (1997) in Zimbabwe.

Further research shows that the hoped for mediation does not take place with the teacher, who may herself have difficulty with the text. For example Peacock (1995) found that in most developing countries, particularly in Africa, teachers are poorly qualified, both in terms of their science content knowledge and in their command of the English language. The textbook, if it is present, is frequently the only resource available to a teacher. However they find it difficult to mediate the text owing to their own lack of background. Other teachers, as found by Rollnick et al. (1998), adopt the approach of predigesting the book themselves and delivering the content in the form of notes copied laboriously and unproductively by learners into notebooks and learnt by rote for tests and examinations. The textbooks in this instance lie unused despite the fact that each learner has a copy (see chapter 9, for example).

Peacock (1995) also found that the expository nature of science text made it particularly inaccessible to second-language learners and found that illustrations did not necessarily help unless well mediated by teachers. Presenting scientific material in accessible discourse has been found to motivate learners and attract them to science. For example Peacock regards the advent of comic forms particularly welcome and they have proved accessible and enjoyable to learners at this level. One such example is the Handspring project in South Africa (Rollnick, Jones, Perold, & Bahr, 1998). Peacock and Gates (2000) found that even newly qualified primary teachers in the United Kingdom selected texts for their learners on the basis of surface features related to accessibility and a relatively high percentage selected the Handspring materials even though they were unfamiliar to them.

A highly motivated teacher with a very sound content background can, with difficulty, mediate scientific discourse to learners but may struggle to motivate them to do so independently. Part of the apprenticeship into acquisition of scientific text is gaining independent access to text. Thus it is important to attain a balance between life-world language and scientific discourse in any texts used in a teaching situation. School learners are not all aspiring to be scientists: many need only enough science to assume a role as a scientifically literate citizen, yet they may need to acquire academic social language for numerous other purposes. Even popular scientific magazines make liberal use of scientific discourse.

In the case of distance learners where contact sessions are few, there is an even greater imperative to keep a balance between the two discourses. Add to this the complication of studying at a distance. This provides an additional challenge to both teachers and learners. A particularly tricky situation is that of access courses. These are programs for adult learners who are interested in accessing university study in science but lack the necessary background in these subjects because of poor schooling or poor subject choice. The great majority of the learners on this program are learning in a language that is not their main language. A study of learners accessing text in this situation can provide insight into how novice scientists may go about acquiring the necessary scientific discourse.

One such study by Rollnick, Green, and Block (2003) is underway with second-language learners on a distance access course in South Africa. The approach used by the writers of the science text was to provide a mixture of discourses with the new scientific discourse carefully mediated in the text, as the following extract from the materials shows.

Solutes and Solvents

You have already been introduced to the concept that any homogeneous mixture can be called a solution. In your everyday life you are used to making solutions. When you take sugar (the solute) and dissolve it in your tea (the solvent), you are, of course, making a solution.

Although the solute does not have to be a solid and the solvent does not have to be a liquid, another solution which is easy to make at home is one involving solid table salt (NaCl) and water. You could make a 1 litre solution of NaCl in a Coke bottle and you could choose to make your solution either concentrated or dilute, depending on much salt you use. A solution which contains a high proportion of solute compared to solvent is said to be *concentrated*. A solution which only contains a little solute mixed with a lot of solvent is *dilute*.

This text appears in the fourth week of study and learners have already been introduced to terms such as "homogeneous." However the section begins by using what is clearly life-world discourse referring to familiar contexts such as making a cup of tea. The point of the passage is to teach the concepts, concentrated and dilute, and solute and solvent. Of interest are the last two sentences, the first of which is clearly in academic social language and the second which is in life-world language. In this way it is hoped that the learner will be able to differentiate between the two ways of expressing parallel ideas.

In research into the accessibility of the materials on a distance foundation chemistry course (Rollnick, Green, & Block, 2003) learners were asked to paraphrase the last sentence in the text given here. Responses fell into roughly three categories.

1. Those who were beginning to appropriate scientific discourse. Mostly these adopted the strategy of using the phrasing of the last section, for example, "The mixture of a solute and solvent where the solute has a low proportion."
2. Those who used life-world language to rephrase, for example, "when you have a litre of water and you dissolve a teaspoon of sugar what is formed is a dilute solution."
3. A category that was referred to as second-language discourse, though this is probably the life-world language of those who use it. The grammar looks rather strange to those outside the discourse community, for example, "The substance that is dissolved in another one when its less than the one which is dissolved in the solution is called a dilute solution."

Within these categories other practices such as rephrasing using an example were also observed. There were also responses that showed an understanding of the sentence that was different to that of the scientific community. No one showed no understanding of the sentence.

What is interesting about these findings is that the use of a sentence in life-world language immediately followed by one in academic social language does not prevent any learners from accessing the text but has the effect of gradually introducing the discourse necessary for the discipline. The evidence here shows that the learners were able to understand the text, though not necessarily actively produce the language themselves. Coincidentally the text also started with lower-order concepts as in the Musheno and Lawson (1999) study referred to earlier.

In another study by Block and Rollnick (2003), students' comprehension of a foundation study manual in geography was investigated. Again the students participating in this study were second-language learners. The study manual in question was written almost exclusively using academic social language and it was taught by a lecturer who recited the manual to the students. This direct exposure to the discourse with little mediation resulted in little learning of the discourse or the acquisition of the practice of the discipline. Students were unable to meaningfully paraphrase sentences from the manual such as

> Altitude in itself induces climatic changes and these give rise to a vertical differentiation in vegetation.

Eighty percent of the students produced sentences with incorrect language and science. For example, one student wrote,

> The vertical differentiation in vegetation rises its climatic changes.

The other 20 percent produced sentences that though correct, had only slight changes in the language of the sentence. In other sentences the performance of the students was much the same. One of the students, when asked to comment on the language used in the study manual wrote:

> Words that are used in the study manual are understandable but the way the information is phrased is impossible to understand.

This statement is consistent with findings elsewhere in the same study (Block, 2002) where students largely showed understanding of individual words used in the manual and were even able to make use of logical connectives in isolated sentences. Their lack of initiation into the discourse was most powerfully illustrated by their inability to apply knowledge from the manual to a situation that called for application of principle taught in the manual in question. Thus direct exposure to academic social language in this case did not result in acquisition of the discourse.

In the distance foundation chemistry course previously referred to, further evidence was gathered by asking pairs of learners to work together on a portion of the text by reading aloud and explaining to each other. This exercise was carried out toward the end of the course. The course consisted of 16 units and they were asked to work on unit 15, which at that stage was the next unit they were to access.

The following excerpt shows how Bongi and Vusi mastered the concept of "spectator ion," something that had puzzled them earlier in the episode where Vusi said,

> V: Well, you have got to ask that . . . They are called spectator . . . . I dunno let's just leave it there.

Later on Bongi reads further in the text. (Underlined passages are read straight from the materials.)

> B: <u>They yield $FeSCN^{2+}$ in aqueous solution plus three chlorine ions in aqueous solution plus potassium ions in aqueous solution.</u> [actually written $FeSCN^{2+}$ (aq) + $3Cl^-$ (aq) + K^+] <u>If you look at reactants and products you will notice that the chlorine ion and the potassium ion are exactly the same on both sides of the equation. So they are unchanged during the reaction and are left out of the ionic equation</u> ooohhh . . . do you understand that? It means the two are the spectator ions because . . .
>
> V: yeah . . .
>
> B: . . . on the reactants side . . . they . . . have not been used . . . on the right . . . on the product side that have not been used. So they are just there . . . as spectators.
>
> V: So it means if it's a spectator ion its still having it in your product the only thing only potassium there you still have it in your products . . .
>
> B: . . . . as it was in the reactants
>
> V: They don't take part . . .
>
> B: It was just a spectator, it was just looking . . . what was happening
>
> V: (Laughs) So that's why they say it's a spectator ion

This excerpt is remarkable for several reasons. First, it illustrates the process through which a difficult concept becomes clear to the two students. Not only do they express their appreciation at seeing an idea they had earlier abandoned but they also display their understanding of the concept in life-world second-language discourse when Bongi says, "*It was just a spectator, it was just looking . . . what was happening.*" Further examples of second-language life-world discourse are provided by the earlier utterance where Vusi says, "*its still having it in your product.*"

The second remarkable aspect of the exchange between the students is the extent to which they have bought into academic social language. This is illustrated by the way in which Bongi reads aloud the portion of the equation. They yield $FeSCN^{2+}$ in aqueous solution plus three chlorine ions in aqueous solution plus potassium ions in aqueous solution [actually written $FeSCN^{2+}$ (aq) + $3Cl^-$ (aq) + K^+]. She faithfully repeats in each case the words "in aqueous solution" when reading the "(aq)" after each ion. This is in stark contrast to another pair who simply omitted the equations from the spoken discourse and a third pair who read SO_2 as "so two," rather than "S" "O" "two." Bongi and Vusi are showing increase in understanding as well as acquisition of academic social language. Appropriately, their discourse still consists of both life-world language and academic social language.

In a study on acquisition of biology concepts, Duran, Dugan and Weffer (1998) maintain that the use of academic social language in formal instruction is important for what they call "ventriloquation" of science language. The learners in their study who were studying in their second language had to become users of the language even if they were insecure in the comprehension of the concepts in the early stages of instruction. This view would correspond with Lave and Wenger's (1991) conception of learners as "legitimate peripheral participants" in the social practice of the discipline. In Duran et al.'s (1998) study, learners at the beginning of the study viewed contextualization of concepts as deviation from the business of learning biology, but by the end of the study were able to contextualize concepts for themselves and use the language of the discourse. Although Duran et al.'s (1998) study was not specifically about accessing text, the spoken discourse of the teacher can be construed as text and the concept of ventriloquation may well be applied to written text.

The three studies cited here provide insight into a possible model for understanding the way in which second-language learners may access text material in order to enter the discourse of the discipline. I have been using Gee's (2001) concepts of "life-world language" and "academic social language." Gee's emphasis is on the acquisition of academic social language by learners who use the language of learning and teaching (in this case, English) as their main language. The question raised here is slightly different since it concerns learners who are learning through the medium of a language that is not their primary language. Gee maintains that to become part of the scientific community, a learner must be able to use academic social language or they will not become part of the community of practice, in this case of science.

A distinction also needs to be made between accessing discourse and producing discourse. Learners reading text and showing the ability to paraphrase the text meaningfully in life-world language have successfully accessed the text, but have not necessarily displayed the ability to produce the required academic social language. To become part of the community of practice this last step is essential, but I suggest that the first stage of accessing the text can be regarded as an essential transition stage. It is likely that the second stage of producing scientific discourse would require mediation by the teacher who would need to use meta-cognitive strategies to highlight the distinction between the two discourses for the learners. In Gee's terms learning would precede acquisition.

In countries where the language of teaching and learning is different to the main language of the learner, the learner actually acquires two life-world languages, one in the main language and a second in the language of learning and teaching. This form of bilingualism is seen as a strength rather than as a weakness (Williams, 1987). The discourse community, often referred to as second-language discourse, overlaps with the life-world language of first-language speakers in the same way as many discourse communities overlap to produce what may be referred to as "standard English."

Where countries such as Malaysia have adopted their main language as the language of learning and teaching, this is often also the main language of the learners. However where the academic social language is different to the learner's main language, it would be difficult to acquire academic social language by accessing texts in the main language. This would necessitate a transfer not only to a different discourse but also to a different language. If the goal of instruction is merely to provide an understanding of some key scientific concepts as may be the case at the primary school level, then the language of the text may be more accessible if it is written as the learner's main language.

A Model for Accessing Text

There are three possible approaches to producing texts for instruction. The first is to use purely academic social language as in Block's study, described earlier. The findings clearly illustrate the difficulties encountered by second-language learners attempting to extract meaning from the text. Unlike in Duran et al.'s (1998) study, the possibility of ventriloquation of concepts does not appear to produce anything further than rote learning. The second possibility is to use a mixed discourse approach. These would be materials that make use of both life-world language and academic social language. The learners in Rollnick et al.'s (2003) study were able to access the materials and in some cases produce academic social language. The materials used in this study do not explicitly point to the difference in discourse but by example slowly introduce the "scientists' way of speaking." What the materials do not do, however is "talk" the second-language discourse of the learners. So the life-world language of the first-language speaker becomes a meeting point for the teacher and the learner on the road to production of academic social language. The third possibility would be to produce materials written entirely in life-world language. Social conventions would mitigate against using the second-language discourse in common use by learners, so the life-world language used would have to be the life-world language of the first-language speaker as described here.

The process of accessing the text could be conceptualized diagrammatically. There are three possible text types as elaborated earlier. The text may be entirely in life-world language, it may be mixed as in the example mentioned earlier, or it may be entirely in academic social language. Figure 8.1 examines the possibilities that exist in the case of the text being entirely in life-world language.

Here it should not be possible at all to produce academic social language as no examples are provided for the learner to access. If the text is transformed meaningfully into L2 discourse or the learner's main language, then it can be assumed that the learner has been able to construct meaning from the text. As figure 8.1 shows, it is also possible to construct meaning using life-world discourse either by first using L2 discourse and then translating into the discourse of the text or by directly using the discourse of the text.

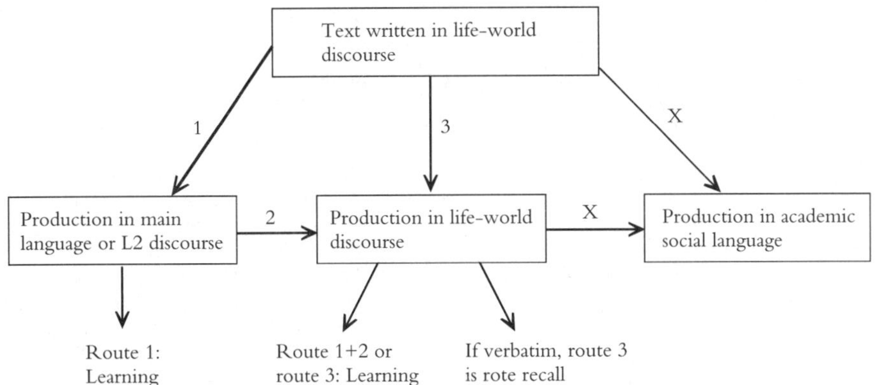

Figure 8.1. Meaningful production from text in life-world language

However, if a learner's production consists of verbatim extracts from the text, one can infer that little meaningful learning has taken place.

Figure 8.2 shows the possible scenarios when the text is in academic social language. As Block's study shows, very few meaningful productions were made by the learners, suggesting that the routes described in figure 8.2 are mostly theoretical and unlikely in practice. The most common likely route of those shown is the verbatim route that is not strictly meaningful learning.

Figure 8.3 shows the third scenario, that of text produced in mixed discourse. As can be seen in figure 8.3 there are two possibilities for rote recall, but in both cases these will easily be detectible as they will be verbatim productions from the text. The possible routes for acquisition and learning are similar to those for academic social language but they are more likely to occur with this type of text.

One last possibility needs to be considered and that is the role played by ventriloquation as defined by Duran et al. (1998). Figures 8.1–8.3 include verbatim reproductions but dismiss them as rote recall and hence not meaningful. However Duran's study

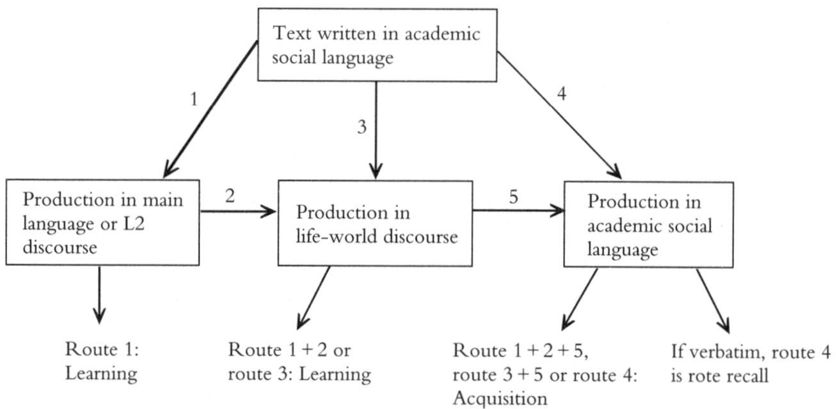

Figure 8.2. Meaningful production from text in academic social language

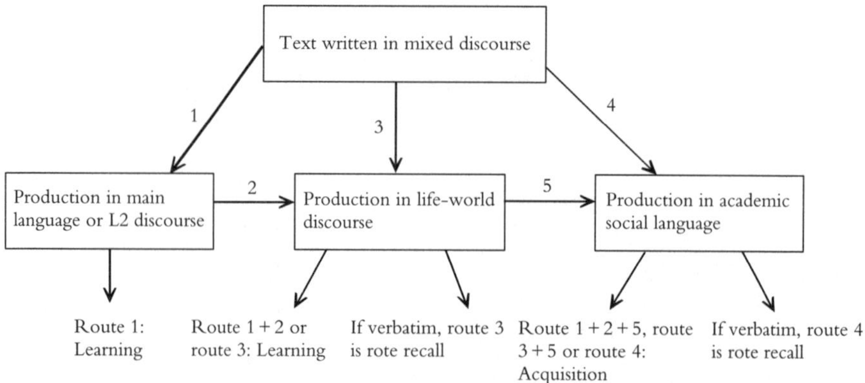

Figure 8.3. Meaningful production from text in mixed discourse

shows that learners may start by using academic social language by merely imitating the discourse they are exposed to. This discourse later becomes meaningful through its use in practice and is thus acquired. According to Vygotsky (1986) infants learn to speak by this method. However an important prerequisite for this type of acquisition is continuous exposure to the discourse as it is used by competent practitioners. In the context that second-language learners often access texts, this exposure is not available and hence a mediated route is necessary with conscious pointers to the difference between the discourses.

CONCLUSION

Why then, do learners have difficulty accessing text? One obvious answer lies in making the text sufficiently interesting and attractive as mentioned earlier, sufficient motivation will allow learners to access text well above their normal reading level. On the other end of the spectrum there are the ponderous school textbooks, particularly in science and particularly when accessed by second-language learners where the chances of learners accessing text or of raising interest are minimal. There is the further interest of some misguided authors or teachers particularly in mathematics and science who feel that the language in such books should be difficult for them to preserve their status of custodians of a difficult subject. This allows them to attract only the upper end of the ability spectrum. This is the view expounded by Michael Young (Young, 1971) in the early 1970s. The manual discussed in the Block (2002) study was deliberately turgid in what was probably a misguided attempt at "raising standards." The point about scientific discourse is that it is not just a matter of joining a club or a secret society that speaks a coded language. Scientific discourse evolved in the way it did because it has a functionality and ultimately it is needed to adequately express scientific ideas.

Gee's view as presented earlier makes the point that if there is any intention on the part of a of novice to access the world of science, or any academic discipline with a view to participate in its practice, those wishing to do so have to pay the price of acquiring the academic social language. In this chapter I have defined three possible levels of access to texts that may use this language: (1) inability to extract meaning from the text, (2) ability to access meaning but only able to explain in life-world discourse, and (3) able to access meaning and to explain in academic social language.

In the situation prevailing in developing countries, levels of scientific literacy are very low both amongst teachers and learners and merely enabling learners to extract meaning from texts would already be an improvement on the poor situation in the schools. As discussed here, texts are currently inaccessible to the majority of learners, possibly due to the formal register in which they are written. Oversimplification can lead to loss of meaning and even accusations that the texts no longer reflect the discipline they are trying to reflect. The experience we have had with mixed discourse texts seems to provide a way forward, even in a distance learning context; a far more stringent test of a text than one to be used in a situation where a teacher is available to mediate. Where teachers have difficulty in mediating normal scientific texts, the use of distance learning texts may prove useful and increase teacher confidence with the discourse.

In an attempt to turn youth on to science, Mark Shuttleworth, the first African in space coined the term "hip to be square," or in the increasingly popular SMS discourse, "hip2b^2." Perhaps this will provide the opening for youth to aspire to the world of science and scientific discourse that will motivate them to access the texts that may be above their level. However not all learners will fall into this category and the most logical way forward appears to be to improve accessibility by using the type of mixed discourse described here.

References

Block, E.
(2002). *First year university students' understanding of aspects of language in a selected geography topic.* (MSc. Research Report). University of the Witwatersrand.

Bracken, B.
(1982). Effect of personalized basal stories on the reading comprehension of fourth grade poor and average readers. *Contemporary Educational Psychology, 7* (4), 320–324.

Chen, Q. & Donin, J.
(1997). Discourse processing of first and second language biology texts: Effects of language proficiency and domain specific knowledge. *Modern Language Journal, 81* (ii), 209–227.

Clark, J.
(1997). Beyond the turgid soil of science prose: Attempt to write more accessible science text materials in General Science. In M. Sanders (Ed.), *Proceedings of the Fifth Annual Meeting of the Southern African Association for Research in Science and Mathematics Education* (pp. 390–396). Johannesburg.

Cleghorn, A. & Rollnick, M.
(2002). The role of English in individual and societal development: A view from African classrooms. *TESOL Quarterly, 36* (3), 347–372.

Cobb P. & Bowers J.
(1998). Cognitive and situated learning: Perspectives in theory and practice. *Educational Researcher, 28* (2), 4–15.

Crook, N.M.
(1977). A study of the validity of the Fry readability graph. *Journal of Social Studies Research, 1* (2), 53–59.

Doidge, M.
(1997). How readable is your biology textbook? Can you be sure? In M. Sanders, (Ed.), *Proceedings of the Fifth Annual Meeting of the Southern African Association for Research in Science and Mathematics Education* (pp. 396–400). Johannesburg.

Duran, B.J., Dugan, T., & Weffer, R.
(1998). Language minority students in high school: The role of language in learning biology concepts. *Science Education, 82* (3), 311–341.

Gee, J.P.
(1996). *Social linguistics and literacies: Ideology in discourse.* London: Falmer.

Gee, J.P.
(1997). Thinking, learning and reading. In D. Kirshner & J.A. Whitson (Eds.), *Situated cognition: Social, semiotic, and psychological perspectives* (pp. 235–260). Mahwah, N.J.: Erlbaum.

Gee, J.P.

(2001). *Language in the science classroom: Academic social languages as the heart of school-based literacy*, unpublished manuscript, University of Wisconsin-Madison.

Glyn, S.M. & Takahashi, T.

(1998). Learning from analogy enhanced science text. *Journal of Research in Science Teaching, 35* (10), 1129–1149.

Gordon, R.M.

(1980). The readability of an unreadable text. *English Journal, 69* (3), 60–66.

Johnstone, A.H. & Wham, A.J.B.

(1982). The demands of practical work. *Education in Chemistry, 19,* 72–75.

Kearsey, J. & Turner, S.

(1999). Evaluating textbooks: The role of genre analysis. *Research in Science and Technological Education, 17* (1), 35–42.

Lave, J. & Wenger, E.

(1991). *Situated learning: Legitimate peripheral participation.* New York: Cambridge University Press.

Lemke, J.

(1982). Talking physics. *Physics Education, 17,* 263–267.

Lemke, J.L.

(2001). Articulating communities: socio-cultural perspectives on science education. *Journal of Research in Science Teaching, 38* (3), 296–316.

Lemke, J.L.

(1990). *Talking science: Language, learning and values.* Norwood, New Jersey: Ablex Publishing Corporation.

Linkonyane, J. & Sanders, M.

(1997). South African matric biology textbooks as possible sources of erroneous ideas about respiration. In M. Sanders, (Ed.), *Proceedings of the Fifth Annual Meeting of the Southern African Association for Research in Science and Mathematics Education* (pp. 421–428). Johannesburg.

MacDonald, C.A.

(1990). *School based learning experiences: A final report of the Threshold Project.* Pretoria: Human Sciences Research Council.

Moje, E.B.

(1995). Talking about science: An interpretation of the effects of teacher talk in a high school science classroom. *Journal of Research in Science Teaching, 32* (4), 349–371.

Moje, E.B., Collazo, T., Carrillo, R., & Marx, R.W.

(2001). "Maestro, what is 'quality'?": Language, literacy, and discourse in project–based science. *Journal of Research in Science Teaching, 38* (4), 469–498.

Musheno, B. & Lawson, A.E.

(1999). Effects of learning cycle and traditional text on comprehension of science concepts by students at different reasoning levels. *Journal of Research in Science Teaching, 36* (1), 23–37.

Peacock, A.

(1995). An agenda for research into text material in primary science for second language learners of English in developing countries. *Journal of Multilingual and Multicultural Development, 16* (5), 389–401.

Peacock, A. & Gates, S.
(2000). Newly qualified primary teachers' perceptions of the role of text materials in teaching science. *Research in Science and Technological Education, 18* (2), 155–171.

Prophet, R. & Towse, P.
(1999). Pupils' understanding of some non-technical words in science. *School Science Review, 81,* 79–86.

Rollnick, M. Green, G., & Block, E.
(2003). The loneliness of the long distance learner: Accessing Chemistry Foundation texts. In V. Kelly (Ed.), *Proceedings of the 11th Annual Conference of the Southern African Association for Research in Mathematics, Science and Technology Education* (pp. 657–663). Swaziland.

Rollnick, M., Jones, B., Perold, H., & Bahr, M.
(1998). Puppets and comics in primary science: The development and evaluation of a pilot multimedia package *International Journal of Science Education, 20* (5), 533–550.

Rollnick, M., Manyatsi, S., Lubben, F., & Bradley, J.
(1998). A model for studying gaps in education: A Swaziland case study in the learning of science. *International Journal of Education Development, 18* (6), 453–465.

Rumelhart, D.E.
(1980). Schemata: The building blocks of cognition. In R.J. Spiro, B.C. Bruce, and W.F. Brewer (Eds.), *Theoretical issues in reading comprehension* (pp. 33–58). Hilldale, N.J: Erlbaum.

Rush, R.T.
(1985). Assessing readability: formulas and alternatives. *Reading Teacher, 39* (3), 274–283.

Ryf, A. & Cleghorn, A.
(1997). The language of science: Text talk and teacher talk in second language settings. In M. Sanders (Ed.), *Proceedings of the Fifth Annual Meeting of the Southern African Association for Research in Science and Mathematics* (pp. 437–441). Johannesburg.

Tendencia, C.P.
(1999). English words that Bruneian children find difficult in upper primary science textbooks. In M.A. Clements and L.Y. Pak (Eds.), *Cultural and language aspects of science, mathematics and technical education.* (pp. 103–112) Gadong: Universiti Brunei Darussalam.

Vygotsky, L.S.
(1978). *Mind in society: The development of higher psychological processes.* Cambridge, M.A.: Harvard University Press.

Vygotsky, L.S.
(1986). *Thought and language.* Cambridge, M.A.: MIT Press.

Williams, I.
(1987). Science and mathematics—the final frontier for bilingual *education. Education for Development, 11,* 40–54.

Young, M.F.D.
(1971). *Knowledge and control: New directions for the sociology of education.* London: Collier-Macmillan.

9

Using Science Textbooks in Kenyan Primary Schools

Beatrice Murila

There have been several studies of the quality of instruction in developing country classrooms that underline the paucity of text and other learning materials (e.g., Eisemon, Nyamete, & Cleghorn, 1989; Heyneman & Jamison, 1980; MacDonald, 1990; Ochola, 1983; Wandiga, 1994). The implications drawn from this research are that the quality of instruction would improve if text materials were more plentiful; that student instruction would improve if text materials were more plentiful; students would become more efficient readers if more books were available; scores on national tests would improve; more students would graduate from secondary school and so on.

Few studies however have looked closely at the ways text materials are actually used in developing country classrooms by students and teachers. Even fewer have explored this matter comparatively, for example to see if there are differences in use where textbooks are in short supply. Yet evidence such as this is crucial in determining whether or not text material can make the differences claimed by research. If text material exists but is not used, or if use by pupils is not encouraged, then the gains predicted from a supply of such materials will not be realized. This study therefore set out to compare the use of science text material in primary schools in different socioeconomic and sociolinguistic contexts.

SETTING OF THE STUDY

The purpose of this research was to find out how teachers and pupils used Science textbooks in differing types of Kenyan primary schools. Standard 4 classes were chosen for the study, since this is the stage at which children begin to study their subjects in English, as opposed to the vernacular language used in standards 1–3. A pilot study was

Table 9.1. Distribution of schools in sample

	Nairobi	Western Province
High cost schools	2	2
Low cost schools	2	2

conducted, followed by data gathering in eight schools chosen to represent differing locations and language populations, as shown in table 9.1.

High-cost schools (usually private) charge tuition fees and are usually run by individual entrepreneurs or companies. They tend to be located in larger urban areas and are well resourced in terms of facilities such as classrooms with desks and windows, libraries, furniture (such as bookshelves and lockable storage) and textbook and other learning materials. Their pupils, often from better-off homes with literate parents, tend to do better in national examinations. Low-cost schools are mainly government schools, run through district authorities, and lack good physical facilities. The government pays teachers' salaries, but much of the physical structure of the school is the responsibility of the parents or community. As a consequence of historically rapid population growth in Kenya, they often have large class sizes and few resources, often extending to a lack of books and storage space. Though tuition fees may not be charged by the government, in reality schools levy fees for such items as uniforms, fees which, however small, can often be beyond the reach of parents involved in subsistence agriculture.

Some government schools may be high-cost, whilst some private schools may be very basic. The key distinction is that high-cost schools operate almost exclusively in English as the medium of instruction, whilst in low-cost schools, Kiswahili or vernacular languages will be used up to standard 4 and often beyond, even though the official language policy requires English. Textbooks for standard 4 and above are exclusively in English.

METHODOLOGY

The study involved classroom observation, taped interviewing of pupils and teachers and observing/listening to pupils reading from the textbook, after which pupils were tested on their knowledge of the double-page spread used. The teacher interviews were unstructured, whilst pupil interviews used a semi-structured interview schedule. Eight teachers and 24 pupils were interviewed in depth.

All teachers were interviewed in English. Pupils, however, were interviewed according to their preference in English, Kiswahili, or Luyha, the vernacular language of the schools in the Western Province and the first language of the researcher. Pupils' reading was analyzed using methods adopted from the Primary Language Record Handbook (Barrs, Ellis, Hester, & Thomas, 1992). The evidence below is first presented in the form of detailed discussion of case studies, followed by a summary of the more general evidence from the pupil observations and interviews.

Case Studies of Teachers in Three Schools

The three examples chosen were taken from a rural low-cost school, an urban low-cost school, and an urban high-cost school. They varied in terms of availability of books, space and resources for teaching and learning, and language used in the classroom.

Case Study 1: Rural Low-Cost School—Standard 4

The school, was not well equipped, and generally three pupils shared a desk designed for two. The teacher spoke the same vernacular language (Luhya) as the pupils, as well as English: pupils spoke their mother-tongue most of the time, even in class. Their knowledge of English did not extend much beyond the names of items like books, table, chair and a few short phrases read to them and repeated.

A 30-minute science lesson was observed, which began by the pupils standing up and chorusing, in English, "good morning our teacher and our visitor." The teacher then asked a few questions in English about what she had taught in the previous lesson, on soil. The questions were directed to the class, and so chorus answers were given back, which appeared to be rehearsed, as follows:

Teacher:	What is soil made of?
Pupils:	Dead animals, dead leaves, broken rocks
Teacher:	Is the soil the same (*sic*)?
Pupils:	No, the soil is not the same.

After this revision, the teacher wrote TYPES OF SOIL on the chalkboard and introduced the topic again by telling pupils that soil has different types, like loam, clay, and sand. She wrote these words on the board, and went on to give an explanation of their meanings. In the course of this, she asked pupils the meanings of words, like "sticky"; where none of them knew, she provided explanations in the mother-tongue, as follows:

Teacher:	"Sticky" nikhuli shindu nishihandi menya ikamu (*sticky is when something sticks like glue*). Muhulili? (*Have you understood?*)
Pupils:	Yee madamu (*yes madam*).

Pupils were then asked to get out the soils they had been asked to bring; each of the 31 pupils had brought a small bag of soil. They were asked to feel the type of soil they had brought, and to say aloud which type of soil was theirs. Hands were put up, and the teacher chose a few pupils to give answers. Most of them had loam soil from their gardens at home.

The teacher then sent two pupils to the school kitchen (where teachers' tea is prepared) to bring a jerry-can of water. After the water arrived, pupils were asked to move to the back of the class; plastic bags were spread on the floor, and in groups, pupils mixed their soils with a little water, while kneeling down. There was not much space around the plastic sheet, so some pupils did this on their desks. During the activity, there was a lot of talk in Kiswahili or the mother-tongue, and a lot of laughter. Observing pupils, it was clear that most conversations were about the task in hand; pupils made observations like "yako inaanguka" (*yours is falling apart*). After the experiment, they were again asked about the types of soil they had brought, and to test each other's. Eventually they were asked to go out and wash their hands in the remaining water, then come back to class. While they were out, the teacher drew this table on the board:

Type	Colour	Texture
Loam		
Clay		
Sand		

After the pupils returned, they drew the table in their exercise books and were asked to discuss the types of soil they had. The teacher explained the word "texture" as rough, fine, or smooth. Pupils were asked to describe the color of their soil (now wet); colors varied a lot. Answers in each column and row varied as a consequence. The teacher then told pupils that "loam had a fine texture."

No textbook was used at any stage of this lesson. The teacher's notes were taken from the textbook, which she referred to regularly throughout the lesson. Pupils did not ask questions, and did not open their own copies of the textbook at any time. Later, the teacher explained that she had to share a copy of the textbook with another teacher in the other standard 4 class, which is why she worked from notes. She also reiterated the view that pupils had no textbooks to work from.

However, out of the five pupils interviewed, two had their own textbook, which had been bought by parents or passed down by siblings: when asked if they carried their books to school, they answered yes, but that the teacher never asked them to refer to them in class, since few others had them. The two pupils in question explained that they used the books themselves at home, for revision; homework was never set, hence most pupils never used a textbook in science lessons.

The five pupils were then asked to read a short passage from the text and answer questions. One did not need any assistance, and answered most questions correctly. When he could not remember, he reread the passage to get the answer, without assistance or prompting. Three others needed assistance, and so the researcher drew their attention to the relevant passages, which they then reread before answering questions.

It appeared that, in this class, no attempt was made by the teacher to utilize the textbook as a learning aid for pupils, and this was rationalized on the grounds of inadequate supply. As a consequence, the majority of pupils had developed few skills for using the text to obtain information.

Case Study 2: Urban Low-Cost School—Standard 4
This school was located in one of the poorest areas of Nairobi, and did not have big classrooms, so pupils were crowded together. Unlike the rural school, however, pupils each had a desk that could be locked, and an individual chair. The teacher in this standard 4 class had 25 years experience and was very confident. Pupils felt free to ask

her questions. The lesson observed was a double science period of 70 minutes. The lesson began in English as follows:

> Teacher: Our topic today is about floating and sinking. Do you know what these two words mean?
>
> Pupils: (in chorus): Staying on top of the water, going to the bottom.

The teacher then wrote FLOATING AND SINKING on the board, from the Primary Science Standard 4 textbook. All the information the teacher gave to the pupils was taken from this book. She explained that they would do experiments to find out which objects floated or sank, and she had brought some of the apparatus that were illustrated in the book. She called all 40 pupils round her table, and put a plastic container in front of them. However, there was not enough room for them to see, so some stood on desks to see the demonstration of the activity described in the book. The session began like this:

> Teacher: I will pour some water into the container. I will then put some maize seeds and two nails into the water. What is (*sic*) happening to them?
>
> Pupils: The nail is sinking and the seeds are float.

She dropped the objects in and removed them, then added some sugar to the water. On the table, she had two eggs, salt, nails, and maize seeds. She asked two pupils to go forward and mix sugar and salt with water in separate containers. They continued stirring until the sugar and salt had dissolved. She then put an egg in each of the containers, and spoke to the pupils as follows:

> Teacher: Look at the container that has the sugar. Come close so that you can see.
>
> Pupils: It is floating.
>
> Teacher: Look at the other container. Has the egg sunk?
>
> Pupils: No, it is floating.

In the textbook, other items like petrol and paraffin were recommended for this experiment. The teacher paused to explain what had happened (salt had made the water denser), even though in the textbook the pupils were supposed to do the experiments themselves and suggest reasons why the eggs floated. She continued to explain that objects that were lighter than water floated, and those that were heavier sank. However, sinkers could be made to float, as in the experiment.

The teacher then asked one pupil to fill a container with water and put a plastic lid into it. It floated. The teacher then asked him to put maize seeds onto the lid, and asked what was happening; he said that "the lid was floating." Pupils added more seeds, until the lid began to sink. She asked other pupils what was happening. The discussion was held entirely in English. At times, pupils were asked to repeat what the teacher said, for example:

> Teacher: Heavy objects sink in water, What do heavy objects do?
>
> Pupils: (in chorus) they sink in water.

Pupils were clearly used to only responding in chorus, since none of them ever put up their hands to answer a question.

They were then told that they would go outside the classroom to do the experiment, using the containers and materials they had brought. They were divided into five groups. The repeated experiment was carried out in the classroom, and the teacher went round asking questions about which objects floated. Pupils talked in Kiswahili and English.[1] They often also mixed languages, when they did not know the relevant word, for example:

"kalamu in float" (*the pen is floating*)
"mawe ina sink" (*the stone has sunk*)

Unlike in the previous class, the teacher now also used Kiswahili. After 15 minutes, they returned to the classroom, settled down and drew a table that the teacher had copied from the textbook onto the board. Pupils were asked to copy it into their books and complete it, by adding the objects they had tested. There were some arguments, in Kiswahili, between groups, about whether things had floated or sunk. The teacher repeated that they had to write what they had done, not what the teacher had done. She circulated around, ticking correct answers.

Most of the work pupils were asked to do was from the textbook. The teacher explained that the experiment was actually combined from two textbooks. However, most pupils did not have books with them. When interviewed, one in five claimed to own a textbook; the others all claimed to borrow them for homework.

Four of the pupils did not read well. They found words like "oxygen" and "carbon dioxide" difficult to pronounce, and did not answer many questions correctly. The researcher asked them to go back to the passage to find their answers: one pupil saw no connection at all between the passage and the questions and so attempted to answer from his general knowledge. Pupils said that words like "starch" and "photosynthesis" were difficult to understand. The teacher had already explained, in her interview, that it had taken her a long time to explain the title of the topic ("Properties of Matter"), and that she also found these terms difficult. She rarely gave homework, because she claimed that very few pupils had books.

It was clear in this case that the teacher relied on the science textbook, mainly she said because the pupils had no access to books. However, she also felt that the book was merely a prescription of what to teach, and not a learning resource in itself. For example, she consistently changed what the book prescribed, and explained this on the grounds that she had to simplify it so that pupils could understand. However, what was changed was the process, not the content.

Case Study 3: Urban High-Cost School
This school had very good facilities, paid for by parents, which included sufficient textbooks and even a science laboratory. The teacher observed was a graduate of a Kenyan teachers college, with 15 years experience. The lesson began with a brief revision of the previous lesson, on "grouping animals collected." The discussion opened as follows:

Teacher: How were animals grouped in our last lesson?
Pupil 1:   Animals with or without wings
Pupil 2:   Animals that have 2 legs and 4 legs

In this class, pupils raised their hands and were chosen to answer by the teacher. There were no chorus answers. The teacher then wrote DIFFERENCES BETWEEN LIVING AND NONLIVING THINGS on the board, after which she asked pupils to open their textbooks on page 27, where the topic began. Apart from one pupil who shared, the remaining 38 had their own book, which they kept in their desks, and took out at the beginning of the lesson without being asked to do so.

The reading ability of this class was well above average. All pupils read confidently, except for the word "photosynthesis," which they found hard to pronounce. However, they all knew what it meant, and all five pupils interviewed answered all questions correctly, referring at times to the passage to find the answer.

The teacher asked individual pupils to read aloud from the book. There were eight short sentences, so eight pupils read, in order from the front of the class. The reading included instructions about what pupils were required to do: for example, "go outside the classroom and collect many things." During the course of their reading, one pupil could not pronounce the word "reproduce" correctly; the teacher repeated the correct pronunciation, followed by the pupil. She explained it meant "having young ones."

Pupils were then asked to take out the materials they had brought, and place them on their desks. Some had brought stones, wood, and beetles in jars. They held up their specimens, at the teacher's request, so others could see. During this session, all the talk was in English. The teacher then wrote on the board:

Living things grow, breathe, feed, reproduce and move. Examples are ———— and ————.

Nonliving things do not feed, grow, breathe and move. Examples are ———— and ————.

The pupils were to fill in the blanks from what they had observed, then complete a table according to the prescription in the textbook, and write a conclusion. However, the teacher side-stepped this activity by writing a few sentences on the board, which summarized the table and that required them again merely to fill in the correct answers. After being given time to do this, pupils were again asked to read out their answers. The teacher asked questions, such as "in which category do sticks belong?" The pupils discussed amongst themselves and agreed that they were nonliving because they could not grow or reproduce.

The teacher then copied out more sentences onto the board from a book called *Learning Science and Agriculture*, which the pupils did not have. Before the lesson ended, she gave pupils homework from their science textbooks. They were to study a diagram that had pictures of both living and nonliving things, and were required to copy another table, which she drew on the blackboard, and fill it in.

It was evident here that pupils used the textbook for both class work and homework. When interviewed, the teacher was confident that her pupils were able to use the books on their own, and often did so in class with minimal direction from herself. Pupils confirmed this in their interviews. The fact that most pupils had books made work easier for the teacher. Pupils were in the habit of opening their books and using them to learn. The teacher followed the book closely, and did not add much from other sources. In such a context, textbooks played a central role in the teaching and learning that went on in the classroom.

GENERAL FINDINGS

The main aim of the observation phase was to find out the extent to which textbooks were actually used by pupils in the classroom, and how. It was observed that half of the teachers did not use textbooks at all in their teaching; this was justified on the grounds that they did not have a copy, or they were unable to obtain copies for class use. Only a minority of pupils used them, since some teachers' use was simply for copying items onto the board. Interviews revealed that pupils' use of text was mainly for doing homework and revision exercises. However, pupils stressed that they were never given opportunities during lessons to ask questions about sections of the homework that they had not understood.

Teachers usually came into class and placed their copy of the textbook on the table. They then opened a separate exercise book, in which they had made lesson notes, and taught using their notes, even though these (and their diagrams) were often copied directly from the textbook. When teachers did use textbooks, however, there was no reference whatsoever to tables and other illustrations. Most teachers explained this on the grounds that pupils did not have textbooks, although this was not entirely the case, as table 9.2 indicates. They also felt that the textbook needed to be simplified, to save lesson time. However, pupils often said that they were asked to copy diagrams from the textbook for homework.

This evidence raised questions about pupils' understanding of the text and illustrations, since they rarely encountered or used them. These were therefore dealt with through the reading comprehension phase of the study.

Reading Comprehension

Pupils were asked to read about "How Animals and Plants Move" from a double-page spread of a widely used standard 4 Science textbook. After reading aloud, they were categorized as good, average, or poor readers (Barrs et al., 1992) then asked questions about their reading of the page, followed by factual questions to see if they had understood the content. Table 9.3 analyses their use of the illustrations, first reading a passage from the left-hand page without being asked to look at the illustrations, then again reading from the right-hand page after being asked to use the illustrations to help them.

Table 9.2. Availability of textbooks to pupils ($N = 51$)

Availability	No. of pupils
Had their own personal copy	22
Did not have a personal copy	29
Shared with 1 other pupil	20
Shared with 2 others	11
Shared with 3 others	4
None available even for sharing	16

Table 9.3. Pupils' reading of two passages from the text, in relation to their use of illustrations

Reading ability	No	When not specifically told to look at illustrations	No	When asked to use illustrations	No
Good readers	27	Looked	17	Looked	27
		Did not look	10	Did not look	0
Average readers	11	Looked	5	Looked	8
		Did not look	6	Did not look	3
Poor readers	10	Looked	1	Looked	8
		Did not look	9	Did not look	2
Non-readers	3	Looked	0	Looked	0
		Did not look	3	Did not look	3
Totals	51		51		51

Table 9.4. Pupils' content knowledge of the text

Reading ability	All correct	Some correct	None correct	Totals
Good	22	5	0	27
Average	2	9	0	11
Poor	0	2	8	10
Non-readers	0	0	3	3
Totals	24	16	11	51

Table 9.3 indicates that the more able pupils were as readers, the more likely they were to make reference to the illustration without being prompted. However, a substantial number (28) did not, even though the written text specifically asks them to. When told to look at the pictures to answer the questions, all but eight pupils did. Those that did not were all amongst the weaker readers.

When asked about the purpose of the illustrations, some pupils explained this in relation to the content of the text (e.g., to show plants and animals, to show how they move). However, many responded with statements such as, "to make the book look smart," "to show examples," or "to help me answer questions," even though they had not used them. Others could not explain why the illustrations were there. This reinforces observations that many teachers did not encourage use of the visuals as they taught, and indeed during the interviews, some teachers said that they did not always understand the illustrations themselves, so they could not draw pupils' attention to them.

Pupils' understanding of science concepts on the two pages of text were identified by the final set of questions. The findings are set out in table 9.4. The evidence indicates clearly that comprehension of the science messages is strongly related to reading ability, which in turn is related to use of illustrations. Hence pupils who do not or cannot see the purposes of illustrations, or who do not or cannot interpret them, are doubly handicapped in terms of comprehension, and are not helped by the lack of provision of opportunities to ask questions during lessons.

Final Thoughts

Pupils in low-cost schools have access to very few science resources, are generally poorer readers than their peers in high-cost schools and their teachers have less confidence in teaching science. In such a context, the textbook is probably the most important science learning resource for the pupils. It is a paradox therefore that in such schools, pupils often do not have access to a textbook; and even when they do, little or no use of it is made by teachers during lessons, reinforcing pupils' weak literacy skills in both written and graphic terms. Traditional teaching methods that emphasize rote learning and chorus responses are still widely used, as the case studies show: these methods also discourage pupils from direct engagement with the text.

Little or no teaching is done, for instance, which helps pupils to construct or interpret tables, diagrams, and other illustrations, even though these constitute a large proportion of expository text material. Yet most poor readers in the study did not even look at the illustrations, even though these were specifically designed to provide information: these pupils perceived no link between words and pictures. In the high-cost school, on the other hand, where the teacher deliberately used the text, pupils showed confidence and ease in interpreting both written and graphic information, and in relating these to each other to make sense of the science ideas.

The textbook was not seen by most teachers as a source of information or enquiry for pupils to use independently, except for mechanical homework exercises; pupils claimed they were not given work to do from the textbook. Even where pupils did homework from the textbook, no time was made in subsequent lessons to ask questions or follow up the work done. Yet many textbooks that have been available in Kenyan schools over the past 25 years are of good quality, and provide excellent models of effective teaching and learning, if used as intended by their authors. A majority of teachers interviewed claimed to prefer one particular text because it had many experiments for pupils to find out by doing, yet no teacher was seen to use a text in this way throughout the whole study. As in Ochola's (1983) earlier study in Kenya, teachers still used text primarily to provide information on which to base lessons; the role of enquiry was not evident, despite its importance being emphasized in both government and commercial primary science books throughout the 1970s and 1980s.

Some of the difficulties outlined earlier may be due to the teachers' own problems with illustrations. It is likely that their own teacher training had not placed much emphasis on this. Most primary teachers in Kenya have no choice but to teach science, even though they have had little prior study of the subject. In-service training is rare in Kenya, and so these problems persist and weak teachers get no chance to improve their practice.

The study also shows that, as in other anglophone African countries, teaching in a second or third language creates major problems for pupils, especially where the teacher herself is not fluent in the language of instruction. A major problem is the discontinuity between language teaching in the early years of schooling, and the textbooks used in the second language from standard 4 onward, as also pointed out by van Rooyen (1990) in South Africa, Jegede (1982) in Nigeria, Chimombo (1988), Cleghorn, Merrit, and Abagi

(1989), and Cleghorn (1992) in Kenya. Commercial publishers of language schemes and science textbooks could usefully address this, by integrating the development of these different types of material more closely through use of common vocabulary, format, and text structures.

Textbooks are still the main resource for science teaching and learning in most Kenyan primary schools; yet the evidence of this study is that they are underused or misused by the majority of primary teachers. Moreover, these teachers often see good reasons for this, arising out of other pressures. This needs to be addressed not only by initial teacher training, but also by the producers of textbooks and by those responsible for the format of national examinations. In the latter case, Kenya has in the past been in the forefront of effective innovation; teachers need to see that exams, textbooks, syllabus and training are all working in the same direction toward the same learning goals for their pupils.

Yet the underlying point emerging from this study is that the mere provision of good text material is a necessary but not sufficient condition for improvement in pupils' learning. In most schools, we have seen that all the other constraints on teaching and learning (such as language, socioeconomic status of pupils, teachers' skill levels, commitment and pedagogical mind-sets, the pressures of national examinations) are working against the effective use of text material. Until these other constraints are tackled, particularly but not exclusively during training, then even where every pupil has a good textbook, it may not be used to produce the learning that effective use could generate. In this respect, unless teachers are trained in text use and are free to use text as intended, there may be little difference between high- and low-cost schools. International agencies have often invested in textbook provision, yet providing large numbers of textbooks without first paying attention to the issues of training, examinations and mind-sets could well be very cost-ineffective.

Note

1. In Kenya there are more than 40 different mother-tongue languages. In the urban schools classes are linguistically mixed thus Kiswahili and English are used as lingua franca.

References

Barrs, M., Ellis, S., Hester, H., & Thomas, A.
(1992). *The primary language record handbook for teachers.* London: Webber Row.

Chimombo, M.
(1988). *Readability of subject texts: Implications for ESL. Teaching in Africa.* Paper presented at the 22nd Annual TESOL Convention, Chicago.

Cleghorn, A.
(1992). Primary level science in Kenya: Constructing meaning through English and indigenous languages. *Qualitative Studies in Education, 5* (4), 34–323.

Cleghorn, A., Merrit, M., & Abagi, J. O.
(1989). Language policy and science instruction in Kenyan primary school. *Comparative Education Review, 33* (1), 21–39.

Eisemon T.O., Nyamete A., & Cleghorn, A.
(1989). A note on the language of instruction, teaching and cognitive outcomes of science instruction in primary schools in Kisii and Kwale Districts, Kenya. *Kenya Journal of Education, 4* (2), 153–165.

Heyneman, S. & Jamison, D.
(1980). Student learning in Uganda: Textbook availability and other factors. *Comparative Education Review, 20* (2), 206–220.

Jegede, O.
(1982). Readability and science curriculum development in cultures where English is a Second Language. *Journal of Curriculum Studies, 14* (3), 289–291.

MacDonald, C.A.
(1990). *School based learning experiences: A Final Report of the Threshold Project.* Pretoria: Human Sciences Research Council.

Murila, B.
(2002). An investigation into the use of science textbooks in selected primary schools in Kenya. Unpublished Masters thesis. University of Exeter, UK.

Ochola, J.A.
(1983). Investigating the relevance of some suggested textbooks for teaching new chemistry syllabus in Kenyan secondary schools. *African Studies Curriculum Development and Evaluation.* No. 88, KIE, Nairobi.

van Rooyen, H.
(1990). *The Disparity between English as a subject and English as the medium of learning* (a Final Report of the Threshold Project). Pretoria Human Sciences Research Council.

Wandiga, S.O.
(1994). *Educaton and science in Africa: Possible ways of improvement in the next decade.* Paris: UNESCO.

10

Do Virtual Environments Lead to Virtual Learning?

P. Karen Murphy and Theresa A. Holleran

The primary motivation for using computer technologies in education is the belief that such technologies will, in some way, enhance learning (Means, Blando, Olson, Middleton, Morocco, Remz, & Zorfass, 1993). In the early 1960s, programers at Stanford and the University of Illinois began adapting lessons for presentation by computer. From these early projects, researchers concluded that students could learn basic subject matter just as well from a computer as from books, films, or teachers (Hackbarth, 1996). While the computer appears to have many advantages over other media in the educational environment (e.g., immediate feedback, presentation with animation and sound, active interaction, and individualization), it is also more likely to motivate students to learn when compared to any other medium (Bagui, 1998; Hargis, 2001). In addition, computers offer extremely powerful ways to access and process information, going far beyond other types of media (Bonime & Pohlmann, 1998).

Thus, on the surface, it would appear that technology is a blessing to educators and to students because it affords almost instantaneous and seemingly limitless access to a universe of information on any conceivable topic. With the click of a few keys, high school students can explore Pompeii, walk the Great Wall of China, watch the weather unfold in their own neighborhoods, or investigate Elizabethan England. College students no longer need to go to the library. Rather, they can sit down in their own dorm rooms or apartments and enter the world's virtual library—the World Wide Web (WWW). More subject-matter content can be downloaded to a computer disk than can be stored in even the most weighty school textbooks. Further, these disks come with animation and audio tracks that traditional books lack (Anderson-Inman & Reinking, 1998). No matter how real on-line environments may seem, however, they are necessarily *virtual*. That is, they are approximations or re-creations of real-time events.

Dewey (1913), seemingly clairvoyant on this matter, warned of the dangers of *near* experiences almost a century ago. During his lifetime, Dewey was concerned about students' reading of subject-matter knowledge, rather than actually experiencing objects of knowledge. For instance, Dewey would opt for real experiments in science or taking students to a nearby battlefield instead of reading about these events in a textbook [or on a computer screen]. Dewey's perspective on the importance of actual experience was shared by many of his contemporaries (e.g., James, 1977 or Emerson, 1837). For example, Emerson felt strongly that students should spend the majority of their time experiencing nature instead of reading books, because "books are for the scholar's idle times. When he can read God directly, the hour is too precious to be wasted in other men's transcripts of their readings" (Emerson, 1837, p. 17).

Although Emerson was mainly referring to teachers' and students' preoccupation with *books*, we can easily speculate that the problem increases exponentially with computers since computers, when programmed correctly, have the potential to replace books and activities (e.g., science experiments). For instance, rather than students' recycling their trash at home, they can merely take part in on-line virtual recycling. This form is not actually recycling but a form of virtual or approximate recycling. When participating in these types of activities, it remains unclear whether students can actually transfer this type of knowledge to real-time experiences. It is just this type of learning that we refer to herein as virtual learning. Specifically, we understand virtual learning to be the outcome of students' interactions with or in virtual environments that may include everything from "Leap Frog"® learning books where the child waves a wand over the words of a storybook and the words are echoed through a small speaker, to the extreme situation in which students receive all of their instruction in or through an on-line environment—the twenty-first century's virtual classroom. While billions of dollars are being invested in these virtual environments, researchers know very little about the effects of these environments on learning (Cuban, 2001). Indeed, Cuban suggests that much of America's investment in virtual environments is based on inflated expectations of learning gains rather than empirical research.

As James (1977) mentioned in *Principles of Psychology* (McDermott, 1977), concepts and precepts guide future understandings and behavior. Specifically, what one knows and believes to a great extent, can determine his or her behavior. In fact, James believed that precepts or beliefs had the potential to influence one's behavior more than his or her storehouse of knowledge (e.g., Murphy, 2001). For example, if a person believed that large ocean liners were sinkable, then he or she would avoid ocean voyages. The same line of reasoning would follow with computer technology and virtual environments. If teachers perceive that computers will enhance student learning, then they are more likely to use them in their teaching. Similarly, if students perceive virtual visits to foreign countries as more exciting or interesting, then it is likely they will spend more time exploring on-line worlds than reading their geography textbooks. Thus the overarching purpose of this chapter is to briefly explore student learning in various virtual environments, as well as some perspectives on pedagogy in virtual environments.

LEARNING IN VIRTUAL ENVIRONMENTS

Not only is there very little research pertaining to how students learn in virtual environments and from various forms of virtual texts, but also many teachers, parents, administrators, and politicians believe that computers and virtual environments will solve what ails American schools. In the paragraphs that follow, we overview some of our research in this area. Our own findings have failed to confirm some of the prevailing perceptions about computers.

Linear, Computerized Text

To investigate whether students were more persuaded by what they read on-line versus what they read in traditional written texts, our research team devised a study in which we had 131 undergraduate students (64 males and 67 females) read two articles that had appeared in *Time* magazine. One article discussed the pros and cons of doctor-assisted suicide for terminally ill patients while the other explored the failure of school integration in the United States. Both articles had been previously judged by experts as being two-sided refutational texts, which are the most persuasive form of text. Such a text presents both sides of an argument, and then refutes one side of the argument. By comparison, texts that present only one side of an argument or present both sides in a more neutral fashion have been found to be less persuasive (Murphy, 1998).

Before reading these articles, the students were randomly assigned to one of three groups that were approximately equal in size. One group of students read the articles in their traditional text form and responded to questionnaires on paper. A second group read the articles in a computerized format from a Web page that we designed and then answered questionnaires on paper. The final group read the articles and answered the questionnaires in a computerized on-line format. The only difference between the traditional text and the computerized text was that the computerized text had been scanned into a digital form to appear on our Web page. The questionnaires administered to all the groups were exactly the same, querying students about their knowledge and beliefs relative to the articles. Similar versions of the questionnaire were administered before and after reading, with the addition of a series of questions about their perceptions of the text after reading the articles.

The results revealed that regardless of the group, all students increased their knowledge about the article topics, and students' beliefs became more closely aligned with those espoused by the author in the article. Moreover, the changes in these variables did not differ significantly among the groups. Unlike the data relating to students' knowledge and beliefs, however, we did find statistically significant differences in students' reactions to the text that appeared to be attributable to their group. Specifically, students in the paper group found the texts to be much more understandable than respondents who *read* the texts in a computerized form, regardless of whether they responded to our questions on paper or computer. While students at the college level are likely to have a repertoire of strategies that they use to comprehend and remember printed text, it may be that the students failed to transfer those same strategies to reading the computerized text. For instance, young students are frequently taught to conceptualize specific genres of text (e.g., expository or narrative) as an aid for comprehension and understanding. Therefore we expected students to employ whatever strategies they might generally use for reading printed text to any format. Some of those common reading strategies might be rereading, relating the article content to one's background knowledge, finding the main idea, or elaborating on ideas or sentences in the text.

However, if one were to consider all forms of computerized text as a genre in its own right, then students might simply have been employing the wrong strategies for reading our computerized text. Indeed, it may be that the strategies required for comprehending traditional printed text are likely not to be the same strategies required to comprehend on-line texts. The technology literature would suggest that students require more sophisticated strategic processing abilities when attempting to read and comprehend on-line text (e.g., Lawless & Kulikowich, 1996). Among the on-line processing strategies offered by Alexander (in press) as being necessary for understanding text are: locating strategies (i.e., situating oneself within the Internet and navigating from one node to the next); accessing strategies (i.e., narrowing the pool of information, judging relevance and suitability of sites, and using associated sources or supports); and application strategies (i.e., actual use of the information). Of course, our knowledge and understanding of these on-line strategies is only in its infancy.

In addition, when reading the doctor-assisted suicide text, those reading the computerized text found it to be less interesting than those reading the paper version. Given that the words, paragraphs, and a small picture were exactly the same in all three groups, we would argue that the students simply found the computerized text less interesting because it was computerized. While we cannot be sure, it may be that the understandability of the text is the key to students' reactions to other aspects of the text. When students encounter difficulty in understanding the text, it may influence their perception of the interestingness of the text. Though we were unable to find support for such a contention in the persuasion literature, there is strong evidence in the literacy research to suggest that students do not find interest in what they are unable to understand (Alexander & Jetton, 1996).

When reading the text on integration, students in the paper group found the author to be significantly more credible and the arguments to be significantly more persuasive than those students who read the computerized text. As mentioned previously, it may be that the understandability of the text also influenced students' perceptions of the author and his arguments. We would posit that individuals who do not understand the message would be unable, to a certain extent, to link the message to their prior knowledge and beliefs. As such, the reader might not judge the author to be credible or find the arguments as persuasive as an individual who had understood the message.

Another plausible explanation for these results pertains to the resolution of on-line materials versus traditional printed materials. While we did not attempt to control the lower resolution of computer screens compared to traditional texts, computer experts would likely agree that resolution plays a role in on-line reading. In fact, there are several on-line software packages (e.g., Microsoft e-books) available that purport to provide a more eye friendly medium for reading on-line materials. The role of resolution in on-line reading and comprehension is certainly an important avenue for future research, but at this point, the role of resolution can only be conjectured.

Perhaps the most important implication of these findings applies to educational practice. Specifically, the use of these simple computerized texts does not guarantee enhanced learning (i.e., changes in knowledge and beliefs) beyond traditional paper texts. Given that there is such an emphasis on using computers in the classroom, this study gives educators reason to pause and examine the alleged benefits associated with computer use in classrooms. Simply put, the results of this study suggest that students find paper texts easier to understand and somewhat more convincing. If anything, the study results suggest that computerized texts may even present additional hurdles for less competent readers. While this remains an empirical question yet to be investigated, it was certainly evident that the students who read the computerized text found it more difficult to understand than those reading the traditional paper text. Moreover, as computerized texts become more enhanced, it would seem that poorer readers might have even more difficulty gleaning understanding from the texts.

Nonlinear, Hypertext, and Hypermedia

In comparison to the linear texts used in the previous study, nonlinear (Alexander, Kulikowich, & Schulze, 1994; Gillingham, Young, & Kulikowich, 1994) or multilinear (Bolter, 1998) texts are not structured to be processed linearly from left to right. Indeed, in some cases, nonlinear texts are not intended to be processed in any particular order; rather they are intended to be fluid and dynamic, offering the reader multiple paths for navigation and understanding. As such, one could consider the entire WWW as one huge, interconnected nonlinear text containing infinite possibilities for learning pathways. While there are many forms or subcategories of nonlinear text, two prominent forms in the educational technology literature are hypertext and hypermedia. Hypertext is a term that was coined in the 1960s to represent a text that was meant to be processed in a nonlinear or nonsequential way (Nelson, 1974). Since that time, researchers have begun to more closely differentiate between the various kinds of text that require alternative processing. Specifically, a *hypertext* can be understood as a computer-based text, written in a nonlinear fashion and organized in multiple dimensions, so that there are "clickable" choices represented by icons, which allow the user to make navigational selections and direct his or her own sequence of learning (Landow, 1992).

Like hypertext, hypermedia is also nonlinear. However, *hypermedia* comprises a combination of nonlinear text, sound, still pictures, graphics, and motion video arranged nonlinearly in linked nodes so that a user can go directly from one node to another. The emphasis in hypermedia is on the media and its navigation, rather than the text. Thus it requires that a reader should have strong learning goals and search strategies for comprehension (Lawless & Kulikowich, 1996). As such, with hypermedia there is a built-in increase in the learner's control over the subject matter and how it is approached. A meta-analysis of 35 studies performed by Liao (1998) compared the effects of traditional instruction to hypermedia and found interesting results. Twenty-four of the studies reported significant learning gains using hypermedia instruction, whereas ten of the studies favored traditional instruction. Only one study found no significant differences between the two methods of instruction. Liao concluded that "hypermedia instruction has moderately positive effects on students' achievement over traditional instruction" (p. 352). Almost 60 percent of those studies involved the teaching of language, reading, writing, medicine, or science, which implies that for disciplines other than those (e.g., math), the effects of hypermedia on learning may be different from traditional patterns. Of particular importance were effects due to class size, for the analysis suggested that positive effects might only occur when hypermedia is used with small to medium-sized (less than 80) groups. Additionally, the author concluded that hypermedia might be more effective when used as a supplement rather than as a replacement to traditional instruction.

Hyperlinking capabilities open up entirely new ways of presenting information in a nonlinear dynamic form, because ideas can be presented in a manner more closely resembling the way in which we think, without adhering to a specific order (Bonime & Pohlmann, 1998). In addition, links can be established between any two existing Websites, so the reader can then navigate freely from one site to another by simply clicking on the highlighted existing link indicators (Romiszowski, 1997). These links have the potential to lead one to an array of information in text, graphical, audio, and video form. Yet, the selection of possible paths becomes quite unpredictable once the reader discovers a link to another potential site.

Our own work in this area has revealed that students may feel very little need to travel from page to page using the in-text links (Murphy, Long, Holleran, & Esterly, in press; Long, Holleran, & Esterly, 2001). In fact, in the second phase of our research, we found that less than 17 percent (11 out of 65) of our college participants actually bothered using links embedded in text pages. Indeed, the students showed very little effort in spite of the fact that they knew they were going to be tested over the material. Action research by the first author and other colleagues (Murphy, DeHaus, & Banyasz, 2002) revealed similar findings with 4th and 5th grade students. Specifically, these students were presented with a central Website introducing the topic of Monarch butterflies. On the main Web page, the layout included links to two other Web pages. One of the pages was a linear, computerized text on Monarch butterflies with no pictures or links (page 1). The other page consisted of minimal text and several pictures of butterflies indicating links to additional information (page 2). The links on page 2 allowed the students to access five additional web pages containing the balance of all the information contained on page 1. There was no difference in text content between the two pages; only colorful pictures of butterflies were added. Sadly, only one child out of 40 realized that page 1 and page 2 presented the very same information, and most felt that page 1 was more accurate than page 2. At the very least, these results suggest that we need to know more about how and why students process on-line information.

Pedagogy and Virtual Environments

As we have mentioned, virtual environments (e.g., WWW) present enormous possibilities for education. Certainly, pedagogy presents one mechanism for promoting real learning in virtual environments. The caveat, however, is that Web-based and computer-enhanced instruction present teachers with novel problems in classroom instruction (Reeves & Reeves, 1997). As a result, educational researchers and practitioners will need to reinterpret and retest much of what is known about designing and developing instruction for the classroom, for textbooks, for audio, for video in this new environment. Educators need to rethink how this new medium fits into their classroom, affirming that students want to interact with this new place. As we create these spaces, they should invite lively interactions and interchanges (Boettcher, 1998).

Although the amount of information in the world is estimated to be doubling every seven years (Hargis, 2001), the vastness of the Web as a data source is also a source of its weakness (Fetterman, 1998). "The more information there is, the more it tends to become difficult to find the specific information that may be of particular relevance to a particular activity or problem situation that we may be facing at a particular point in time" (Romiszowski, 1997, p. 26). It appears that educators will have to find ways for making this information easily available and helping students effectively navigate through educational sites (Gillani, 1998).

The Web can be a powerful medium for instruction when used to its best advantage—for information access, communication, collaboration, and sharing. The ultimate concept of Web use in instruction, however, is to set up a structure where both teachers and students are able to share knowledge and skills, while learning how to access necessary resources, create new knowledge, and disseminate it (Sherry & Wilson, 1997). The Web is changing the lifestyle of millions of people who have grown to rely upon it as a source of entertainment, information, and communication (Kaye & Medoff, 1999). As was true of previous technologies, the Web offers us tools for dealing with the new challenges that a dynamically changing society encounters and it also contributes to the challenges that these changes generate (Romiszowski, 1997). Use of the Web for instruction will either force change or cause resistance. By introducing new capabilities into existing instruction, the Web is redefining the rules and expanding the frontiers of curriculum and instruction (Sherry & Wilson, 1997).

For example, Skarecki and Insinnia (1999) reported on using the Web in their 8th grade language arts class. From both the students' and teachers' perspectives, the Web dramatically changed the approach to teaching and learning previously used in their classroom. Students remembered information that they found on the Web, used higher-level thinking skills in acquiring the information, spoke knowledgeably and impressively about the information found, and were able to draw conclusions about the information on their own. Students also took an active role in their own learning. Traditional methods (e.g., handouts) of presenting information became meaningless to many of the students once the Web was introduced. In addition, the Web changed the way the two teachers approached the classroom. Instead, they became guides and facilitators, sharing in the learning process with their students.

However, the introduction of virtual environments must be accompanied by technology instruction so that student learning is enhanced (Dockstader, 1999). Over the past 20 years, K-12 schools have invested billions of dollars on computers for instructional use (Moursund, 1998), but research on the effectiveness of these computers and their related technologies in education remains minimal (Charp, 1998; Moursund, 1998). Preliminary reports indicate that to be effective, integrating technology requires new methods and materials (Charp, 2000; Kelly & Leckbee, 1998) coupled with sound practices (Wetzel, 1999). If thoroughly integrated, technology should appear in all aspects of education: planning, curriculum, instruction, assessment, and so on (Moursund, 1998). Teachers must be proficient in instructional techniques and technology in order to integrate technology into instruction (Dockstader, 1999) and to incorporate instruction into technology. According to Charp (2000) "the success or failure of technology and its integration into the instructional program is more dependent on human and contextual forces than on hardware, software, or connectivity" (p. 10).

Another complicating factor is that technology is continuously changing. Just as soon as educators get comfortable with one concept and the accompanying investments in hardware, software, training, and curricular adjustments, the technology changes again (Fulton, 1998). Of course, teachers are expected to keep up with these changes, often embracing technology on their own time when it comes to training (Tomei, 1999). Most feel that neither their pre-service training nor their present level of performance has prepared them to use technology and/or to keep up with the steady changes (Roblyer & Erlanger, 1998). Research confirms that teachers want guidance in using technology effectively, yet only a fraction of teachers actually receive any in-service training (Roblyer & Erlanger, 1998).

Nevertheless, training teachers to use technology is money and time well spent. According to Archer (1998), students scored higher on the math section of the National Assessment of Educational Progress test when they were instructed by teachers who had been trained to use computers in their curriculum. Since teachers have neither the sufficient technological expertise nor the time to develop such expertise on their own (Zhao, 1998), planned in-service training is needed.

Rups (1999) reported on a total of 67 faculty members who participated in an intensive week-long institute. The goal of the institute was to get faculty started on their own projects and to give them time to follow through with the guidance of the computing services staff. For the participants, one of the most rewarding aspects of the institute was the open lab times. In addition, the institute provided an opportunity for the technology staff to demonstrate the digital equipment (e.g., scanner, digital camera) that was available for faculty use. By the end of the program, faculty had become confident in using the technology on campus and were familiar with the computing services staff. This made them more likely to approach the technology support staff with questions and requests for assistance on future projects.

According to Roblyer and Erlanger (1998) the skills needed to integrate technology cannot be passively learned by listening to an instructor or watching demonstrations—learners must be active participants. Participants must be able to navigate through programs and experience the joys of creating new products and the frustrations of making mistakes. Using hands-on training over time with an instructor who models, mentors, and coaches will make technology training more useful. During this training, "the focus must be on *how* to use the technology resource in the classroom, not just technical skills" (p. 59).

From these authors we conclude that teachers need to experience learning in much the same way their students are expected to experience it. In fact, Gagné and Briggs' guidelines (1979) still hold true today, even though they were written almost a quarter of a century ago. Regardless of the available technology or medium, instruction should be designed to ensure that: subject matter is presented in a manner consistent with the type of outcome sought (e.g., application of a principle, change in attitude, performance of a skill); subject matter is in accord with students' abilities (e.g., level of intelligence, prior experience, or knowledge); students are engaged actively in the learning process (e.g., by providing them with opportunities to relate new knowledge to what they had previously learned and with strategies for doing so); students are called on to demonstrate progress so their accomplishments can be analyzed and informational feedback given to confirm success, correct error, and guide subsequent effort; and students are given ample practice under a variety of conditions to ensure retention and transfer.

In virtual environments such guidelines are important in giving way to success (i.e., learning). As Cuban (2001) so clearly suggests, computer technologies are here to stay. It is their eventual impact on learning that remains in question. Our research has shown that students and teachers alike require sufficient access to and instruction in hardware and software in order to use these tools to enhance learning. Moreover, it is clear that much more research is required before educational researchers can actually grasp the influence these technologies may have on learning. At present, it seems inevitable that virtual environments will lead to virtual learning.

References

Alexander, P.A.
(in press). *Psychology in education.* Columbus, OH: Merrill.

Alexander, P.A. & Jetton, T.L.
(1996). The role of importance and interest in the processing of text. *Educational Psychology Review, 8* (1), 89–121.

Alexander, P.A., Kulikowich, J.M., & Schulze, S.K.
(1994). How subject-matter knowledge affects recall and interest. *American Educational Research Journal, 31,* 313–337.

Anderson-Inman, L. & Reinking, D.
(1998). Learning from text in a post-typographic world. In C.R. Hynd (Ed.), *Learning from text across conceptual domains* (pp. 165–191). Mahwah, NJ: Lawrence Erlbaum Associates.

Archer, J.
(1998). The link to higher scores. *Education Week, 18* (5), 10–20.

Bagui, S.
(1998). Reasons for increased learning using multimedia. *Journal of Educational Multimedia and Hypermedia, 7* (1), 3–18.

Boettcher, J.
(1998). The journey to the Web: Simple adaptations or new curricula? *Syllabus, 11* (5), 48–52.

Bolter, J.D.
(1998). Hypertext and the question of visual literacy. In D. Reinking, M.C. McKenna, L.D. Labbo, & R.D. Keiffer (Eds.), *Handbook of literacy and technology: Transformations in a post-typographic world* (pp. 3–13). Mahwah, NJ: Lawrence Erbaum Associates.

Bonime, A. & Pohlmann, K.
(1998). *Writing for new media: The essential guide to writing for interactive media, CD-ROMs, and the Web.* New York: John Wiley & Sons, Inc.

Charp, S.
(1998). Measuring the effectiveness of educational technology. *T.H.E. Journal., 25* (7), 6.

Charp, S.
(2000). Technology integration. *T.H.E. Journal, 27* (7), 8–10.

Cuban, L.
(2001). *Oversold and underused: Computers in the classroom.* Cambridge, MA: Harvard University Press.

Dewey, J.
(1913). *Interest and effect in education.* Boston: Riverside.

Dockstader, J.
(1999). Teachers of the 21st century know the what, why, and how of technology integration. *T.H.E. Journal, 26* (6), 73–74.

Emerson, R.W.
(1837). *An oration delivered before the Phi Beta Kappa Society, at Cambridge, August 31, 1837.* Boston: James Monroe and Company.

Fetterman, D.
(1998). Webs of meaning: Computer and Internet resources for educational research and instruction. *Educational Researcher, 27* (3), 22–30.

Fulton, K.
(1998). Learning in a digital age: Insights into the issues. *T.H.E. Journal, 25* (7), 60–65.

Gagné, R.M. & Briggs, L.J.
(1979). *Principles of instructional design.* New York: Holt, Rinehart, & Winston.

Gillani, B.
(1998). The Web as a delivery medium to enhance instruction. *Educational Media International, 35* (3), 197–202.

Gillingham, M.G., Young, M.F., & Kulikowich, J.M.
(1994). Do teachers consider nonlinear text to be text? In R. Garner & P.A. Alexander (Eds.), *Beliefs about text and instruction with text* (pp. 201–219). Hillsdale, NJ: Lawrence Erlbaum Associates.

Hackbarth, S.
(1996). *The educational technology handbook: A comprehensive guide.* Englewood Cliffs, NJ: Educational Technology Publications.

Hargis, J.
(2001). Can students learn science using the Internet? *Journal of Research on Computing in Education, 33* (4), 475–487.

James, W.
(1977). The principles of psychology. In J.J. McDermott (Ed.), *The writings of William James: A comprehensive edition* (pp. 21–74). Chicago: University of Chicago Press. Original work published in 1890

Kaye, B. & Medoff, N.
(1999). *The World Wide Web: A mass communication perspective.* Mountain View, CA: Mayfield Publishing Company.

Kelly, T. & Leckbee, R.
(1998). Reality check: What do we really know about technology, and how do we know it? *Syllabus, 12* (1), 24–26, 53.

Landow, G.P.
(1992). *Hypertext: The convergence of contemporary critical theory and technology*. Baltimore: Johns Hopkins University Press.

Lawless, K.A. & Kulikowich, J.M.
(1996). Understanding hypertext navigation through cluster analysis. *Journal of Educational Computing Research, 14*, 385–399.

Liao, Y-K.C.
(1998). Effects of hypermedia versus traditional instruction on students' achievement: A meta-analysis. *Journal of Research on Computing in Education, 30* (4), 341–359.

Long, J.F., Holleran, T.A., & Esterly, E.
(2001). The effectiveness of persuasive messages: Comparing traditional and computerized texts. *Theory into Practice, 40* (4), 265–269.

McDermott, J.J. (Ed.)
(1977). *The writings of William James: A comprehensive edition* (pp. 21–74). Chicago: University of Chicago Press. Original work published in 1890.

Means, B., Blando, J., Olson, K., Middleton, T., Morocco, C.C., Remz, A.R., & Zorfass, J.
(1993). *Using technology to support education reform*. Washington, DC: U.S. Department of Education, Office of Education Research and Improvement.

Moursund, D.
(1998). Is information technology improving education? *Learning & Leading With Technology, 26* (4), 4–5.

Murphy, P.K.
(1998). *Toward a multifaceted model of persuasion: Exploring textual and learner interactions*. Unpublished doctoral dissertation. College Park, MD: University of Maryland, College of Education.

Murphy, P.K.
(2001). Teaching as persuasion: A new metaphor for a new decade. *Theory Into Practice, 40* (4), 224–227.

Murphy, P.K., DeHaus, T., & Banyasz, R.
(2002). Understanding 4th and 5th graders processing of online texts. Unpublished manuscript.

Murphy, P.K., Long, J.F., Holleran, T.A., & Esterly, E.
(in press). Persuasion online or on paper: A new take on an old issue. *Learning and Instruction*.

Nelson, T.H.
(1974). *Dream machines/Computer lib*. Chicago: Nelson/Hugo Book Service.

Reeves, T. & Reeves, P.
(1997). Effective dimensions of interactive learning on the World Wide Web. In B. Khan (Ed.), *Web-based instruction* (pp. 59–66). Englewood Cliffs, NJ: Educational Technology Publications.

Roblyer, M.D. & Erlanger, W.
(1998). Preparing Internet-ready teachers. *Learning & Leading With Technology, 26* (4), 58–61.

Romiszowski, A.
(1997). Web-based distance learning and teaching: Revolutionary invention or reaction to necessity. In B. Khan (Ed.), *Web-based instruction* (pp. 25–37). Englewood Cliffs, NJ: Educational Technology Publications.

Rups, P.
(1999). Training instructors in new technologies. *T.H.E. Journal, 26* (8), 67–69.

Skarecki, E. & Insinnia, E.
(1999). Revolutions in the classroom. *Learning & Leading With Technology, 26* (7), 23–27.

Sherry, L. & Wilson, B.
(1997). Transformative communication as a stimulus to Web innovations. In B. Khan (Ed.), *Web-based instruction* (pp. 67–73). Englewood Cliffs, NJ: Educational Technology Publications.

Tomei, L.A.
(1999). The technology façade. *Syllabus, 13* (2), 32–34.

Wetzel, K.
(1999). Getting in the technology game. *Learning & Leading With Technology, 27* (2), 32–35.

Zhao, Y.
(1998). Design for adoption: The development of an integrated Web-based education environment. *Journal of Research on Computing in Education, 30* (3), 307–328.

11

The Constraints of Commercial Publishing

Thomas Hardy

What is meant by the term Commercial Constraints? The fundamental commercial constraint that applies to publishing is that the process should be profitable. Commercial publishers must, by definition, run financially viable operations. Those that do not, certainly if nonviability is practised over several years, will cease to exist. So those that do exist must, at least in the medium to long term, be financially viable. And financial viability here means that the income to the publisher must exceed the costs by a margin sufficient to cover overheads, shareholder requirements and future investment needs.

Commercial publishing is undertaken by companies and other organizations that are operating within the open market. Structurally these organizations may be of varied constitutions: they may be public corporations, privately owned companies, charitable trusts or educational establishments, but if they undertake commercial publishing, by definition they are operating in the open market. Their sole source of income is revenue from the sale of books and products into the open market. Other organizations such as government departments and quasi nongovernmental organizations may also publish, but usually these are not operating in an open market, and so are not subject to commercial constraints. For example, a Curriculum Development Centre, which is part of a Ministry of Education, may publish school textbooks, but it would not usually be obliged to make a profit on the sale of these books. It is therefore not ruled by commercial constraints in the way that other publishing organizations are.

So the key commercial constraint applying to commercial publishing projects is the need to ensure that the income from the operation exceeds the costs by an adequate margin. Logically therefore, commercial constraints can be met in three ways: by increasing income, by decreasing costs or by reducing the size of the margin deemed to be adequate. In practice publishers pursue all three of these strategies.

There is a fundamental financial relationship here. Commercial publishing is constrained to operate in a way such that sales revenue exceeds production and other costs by a margin adequate for covering overheads, shareholder demands and future investment needs. This basic commercial relationship is the source of the constraints that affect publishers. There are tactics that can increase sales revenue and income, there are tactics that can reduce production and overhead costs, and there are tactics that minimize the margin of profit needed by a publisher. In this article, we look briefly at some of the tactics practised in each of these three areas. To do this it is useful to have a view of what is involved in publishing a book or series of books, and then to explore the financial structure of an example project.

The Publishing Process

Publishing takes a long time, because there are many things that have to be done. It is often a shock and disappointment to new authors just how long the process can take. It is also a continual cause of frustrations to customers and users who may be waiting to get their hands on some new books, but who have to wait. The principal stages for publishing an individual book are listed in table 11.1. Where processes take a period of time, a typical time period has been indicated. Some of the processes are either instantaneous, or occur alongside others, and do not therefore impact on the final publication date.

Stages 1–17 are the Pre-press stages of a project (or in some companies the Plate or preprinting costs). Stages 18–20 are the Paper Print and Binding stages (PPB). Stages 21–25 are the marketing and distribution stages, which also have their own costs. In the financial management of a project, which we consider next, these different stages have different financial characteristics.

Financial Structure of a Project

In order to manage the risks involved in commercial publishing projects, publishers undertake profit and loss forecasting, as shown at stage 2 in table 11.1. This is usually done on a project by project basis, on the assumption that if each project individually is profitable, then the publishing company as a whole will be commercially viable. Most publishing companies plan the budgets for each publishing project in a similar way. Each project is expected to generate an adequate margin on its investment, and the size of this is calculated in the following way.

In educational publishing one refers to "publishing projects" rather than "books," because most publishing decisions are to do with deciding to produce a course in a particular subject area at a particular level, for example a Key Stage 3 Maths course for the United Kingdom, or a High School Social Studies course. Each course may consist of several pupil books, perhaps one for each year, with supporting teacher's guides, assessment resources and so on. The decision is made whether or not to do the whole social studies course, rather than separately deciding to do each book. It would be pointless to decide not to do the Grade 11 textbook, if the publisher had already decided to do the Grades 10 and 12 books. However, in the example that follows, I am assuming the project is just one book, for simplicity.

Table 11.1. The main stages in the publishing process, with time estimates for each stage.

Process	Approx. time taken
1. Research and planning. This will involve identifying needs, collecting syllabuses, checking market needs and assessing competition.	Anything from 0 to 6 months
2. Estimating, forecasting and predicting financial viability, using the publisher's standard techniques	1 month
3. Decision to go ahead, usually made by a Managing or Publishing Director, or Publishing Committee	
4. Selection and commissioning of the author team, by the Commissioning Editor	2 months
5. Contracting authors	
6. Writing process, with the authors being supported by the Commissioning Editor	6 months
7. Review of sample materials by Commissioning Editor and completion of first draft by authors	1 month
8. Review by consultants and advisers. Sometimes school trials may be necessary at this stage	2 months, or 6 months if trialling is involved
9. Completion of final draft by authors	2 months
10. Copy-editing by in-house or freelance copy-editor	1 month
11. Design and page layout by design studio	1 month
12. First proofs available for checking	0.5 month
13. First proofs corrected	0.5 month
14. Illustrations drawn by commissioned artists and photographs collected from author or from photo libraries	This happens at the same time as the page layout
15. Second proofs available for checking with illustrations and photographs in place	0.5 month
16. Cover designs prepared by design studio	
17. All work prior to printing (Pre-press work) now completed and book sent off to printer	1 month
18. Printing by printer, often in South-east Asia, where print prices are much less than in the UK.	1 month
19. Binding, trimming, finishing and then packing and shipping to publisher	0.5 month
20. Receipt at publisher's warehouse. The time taken here depends on where the warehouse is! From a printer in Hong Kong to a warehouse in Lusaka takes 3 months.	2 months
21. Release of promotional copies and marketing leaflets	
22. Entry in Publisher's catalogue	
23. Publication	
24. Distribution to bookshops, or directly to customers	1 month
25. Books used by customers	
Total time taken from the initial idea to the books being created and in use by the customers can be as much as	Two years

Sales Revenue

To calculate the sales revenue from a publishing project, we need to forecast the sales, predict the price and know the discount that the publisher will offer to retailers, schools or other suppliers. Sales revenue is units sold multiplied by the unit price, less the discount offered. Projects are usually costed over three years so as to give a project time to reach its highest level of sales per annum, but not so far into the future that the crystal ball becomes too murky. In this example (see table 11.2), we assume the project consists of one book, priced at £10, with sales rising to 20,000 per annum after three years, being sold through school suppliers taking a 20 percent discount.

In this case, the total revenue over the three years is £312,000. Most publishers would want to make a margin of about 40 percent over the three-year period. To achieve this, our development, production and other costs must not be more than £187,200 (60 percent of £312,000). So let us look in more detail at the costs.

Pre-Press Costs

Publishing costs are divided into three main parts as follows: Title costs, which are further divided into Pre-press or Plate costs, and Paper, print and binding costs. Overhead, marketing and administrative costs. Pre-press costs are those required to drive stages 1–18 in table 11.1. They may include any or all of the following as given in table 11.3.

The process of creating a book as far as sending it to the printer can be long and expensive. It is necessary for publishers to manage these costs, and to make sure that they do not increase beyond the budgeted costs. For our example project, let us assume some figures (see table 11.4).

In our example the pre-press costs are £32,890 (US$54,926). Clearly each of these categories of pre-press cost offers an opportunity to minimize costs, and publishers normally make every effort to do so. This is one key aspect of meeting the constraints of commercial publishing, that of controlling the pre-press costs.

We have considered the pre-press investment required for a single book. It was noted earlier, that in practice most publishing decisions in the educational publishing business are to do with projects, which may consist of five or more textbooks, a matching number of teacher's guides and other resources. So publishers are making investment decisions of the order not just of £32,000, but of perhaps five or eight times that: £150,000–250,000. These are significant sums that are being invested in new products completely at the publisher's own risk. There is no bailout clause if the new product is a failure. There is no insurance against books that do not meet market needs or that fail to sell for whatever reason. So it is only to be expected that publishers often take their time in making these large investment decisions.

Print Costs

Print costs are the paper, printing and machining costs and the binding costs (usually known as PPB), shown as stages 18–20 in table 11.1. Most modern printing machines are very complex and have a substantial set-up time. This requires a skilled and (in the United Kingdom) highly paid operative to prepare the machine, install the printing

Table 11.2. Sample project sales revenue over three years

Forecast year	2003	2004	2005	2006	Total
Sales forecast (units)		4,000	15,000	20,000	39,000
Price (£)		10	10	10	
Discount offered (%)		20	20	20	
Sales revenue (£)		32,000	120,000	160,000	312,000

Table 11.3. Sources of preprint costs

Writing fees	For authors who prefer a fee to a royalty on low-selling, low-revenue books such as Teacher's Guides.
Consultancy fees	Educational books may benefit from the opinions of a well-known consultant, a Chief Examiner or an influential name.
Advisers' reports	These may be needed in addition to a consultant's view.
Trialling	School trialling can be very valuable in the development of really functional classroom materials, but it can add a lot of time and cost to a project. It will often double the development time for a project, which may make it impossible to conduct if there are publication deadlines to be achieved.
Rewriting fees	Necessary if the author is perhaps someone who knows the subject, or the market and users well, but is not so experienced at the graft involved in completing a whole publishing project.
Typing	Where there is no electricity supply for word processors.
Translation fees	This usually only arises in international publishing projects, but there are examples of primary science courses written in English that had to be translated into the teaching medium of Kiswahili before publication.
Structural editing	Again, necessary where the author is less well-experienced.
Copy-editing	This is a standard and invaluable process for typescripts of all standards. It involves the clarification of meaning, organisation of the content, checking of spelling and grammar and final completion of all components.
Proof-reading	Usually done at a later stage by the copy-editor.
Typesetting	These costs are very much reduced these days, now that most authors deliver word-processed files on disc which the typesetter can use directly, without the need for re-keying the material.
Design	A key publishing skill, which can be noticeably missing from projects produced by nonpublishers.
Illustrations	This is a key part of educational books. Illustrations may be diagrams for science and maths books, maps and plans for geography, or figurative illustrations for history and other subjects. Each type of illustration requires a specialist artist. If the books are for a specific market, say language schools in Argentina, the illustrator must be familiar with the expectations of the market, must know what Argentine students aspire to look like, and must have some understanding of the culture. For a secondary physics text, the illustrator must be familiar with the conventions of scientific

Table 11.3. (Continued)

	illustration. Knowing, commissioning and finding suitable illustrators are important skills.
Photographs	Photographs may be commissioned from a photographer for the book, or may be collected from photo libraries. Reproduction fees are typically £75 per photograph for a small picture, so these costs will mount up.
Proofing	Charged by the design studio.
Origination	This is the process of creating printer's film from the final camera-ready copy. Today, this camera-ready copy is a computer image sent as Quark or Zip files to the printer.
Cover designs	And additional design cost, but one that is very important. The cover is essentially a marketing tool for the book, and it is necessary that it is attractive as well as being representative.
Cover photographs	Cover photograph permission fees are much more than for photographs inside the book.

Table 11.4. Pre-press costs for the sample project. Note that all of these are incurred before publication and sales can start

Pre-press work	In pounds	Assumptions for example project
Writing fees	—	Assume author takes a royalty
Consultancy fees	500	We need a good name to be associated with this book
Advisers reports	—	
Trialling	—	No time to do this; book is needed urgently
Re-writing fees	—	
Typing	—	Author delivers word-processed disc
Translation fees	—	Publishing in English
Structural editing	450	Author's material has to be sorted, and some more questions added
Copy-editing	1,800	256 pages at £7 per page
Proof-reading	750	256 pages at £3 per page
Typesetting		
Design	7,680	Typesetting, design and page layout for 256 pages at £30 per page
Page layout		
Illustrations	10,500	200 illustrations at £40 each and 100 diagrams at £25 each
Photographs	7,500	100 photographs at £75 each
Proofing		Extra copies of proofs needed to go to author and Exam
	500	Board
Origination	2,560	256 pages at £10 per page
Cover designs	250	
Cover photos	400	
Total pre-press cost	32,890	

plates, apply the inks, run many sample pages to get the ink balance correct and then to prepare for the actual print run. As a result, machining costs for 500 copies may be very little different to those for 5,000 copies. Print runs longer than 5,000 do take additional machine time, but very short print runs (such as 500) are notoriously uneconomical.

Paper Costs

Paper costs, on the other hand will be approximately proportional to the number of copies printed. Note that most modern printing machines print 16 pages at once (assuming a conventional page size), because they use large standard-sized sheets of paper that are at least eight (often 16) times the size of a conventional page. This has two consequences. First, most books therefore have to be of a conventional page size. The commonest sizes are 248 × 187 mm, 276 × 219 mm and 298 × 210 mm (A4).

The second consequence is that books whose number of pages is an exact multiple of 16 will make the most economical use of paper. A 160-page book will require exactly ten sheets of printing paper eight times the size of the book's page (double-sided). If the book is 158 or 153 pages long, it will still require the same amount of paper. If the book is 170 pages, or even if it is 161 pages, it will require 11 sheets of paper, and its paper costs will have increased by 10 percent from the 160-page book. As a result, most books have page lengths, or extents, which are multiples of 16. These are the economical workings. Table 11.5 shows our sample PPB costs.

Profit Margin

In addition to the specific title costs that we have been looking at, publishers also have other costs, which can be very substantial. These include many of those in the following list. They may be grouped under marketing and selling costs on the one hand, and administrative and overhead costs on the other (see table 11.6). These considerations give us a final profit and loss forecast as shown in table 11.7.

You will observe, that the budget for the production costs on this project are £97,990, including the author's royalty, the pre-press costs and the PPB costs. This seems well within our target of £187,200. However when the marketing and overhead

Table 11.5. Unit printing costs reduce dramatically as the print quantities increase

Paper, Print and Binding			
Quantities	4,000	15,000	20,000
Paper costs (£)	1,200	4,500	6,000
Print and binding costs (£)	6,200	7,800	8,200
Total PPB (£)	7,400	12,300	14,200
Unit cost (£)	1.85	0.82	0.71

Table 11.6. Publishers' other costs

Marketing and Promotional costs	This will include advertising, leaflets and catalogues
Sales commissions	Commissions may be payable in some markets
Sales reps costs	Freelance reps costs can be put against a project
Warehousing	Even those publishers who have their own warehouses usually identify these costs separately
Distribution	Distribution is often undertaken by a third party
Total marketing costs	18% of total sales revenue of the project
Administration	All the publishing staff who are not in the editorial or marketing departments
Computer costs	Publishers' IT departments get bigger and bigger.
Office overheads	The cost of running big glossy Central London offices can be very high
Non sales staff pay	The editorial, marketing and other staff salaries
Total overhead costs	12% of total sales revenue of the project

Table 11.7. The profit and loss forecast for our sample project

						% of sales revenue
Discount		20%	20%	20%		
Sales revenue (£)	—	32,000	120,000	160,000	312,000	100
Costs						
Pre-press costs (£)	32,890				32,890	11
Author's royalty		3,200	12,000	16,000	31,200	10
Paper print and binding (£)		7,400	12,300	14,200	33,900	11
Total title costs (£)	32,890	10,600	24,300	30,200	97,990	31
Gross margin per year (£)	32,890	21,400	95,700	129,800	214,010	
Marketing costs (£)		5,760	21,600	28,800	56,160	18
Overheads (£)		3,840	14,400	19,200	37,440	12
Profit (before tax and int.) (£)	32,890	11,800	59,700	81,800	120,410	39

costs are added in, the total cost is £191,610, some £4,500 over our budget. And if we look at the eventual profit before tax and interest, we see that the profit is 39 percent, rather than the 40 percent we were looking for.

This is a typical situation. The project has been assessed and forecasted, and while it is clearly a quite promising project, it is not yet reaching the level of profitability that will ensure that it is signed off by the Publishing Committee and approved for implementation. So what happens now? In practice, the Publishing Director and the Commissioning Editor will scrutinize every single figure in the profit and loss forecast shown here, and will look for opportunities to save pre-press or PPB costs, or try to find ways of increasing the sales revenue. This is where the constraints of commercial publishing begin to bite. Every cost will be examined, and every source of revenue reconfirmed. The budgets must be trimmed back so that we reach a level where the project is viable.

Controlling the Costs

In our example, the pre-press costs are listed in table 11.3. The editor will look at every one of these figures to see if they can be reduced. Do we need the consultancy fee? Does the author really need all those photographs? She might also enquire whether 224 pages, rather than 256 pages, wouldn't be long enough to get everything in. She will look at the design costs, at the illustration costs and at the cover costs. We noted that those costs that are directly proportional to the extent of the book are the ones where shortening the books is most effective in controlling costs. The editor may even ask the author if she is sure she needs such a big royalty as 10 percent! This last is, perhaps not surprisingly, the figure that is hardest to change in these costings.

Note that the quantities that are dependent on the extent of the books, for example the copy-editing, the design and page layout and the origination are those that are most affected by shortening or lengthening the book. Similarly, the number of illustrations and photographs has a direct and unavoidable impact on the cost of production of the book. As a rule, authors will want their book to be as lavishly illustrated as they can get away with, so publishers have to set limits and insist on their inviolability, in order to prevent the supposed 300-long illustration list being stretched by the author to 370 or 390.

Once the revised costs have been agreed, they represent the new budget for the project. Within a publishing company it is the responsibility of editors and production staff to ensure that projects run within their budgets. Professional reputations and even jobs are on the line here, and it is this pressure that leads to editors being so miserable and unhelpful when authors suggest for example that surely 317 illustrations is not so much worse than the 300 agreed in the budget.

The necessity to control pre-press costs during the page layout and illustration stages can have unfortunate consequences. For educational materials, the relationship between text, diagrams, illustrations and photographs as they appear on the page is very important. It is the page designers in the design studio who have the task of making this relationship as effective as possible. Many authors would like to contribute to this process of laying out their material, but in practice the time and costs involved in having the author and designer sitting together and discussing page layouts as they are done would be beyond the specified budgets. Generally designers do a very good job of laying out pages in a consistent and intelligible manner, but sometimes there can be issues that only an author is aware of. The author's input in this case has to come through his corrections to the proof stages.

In addition to cutting the costs of production, and in addition to ensuring the revenue forecast is met or exceeded, which is considered in the next section, there is a third way of improving commercial viability, which is to reduce the size of the profit margin considered to be necessary. This can be done by reducing the overheads, operating as a privately owned company so as to avoid shareholder demands, or limiting future investment. Reducing overheads may mean reducing the numbers of staff employed, moving offices from high-rent districts in central London to a business park in the midlands, for example, or cutting the training budget. This last tactic is a favorite of finance directors, as it seems to cause no immediate ill-effects, and in fact actually increases the number of working days per staff member per year. Generally speaking, however, companies have limited room for manoeuvre in changing their ongoing costs, and accepting reduced margins on publishing projects has been the first step on the road to ruin for many companies.

Searching for the ideal mix of editorial quality, production specifications and value for money that will ensure the viability of a project, is what discussions are all about within a publishing company. It is easy to caricature the tensions aroused by these discussions! Within a publishing company, the different functions tend to take different views as to what is required to ensure a book's commercial success. I hope my colleagues will forgive these caricatures, but I think they make the point. Editors love books. They want their books to be as big and luxurious as possible. Full color, leather binding and even gold edging to the pages are all good stuff. The more lavish a book, the more prestigious it is to have worked on it, and the more they are convinced that the customers will buy it in large numbers. Also the more they enjoy their lunches with their authors. Production, however, have their professional reputations—and probably their bonus plans—linked to keeping within production budgets, and producing the books for the lowest possible cost. So they will want to use black and white only, print on cheap paper and bind in the Far East where prices are lower, even though it may take three months for the stock to reach the United Kingdom. And Sales and Marketing, of course, don't care what the book is like, as long as they don't get embarrassed by its lack of content when they try to sell it, and as long as there is stock in the warehouse by yesterday's breakfast.

Ensuring the Sales Revenue

To ensure that the sales revenue that was forecast is in fact achieved, the publisher's sales and marketing departments have to do two things: they have to ensure that the set price is acceptable to the market, and they have to ensure that the forecast numbers of books are in fact sold. Price is determined by several features, of which the two principal ones are the costs of production and the prices being charged by the competition already in the market. Pricing to production cost is a pleasantly reliable way of achieving the desired profit margin. All one does is to increase the price until the required margin is obtained. However, this is likely, certainly in the field of educational publishing, to pitch the price much higher than that of the competition. In this field, the competition effectively sets a ballpark within which one must price one's books, if they are to compete. Setting the price to the competition, and assuming a realistic sales volume, will, as we have seen, in the end determine the production budget. Getting the production to work successfully within the budget set is where the constraints of commercial publishing are keenly felt.

However, in looking to try and ensure the viability of a project, the publisher's marketing director will consider if the price of the book can be raised without affecting sales numbers or whether by reducing the price, increased numbers of books will be sold, and hence increased sales revenue will be achieved. Setting the price is not by any means a straightforward issue. Some markets are highly price-sensitive, and here even a small price change can affect sales numbers. This is true of retail market products where there is plenty of competition, such as potato crisps, for example. Novels tend to be less price-sensitive; customers will probably buy the new Fay Weldon whether it is £5.25 in paperback or £5.75. Educational books sold through bookshops are quite price-sensitive. Here individuals are buying the books for themselves, or for their children, and the price of books as compared with the competition is a key issue. Teenagers buying GCSE revision guides will be very tempted to buy the one costing £3.50 rather than the one costing £4.25: doing so gives them 75p more pocket money, which is of significant value to them. Whether or not the £4.25 books would prepare them better for the examination is an issue they are not well placed to decide. It is not part of their buying decision making process. The £4.25 book may well be longer, but increased length is not always seen as an asset in these contexts. Teenagers would prefer to believe that they can adequately revise for their examinations in less time, rather than more time, so the "benefit" of a longer book is not seen as a benefit, but as a disadvantage.

Prices are therefore very sensitive in books sold through the retail bookshop trade, to customers on very limited budgets. This applies to both primary and secondary books. Although primary-aged children may not be making their own purchase decisions, their parents will, and they too are influenced considerably by price differentials.

Where school textbooks are sold as bulk orders to Ministries of Education by direct order, as happens in many African countries, the price of the books is much less sensitive. Whether a contract to supply 100,000 sets of a four-level course, complete with pupil textbooks and teacher's guides, comes to £1,500,000 or £1,800,000 in total, is probably not significant to the Ministry budgets, or to the Donor Agencies that may be funding them. Here the price of the individual books is much less sensitive, and the publisher may well look to increasing the price as a way of ensuring the viability of the project in financial terms.

An example of a bulk purchase market is The Gambia. Here the market is insufficiently large for it to be worth dividing up between competitors. In this case the Ministry of Education retains the purchasing power, and buys a single product, in each subject area, which then is distributed throughout the country. This rules out competition, which helps to ensure that publishers are working with viable printing quantities, but also means that teachers and schoolchildren do not have any effective choices.

The publisher's sales and marketing teams must also ensure that the sales numbers that have been forecast are in fact sold. In the open market, products are offered to customers in a competitive environment, so that customers have the opportunity to choose from several different suppliers, the products they will buy. To have their books purchased in the necessary quantities, publishers must persuade their customers that their books are to be preferred. The reasons for the preference may be to do with quality, content, value, price, placement on an Approved List, compliance with instructions (from an education authority or Ministry of Education, for example) or for other reasons. Whatever the reasons, these are an important part of the commercial constraints that operate: the need for publishers to have their books preferred over those of their competitors, so as to increase sales revenue.

Educational publishing clearly differs from fiction publishing, in that several publishers may produce books designed to meet exactly the same market needs. If a school needs to educate its pupils in geography so that they will all get Grades A–C at Geography GCSE, to take a U.K. example, they may consider that they need a geography textbook to help them achieve this. At the moment, there are at least eight products from different U.K. publishers, which claim to meet exactly this need. So to have their products preferred a publisher must have features that will make their book preferred.

It is these features of books, and the need to make them superior to those of the competition, which publishers try to build into their projects, but which are affected and indeed controlled by the budgetary constraints that we have looked at. Many of the desirable features of a book will, however, have financial implications. Some of these are suggested in table 11.8. There are many others.

Table 11.8. Cost implications of desirable features of a book

Use of a famous or popular author	Established authors, with a strong reputation may be able to insist on higher royalty rates.
Use of full color illustrations	Full color books are more expensive to produce, and much more expensive to print than one color or two color books.
Use of plenty of photographs in the book	Every photograph used has to be paid for. Either this will be a permissions fee to a photo library, or a fee to a photographer.
Evidence of successful school trials	School trialling for educational books is undoubtedly a valuable way of ensuring the usefulness, effectiveness and user-friendliness of new books. However, because of the need to develop draft trial materials for testing, and then take the time to redraft and to revise them after trialling, this process can easily add 50% to the pre-press costs of a project, and at least six months to the time taken to final publication.
Compliance with new syllabus or teaching approach	This is essential, of course, but can be made more explicit by using chapter titles that match syllabus topics. Explicit alignment with a new approach, such as the Numeracy Framework, will also encourage sales.

The Customers for Educational Textbooks

Educational publishing is unusual in that its market is not a simple homogenous mass of retail customers, as may be the case for, again, potato crisps. In educational publishing there are at least three "customers" who are involved in determining the commercial success of the books. The end users for whom the product is designed are the pupils. The teachers in many markets have the power to select books.

In many international markets, there is a purchasing authority. This may be a Ministry of Education, or a donor agency, and where they are involved, they tend to retain the purchasing power (i.e., the money) that in other markets is devolved to the teachers. Because of this, it is often the case, that the key features that may be of benefit to the end users, the schoolchildren, are not necessarily the key features that will generate competitive advantage in the market. If the customer with the purchasing power is a Ministry of Education, they may well hold different criteria relating to their purchasing decisions from those which the end users may hold. For example, there are Ministries that as a matter of policy want to provide school textbooks with material presented in child-centered active learning ways. But these are to be used in markets where both the teachers and the pupils are quite inexperienced in the use of textbooks, do not have the space or the experience to handle child-centered learning approaches, and undoubtedly feel more comfortable using a more didactic style of textbooks. Or again, Ministries are sometimes advised by international teams of educational consultants funded by donor agencies. In order to secure the funding from the donor agencies, Ministries may agree to features of the books, such as inclusion of regular diagnostic assessment tests, which are not necessarily a feature demanded by the teachers who will be using the books. As ever, he who pays the piper calls the tune. One would prefer to see the end users of the books, the learners themselves, being able to call the tunes, but in many markets this is a long way from happening. The problem is that since the actual customers are not usually the learners, then the constraints imposed by the technical issues and by the issues of who is paying for the products, and who is the customer, will continue to exert much more influence than any new research on the learning processes of readers, and the understandings we are developing about the ways in which learners use and learn from textbooks.

Ensuring that the forecast sales volumes are achieved means that marketing have to work with whoever has the purchasing power. In markets where this power is devolved to teachers, this will entail teams of sales representatives visiting schools to show books to teachers and to discuss whole school purchases. Here, good illustrations, appropriate text and full syllabus coverage may well be the features that hold the key to success. In markets where the purchasing power is retained centrally, it means marketing staying close to the government decision makers and being ready to respond as soon as requirements are expressed. Here other criteria, particularly price or delivery deadlines, will become more important than the illustrations or text. This latter system is open to charges of inappropriate and even improper decision making, as the process may not be transparent and open.

In many markets in Africa there is now developing a system of approval procedures, which are open and transparent. Once a book has been approved by the relevant authority—usually the Ministry of Education or the Curriculum Development Centre

(CDC)—the book is placed on an Approved List. Teachers, or sometimes educational districts as in Tanzania, for example, are permitted to select books from the Approved List. Books purchased from this list may benefit from donor funding, as in Kenya for example. Where this approval procedure is well developed, the authority may even specify the criteria for approval. These will be divided into technical criteria, to do with the book size, paper weight, type size, binding quality and so on, and content criteria to do with whether the book covers the relevant syllabus, whether it has an appropriate reading level, whether the illustrations are relevant and useful and whether it has enough assessment material, for example. The pre-publication of these approval criteria has the result of ensuring that all publishers know what is expected of their books, but also of creating a rather dull uniformity, which means that users in fact end up with less choice.

For all the publishers to be working in a level playing field, where they all know what is expected, is fine for all of them except those who happen already to have this knowledge, perhaps through greater experience, and closer contacts with Ministries of Education and CDCs. Evening things out can encourage new participants in the publishing process, but it also removes the advantages that experienced and successful publishers carry. Whether this is a good thing or not is a discussion beyond the scope of this chapter. But creating dull uniformity throughout all the books available to schools and to children is in nobody's interests.

THE FUTURE

As with all commercial operations, publishing is continually changing. However, the last 20 years have seen a change that is as significant to publishing as was the invention of the printing press. This is the development and use of new technology in typesetting, page layout and design. Almost all educational books are now produced using Apple Macintoshes and Quark software. This has dramatically reduced the cost of these stages of the process, and made them quicker and more flexible. Reducing the costs has opened up access to these processes to many more individuals and organizations outside the existing publishing community. In the United Kingdom, individual schools and even individual teachers are now able to produce at least some of the educational materials they want to use with their classes. In international markets, setting up a publishing business is no longer prohibitively costly, so there is more new start-up competition. In developing countries, publishing is now the kind of low-cost start-up business that many governments are trying to encourage.

New technology has reduced publishing investment costs and in particular made small project publishing more viable. Printing costs are also reducing, with direct output from the design studio to the printer's plates. These cost reductions make book production more accessible to more groups. To some extent the rules about the constraints of commercial publishing are changing. Older constraints, such as the cost of preparing photographic plates, are now being overcome by high-resolution scanning, but new ones are subtly appearing. Anything that Quark and a Mac cannot easily do, for example embedding complex screen illustrations from other software, cannot in general be done. Other constraints continue: printing still tends to be either a full-color or a black and white process, without much opportunity for part color and part black and white books, because large-volume printing machines are still either only black and white machines or four-color machines. And if you are using a four-color machine to print the books, there is little saving in choosing not to have full color on every page.

It is likely that in some markets, some of the functions of textbooks will be taken over by the new information and communications technologies. The Internet already provides a huge reference and research resource for those learners who have ready access to it, and as a consequence, textbooks in Europe and the United States are increasingly consisting of learning activities and programs, and less and less do they contain reference material. Publishers are producing whole-syllabus revision resources, where the content is available on CD-ROM or on-line, and often with on-line access to help services or tutorial guidance. In markets where institutions can afford to provide learners with genuinely adequate access to these resources, on-line publishing will become an increasingly important medium for educational publishing. And here many of the technical issues are significantly different. Screen layouts are not permanent in the way that pages are, so they can be changed and updated regularly in response to user feedback. Again, color is available from scratch, rather than being a higher level of provision, as in books. Animation, movement and sound are also available, and it is these which perhaps represent the higher level of provision in this medium, as they are significantly more costly to produce than static screen displays.

Although very few are predicting the imminent demise of the book as a medium, and in particular, of the textbook as an educational resource, there is no doubt that the new technologies are going to provide an increasingly important medium for the provision of educational materials. The financial structures for this type of publishing are inevitably less well established than those for book publishing that we looked at earlier, and they will be developed more fully over the years to come. Nevertheless, the fundamental constraints of commercial publishing, that the revenue must exceed the costs by a satisfactory margin, will continue to hold.

But technical and media issues are not the only constraints to commercial publishing. Economic and infrastructure development issues also apply. Where the purchasing power resides, and what criteria the purchaser uses to come to a decision, remain major issues that constrain commercial publishing. The more that book purchasing power can be devolved to the end users, the more it will be the case that books meet the needs of these end users. At the moment in some markets, such as the United Kingdom, purchasing power has been devolved at least as far as Heads of Department in individual schools. Although there may be practical difficulties, it would be interesting to see it devolved further, to the actual schoolchildren themselves. In the United States and in many international markets, state governments operate approved lists, which offer restricted choice, but that inevitably involve approval selection criteria that will tend to homogenize those books listed. And where purchasing power remains centralized, there is the greatest danger that the constraints being applied to commercial publishing will have less relevance to the schoolchildren themselves. These are the development and infrastructure issues that constrain commercial publishing. Together with the financial and technical constraints that we have discussed, they make the whole process of educational publishing a fascinating, complex and ever-developing business.

12

What is Difficult to Read, Why Might This be So, and What Could, or Should, be Done About It?: An Overview of Section Two

Mitch O'Toole

This chapter will indicate some of the literature dealing with reading difficulties and draw the discussion comprising section two together. It will also report some contemporary research that makes use of tools for the quantitative prediction of text difficulty (Zakaluk & Samuels, 1988) and exposure of actual student difficulty with particular texts (Alderson, 1983; Taylor, 1953). The chapter will close with suggestions of potentially fruitful areas for future development. These suggestions will distinguish between the two groups most concerned with text comprehensibility: teachers who select, modify and use text resources and authors and publishers who produce them.

READING

Reading has long been recognized as a complex interaction between text and reader (Klare, 1988). The ability to access information from a particular written source will depend on overall reader competence (Engen & Høien, 2002), which interacts with motivation to read the particular text (Breen & Lindsay, 2002), background knowledge of content, of which the source presents a sample (McNamara, Kintsch, Songer, & Kintsch, 1996), control of the specialist style within which the source is written (O'Toole, 1998) and the general readability level of the material (Daniels, 1996). Successful episodes of access to the information in various sources will progressively build up the reader's overall competence. Reading is an important skill in its own right, but it is also a vehicle for the acquisition of a great deal of knowledge, the development of many important skills and the growth of significant attitudes. This mix of intrinsic importance and instrumental utility may go part way toward explaining the amount of controversy that can surround reading issues (Krashen, 2002).

This section has dealt with reading issues in a variety of contexts. Peacock and Murila have written concerning primary (or "elementary") schooling, Leahy, Cooper and Sweller have discussed research based on a range of reader ages and Rollnick writes from a multilingual tertiary (or "college") context. Some data from original research with secondary (or "high") school students will be presented later in this chapter. The section's focus on reading in science is in line with wider concerns. The movement for text simplification associated with the development of quantitative measures of readability grew out of recognition of children's difficulties with the language of their junior secondary science books (Lively & Pressey, 1923) and student access to text through reading has continued to be of concern (Bowen & Roth, 2002; Humphreys, 2002; Koch & Eckstein, 1995; Paterson, 1996; Peacock, 1996; Peterson & Van Der Wege, 2002). Concerns for student language access and production are often expressed as discussions of "literacy" (Anstey & Bull, 1996; Cope & Kalantzis, 2000; Kirkpatrick & Mulligan, 2002; Wellington & Osborne, 2001). Much previous literacy work (Robinson, 1980; Swales, 1985) was prompted by concern for the progress of various types of "nontraditional students" such as domestic language minority students, international students for whom English is one of a number of languages in which they are variously competent and domestic students from social groups with traditionally low access to tertiary study (Rosenthal, 1996). These concerns are reflected in the present collection. However, this recognition of the needs of the "disadvantaged" (Borland & Pearce, 2002) can obscure the difficulties that specialist language styles can cause for supposedly adept monolingual "mainstream" students. All students are expected to read as part of their education and reading in specialist areas can be problematical for a very wide range of people for a variety of reasons (O'Toole, 2000; Swales, 1993; Sweller, van Merrienboer, & Paas, 1998).

Earlier in this section, Peacock, Rollnick, Murila and Murphy and Holleran all noted the central role of the textbook at various levels of schooling and in various national and linguo-cultural contexts. This echoes the findings of much wider studies such as those by Valverde, Bianchi, Wolfe, Schmidt and Houang (2002, p. 3).

> Textbooks are artifacts. They are a part of schooling that many stakeholders have the chance to examine and understand (or misunderstand). In most classrooms they are the physical tools most intimately connected to teaching and learning. Textbooks are designed to translate the abstractions of curriculum policy into operations that teachers and students can carry out. They are intended as mediators between the intentions of the designers of curriculum policy and the teachers that provide instruction in classrooms. Their precise mediating role may vary according to the specifics of different nations, educational systems, schools and classrooms. Their great importance is constant.

Recognition of the importance of textbooks is not a recent phenomenon and it is continuing (Farris, Kissinger, & Thompson, 1988; Harris, 1990; Kearsey & Turner, 1999; Lively & Pressey, 1923; Morris, 1989; Swales, 1981; Taylor, 1979; Wellington, 2001).

A number of other issues come into focus once textbooks are recognized as an important part of schooling. The ease with which students access information in textbooks is often discussed under the label of *readability* (Binkley, 1988; Daniels, 1996; Kerr, 1972; Long, 1991; MacInnis, 1979). An account of an empirical investigation of the use of some readability formulae follows. All such formulae depend on counts of surface features of the text and this limited approach is not sensitive to features such as *graphic use*, which can cause significant reading difficulties for students (Henderson, 1999; Pintó & Ametller, 2002). Peacock, Leahy, Cooper and Sweller, Murila and Murphy all referred to the role of graphics in this section. Readability formulae are also too crude to recognize differences in *specialist language styles* (Anderson, 2003; Henderson & Wellington, 1998; Kaldor & Rochecouste, 2002; O'Toole, 1996; Rollnick, 2000), which were considered in the chapters of this collection. *Formal instruction* in reading has been a source of great controversy and the papers by Peacock as well as Leahy, Cooper and Sweller have both dealt with it in different contexts (see also Allington, 2002; Krashen, 2002; Rivard & Yore, 1992; Scott, 1995).

What is Difficult to Read?

Readability formulae were developed in an attempt to determine an answer to the first of our questions, and avoid a situation where according to Zakaluk and Samuels (1988, p. xi),

> … people (in evaluation committees) argue and counter-argue, trying to decide whether materials are of a certain difficulty or appropriate for certain children. At the end the issue is resolved on the basis of personal opinion, having in mind some abstract child selecting texts that are too difficult for children and forcing them to suffer frustration …

Such discussions as these still occur. The relevance of the formulae, and the importance of understanding their scope, is enhanced by their inclusion in many widely used word-processing packages. Earlier in this section, both Peacock and Rollnick remarked on the limitations of quantitative approaches to readability. The potential and limitations of a quantitative approach to reading difficulty can emerge quite clearly if they are closely examined in use.

An Empirical Comparison of Quantitative Approaches to Text Difficulty

The study made use of three parallel passages, each of approximately 200 words. The original (passage 1) describes an Australian innovation in sewage treatment, and is taken from a government information book prepared for use by schools and industry (CSIRO, 1988). This book was revised, expanded and adapted for use in science classrooms. The first adaptation produced a typescript that was subsequently revised before publication (O'Toole, 1995). This revision process produced two more portions of text parallel to the first, but with different apparent readabilities (passage 2 and passage 3). The readability of the passages was determined according to seven readability formulae (Gilliland, 1972). FOG, Flesch and Flesch/Kincaid are built into the grammar module attached to WORD5 on Macintosh and Fry's Graph, SMOG,

Rix and Flesch 1948/58 were applied manually. The readabilities obtained appear on figure 12.2.

A cloze test (Robinson, 1981) was constructed from each of the passages, and administered to secondary science classes. Five schools in Sydney, Australia, were involved in the study, providing 18 intact science classes and a total of 447 students. The cloze tests all involved the deletion of every fifth word, and all were marked under the "strict regime," which accepts only exact replacement. This marking regime allows the use of criterion scores regarding predicted student access to the text (Bormuth, 1965). Figure 12.1 includes an indication of Bormuth's suggested boundary between the frustration and instructional levels at a group mean of 37 percent and shows each of the individual class means. Classes from the same school are indicated by the use of identical typeface.

The cloze tests all proved to be highly reliable. The following, and all subsequent statistical descriptions, were obtained by use of SPSS Version 4 (Macintosh). Cronbach's Alpha on the test based on passage 1, used with 119 students, was 0.95, the test on passage 2 (117 students) yielded 0.79 and that on passage 3 (221 students) gave an alpha value of 0.93. Comparison of the intact class means by ANOVA techniques yielded an F score of 61.64, with a significance level of 0.0000. These statistical details indicate that the data on Graph 1 is interpretable. Notwithstanding the optimism of some of the formulae, the cloze scores indicate that *none* of the classes involved in this study would be able to use any of these passages independently. The formulae do provide a relative indication of difficulty, and some may be of use for particular purposes. The machine Flesch grade seems to give a reasonable prediction of use in more able classes, while Fry's Extended Graph may be useful if the classes concerned are of lesser ability. SMOG could be used instead of machine Flesch if the computing facility is not available.

Although the trend in difficulty shown in figure 12.2 was the same in all cases, different readability formulae yielded different scores for the same text. That is, every

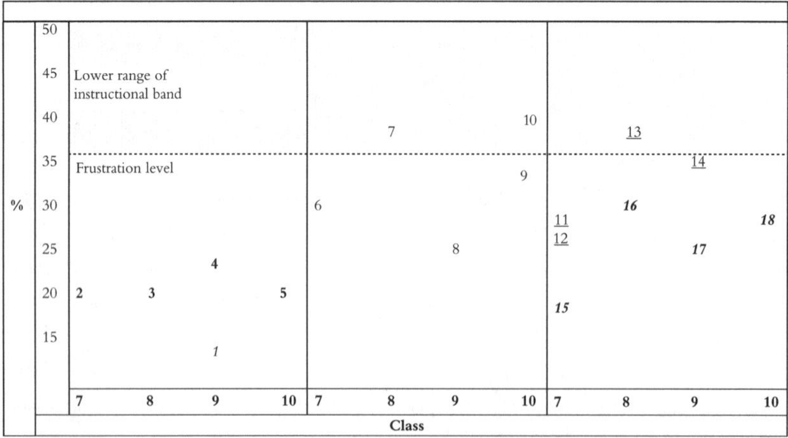

Figure 12.1. Mean cloze score by class (classes from the same school, taking the same test, are in similar typeface)

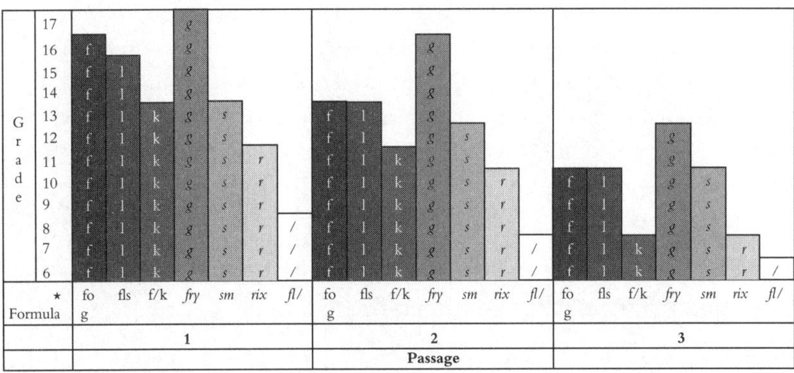

Figure 12.2. Readability score by formula

fls = machine Flesch; f/k = Flesch/Kincaid; fry = Fry's graph (ext); sm = SMOG; fl/ = Flesch 48/58 manual.

formula scored the difficulty of the passages in the same order (passage 1 as most difficult, followed by passage 2, then passage 3) but each formula gave different grade levels for the individual passages. The readability scores can differ by one to nine grade levels. This latter grade range (on passage 1) is greater than the entire span of secondary schooling. However, differing calibrations are not necessarily fatal to an instrument. Celsius and Fahrenheit temperature conventions differ by up to 112 units for the same phenomenon. Although this does not mean that we stop using thermometers, the variation does mean that the convention should be chosen with care and clearly indicated.

The trends in cloze score results are not as neat as those in readability scores. These irregularities in the trends underline the interactive nature of reading. Readability formula may give half the story, but the class concerned gives the other half. The difference in the cloze scores for classes 9 and 10 represent the effect of science ability and the difference between the average cloze scores on passage 1 for classes 1 and 4 reflect a similar effect compounded with a difference in ethnic composition. The question of the readability of a text does not mean very much without the focusing questions: readable by whom and for what purpose? The cloze tests seem to be responding to some of these wider issues. Cloze tasks may be more effective predictors of reading difficulty, as they allow particular texts to be tested against particular groups of readers.

The readability formulae used for the passages read by these groups can provide a prior indication of possible difficulty. This is useful, but it should form only one part of the decision process. Factors inside *and* outside the reader's head are both important (Zakaluk & Samuels, 1988, p. 121). When reading is used instrumentally, "inside head" factors are sometimes beyond the control of the person designing or choosing the text, while at other times dealing with them represents a return to fundamentals, which that person does not wish to make. In situations such as public health, advertising, journalism and technical popularization, focus will shift to the "outside head" factors. Competence and motivation do not cease to be important, but emphasis shifts to the readable communication of content. The readability formulae may be of use at such times in much the same way as a simple thermometer is of use in health care. A change in temperature is only one factor in an accurate diagnosis but it is a useful one, so long as the characteristics of the thermometer are understood. Some things are clearly more difficult to read than others and an appropriate readability formula can provide a useful prediction of relative difficulty when access to the actual readers is not practical. However, it also seems from this study that most of the formulae can *underestimate* the difficulty readers may have.

Why are Some Things Difficult to Read?

The second of our questions also involves "inside head" and "outside head" factors. John Sweller and a succession of co-workers have developed answers to this question on the basis of human cognitive architecture. This section contains an account of this work, which might be grossly simplified as "some things are hard to read because they make too great a demand on the reader's short term memory." Sweller and his co-workers have identified a number of implications of this deceptively simple idea. The most relevant to our present discussion is the notion of "interactivity," which refers to the number of elements that must be held in short-term memory while a concept is processed for movement into long-term memory. This provides a cognitive base for the impact of background knowledge and the control of specialist language style (both of which provide long-term schemas that reduce the cognitive load of highly interactive text) and the increasingly recognized difficulty students have in interpreting graphics (which are composed of elements that must be simultaneously interpreted if the graphic is to be interpreted).

Background Knowledge

Groups of students possessing greater familiarity with the content of a passage could be expected to have less difficulty reading it and this emerged in the cloze means for classes 10 and 11 in the readability study that was described earlier. Other workers have found background knowledge to be important in student response to the organization of instruction (Schönwetter, Clifton, & Perry, 2002) and it has long been recognized as central to student comprehension (Finley, 1991). However, the background knowledge possessed by readers is often beyond the control of those who prepare educational resources and, at its widest, a concern for background knowledge is indistinguishable from a concern for education within particular subject areas.

The Role of Graphics

Graphics are a paradoxical feature of text. They are usually included to make the meaning of a passage clearer (Cheng & Shipstone, 2003), but may be problematical in themselves (Flugelman, 1986). As we move deeper into the digital society, some are signaling the triumph of the graphical representation of information. Whether such enthusiasm is warranted or not, it is very unlikely that graphics will become *less* important! The following discussion will use "graphics" to mean nonlexical elements of a text, such as photographs, diagrams, graphs, tables, drawings and page layout.

The most disturbing, although potentially the most easily addressed, difficulties arise when the graphic contains factual errors such as misleading labelings (Soyibo, 1994) or incorrect representations (Gauld, 1997). Student tendency to read a graphic as a narrative (Pintó & Ametller, 2002) is more difficult to address. The workers in the multinational study that Pintó and Ametller bring together found that students had difficulty with incomplete or contextually loaded diagrams, which echoes the earlier findings of both Soyibo and Gauld. The students seemed to apply real-world interpretations, or emphases, to graphics that were not intended to be so interpreted, which echoes the comments of Peacock, over the last of whom indicated that use of diagrams was a strong indicator of reading ability and content knowledge in students participating in Murila's Kenyan study. Other workers have noted the modifications graphics undergo as they move from specialist to pedagogical publications (Bowen & Roth, 2002) and that even such ubiquitous features as tables may be more problematical than anticipated (Eshach & Schwartz, 2002). On the other hand, others have provided guidance toward the more effective use of graphics in instruction (Lowe, 1993). Reader difficulties with graphics may be appreciated by reference to the wide range of illustrative figures in this book.

Specialist Language Styles

Graphic use is a central part of several of the specialist language styles that students encounter but they are not the only feature. A description of an empirical study of the difficulties posed by the language that is characteristic of secondary science textbooks follows.

This investigation used a language test based on an enhanced version of cloze technique (McKenna, 1976) to identify the features of the language of science that were causing difficulty for 870 junior secondary school students from schools in four nations. Three schools in Australia were involved as were two schools each in Singapore and the Philippines and one school in Britain. The students were asked to replace every fifth word deleted from a passage from a secondary science textbook. Their entries were coded so that conceptually correct entries were accepted and only clear errors were counted. Each deleted word was coded by its traditional (or dictionary) classification and its modern grammar category.

The distribution of total scores for both conceptually correct replacement of deleted items and error scores were both adequately normal to allow the use of multivariate statistical tools. The data also satisfied the other assumptions implicit in such tools, such as linearity, independence and absence of influential outliers or leverage points. The conceptually scored results of the cloze test at the core of this investigation exhibited a reliability of 0.94, enabling some confidence in the interpretation of the data. The reliabilities of the language feature subtests extracted from the cloze test were lower but still allowed meaningful comparison of the scores. MANOVA techniques (taking language category as the dependent variable and heritage language as the independent variable) indicate that there is a less than 5 in 1,000 probability of the differences between the means shown in table 12.1 being due to chance. The results are robust enough to allow meaningful discussion.

Students' results on the cloze test described earlier were compared on the basis of the status of the school they attended, their age and the language they specified as being spoken in the homes from which they came. In general, it appeared that students from higher-status schools had less difficulty with all language features than those from lower-status schools and older students had less difficulty than younger students. These results are fairly predictable. However, the results that emerge when students claiming linguistically diverse backgrounds were compared with those admitting to monolinguality are more surprising. Many people would expect the monolingual students to have less difficulty than their more linguistically diverse fellows. However, the two groups experienced the same level of difficulty for four of the eight categories (articles, verbs, passive voice and cohesion) and a *greater* degree of difficulty with nouns and word stacks.

The result cells on table 12.1 represent the percentage of category deletions that students who claimed the particular heritage language could not process correctly. For example, the 167 English language background students in this sample got 44 percent of the noun-deletions clearly wrong on the particular cloze test, compared to a total group mean difficulty level of 43 percent, yielding a comparison score of +1 for noun difficulty. Students who identified English as the only language spoken in their homes were unable to conceptually replace correctly, an average of 36 percent of the deletions making up this cloze test and that percentage also indicated the total mean level of difficulty (the error total) for this cloze test.

Students' difficulties with nouns and technicality are predictable but difficulties with verbs, prepositions and cohesive devices may come as more of a surprise to mainstream science teachers. The relatively high degree of difficulty experienced by students who indicated they came from monolingual English-speaking homes is particularly notable (comparatively: nouns +1, technicality +4, word stacks +5). Such difficulties can have real consequences for student learning and their demonstration of it: after sifting markers' comments on almost 9,000 Physics scripts, Australian examiners remarked, "Candidates did not always observe the instruction of the key verb in each question. This omission often resulted in a loss of marks, for example if a candidate only provided a description when an explanation was required" (BofS, 2002, p. 5). Table 12.1 indicates a mean verb difficulty of 39 percent, ranging from 24 percent to 57 percent. The monolingual difficulty level of 38 percent leaves scant room for complacency. The difficulties identified thus far in this ongoing study seem to be reflected in responses to high-stakes testing.

Much resistance to direct treatment of language issues in mainstream classrooms rests on arguments of "majority equity": "Most of my students are ordinary regular English-speaking children (meaning monolingual speakers of the local prestige dialect of English), why should I slow them down for the sake of the few who are having trouble with the language I use?" This data (and that presented in O'Toole, 2000) demonstrates that even the supposedly linguistically adept are having trouble with the language of science. It is likely that action designed to help those students who are

Table 12.1. Who is having trouble with what?

Student specified heritage language	No. (% of sample)	Noun % wrong comp. sample d'fclty	At'cle % wrong comp. sample d'fclty	Verb % wrong comp. sample d'fclty	Prp'n % wrong comp. sample d'fclty	Tchlty % wrong comp. sample d'fclty	Word stacks % wrong comp. sample d'fclty	Pas've voice % wrong comp. sample d'fclty	Cohsv device % wrong comp. sample d'fclty	Overall d'fclty % wrong comp. sample d'fclty
English	167	44	28	38	40	36	24	35	40	36
	(19.2)	+1	0	−1	−6	+4	+5	−1	−5	0
Patwa (spoken by Londoners of W. Indian ethnicity)	12	56	43	48	57	49	43	44	54	49
	(1.4)	+13	+15	+9	+11	+17	+24	+8	+9	+13
Greek	9	50	38	57	47	46	33	70	48	50
		+7	+10	+18	+1	+14	+14	+34	+3	+14
Mandarin	166	33	18	26	37	22	13	18	35	25
	(19.1)	−10	−10	−13	−9	−10	−6	−18	−10	−11
Cantonese	19	41	21	28	37	29	19	28	40	30
	(2.2)	−2	−7	−11	−9	−3	0	−8	−5	−6
Hokkien	32	32	21	29	41	21	13	26	38	28
	(3.7)	−9	−7	−10	−5	−11	−6	−10	−7	−8
Other Chinese	48	34	18	24	35	24	15	24	36	26
	(5.5)	−11	−10	−15	−11	−8	−4	−12	−9	−10
Pilipino	369	48	33	48	55	36	19	45	52	42
	(42.4)	+5	+5	+9	+9	+4	0	+9	+7	+6
Other Philipino	12	43	43	54	63	30	19	53	54	45
	(1.4)	0	+15	+15	+17	−2	0	+17	+9	+9
Average feature difficulty	834	43	28	39	46	32	19	36	45	36

Notes: Table 12.1 is based on analysis of student responses on a single cloze test. Student data was recoded so that a clear error = 1 and acceptable replacement or defeat was = 0. Cloze test deletions were classified by language category. Two SPSS routines were written ("dictionary categories" + "modern grammar categories").

These did the following:

1 Count number of items representing a particular language category (e.g., nouns) a student got wrong.

2 Divide that number by the number of items representing that category (e.g., nouns) deleted (in this case, 18) to give the mean category (in this case, noun) difficulty.

3 Multiply that mean by 100 to yield a percentage.

experiencing greater difficulty will be of assistance to those of their classmates who might be expected to experience less.

Formal Instruction

The role of formal instruction in language, and in reading in particular, has been an area of much conflict. As the preceding comments indicate, this writer sees a place for direct intervention to help students gain control of the specialist language styles that can act as a barrier to access for many of the students in our classes. As some of the heat comes out of the controversy, teachers will able to locate resources that might be able to help their students expand their life options by increasing the access that reading can give them (Hennings, 1982; Koch & Eckstein, 1995; Morris & Stewart-Dore, 1984; Peterson & Van Der Wege, 2002; Rivard & Yore, 1992; Sutton, 1989; Valleley & Shriver, 2003; Wellington, 2001).

Students in our classes seem to be having difficulties that can be predicted, noted and described. These difficulties affect more of our students than we may have previously realized. Strategies exist to allow us to help our students to gain greater access to text than they have at the moment. It would seem strange if we chose to ignore their difficulties. Many people deeply involved in the conflicts have indicated the need to look closely at the needs of specific contexts, from both whole language (Krashen, 1991; Turner, 1991) and systemic (Mohan, 1986; Moore, 1987) viewpoints. It might be time to listen to them.

Prospects for Change

A number of the contributors to this section have commented on teachers' stated dissatisfaction with published reading resources and their tendency to modify commercial material for use in their particular contexts. However, Peacock and Rollnick both indicate that such teacher modifications are not always easier for students to access than the original text from which the teacher worked! Teachers are part of the communities that produced the texts they use (although they may not be considered full members), so it is not surprising that the text they produce should show signs of their own training. Such modified text is rarely shared with anyone but their own class, so it is not surprising that students are attempting to use it without any of the editing steps that are applied to commercial material. Consequently, teacher modified text will often avoid some barriers to student access while erecting others. Teacher-written worksheets may not necessarily remove "outside the head" reading difficulties, but when teachers deal communicatively with language issues they can be of great assistance with "inside the head" student difficulties (Warwick, Stephenson, & Webster, 2003).

Murphy and Holleran have referred to the hope some people place in technological change. This hope connects with Peacock's call for changes in teacher education (Knezek & Christensen, 2002), although there is no indication that he would welcome a move to virtual education. Recent work points to the use of multimedia (Cannings & Talley, 2002), email (White & Cornu, 2002) and the virtual library (Gibson & Ruotolo,

2003) in teacher education. However, Murphy & Holleran are not alone in their concern about developments such as these (van Weert & Munro, 2003).

In the present context, it is worth noting that students will still be reading, even if the book (or worksheet) is replaced by a screen. Some have argued that the change in mode represents a fundamental shift in task (Gardner, 2003) but such assertions are not persuasive. The screen is a highly flexible page, allowing animation, illustration and rapid reader control of the experience but users still need to read and Murphy & Holleran's work indicates that students may find pages easier to read than screens. If that is the case, the change from ink stains on paper to light emerging from a colored screen will increase the difficulty of the reading task. This would make increasing the comprehensibility of the text that is common to both modes even more urgent, leaving aside the fact that such technology is beyond the reach of many students in contexts from which contributors to this section wrote.

It seems that change remains in the hands of those who prepare commercial teaching material and those who select, modify and use it. Teachers have access to both "inside-" and "outside-head" factors affecting comprehensibility and therefore would seem to have the greatest power (and responsibility) to bring about change, which is in the long-term best interest of their students. Indeed this realization can be sensed as an unstated thread running through the writings of most of this section's contributors.

WHAT COULD, OR SHOULD, BE DONE ABOUT READING DIFFICULTIES?

It seems that access to information contained in specialist text is being hampered by student difficulty in reading it. It may be that this gate-keeping function is legitimate and that using reader competence as a filter to select those who will move through the educational system and into particular specialist communities is efficient and defensible. However, reading competence seems a less equitable filter than under-standing of the intellectual products of those communities. It would seem hard to defend a position that supported exclusion on any basis other than lack of potential to make a real and ongoing contribution. Using reading as the barrier to communal access is quite likely to keep out some students whose potential contributions could be very valuable.

Thomas Hardy, who was the penultimate contributor to this section, clearly laid out the process that leads to provision of commercial resources for educational institutions. The complexity of the task of educational publication explains the cost, in time and money, of these books of which teachers can be so critical. The process, however, does allow the time for the editing that can move a text so much closer to the needs of the student who will read it.

Specialist teachers, and other people interested in text comprehensibility, need to take control of the text that they put before their clients. Teachers do not have the time to rewrite all the resources of which they make use. However, they choose resources and they need to carefully control the level of those documents that they do prepare. As recognized earlier in chapter 6, some text prepared by teachers and trainers can be as difficult as many textbooks. If such people have access to their target groups, they would be well advised to construct cloze tasks based on "typical" samples of the text they are considering. When they are used with the particular group for whom the text is intended, such tasks give a direct indication of difficulty, and they seem to be sensitive to both inside and outside head factors. If such access is not available, appropriate readability formulae may be useful. We need to decide what is important in what we expect of our classes, and then use tools such as appropriate readability formulae to indicate whether we are expecting more than we realize. Different formulae will be appropriate for different groups, just as different thermometers are appropriate for different circumstances. They are rather blunt instruments, but there are times when blunt instruments are useful. One would not want to play cricket with a rapier!

The formulae are also useful as an aid to editing. Use of the appropriate formula should send the writer back to the text in a quest for greater clarity. A competent nurse would not treat a patient's fever by chilling the thermometer, and a competent writer should not treat inaccessible prose by simply splitting up sentences. However, both would be unwise to abandon the instrument because its uses are limited. Figures 12.1 and 12.2 may provide some guidance as to which formula is most useful in a particular context.

However, the formulae will only identify difficulty, they will not explain it nor suggest ways in which it could be surmounted. Recognition of the difficulty of particular texts should lead to an examination of them to identify features that might contribute to student problems. The impact of graphics and specialist language styles can both be explained in terms of the burden interactivity places on finite components of the human cognitive architecture. The information on table 12.1 would therefore have a number of uses. Teachers could use it to provide advance warning of the features of scientific English, which might cause difficulties for students in their classes. For example, the results for the small number of students from Greek-speaking homes suggest that such students might have difficulty with the Passive Voice in English (70% of Passives wrong, comparative $+34$) and so teachers might choose to use the structure less *or* to teach it directly in science classes containing significant numbers of students from Greek-speaking homes. The fact that monolingual students were unable to correctly replace an average of 35 percent of these items indicates that such direct treatment would do them no harm either!

This raises the choice between simplification and formal instruction. There will be occasions where a language feature or graphic convention is not necessary for a group of students in a particular place, at a particular stage in their education. In such cases that feature or convention should be removed so that the simplified material may be better understood. There will be other occasions when the teacher decides that the feature or convention is necessary to students' effective understanding of the work at hand. At such times, the feature or convention should be directly taught.

Difficult features such as graphical and stylistic conventions may well benefit from direct treatment in commercial resource material. This often makes use of questions and activities and the inclusion of language development tasks would provide both help and guidance for busy teachers. Explicit instruction in features that have been identified as both difficult and important will increase the students' access to more widely available material, their chance of successful reading experiences, their background knowledge within the subject and, consequently, their reading competence. The reading cycle that began this chapter will act as a productive spiral, as our students move toward membership of the literate communities that they have chosen.

Acknowledgments

The author would like to thank Prof. Ma. Christina Padolina, Dr. Goh Ngoh Khang and Mr. Seamus O'Mahoney for their invaluable assistance in coordinating data collection in the Philippines, Singapore, and Britain, respectively.

References

Alderson, J.C.
(1983). The cloze procedure as a measure of proficiency in English as a foreign language. In J. Oller (Ed.), *Issues in language teaching research* (pp. 205–212). Rowley: Newbury House.

Allington, R.L.
(2002). What I've learned about effective reading instruction. *Phi Delta Kappan, 83* (10), 740–747.

Anderson, D.L.
(2003). *Communicating information across cultures: Understanding how others work* [internet]. Pantaneto Forum. Retrieved December 17, 2002, from the World Wide Web: http://www.pantaneto.co.uk/issue9/anderson.htm.

Anstey, M. & Bull, G.
(1996). *The literacy labyrinth.* Sydney: Prentice Hall.

Binkley, M.R.
(1988). New ways of assessing text difficulty. In B.L. Zakaluk & S.J. Samuels (Eds.), *Readability: Its past, present and future* (pp. 98–120). Newark: International Reading Association.

BofS.
(2002). *2001 HSC Notes from the Examination Centre: Physics.* Sydney: Board of Studies, New South Wales.

Borland, H. & Pearce, A.
(2002). Identifying key dimensions of language and cultural disadvantage at university. *Australian Review of Applied Linguistics, 25* (2), 101–127.

Bormuth, J.R.
(1965). Validities of grammatical and semantic classifications of cloze test scores. In J.A. Figurel (Ed.), *Reading and inquiry* (Vol. 10, pp. 303–306). Newark: International Reading Association.

Bowen, G.M. & Roth, W.-M.
(2002). Why students may not learn to interpret scientific inscriptions. *Research in Science Education, 32* (3), 303–327.

Breen, R. & Lindsay, R.
(2002). Different disciplines require different motivations for student success. *Research in Higher Education, 43* (6), 693–725.

Cannings, T.R. & Talley, S.
(2002). Multimedia and Online Video Case Studies for Preservice Teacher Preparation. *Education and Information Technologies, 7* (4), 359–367.

Cheng, P.C.-H. & Shipstone, D.M.
(2003). Supporting learning and promoting conceptual change with box and AVOW diagrams. Part 1: Representational design and instructional approaches. *International Journal of Science Education, 25* (2), 193–204.

Cope, B. & Kalantzis, M. (Eds.).
(2000). *Multiliteracies: Literacy learning and the design of social futures.* London: Routledge.

CSIRO.
(1988). *CSIRO research for Australia: Water.* Canberra: CSIRO.

Daniels, D.
(1996). A study of textbook readability. *Australian Science Teachers Journal, 42* (3), 61–65.

Engen, L. & Høien, T.
(2002). Phonological skills and reading comprehension. *Reading and Writing, 15* (7–8), 613–631.

Eshach, H. & Schwartz, J.L.
(2002). Understanding children's comprehension of visual displays of complex information. *Journal of Science Education and Technology, 11* (4), 333–346.

Farris, P.J., Kissinger, R.W. & Thompson, T.
(1988). Text organisation and structure in science textbooks. *Reading Horizons, 28,* 123–130.

Finley, F.N.
(1991). Why students have trouble learning from science texts. In C.M. Santa & D.E. Alvermann (Eds.), *Science learning: Processes and applications* (pp. 22–27). Newark, DE: International Reading Association.

Flugelman, P.
(1986). Moonstruck. In M. Aldhamland (Ed.), *Science and the ESL student* (pp. 57–58). Canberra: Australian Government Publishing Service.

Gardner, C.
(2003). Meta-Interpretation and Hypertext Fiction: A Critical Response. *Computers and the Humanities, 37* (1), 33–56.

Gauld, C.
(1997). It must be true—it's in the textbook! *Australian Science Teachers Journal, 43* (2), 21–26.

Gibson, M. & Ruotolo, C.
(2003). Beyond the Web: TEI, the Digital Library, and the Ebook Revolution. *Computers and the Humanities, 37* (1), 57–63.

Gilliland, J.
(1972). *Readability.* London: University of London Press.

Harris, D.P.
(1990). The use of organising sentences in science textbooks. In U. Connor & A.M. Johns (Eds.), *Coherence in writing: Research and pedagogical perspectives* (pp. 67–86). Alexandria: Teachers of English to Speakers of Other Languages.

Henderson, G.
(1999). Learning with diagrams. *Australian Science Teachers Journal, 45* (2), 17–25.

Henderson, J. & Wellington, J.
(1998). Lowering the language barrier in learning and teaching science. *School Science Review, 79* (288), 35–46.

Humphreys, J.W.
(2002). There is no simple way to build a middle school reading program. *Phi Delta Kappan, 83* (10), 754–757.

Kaldor, S. & Rochecouste, J.
(2002). General academic writing and discipline specific academic writing. *Australian Review of Applied Linguistics, 25* (2), 29–47.

Kearsey, J. & Turner, S.
(1999). Evaluating textbooks: The role of genre analysis. *Research in Science and Technological Education, 17* (1), 35–42.

Kerr, A.H.
(1972). Psycholinguistics and a new empirical approach to the measurement of comprehension and readability of French as a second language. In W.S. Simpkins & A.H. Miller (Eds.), *Changing education: Australian viewpoints* (pp. 278–295). Sydney: McGraw Hill.

Kirkpatrick, A. & Mulligan, D.
(2002). Cultures of learning: Critical reading in the social and applied sciences. *Australian Review of Applied Linguistics, 25* (2), 73–99.

Klare, G.R.
(1988). The formative years. In B.L. Zakaluk & S.J. Samuels (Eds.), *Readability: Its past, present and future* (pp. 14–35). Newark: International Reading Association.

Knezek, G. & Christensen, R.
(2002). Impact of new information technologies on teachers and students. *Education and Information Technologies, 7* (4), 369–376.

Koch, A. & Eckstein, S.G.
(1995). Skills needed for reading comprehension of Physics texts and their relation to problem-solving ability. *Journal of Research in Science Teaching, 32* (6), 613–628.

Krashen, S.
(2002). Whole language and the great plummet of 1987–1992. *Phi Delta Kappan, 83* (10), 748–753.

Krashen, S.D.
(1991). Sheltered subject matter teaching. *Cross Currents, 18,* 183–189.

Lively, B.A. & Pressey, S.L.
(1923). A method for measuring the "vocabulary burden" of textbooks. *Educational Administration and Supervision, 9,* 389–398.

Long, R.R.
(1991). Readability for science: Some factors which may affect the students' understanding of worksheets etc. *School Science Review, 73* (262), 21–31.

Lowe, R.
(1993). *Successful instructional diagrams*. London: Kegan Paul.

MacInnis, P.
(1979). *Readability and science testing* (Vol. 5). Sydney: School Certificate Development Unit, New South Wales Department of Education.

McKenna, M.
(1976). Synomic versus verbatim scoring of the cloze procedure. *Journal of Reading, 20* (2), 141–143.

McNamara, D., Kintsch, E., Songer, N.B., & Kintsch, W.
(1996). Are good texts always better? Interactions of text coherence, background knowledge, and levels of understanding in learning from text. *Cognition and Instruction, 14*, 1–43.

Mohan, B.
(1986). *Language and content*. Reading: Addison-Wesley.

Moore, H.
(1987). "Process" vs. "product" or down with the opposition. In M.A.K. Halliday, J. Gibbons, & H. Nicholas (Eds.), *Learning, keeping and using language* (Vol. 1, pp. 379–401). Amsterdam: John Benjamins.

Morris, A.
(1989). Textbooks: Over-relied on but under-utilised. *Australian Journal of Reading, 12* (4), 312–329.

Morris, A. & Stewart-Dore, N.
(1984). *Learning to learn from text: Effective reading in the content areas*. Sydney: Addison-Wesley.

O'Toole, J.M.
(1995). *Water*. Melbourne: Cambridge University Press/CSIRO.

O'Toole, J.M.
(1996). Science, schools, children and books: Exploring the classroom interface between science and language. *Studies in Science Education, 28*, 113–143.

O'Toole, J.M.
(1998). Climbing the fence around science ideas. *Australian Science Teachers Journal, 44* (4), 51–56.

O'Toole, J.M.
(2000). *Getting into the game: Language development in science classrooms*. Seven Hills: Five Senses Education.

Paterson, C.C.
(1996). Comprehending biology text using plasticine. *Australian Science Teachers Journal, 42* (1), 35–36.

Peacock, A.
(1996). Children's learning from science texts: A critique of "EXIT into Understanding." *Reading, 30* (3), 32–36.

Peterson, D. & Van Der Wege, C.
(2002). Guiding children to be strategic readers. *Phi Delta Kappan, 83* (6), 437–439.

Pintó, R. & Ametller, J.
(2002). Students' difficulties in reading images. Comparing results from four national research groups. *International Journal of Science Education, 24* (3), 333–341.

Rivard, L.P. & Yore, L.D.
(1992). Review of reading comprehension instruction: 1985–1991. *ERIC Document* (ED 354 144).

Robinson, C.G.
(1981). Cloze procedure: A review. *Educational Research, 23* (2), 128–133.

Robinson, P.C.
(1980). *ESP (English for specific purposes): The present position.* Oxford: Pergamon Press.

Rollnick, M.
(2000). Current issues and perspectives on second language learning of science. *Studies in Science Education, 35,* 93–122.

Rosenthal, J.W.
(1996). *Teaching science to language minority students.* Avon: Multilingual Matters.

Schönwetter, D.J., Clifton, R.A., & Perry, R.P.
(2002). Content familiarity: Differential impact of effective teaching on student achievement outcomes. *Research in Higher Education, 43* (6), 625–655.

Scott, M.
(April 27, 1995). Reading: The new testament. *Sydney Morning Herald,* p. 9.

Soyibo, K.
(1994). Misleading labellings in biology textbook drawings. *Australian Science Teachers Journal, 40* (2), 10–14.

Sutton, C.R.
(1989). Writing and reading in science: The hidden messages. In R. Millar (Ed.), *Doing science: Images of science in science education.* Lewes: Falmer Press.

Swales, J.
(1981). The function of one type of participle in a chemistry textbook. In L. Selinker, E. Tarone, & V. Hanzeli (Eds.), *English for academic and technical purposes: Studies in honor of Louis Trimble* (pp. 40–52). Rowley: Newbury House.

Swales, J.M.
(1985). *Episodes in ESP: A source and reference book on the development of English for science and technology.* Oxford: Pergamon Press.

Swales, J.M.
(1993). Genre and engagement. *Revue Belge de Philogie et d'Histoire, 71,* 687–698.

Sweller, J., van Merrienboer, J., & Paas, F.
(1998). Cognitive architecture and instructional design. *Educational Psychology Review, 10,* 251–296.

Taylor, C.V.
(1979). *The English of high school textbooks.* Canberra: Australian Government Printing Service.

Taylor, W.
(1953). Cloze procedure: A new tool for measuring readability. *Journalism Quarterly, 30,* 415–431.

Turner, L.
(1991). Process vs genre: non-issue in the whole language classroom. *TESOL in Context, 1* (2), 8–13.

Valleley, R.J., & Shriver, M.D.
(2003). An examination of the effects of repeated readings with secondary students. *Journal of Behavioral Education, 12* (1), 55–76.

Valverde, G.A., Bianchi, L.J., Wolfe, R.G., Schmidt, W.H., & Houang, R.T.
(2002). *According to the book: Using TIMSS to investigate the translation of policy into practice through the world-wide use of textbooks.* Dordrecht: Kluwer Academic Publishers.

van Weert, T.J. & Munro, R.K. (Eds.).
(2003). *Informatics and the digital society: Social ethical and cognitive issues.* Dordrecht: Kluwer Academic Publishers.

Warwick, P., Stephenson, P., & Webster, J.
(2003). Developing pupils' written expression of procedural understanding through the use of writing frames in science: findings from a case study approach. *International Journal of Science Education, 25* (2), 173–192.

Wellington, J.J.
(2001). School textbooks and reading in science: Looking back and looking forward. *School Science Review, 82* (300), 71–81.

Wellington, J.J. & Osborne, J. (Eds.).
(2001). *Language and literacy in science education.* Buckingham: Open University Press.

White, B. & Cornu, R.L.
(2002). Email Reducing Stress for Student Teachers. *Education and Information Technologies, 7* (4), 351–357.

Zakaluk, B.L. & Samuels, S.J. (Eds.).
(1988). *Readability: Its past present and future.* Newark: International Reading Association.

Section Three

How Can Text and Other Learning Materials be Better Matched to the Preconceptions, Expectations, and Inclinations of Learners and Teachers?

13

Introduction

Alan Peacock and Ailie Cleghorn with Mirjamaija Mikkilä-Erdmann

The third section of this book addresses the question: *how can text and other learning materials be better matched to the preconceptions, expectations and inclinations of learners and teachers?* We begin this introduction to the section with a focus on the Teacher–Learner–Text relationship that stems from comparative research in three settings, England, Canada and Finland.[1]

Over the past 20 years, there has been an emerging globalization of the way in which school texts are commissioned, constructed, published and marketed (Altbach, 1987; Apple & Christian-Smith, 1991). Nevertheless, the premises upon which school texts are produced remain largely unquestioned; while millions of dollars are spent annually on the production of school texts, many are underused or ineffectively used (Stinner, 1995). Many reasons have been advanced for this state of affairs, including lack of training, poor quality text, and the mismatch between the pedagogical messages in the text and culturally determined teaching styles (Peacock, 1991, 1995a; Peacock & Perold, 1995). In addition, language issues remain crucial: it is of note that today there are reportedly more than 700 million children worldwide learning via English as a second language (Crystal, 1997), yet the majority of science texts, for example, are written by first-language speakers as if for first-language teachers and learners. As earlier chapters have demonstrated, issues surrounding the language in which science is taught thus join long-standing concerns about the language of the texts themselves (Rollnick, 1998; Van Rooyen, 1990; White & Welford, 1988). The Teacher–Learner–Text (TLT) relationship takes on an added dimension when culturally unfamiliar concepts are taught via a language that is a second or even third language for pupils and sometimes even for the teachers (Cleghorn, Merritt, & Abagi, 1989; Cleghorn, 1992; Cleghorn & Rollnick, 2002; Ryf & Cleghorn, 1997).

Language is not, of course, the sole issue in text comprehension. Research already referred to from many contexts has indicated that pupils and teachers also experience difficulties with the visual elements, the format and the design of texts, and the messages about the nature of science implicit in them (see this volume, Gates, chapter 16; Peacock, 1995b; Peacock & Gates, 2000). The vast majority of school science text material, for example, is written from a specific perspective or worldview, and usually embodies "Western" models of science and knowledge; correct or not, these may conflict with teachers' and pupils' perceptions of science knowledge and "doing science." This is as true in culturally diverse classrooms of the north, where students represent a variety of cultural backgrounds as it is in countries in Africa, for example, where notions about the nature of science are sometimes very much at odds with Western explanations of natural and other phenomena (Aikenhead & Huntley, 1999; Clark & Ramalhalpe, 1999; Cobern & Loving, 1998; Ogunniyi, Jegede, Ogawa, Yandila, & oladele, 1995; Shumba, 1995).

School text is also predominantly written to enrich (i.e., to add new information) rather than to help learners reorganize their knowledge and correct misconceptions, in line with constructivist theories of learning (Mikkilä, 1997; Mikkilä & Olkinuora, 1994). Our concerns in this section therefore touch on many complex issues such as:

- bridging cultural discontinuities between the ideas of science educators, the prescribed curriculum and pedagogy of primary schools and the perceptions of teachers;
- clarifying teachers' and learners' notions of the function of text in teaching;
- developing ways in which text quality can be improved to facilitate more effective learning;
- acknowledging within materials the differences in "worldview" stemming from cultural differences among learners;
- responding to the complexity of learning under second-language conditions in school communities in the "north" as well as the "south";
- addressing training needs in relation to text development and use;
- exploring the potential of electronic media to provide new forms of learner–text interaction.

The TLT relationship (Figure 13.1) encapsulates the interactions that are central to the learning environment. On the one hand textbooks can be seen as a crucial, and in some contexts the only, science teaching resource (Armbruster, 1986; Orevbu, 1984; Ogawa, 1995). On the other hand their inappropriateness in a given sociocultural context can be a constraint on high-quality learning (Chimombo, 1989; Gordon, Schumm, Coffland, & Doucette, 1992; Kress & Van Leeuwen, 1996; Langhan 1993; MacNamara, Kintsch, Songer, & Kintsch, 1996; O'Toole, 1996, 1997).

Depending on the particulars of the geographical and social context of instruction, one finds enormous variation in the nature, availability and status of science texts (McEneaney, 1999; Valverde, 1999), as well as in language policies, training and pedagogic practices. All these have an impact on the TLT relationship. Nevertheless, there have been few attempts to understand and communicate improved approaches to the selection and use of text in actual primary classrooms across different sociolinguistic and cultural contexts.

Previous research has focused our attention on the sociocultural context in which school text is used and the demands placed on teachers and learners by the text itself,

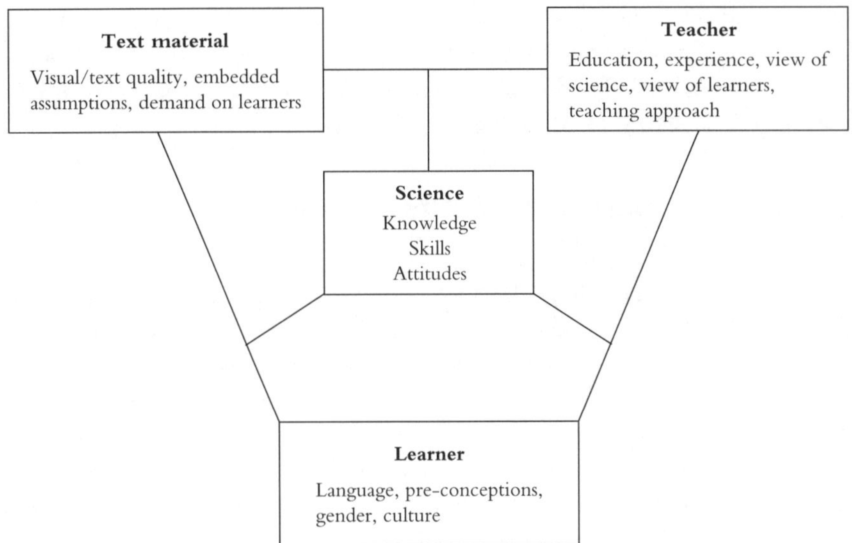

Figure 13.1. The Teacher–Learner–text triangle

in terms of choice of text available to teachers, language, visuals, format, conceptual development and cultural compatibility of content. We hypothesize that teachers choose and use (or reject) text in science lessons primarily by taking account of the "opportunity cost" determined by a range of constraining factors within the TLT relationship as they experience it. These decisions may also be influenced by extra-contextual matters such as the extent to which particular textbooks are mandated, their cost and availability, the perceived systemic constraints and teachers' own conceptions about text use, probably arising from their training (Ball & Feiman-Nemser, 1988; Shumba & Cleghorn, 2002).

We have taken as our first priority the delineating and understanding of the TLT relationship, and have begun by investigating the following dimensions:

1. teachers' attitudes to teaching science in culturally and linguistically diverse settings (the Teacher–Learner dimension);
2. the role that school text is perceived to play during instruction and how it can be developed (the Teacher–Text dimension);
3. the potential for text to effect conceptual change in learners (the Learner–Text dimension).

We have explored these interrelated issues from multiple perspectives, under naturalistic as well as experimental conditions, in culturally diverse as well as homogenous school settings in three countries of the north (Canada, United Kingdom, Finland). We have then attempted to integrate theoretical perspectives from sociolinguistics, pedagogy and cognitive psychology, using both qualitative and quantitative methods of data collection and analysis as appropriate to the questions being asked. A corpus of data is being built up to allow more specific questions to be explored later through a series extension studies in other sociocultural contexts. The design and findings of our studies are reported in detail elsewhere (Cleghorn, D'Amico, & Prochner, 1999; Mikkilä 1999; Peacock & Gates, 2000). This introduction summarizes and draws together their results in order to set a context for the subsequent chapters.

Text Use in the Linguistically Diverse School Setting of Quebec

Our study was carried out in grades five and six in English-medium, French-medium and French Immersion schools. Semi-structured interviews asked teachers for their opinions about the quality and use of available science text material.[2]

Teachers' views about science learning and teaching were intertwined with many factors, colored by the different linguistic school cultures in which they operated. In particular, teachers' expectations of their pupils' ability to tackle science in specific ways appeared to vary from first-language to second-language settings. For example, reading of text was more emphasized in second-language settings, whilst hands-on science was more emphasized with first-language learners. This suggests that, where language learning (first or second) is considered a problem or a primary aim, science content may become a secondary consideration. Evidence to support this is emerging also from the United Kingdom, where the government's National Literacy Strategy (DfEE, 1998) has mandated a Literacy Hour in all primary schools. This has not only limited the time spent on science lessons, but has also shifted the focus from scientific literacy to using science for literacy purposes (Murphy, 1999).

Quebec teachers' views of the texts in use appeared to be closely connected to their views of learners' abilities and needs, which in turn were related to the ethno-linguistic/socioeconomic make-up of the school. This determined such things as, for example, whether the teacher used the science text with the children or decided it was "too hard for the kids" and therefore used it instead for preparation of appropriate other activities.

There is no mandated text for science in either the French or English-medium schools, rather a number of textbooks are recommended. So far, however, the text most often used in the English-medium schools has been the Silver Burdett-Ginn Science Canadian Edition (Agincourt, Ontario: GLC Publishers, 1989). The manner in which teachers use it does vary considerably, depending on their perceptions of the difficulty of the text and on their perceptions of the children's learning needs. Thus in one school it was seen as too easy and in another it was seen as much too difficult. In the first instance the teacher rarely referred to the text; in the latter case the teacher reported making extracts from the text that would give the children "what they needed to know." The implications of these findings for teacher education are taken up in chapter 15 in this volume.

In French-medium schools, instruction was said to be switching to being more language-based, in order to strengthen the French mother-tongue. This is reported by teachers as well as in the media to be due to the paucity of French books in some homes, the pervasive influence of English language television and a long-established trend in Canada to use anglicisms rather than actually available and appropriate French words and terms.

In French-medium schools the *Graficor Memo* series was found to be in use. *Memo* consists of 10 booklets and workbooks per grade, and is an integrated series in which science is subsumed within the Language Arts curriculum. The program is geared toward first-language development, which in this case is French, and comes with prewritten worksheets and tests, suggesting a high level of prescriptiveness for teachers' use. Twelve out of 69 pages were devoted to topics in natural science while the remainder covered topics in social science, personal and social development and reading. There were three experiments proposed, one of which would not have been possible to carry out in the classroom. The series was used for approximately 63 percent of teaching time, though it is difficult to separate out how much of that was devoted to science learning as against the percentage for Language Arts.

Some teachers, particularly the older and more experienced, believed that they do not teach science "the way it ought to be taught." While a few teachers related this to constraints on time and money, others seemed to hold a traditional view of the nature of science that appeared to be at odds with the prescriptions in the texts that advocated a more constructivist teaching approach. Thus it appears that the way these teachers had been socialized to think about teaching science persisted despite the overlay of more recent approaches. The net effect was to undermine the confidence that could have evolved from many years of teaching experience. These teachers reported a lack of confidence in teaching science, and used text mainly as reference material to compensate for their perceived inadequacies. Some teachers reported that the theory as presented in the textbook did not link well with the practical exercises that the same text suggests, a factor that may have inhibited text use.

The findings thus reveal two clearly divergent trends. On the one hand, there was an overwhelming advocacy of hands-on, investigative approaches to science, with little reliance on the textbook, even when the text is practical, constructivist and learner-centered. On the other hand, teachers felt constrained by a back-to-basics structured approach to learning, emphasizing mastery of content (facts and skills) through language and utilizing direct teaching and testing of facts and procedures, through reading and writing. The role of text was seen as being greater here.

U.K. Teachers' Perceptions of the Role of Text in Science Teaching

This study used a phenomenographic methodology (Marton, 1994) to investigate the perceptions of 23 newly qualified primary teachers with diverse training and subject backgrounds. It involved extended interviews with teachers followed by analysis of transcripts to identify categories of teachers' perceptions about text use and difficulty. This focused on what they felt they learned during training, and how their use of text had changed in their first teaching post. During the interviews, teachers were also presented with ten examples of different kinds of science text, and given time to decide which if any they might use, and why. The study, conducted by Peacock and Gates (2000) revealed four major points about the Teacher–Text dimension, as described in the following

(1) As in Canada, teachers perceived that learning science through practical investigative activity was of paramount importance. Use of text was subsidiary to this, and peripheral to pupils' science learning. They had limited though specific uses for science text, these being (i) for teachers' own preparation, (ii) to ensure good starts to topics and (iii) to explain practical procedures. Text was rarely used for representing and explaining concepts directly to learners.

(2) Teachers had received little training in the selection or use of science text . They had a limited familiarity with the science text material available, and selected text according to surface features such as length, attractiveness (including color) and proportion of words to visuals. Choices were made without considering the conceptual content or the way concepts were represented.

(3) In spite of a stated preference for approaches originating in detailed commercially published science schemes (rather than individual texts), teachers did not appear to use these systematically with their pupils but preferred to "dip in" to different schemes for activity ideas where needed. Teachers' own schemes of work, and thus the progression in their organization of teaching science ideas, were not influenced by the progression inherent in published schemes. However, shortly after completion of our study, the U.K. Qualifications and Curriculum Authority (QCA) introduced a detailed Science Scheme covering the six years of primary education. Whilst this scheme is not mandatory, it has been adopted as a basis for planning by a significant proportion of schools and teachers. The QCA scheme, however, does not provide or refer to any published text material for teachers to use.

(4) Teachers tended to adapt text before use, the exceptions being the word-free posters and "big books" (i.e., books large enough for the whole class to "read" at the same time) used to start off a topic with the whole class. (The use of "Big Books" to start a lesson was an important strategy developed for the Literacy Hour.) They provided many reasons for this text adaptation, relating to perceived language difficulties, the importance of oral work, differentiation, traditions of teacher autonomy and ownership, and a predilection for customized worksheets. Adaptation was not seen as problematic, but rather as simplifying conceptual language and instructions. However, studies by Macdonald (1990) and van Rooyen (1990) in South Africa have shown that teacher adaptation often serves to introduce ambiguity and hence to confuse pupils, rather than to help them.

As in Quebec, the teachers acknowledged their lack of confidence in teaching science, and stressed the importance of a "good start" to a new science topic, which was how many justified their use of large-format pictures, posters and worksheets. At the same time, the Literacy Hour was focusing their attention on the use of nonfiction text, and thus teachers were beginning to see science text as a vehicle for basic literacy learning. The same divergent trends apparent in Quebec were thus emerging amongst U.K. teachers. However, effective strategies for teaching text use to pupils were not apparent in either system. Approaches to this are discussed in chapter 14 in this volume.

The analysis of science text was advocated by the National Literacy Strategy, yet the methods of analysis focused almost entirely on linguistic elements (Nuffield Foundation,

1998). However, our own studies as well as others referred to in this volume were indicating clearly that analysis of graphic elements and format/design elements were also crucial to "reading the page." The demands and teaching of visual literacy as applied to nonfiction text is therefore discussed in chapter 16 in this volume.

We thus began to develop an Index of Text Demand (ITD), to be used by teachers to assess not only the language of a text but the overall cognitive load, taking account also of the demands created by the science concepts, visuals and format aspects. This idea is further developed in chapter 15 in this volume. It is important to acknowledge that text demand may be very context-specific, in terms of the cultural and linguistic conditions inherent in the classroom where the text is used, as demonstrated by the Quebec study. Focus of the ITD instrument is therefore on analysis of text demand within the specific classroom contexts in which it is intended to be used, at pupils' own particular stage of science concept development, that is, within the Learner–Text dimension.

A final strand of recent U.K.-based developments is the rapid growth of test-related text material for pupils. Such materials now make up the greater part of commercially published text available on the primary school shelves of bookstores, presumably targeting parents who wish to provide their children with additional support. In the United Kingdom, pupils are now tested at ages 7, 11, 14 and 16 by means of nationally administered Standard Attainment Tests (SATs), the results of which are used to construct published "League Tables" of school performance. These league tables are crucially important to a school's perceived standing in the eyes of prospective parents and inspectors, and therefore there is considerable pressure for pupils to perform well, hence the rapid growth of test-based text material for practice. The development and impact of this material is discussed in chapter 17 in this volume.

THE EFFECTS OF REDESIGNED TEXT ON CONCEPTUAL UNDERSTANDING AMONGST FINNISH CHILDREN

This study was based on research into conceptual change from a constructivist perspective, which suggests that the learning of science concepts and principles usually involves major restructuring of pupils' already existing preinstructional conceptions.

There has been a line of research into the possibility of constructing text materials that are capable of bringing about such learning (Beck, Mckeown, Senatra, & Loxterman, 1991; Chi, Slotta, & de Leeuw, 1994; Guzzetti, Snyder, & Glass, 1992; Guzetti, Williams, Skeels, & Wu, 1997; Gyselinck & Tardieu, 1994; Schnotz, 1993). But as yet, pedagogical practice in commercial textbook design rarely takes account of this need to develop meta-conceptual awareness, assuming instead that the new knowledge provided will be compatible with what learners already know. There are exceptions (e.g., the "Spider's Place" series of science texts from South Africa), which have been evaluated during implementation (Peacock & Perold, 1995) to reveal that teachers did not fully understand the importance of the meta-cognitive dimension. Existing science texts in Finland however are not designed to refute common misconceptions and promote cognitive conflict. Instead they teach directly and aim to enrich (add new information) rather than reorganize existing knowledge structures. This learning-by-reorganization can be seen as more difficult (Hatano & Inagaki, 1997; Vosniadou &

Schnotz, 1997), and requires the development of meta-conceptual awareness (Vosniadou, 1994).

Hence the study attempted to redesign a section of text to present cognitive conflict to the learner (designated "refutational text") in order to create this meta-conceptual awareness by alerting pupils to the fact that they may need to change their existing ideas. The study then measured the effects on learning of the refutational text in comparison with the traditional text from which it was developed.

The study used as its example the concept of photosynthesis, where research (Sanders, 1997) indicates that most learners think that plants take their food from the soil, rather than that plants produce their nutrients themselves through photosynthesis. Systematic instruction by "enrichment" text usually "tells" the latter, without refuting the former. The "refutational" text, on the other hand, activates existing schemata ("you may already think that plants take their food from the soil; however, …") and then provides information to counter misconceptions. It was hypothesized that more Learner–Text interaction of this kind would promote cognitive conflict and thus meta-conceptual awareness. The key aspect of conceptual conflict in this case was that all living things need energy from food, but plants differ in that they make their own food. Examples of the traditional text and the revised refutational text are provided in figures 13.2 and 13.3. The study found that text design does play an

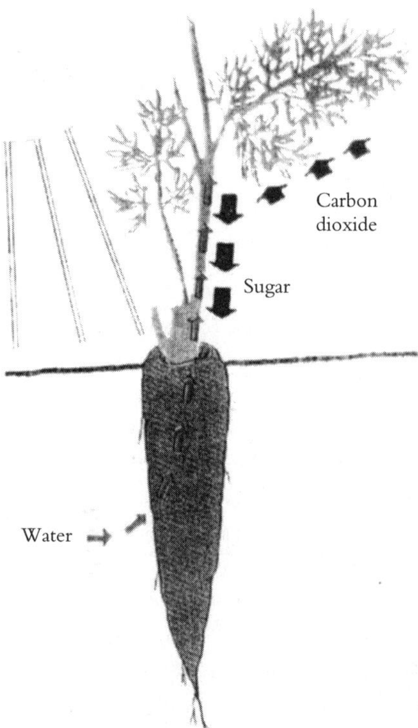

Figure 13.2. Example of conventional text. The carrot's roots take water from the soil, and its leaves take carbon dioxide from the air. The leaves produce sugar from these. The sugar turns into starch and is stored in the main root (Mikkilä-Erdmann, 2002, p. 22)

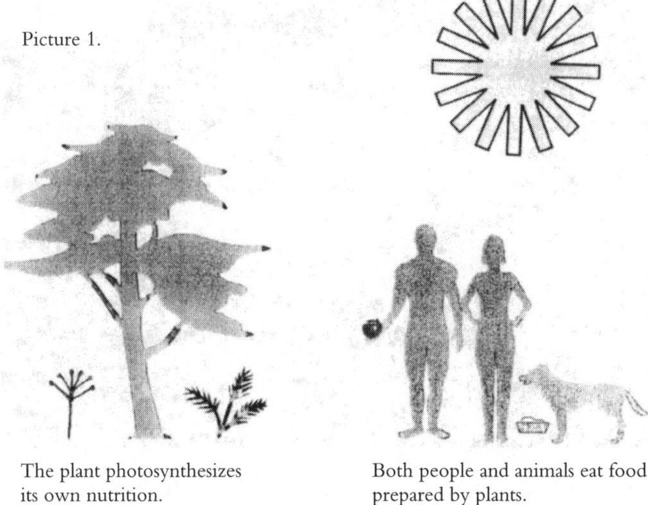

Figure 13.3. Example of refutational text. Plants and animals need energy to live and this comes from food. How plants get their food happens in a different way than we normally think. How does the energy get into a plant? Is water food for a plant? (Mikkilä-Erdmann, 2002, pp. 25 and 27)

important role in learning (Mikkilä, 1999). Pupils using the refutational text scored better on critical distinction questions. Moreover, other strategies for promoting cognitive conflict require major resourcing and pupil–teacher interaction, and have not been found to be sufficient in themselves (Caravita & Hallden, 1994; Limon & Carretero, 1997). However text design, where effective, presents a relatively easy and more economical approach to promoting change in pupils' conceptual understanding. There are implications here for teacher education that are taken up in chapter 15.

The study, being experimental, raised new questions about effective text use in authentic classroom contexts. These include questions about the Learner–Text dimension, such as whether or not there are "critical moments" in reading a text; about the role of visuals in promoting cognitive conflict and about the comprehension of symbols and icons. There are also questions about the Teacher–Learner dimension, such as those concerning improved learning through mediation, for example to help pupils integrate text and visuals by other linking strategies. In this context, the use of multimedia environments where such devices are also developed to enable Learner–Text interaction may have potential. Such issues are discussed in more detail and from a critical–phenomenological perspective by Michael Roth in chapter 18 in this volume.

It is also likely that the nature of science learning varies enormously from one culturally determined teaching context (or worldview) to another. For example, the conceptual development approach described above tends to see preinstructional conceptions (often referred to as "misconceptions") as culturally free entities, variable at the level of the individual. Western constructivist research, for example, has frequently asserted that the same misconceptions recur regardless of pupils' origins (Driver, 1995; Solomon, 1987). Yet in many African contexts, (science) knowledge is seen as pre-determined within their worldview and thus invariable, rather than constructed (Horton, 1971). For example, Jegede (1995) emphasized that collateral learning of two conflicting explanations is not a problem for young African students from traditional backgrounds. Research however has yet to determine whether or not refutational text can be used as effectively in non-Western school contexts; Murila has shown in chapter 9 in this volume how learners are likely to perceive that science text is to be used largely for revision and copying.

Summarizing the Findings: Developing the TLT Relationship

Two of the studies revealed clearly that teachers are subject to conflicting and increasingly divergent trends. Using the United Kingdom as an example, recent influential proposals from the science community such as those of "Science Beyond 2000" (Millar & Osborne, 1999) are moving pedagogy more toward models based on relevant, real-world science issues and an understanding of science as a process: whilst national policies are moving in the direction of a "back-to-basics" emphasis on literacy, numeracy, testing and heavily structured forms of didactic pedagogy that accompany this (DfEE, 1998). Such trends, which are reflected in other countries, may be influenced by the impact of international surveys of science and maths achievement. This creates a dilemma for teachers, especially as the implications of the two trends for text materials are widely divergent.

Newly qualified and novice teachers may also be subject to other pedagogical pressures arising from their experiences during training, particularly the lack of training in use of text (Peacock & Gates, 2000). Hence teachers may have no robust, consistent view of what "good practice" in text use during teaching implies. Given that our studies also indicate teachers' lack of familiarity with a wide range of text types, it is likely that they will be unable to make either informed choices or effective use of text material—print or other. Only where the pedagogy of the text is unambiguously explicit, and in accord with the teacher's actual pedagogical style, is it likely that text will be used systematically. This may account for both the lack of use of text, and also the tendency to adapt it to suit the teacher's style before use. How to pursue this aspect of the Teacher–Text relationship through further research and training is discussed in chapter 15.

Certain cultural conditions may be necessary for teachers to adapt traditional printed text in order to promote cognitive conflict and refute commonly held misconceptions. For example, where there is a cultural fit between the content of the text and the culture of the school/learner, adaptation (and therefore direct learning of science concepts) from the text is facilitated. However, it is unlikely that most teachers currently have the capacity or the time to undertake such adaptation, particularly where there is a poor match between the cultural assumptions of the text and the culture of the classroom. Yet this is often the very situation in which adaptations are attempted. Research evidence suggests that, whilst teachers see adaptation of text as unproblematic, those with a limited background in the conceptual content often make text ambiguous and conceptually more difficult when attempting to simplify (Macdonald, 1990; Van Rooyen, 1990). Thus there is a tension between the need for text modification strategies in practice, and the likelihood that these may not be effective in promoting learning. Publishing of refutational science texts is probably some way off, and will require the cooperation of commercial publishing houses. In the meantime, one productive outcome of this research might be the incorporation into teacher education programs of instruction in the design of text (such as worksheets), which attempts to generate cognitive conflict and meta-conceptual awareness, thus effectively addressing the Learner–Text relationship.

Ultimately, ways of using text more effectively cannot be prescribed without taking account of the specific TLT classroom context. This may best be addressed during teacher education, where knowledge of all three dimensions and of local contexts can be brought to bear on the questions of text use. It will also have to be addressed by authors, illustrators, designers and publishers in the way new text material is developed. And crucially, teacher education and publishing may come together more than at present to resolve the dilemmas faced in the classroom. Our experience as researchers, educators and authors indicates strongly that material which is eye-catching, or which sells well, is not necessarily the most effective in supporting pupils' conceptual learning. Thus there are tensions between the commercial interests of publishers and the educational priorities within the TLT relationship, since more effective texts may appear unfamiliar, even off-putting, and may cost more to produce. The way forward is thus the subject of the final chapter (chapter 18) of this book.

Notes

1. An earlier version of this chapter appeared in 2002 in *Curriculum and Teaching, 17* (2), 55–72.
2. In Quebec teachers trained for the elementary grades are generalists; they do not specialize and thus science education has been but one relatively small part of their teacher education.

References

Aikenhead, G. & Huntley, B.
(1999). Teachers' views on aboriginal students learning western and aboriginal science. *Canadian Journal of Native Education, 23*, 159–175.

Altbach, P.G.
(1987). The oldest technology: Textbooks in comparative context. *Compare, 17* (2), 93–106.

Apple, M.W. & Christian-Smith, L.K. (Eds.).
(1991). *The politics of the textbook.* New York: Routledge.

Armbruster, B.B.
(1986). Schema theory and the design of content-area textbooks. *Educational Psychologist, 21* (4), 253–267.

Ball, D.L. & Feiman-Nemser, S.
(1988). Using textbooks and teachers' guides: a dilemma for beginning teachers and teacher educators. *Curriculum Inquiry, 18* (4), 401–423.

Beck, I.L., McKeown, M.G., Sinatra, G.M., & Loxterman, J.A.
(1991). Revising social studies text from a text-processing perspective: evidence of improved comprehensibility. *Reading Research Quarterly, 26* (3), 251–278.

Caravita, S. & Hallden, O.
(1994). Re-framing the problem of conceptual change. *Learning and Instruction*, *4* (11), 89–111.

Chi, M.T.H., Slotta, J.D., & de Leeuw, N.
(1994). From things to processes: a theory of conceptual change for learning science concepts. *Learning and Instruction*, *4* (1), 27–43.

Chimombo, M.
(1989). Readability of subject texts: Implications for ESL teaching in Africa. *English for Specific Purposes*, *8* (3), 255–264.

Clark, J. & Ramahlape, K.
(1999). Crackles and sparks: stepping out of the world of lightning with the "science through applications project" (STAP). In Kuiper, J. (Ed.) (1999). Proceedings of the 7th annual conference, Southern African Association for Research in Mathematics and Science Education, Harare, pp. 110–120.

Cleghorn, A.
(1992). Primary level science in Kenya: Constructing meaning through english and indigenous languages. *Qualitative Studies in Education*, *5* (4), 311–323.

Cleghorn, A., Merritt, M., & Abagi, J.
(1989). Language policy and science instruction in Kenyan primary schools. *Comparative Education Review*, *33* (1), 21–39.

Cleghorn, A., D'Amico, M., & Prochner, L.
(1999). Teachers' views of primary science in linguistically diverse school settings in Quebec. *Curriculum and Teaching*, *14* (1), 95–109.

Cleghorn, A. & Rollnick, M.
(2002). The role of English in individual and societal development: lessons from African classrooms. *TESOL Quarterly*, *36* (3), 347–372.

Cobern, W.W. and Loving, C.C.
(1998). Defining "Science" in a multicultural world: implications for science education. Paper presented at NARST Conference, April 1998.

Crystal, D.
(1997). *English as a global language*. New York: Cambridge University Press.

Driver, R.
(1995). Constructivist approaches to science teaching. In L.P. Steffe & J. Gale, *Constructivism in education* (pp. 385–400). Hillsdale, NJ: Erlbaum.

DfEE,
(1998). *The national literacy strategy: Framework for teaching*. London: Department for Education and Employment.

Dwyer, F.M.
(1988). Examining the symbiotic relationship between verbal and visual literacy in terms of facilitating student achievement. *Reading Psychology: an International Quarterly*, *9*, 365–380.

Gordon, J., Schumm, J.S., Coffland, C., & Doucette M.
(1992). Effects of inconsiderate versus considerate text on elementary students' vocabulary learning. *Reading Psychology: An International Quarterly*, *13*, 157–169.

Guzzetti, B., Snyder, T., & Glass, G.

(1992). Promoting conceptual change in science: Can texts be used effectively. *Journal of Reading, 35* (8), 642–649.

Guzzetti, B.J., Williams, W.O., Skeels, S.A., & Wu, S.M.

(1997). Influence of text structure on learning counterintuitive physics concepts. *Journal of Research in Science Teaching, 34* (7), 701–719.

Gyselinck, V. & Tardieu, H.

(1994). The role of text illustrations in the construction of non-spatial mental models. In De Jong & van Hout-Wolters, *Process-oriented instruction and learning from text*. Amsterdam: VU University Press.

Hatano, G. & Inagaki, K.

(1997). Qualitative changes in intuitive Biology. *European Journal of Psychology Education, 22* (2), 111–130.

Horton, R.

(1971). African traditional thought and western science. In Young, M.F.D. (Ed.), *Knowledge and control: New directions for the sociology of education*. London: Collier-Macmillan.

Jegede, O.

(1995). Collateral learning and the eco-cultural paradigm in science and maths education. *Proceedings of the Southern African Association for Maths and Science education (SAARMSE) Annual Conference, Cape Town.*

Kintsch, W.

(1994). The role of knowledge in discourse processing: A construction-integration model. In R.B. Ruddell, M.R.Ruddell and H. Singer (Eds.), *Theoretical models and processes of reading* (pp. 951–995). Newark: International Reading Association.

Kress, G. & Van Leeuwen, T.

(1996). *Reading images: The grammar of visual design*. London: Routledge.

Langhan, D.

(1993). The textbook as a source of difficulty in teaching and learning: Final report of the Threshold Project. Pretoria: Human Sciences Research Council.

Limon, M. & Carretero, M.

(1997). Conceptual change and anomalous data: a case study in the domain of natural sciences. *European Journal of Psychology of Education, 22* (2), 213–230.

Macdonald, C.A.

(1990). Standard 3 general science research 1987–88: A final report of the Threshold Project. Pretoria: Human Sciences Research Council.

MacNamara, D.S., Kintsch E., Songer, N.B., & Kintsch, W.

(1996). Are good texts always better? interactions of text coherence, background knowledge and levels of undersranding in learning from text. *Cognition and Instruction, 14* (1), 1–43.

Marton, F.

(1994). Phenomenography. In T. Husen and N. Postlethwaite, *International Encyclopedia of Education* (pp. 4424–4429) (Second edition, vol. 8). London: Pergamon.

McEneaney, E.
(1999). Models of science, experts and Nature: A View from primary school textbooks. Paper presented the Comparative and International education Society conference, Toronto.

Mikkilä, M.
(1997). Inspiring conceptual change through text and pictures. Paper presented at the EARLI Conference, Athens.

Mikkilaä, M.
(1999). The effect of text design on 5th grade learners' comprehension of photosynthesis. Paper Presented at the Comparative and International Education Society conference, Toronto.

Mikkilä, M. & Olkinuora, E.
(1994). Problems of current textbooks and workbooks: Do they promote high-quality learning? In De Jong and van Hout-Wolters (Eds.), *Process-oriented instruction and learning from text.* Amsterdam: VU University Press.

Millar, R. & Osborne, J.
(1998). *Beyond 2000: Science education for the future.* London: King's College School of Education.

Murphy, P.
(1999). Science and literacy moving forward? *Primary Science Review, 59,* 2–3.

Nuffield Foundation,
(1998). *Science and literacy: A guide for primary teachers.* London: Nuffield Fioundation/Collins Educational.

Ogawa, M.
(1995). Science education in a multiscience perspective. *Science Education, 79* (5), 583–593.

Ogunniyi, M.B., Jegede, O.J., Ogawa, M., Yandila, C.D., & Oladele, F.K.
(1995). Nature of worldview presuppositions among science teachers in Botswana, Indonesia, Japan, Nigeria and the Phillipines. *Journal of Research in Science Teaching, 32* (8), 817–831.

Orevbu, A.O.
(1984). School science curriculum and Innovation; an African perspective. *European Journal of Science Education, 6* (3), 217–225.

O'Toole, J.M.
(1996). Science, schools, children and books: exploring the classroom interface between science and language. *Studies in Science Education, 28,* 113–143.

O'Toole, J.M.
(1997). Increasing student access to science Text. Paper presented at the Pacific Science Inter-Congress, University of the South Pacific, Suva, Fiji.

Peacock, A. (Ed.).
(1991). *Science in primary schools: the multicultural dimension.* Basingstoke: Macmillan Education.

Peacock, A.
(1993). A global core curriculum for primary science? *Primary Science Review, 28,* 8–10.

Peacock, A.
(1995a). Access to science learning for children in rural Africa. *International Journal of Science Education, 17* (2), 149–166.

Peacock, A.

(1995b). An agenda for research on text material in primary science for second language learners of english in developing countries. *Journal of Multilingual and Multicultural Development, 16* (5), 389–401.

Peacock, A. & Gates, S.M.G.

(2000). Newly-qualified teachers' perceptions of the role of text material in teaching science. *Research in Science and Technological Education, 18* (2), 155–171.

Peacock, A. & Perold, H.

(1995). Helping primary teachers develop new approaches to science teaching: a strategy for the evaluation of "Spider's Place." *Proceedings of Annual Meeting of the Southern African Association for Research in Mathematics and Science (SAARMSE)*, Cape Town.

Rollnick, M.

(1998). The influence of language on the second-language teaching and learning of science. In. W.W. Cobern (Ed.), *Socio-cultural perspectives on science education* (pp. 121–138). Dordrecht: Kluwer Academic.

Ryf, A. & Cleghorn, A.

(1997). The language of science: text talk and teacher talk in second language settings. *Proceedings of the Annual Meeting of the Southern African Association for Research in Mathematics and Science Education (SAARMSE)*, Johannesburg, January 1997, pp. 437–441.

Sanders, M.

(1997). Developing critical thinking in science education researchers. *Proceedings of the Annual Meeting of the Southern African Association for Research in Mathematics and Science Education (SAARMSE)*, Johannesburg, 16–22.

Schnotz, W.

(1993) Adaptive construction of mental representations in understanding expository texts. *Contemporary Educational Psychology, 18*, 114–120.

Shumba, O.

(1995). Interaction of traditional Socio-cultural variables with instructional ideology and knowledge of the nature of science. *Zimbabwe Journal of Educational Research, 7* (1), 23–56.

Shumba, O. & Cleghorn, A.

(2002). Prospective teachers' views about science for children and science textbooks: Some insights from Zimbabwe. Under review.

Solomon, J.

(1987). Social influences on the construction of pupils' understanding of science. *Studies in Science Education, 14*, 63–82.

Stinner, A.

(1995). Science textbooks: their present role and future form. In S.M. Glynn and R. Duit (Eds.), Learning science in the schools: research reforming practice. Hillsdale, NJ: Erlbaum.

Sweller, J.

(1994). Cognitive Load theory, learning difficulty and instructional design. *Learning and Instruction, 4*, 295–312.

Valverde, G.A.

(1999). Using the timss curriculum study to understand the role of textbooks in conforming structures of educational opportunities across the world. *Paper presented at the CIES Conference*, Toronto.

Van Rooyen, H.

(1990). The disparity between English as a subject and English as the medium of learning (a final report of the Threshold Project). Pretoria: Human Sciences Research Council.

Vosniadou, S.

(1994). Capturing and modelling the process of conceptual change. *Learning and Instruction, 4* (1), 45–69.

Vosniadou, S. & Schnotz, W.

(1997). Introduction. *European Journal of Psychology of Education, 22* (2), 105–110.

Walpole, S.

(1999). Changing texts, changing thinking: Comprehension demands of new science textbooks. *The Reading Teacher, 52* (4), 358–369.

White, J. & Welford, G.

(1988). The language of science. Report prepared for The Assessment of Performance Unit (Science report for teachers: 11). London: Department of Education and Science.

14

Teaching the Page:
Teaching Learners to
Read Complex Science Text

Sharon Walpole and Laura Smolkin

The textual world of science presented for younger readers has changed dramatically over the last number of years. This transformation has been noted not only in textbooks designed to instruct (e.g., Walpole, 1999) but also in trade books written to inform (e.g., Vardell & Copeland, 1992). Martins (2002) suggests that the explosion of eye-catching images, the most readily apparent difference in today's texts, reflects a general societal pattern, visible in advertising and news productions, in part due to modern technology reduced costs in color reproduction, improved abilities to manipulate images, and advances in desktop publishing. Images, explains Martins, are no longer subordinate to text; instead, in many cases, they have "become the core text" (p. 76). Regardless of the source of change, these more complex visual environments, as well as the changes in text that accompany them, present new challenges for young readers and the teachers who work with them.

In this chapter, we bring together work we have each pursued to consider two of the most common text types found in elementary science instruction textbooks and trade books. We start by looking at particular concerns expressed with each of these sources of science. We next present four two-page spreads, two from very different textbooks and two from very different trade books, to show the types of challenges each entails, and report how readers reacted and responded to those texts. From those responses we move to some suggestions for teachers who must not only present today's texts to children but must also assist children in negotiating these pages by themselves.

Texts in Science Instruction

Trade books and textbooks differ in many ways. One very important difference is the way in which they are created. Recently, researchers have described the textbook industry (e.g., Hardy, chapter 12, this volume; Holliday, 2002; Kirk, Matthews, & Kurrts, 2001), and the science textbooks corporate entities create. Three parties play large roles in the creation of textbooks. Academic consultants remind publishers of research results and give guidance on content; graphic designers seek to present content in its most appealing format; and sales experts and teacher focus groups address marketplace concerns. Science trade books, on the other hand, generally reflect the combined artistic (and scholarly) efforts of a single author and a single illustrator. Usually, trade books are seen as supplying more depth on a given topic than textbooks, which must cover numerous topics. Stylistically, trade books are generally more engaging; authors who write pedestrian texts seldom see them published. Both of these important text types have been examined and critiqued for their effectiveness in science instruction. Here, we note some of the major concerns.

Major Concerns with Textbooks as Instructional Tools

Textbooks have traditionally played an extremely important role in science instruction. Research has repeatedly shown that many teachers, perhaps insecure in their own science and/or pedagogical content knowledge (e.g., Czerniak & Lumpe, 1996; Harlen, 1997; Tilgner, 1990) rely solely upon the textbook, to the exclusion of related activities and experiences. However, research and writing on textbooks reveals these instructional resources to be subject to numerous flaws. Most important to our current work is the issue of comprehensibility.

Since the early 1980s, numerous researchers have been concerned with the actual writing of textbooks. Armbruster and Anderson (1981) distinguished between texts requiring little cognitive effort for comprehension ("considerate") and those requiring considerable, conscious, and strategic efforts to comprehend ("inconsiderate"). Texts could be made considerate, suggested Armbruster and Anderson (1984), through careful attention to text elements. Global, or overall, coherence could be improved through clear text structures, strong introductions, headings and subheadings, and tables revealing both the text's structure and its content—features Britton, Gulgoz and Glynn (1993) call "construction instructions." Any information that disrupted global coherence was to be moved to relatively low-profile places in the text. With regard to local coherence (at the sentence level and below), Armbruster and Anderson (1984) suggested increased cohesive ties through pronoun reference and clear conjunctions. Such changes were clearly important; research on students from second through fifth grades (Alvermann & Boothby, 1983; Baumann, 1986; Zack & Osako, 1986) showed clear improvements in children's comprehension for those who read considerate as opposed to inconsiderate text.

The effectiveness of these changes makes particular sense if we consider cognitive descriptions of comprehension. Comprehension is an active process of extracting and constructing meaning, integrating prior knowledge and text content (Rand Reading Study Group, 2002). Kintsch (1994) argues that the process has two distinct levels. At first, the reader processes the text in a very basic way, linking words into phrases and making simple inferences necessary to maintain local coherence. Next, the reader does the real cognitive work of restructuring that basic information hierarchically, drawing on his or her store of prior knowledge. It is at this point that improved global coherence in the text plays its important role. Developing these competencies in children requires teachers to analyze and mediate between the specific demands of the text and the specific skills of the readers.

Concerns with Trade Books as Instructional Materials

Numerous writers (e.g., Barber et al., 1993; Barlow, 1991; Butzow & Butzow, 1988; Smardo, 1982) have suggested that teachers turn to trade books for science instruction. There are, however, several areas of concern about trade book use in science instruction. Generally, accuracy is the largest concern. Children's literature textbooks (e.g., Norton, Norton, & McClure, 2003) indicate that teachers must consider whether authors have the qualifications to write on their selected topics and whether the facts they present are accurate. And while the truth is that there are many misconceptions in trade books (e.g., Donovan & Smolkin, 2001; Rice & Rainsford, 1996), admonishments to teachers to look for inaccuracies may be futile in that many elementary teachers lack the science content knowledge necessary to conduct those analyses.

Another major area of concern with trade book use in science instruction involves the genre of the texts chosen. Numerous writers (e.g., Camp, 2000; Crook & Lehman, 1991; McClure & Zitlow, 1991) have suggested that children's literature-based science instruction will be best achieved by combining genres; usually, the suggestion is to mix nonfiction with either poetry or picture storybooks. However, beginning with Mayer (1995), who noted that her third grade students had picked up a number of misconceptions during the reading of the story *Dear Mr. Blueberry* (James, 1991), researchers have begun to question whether these wholesale recommendations of children's literature for science instruction might be problematic. We (Donovan & Smolkin, 2001; Smolkin & Donovan, 2002) have been particularly concerned about problems that arise when teachers use story, especially fantasy, texts as part of their science instruction.

LOOKING AT DISTINCTIVE TEXTS

Each of us, separately, decided to contrast two texts to highlight the ways readers attempted to make sense of the science appearing on a page. Sharon, interested in textbooks, was fascinated by the differences between two Addison-Wesley editions of their third-grade science offering (Barman et al., 1992; Brummett, Barman, DiSpezio, & Ostlund, 1995). She wanted to know how children would respond to differences in format, as well as to adjunct aids such as subheadings and boldfaced type. She interviewed seven fourth-grade students, four low-ability and three high-ability, having them think aloud as they read these texts and discuss their usefulness in learning science.

Laura, interested in trade books, wanted to understand how teachers presented science from an information book and from what she and colleague Carol Donovan had termed "dual purpose" texts (Donovan & Smolkin, 2001, 2002; Smolkin & Donovan, 2001). Dual purpose texts are "fuzzy" (Pappas, Kiefer, & Levstik, 1999) or "blended" (Skurzynski, 1992) texts that embed information within a story structure, but retain many of the graphic features of more traditional science information books. Selecting Gibbons (1995) *Planet earth/inside out* as the information book and Cole's (1987) *The magic school bus inside the earth as the dual* purpose book, Laura analyzed read-alouds by three first, four second, and four third grade teachers.

In the following sections, we will present data from both studies. Each section will begin with a close examination of the texts and particular two-page spreads to which participants responded. This will be followed by a look at participants' responses.

Study 1: Children's Responses to Textbooks

Addison-Wesley's 1992 Textbook

The 1992 Addison-Wesley third-grade science textbook (Barman, DiSepzio, Guthrie, Leyden, & Ostlund, 1992) might best be described as a traditional textbook. Large and hardbound, it contained four distinct units and thirteen chapters. Chapter twelve, in which our first two-page spread is found (see figure 14.1), is representative of the overall text's structure. With its look at the digestive system, the chapter begins with a story, then quickly moves to two lessons, each with a chronological organization. Following a "considerate" text format, construction instructions clearly indicate the authors' plan. The first lesson traces the path of digestion from the mouth to the stomach to the intestines. The second section retraces those steps, focusing on health issues for the teeth, the throat, the stomach, and the intestines. Each section ends with a skill-building lesson, inviting children to conduct a simple experiment. The entire chapter ends with a technology link, a more complex experiment and then an opportunity for self-assessment.

The running text in the digestion chapter, with 1,259 words, contains many signals for readers. Sixteen words assist readers with the chronological structure of ideas in the text; words such as *before, after, next,* and *soon after* aid readers in connecting new text

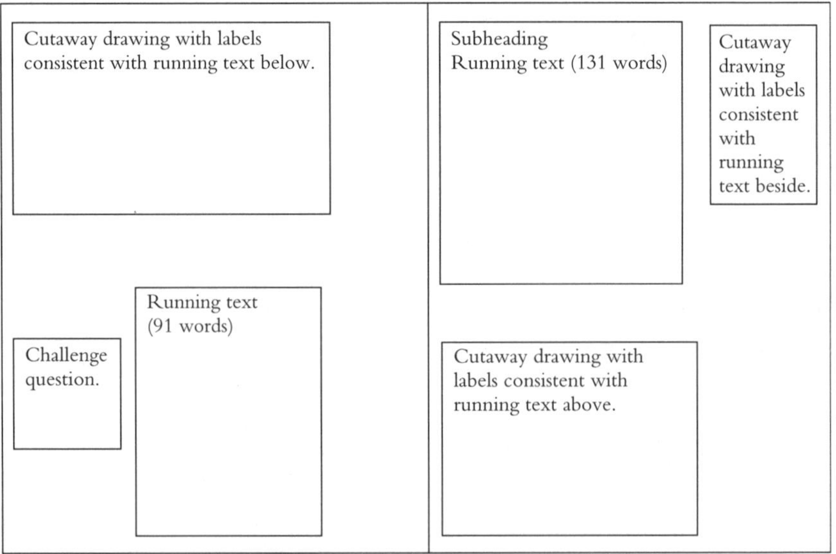

Figure 14.1. Two-page spread from Addison-Wesley's Science (1992)

information with previous information. Boldfaced type is used nine times, signaling new words and concepts within the running text. Boldfaced type also helps readers to attend to important information and directs their attention to information in the book's glossary.

To assist readers in understanding the text–graphics interplay, we created figure 14.1 to represent a two-page spread (pp. 282–283) in the 1992 textbook. On the left-hand side of this spread is a cutaway drawing of the stomach. The illustration contains the following numbered text (Barman DiSepzio, Guthrie, Leyden, & Ostlund 1992, p. 282):

1 Food moves from the esophagus to the stomach.
2 Digestive juices are released in the stomach.
3 Stomach muscles squeeze and mix the food and digestive juices.
4 Food that enters your stomach stays there for a few hours. During this time, the food is digested more. The stomach makes digestive juices.
5 Stomach muscles then squeeze and mix the food with these juices. Soon, the food changes into a soupy mixture.

Running text on this page gives virtually the same information, allowing the reader an additional chance to extract information and make an accurate construction (Barman, DiSepzio, Guthrie, Leyden, & Ostlund, 1992, p. 282).

This structure allows readers to attend first to the illustration and its caption or to the running text and then to the alternate version of the same information, reinforcing their construction of the text's meaning.

Addison-Wesley's 1995 Textbook

By 1995, Addison-Wesley (Brummet, Lind, Barman, DiSpezio, & Ostlund, 1995) had made significant changes to its textbook. Slender softcover volumes replaced the hardbound book, one for each unit. Units began with observations from the children's world and then a detailed experiment. The text information included journal activities, extensions, experiments, and review questions interspersed within the text information. At the end of each unit, a longer extension brought text ideas into the world, an additional experiment extended text content, and assessment had been expanded to include both text information and performance.

In the particular chapter examined, the running text is considerably more compact than in the older textbook. Although the number of pages per unit is fairly consistent (19 in 1992 and 21 in 1995), they are used differently. The 1995 text is quite brief; it has only 65 percent of the words used in running text in 1992. Very few words, only two per chapter, are presented in boldfaced type. There are few temporal signal words to guide reader's construction of ideas across sentences. Instead, there are direct instructions to the reader to feel or do or think: "Feel your outer ear" (Brummet Lind, Barman, DiSpezio, & Ostlund, p. F13); "Notice the long bones in the arms and legs of the dancer" (Brummet Lind, Barman, DiSpezio, & Ostlund, p. F17). This technique is used 11 times in the 1995 text but only 3 times in 1992.

There are striking differences in the use of illustrations and captions in 1995 compared to 1992. Figure 14.2 represents a typical two-page spread from this textbook.

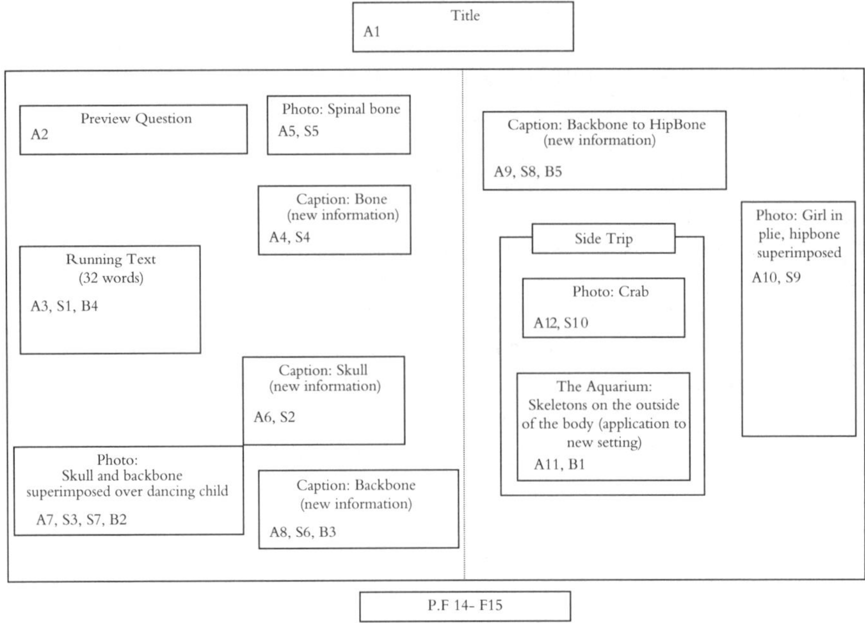

Figure 14.2. Three children navigating two-page spread from Addison-Wesley's *Bones and Muscles* (1995)

Illustrations on these pages are bold photographs of a child in various dance positions; drawings of sections of the skeletal have been superimposed on the photos. The captions for these photographs, set in slightly different print from the running text on the left page, present totally new information. The brief running text on the left page is simply an introduction. The skeleton has many parts. Each part looks different. Some parts move and some do not. Each part is important to the body. You will learn about many parts of your skeleton (Brummet Lind, Barman, DiSpezio, & Ostlund, 1992, p. F14).

The meat of the lesson is presented in the captions to the illustrations. Directly adjacent to the superimposed skull appears this caption: "The skull is made up of thin bones that protect the brain. These bones can be flat or curved" (Brummet Lind, Barman, DiSpezio, & Ostlund, 1992, p. F14). This use of illustrations and captions as a sole source of text content, rather than as an additional source, reflects a very different approach to text construction than the adjunct–aid–oriented 1992 text.

Children's Responses to the Text

Generally, children found the 1992 textbook format daunting; some, however, acknowledged that textbooks are good sources for learning. To high-ability reader Paul, the textbook, "looks like it'd be harder to understand" because "some of the words might be too big," but "it would show you more." Mark, a low–ability reader, commented, "That looks like a fifth grader one, don't it, because it has more words in it." till, he chose the 1992 textbook from several sitting on the table as the best text to learn with because "it shows you pictures and a lot of words." Anne, another high-ability reader, was drawn immediately to the bold-faced words "because you could know what they're talking about, because of the big words. When you read the paragraphs you can find the big words and all you got to do is look on the side and you can find out."

Children surely noticed the differences in illustrations, responding favorably to the newer text. Anne looked at both the 1992 and the 1995 textbook and noted, "Well the difference is that the words are bigger [reference to the font] and it's not like painting pictures, it's real pictures put into the book, and this book [1995] has vocabulary words and I don't think this book does." Mark also noticed that the 1995 text "has more pictures."

All seven children in this study were asked to read and think aloud as they navigated the 1995 text. Figure 14.2 displays the paths of three of the children. Within each text element in the diagram is a navigational notation, represented with a number, referring to a reader, represented with a letter. Their attention to the pages was very different. Anne, one of the high-ability readers in the study, attended to both the title (A1) and preview question (A2) before moving to the running text. And while Shelly, one of the low-ability readers in the study, did not attend to either the title or preview question, she did examine every picture, and read all text except for the Side Trip section on the aquarium. The reading of Brittany, another high-ability reader in the study is markedly different. Perhaps attracted by the highlighted title for "Side Trip," Brittany began her navigation on the right-hand page of the spread (B1). Only after looking at the photo of the backbone and skull and the related caption on the backbone did she finally read the running text (B3). She concluded her reading by swinging back to the right-hand page to read the caption on the backbone/hipbone relationship (B5).

In this visually appealing context, text content and construction instructions included by authors to signal global coherence were used differently by the different children. Of the seven children, only one child read the title. Only two children read the preview question. All but one child read the running text. While all noticed some of the picture-caption relationships, none noticed all of them. These differences in navigational strategies may effect comprehension of content from a science textbook.

Study 2: Teachers' Presentation of Trade Books

The Nonnarrative Information Book

Gail Gibbons's (1995) *Planet Earth/Inside Out* is what we have described as a nonnarrative information book (Donovan & Smolkin, 2001). Unlike narrative information books in which sequence is a very important factor, nonnarrative texts usually feature a series of topics related to an overarching concept, with sections of text often addressing subtopics. *Planet Earth/Inside Out*, a text of 1,944 words, has eight major subtopics. While there are no headings to indicate when a new topic has begun, Gibbons has made use of italics in the running text to indicate the introduction of a new scientific term. Almost always, these terms are found repeated, or reinforced (Hunter, Crismore, & Pearson, 1987), through the labels in her full-color illustrations.

The selected two-page spread, seen in figure 14.3, comes from the topic volcanoes. Its visual format is symmetrical. In the top left-hand corner of page 20 of Planet Earth

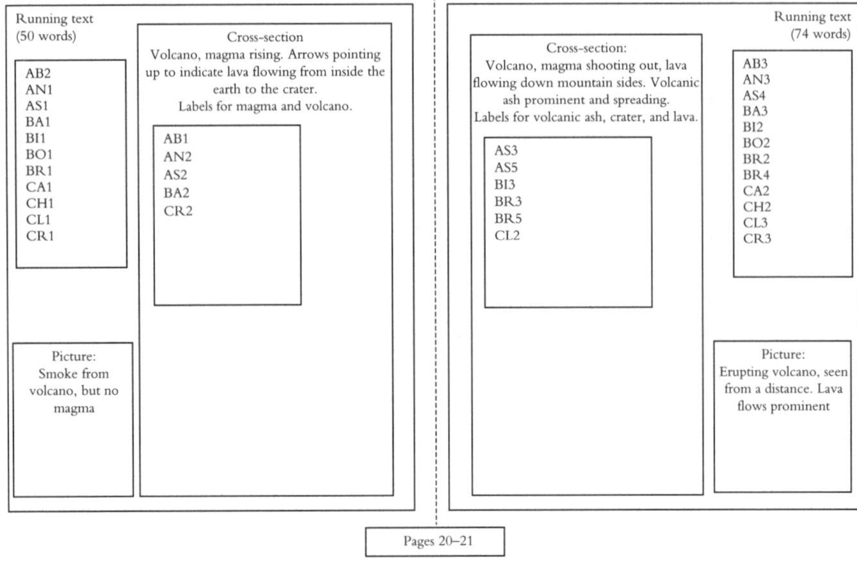

Figure 14.3. Teachers navigating two-page spread from *Planet Earth/Inside Out*

is the running text; below it is a small picture; next to these is a large cross-sectional diagram. This arrangement is mirrored on the right-hand page of the spread. The running text on the left-hand page of the spread includes three italicized words—volcanoes, magma, volcanic eruption. Of these terms, two are repeated in the graphic labels, volcano, and magma. The running text on the right-hand page of the spread contains three italicized terms, crater, volcanic ash, and lava. All three are repeated as labels in the accompanying illustration.

The Dual Purpose Trade Book

The Magic School Bus Inside the Earth (Cole, 1987) was selected because it contained similar content to Gibbons's (1995) *Planet Earth*, but represented a very different generic structure. The story line in this book of 1,423 words begins with teacher Ms. Frizzle and her class completing their unit on animals homes, and her announcement that they will begin a new unit of study on the earth. When her students fail to complete their homework assignment of bringing a rock to school, Ms. Frizzle decides that students will have to go on a field trip. They board the Magic School Bus that turns into various types of machines, which allows the children and their teacher to bore into the earth, stopping at various places to examine different rock types, proceed through the inner core, and exit on a volcanic island. The story line is reflected in the full-page illustrations, and is enhanced by humorous asides from one child to another or comments that appear in the bus's destination window.

The book, however, is more than a story; like all dual-purpose texts, it is also meant to convey information, this time on the topic of the earth. Our analyses of this book indicate that the units bearing the greatest number of informational ideas, from greatest

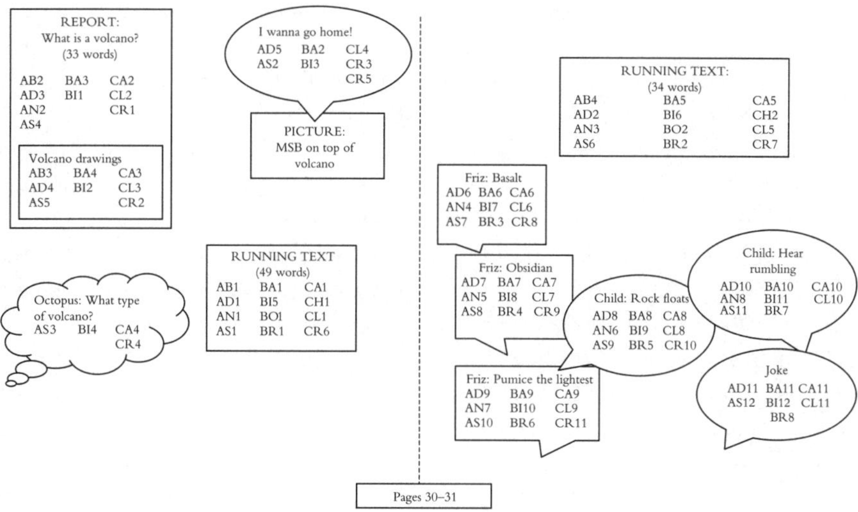

Figure 14.4. Teacher navigating two-page spread from *The Magic School Bus Inside the Earth*

to least, are the reports (notebook pages ostensibly written by children), labeled items within the pictures, Ms. Frizzle's speech balloons (containing instructional commentary), and the running text, in which Ms. Frizzle's comments to her students are also embedded (Smolkin & Donovan, 2002).

Because this is in one sense a storybook, there are no major headings to indicate new sections of content. There are, however, titles on the children's reports; these provide the only "considerate" aspect to those seeking to learn from the text.

The selected two-page spread, seen in figure 14.4, displays a fairly typical two-page display from this text (pp. 30–31). Each page represents a distinct event in the narrative structure. The left-hand side depicts the Magic School Bus at a distance atop a volcanic island. A small speech balloon floats from the bus, in which someone is plaintively exclaiming, "I want to go home!" Below the illustration, set within the ocean, is the running text in which Ms. Frizzle announces their arrival on the island. In the upper left-hand corner appears the notebook paper page on which Rachel (a Frizzle student) has written her illustrated report on "What is a volcano?" Her illustrations depict three different shapes of volcanoes. Below Rachel's report is a smiling octopus who asks readers to name the type of volcano Ms. Frizzle and students are on. The right-hand page of the spread depicts the children's rock collection effort; the running text appears in the sky. Ms. Frizzle, within the picture, is identifying the different rocks through a series of speech balloons.

Teachers' Responses to Information Books and Dual Purpose Text

Figures 14.3 and 14.4 are labeled to show how teachers moved around the pages as they read aloud. First grade teachers are coded with the letter A, second grade with B, and third grade with C. The second letter of each code indicates individuals within those grades; their movements around that pages are indicated by numbers, with 1 being the first place they directed their children's attention, 2 the second, and so forth.

As figure 14.3 shows, there was considerable uniformity in how teachers approached the two-page spread of the nonnarrative *Planet Earth*. All 11 teachers who recorded their readings read the running text on the left-hand page. Only one teacher, Abbott, began her reading with a look at the cross-section; this she did to introduce the topic of the page, and then she, too, read the running text. After reading the running text, four other teachers, Andrews, Ashby, Baber, and Critzer, called children's attention to the cross-section on page 20. At this point, all teachers turned their focus to page 21. First grade teacher Ashby, second grade teacher Bryant, and third grade teacher Clark began with the cross-section (AS3, BR3, CL2) before reading the running text (AS4, BR4, CL3); Ashby and Bryant each returned to discuss the cross-section further with her students (AS5; BR5). All other teachers began their reading of page 21 with the running text; of these, only Bittner (BI3) focused her children's attention on the cross-section. No teachers drew children's attention to either of the small pictures in the lower left-hand and right-hand corners.

In contrast, teachers' navigation of the two-page spread in the dual-purpose book, *The Magic School Bus*, appears far more idiosyncratic. All 12 teachers read the running text on both pages; the orders in which they did so differ markedly. First grade teacher Adams, for example, began with the running text on page 30 (AD1), then left the page on volcanic islands to jump to the running text on the page about volcanic rock (AD2). She next returned to the report on volcanoes on page 30 (AD3) and discussed its accompanying illustration (AD4), before reading her children the humorous speech balloon emanating from the *Magic School Bus* (AD5). After that, she returned to page 31 to read the series of speech balloons belonging to Ms. Frizzle and her students.

Despite its zigzagged path, Ms. Adams's reading included all major information sources on the two-page spread. Second grade teacher Bowen's reading began with the running text on page 30 (BO1) and ended with the running text on page 31 (BO2). This means that the largest sections of scientific information on this two-page spread (the report and Ms. Frizzle's speech balloons) were not read to her students. In fact, examining the report in the upper left-hand corner of figure 14.3 reveals that three of the 12 teachers did not read this information to their students. And looking at Ms. Frizzle's various speech balloons shows this same pattern: one-fourth of the teachers in the study did not read these information-bearing units to their students.

What Our Analyses Suggest for Practice

From our observations of children and adults navigating texts, we believe there are two important aspects of science and text instruction that merit attention from those who work with children and those who work with teachers. We will look first at the issues of text type and purpose, then we turn our attention to where and how to locate important information in science texts.

Different Texts for Different Purposes

What is clear from our examinations is that all texts employed in science instruction are not equal in terms of readers' perceptions. Our texts may be seen as a continuum, both in terms of their visual environments and their uses within the science classroom. On the far left is *The Magic School Bus Inside the Earth*. This book, with its inserted humor and fantastic voyage, will engage young readers. However, its organization and structure prove challenging for those seeking to *learn* from the text, as our 12 adults struggling to navigate the two-page spread demonstrate. These same problems with navigation are apparent with the next text in the continuum, Addison-Wesley's (1995) science textbook. When children are confronted with an engaging but visually unfamiliar layout, as figure 14.2 clearly shows, they, like adults, become unsure of where the important information is located.

Toward the right end of the continuum is Gibbons's (1995) trade book *Planet Earth/Inside Out*. Teachers' reading of this two-page spread contained none of the cross-page zigzagging found in readings of *The Magic School Bus*. They read the running text, and discussed it with their students. Still, lacking headings, the book might not create as clear a text model for readers as the final text in our continuum, Addison-Wesley's (1992) textbook. The children, having examined various science-related books, clearly identified this textbook as the one that would help them learn; it would do so, they explained, because of familiar ways various features were displayed.

We advocate choice and variety within the genre of information books in science instruction, but we now have some insights to direct that choice. *The Magic School Bus* is a very popular series, guiding many children into science because of its engaging features. Teachers might choose to use this or other dual-purpose texts at the beginnings of units of study, simply to stimulate interest. (They will, however, have to prepare to deal with various misconceptions these fantasies introduce, such as the idea that human beings can travel in an air-conditioned bus to the earth's inner core.) The 1995 Addison-Wesley textbook could also prove important in instruction. The 1995 text more closely resembles the eye-catching popular texts Martins (2002) described. It provides a perfect opportunity to guide children in thinking about how readers might strategically approach the visual and verbal information on the page. (Teachers will, however, have to teach children how and why to use the new format to learn.) More considerate text and trade books may be especially effective choices for independent learning as children build the cognitive strategies necessary for effective use of less considerate texts.

Understanding Where, and How, to Look for Information

Teachers need to consider carefully the challenges that more engaging, but less familiar visual environments entail. Our analyses suggest that readers, both young and old, head first generally for the large blocks of running text. Their prior experiences with books have told them that the meat of the meaning is located there. Our analyses also suggest that children and adults make little use of adjunct text aids such as titles, preview questions, and sometimes even pictures. This finding is hardly new: studies (e.g., Miller & Davis, 1993) suggest that even mature readers must have their attention directed to adjunct aids prior to reading to ensure that they will use them. It is for this reason that we stress that teachers must approach science texts two-dimensionally, both assisting them to understand science concepts and preparing them to learn these concepts with written text.

Let us return for a moment to figure 14.3, to examine second grade teacher Bryant's navigation of page 21 of Planet Earth. She began with the cross-section, then read the running text, then returned to the picture to point out text concepts. This processing represents a strategic use of the verbal and the visual. [Interestingly, we can see Shelly making this same type of recursive navigation in her reading of the 1995 Addison-Wesley textbook. See S2, S3, S6, and S7.] Ms. Bryant made these moves to get the science concepts across to her students. But, at no time during her read-aloud did she draw attention to her recursive reading actions. Teachers seldom do so. However, if we want children to make use of adjunct aids, teachers must model their use. The read-aloud event is a perfect context for this modeling because it allows highlighting of strategic efforts at the very moment they are employed. However, this type of incidental attention alone will not be sufficient creating good science text comprehenders.

We encourage teachers, using information science texts during reading instruction, when children are reading texts appropriate to their developmental reading level, to consider making use of the queries of Questioning the Author (Beck, McKeown, Hamilton, & Kucan, 1997). In a Questioning the Author (QtA) discussion, the teacher directs children to read a specific portion of text and then stops and asks a question. The question sparks a short discussion highlighting the during-reading thinking that expert readers do. That procedure is easily adapted to the goal of teaching the page for information text.

For example, a teacher using the text *Planet Earth/Inside Out*, could begin with a traditional QtA query: What is the author trying to say here? She could follow up with a query specific to the format of information text: What is Gail Gibbons trying to say with her illustration? How does the information in the illustration connect to what the Gail Gibbons has already told us in the running text? Why do you think she has chosen to tell us this now? Some pages of the text include illustrations that represent a process, with a series of drawings. Construction of meaning from those pages could be supported by queries specific to the layout of the drawings. Why do you think Gail Gibbons has presented information this way? Is it presented clearly? Or to help children more strategically approach the cross-sections of the book, we could ask another series of questions. Why do you think Gail Gibbons chose to label the illustrations in this way? Does it make sense to look at the illustrations and labels before reading, during reading, or after reading? Such queries could spark the type of metacognitive discussion that would teach children to make purposeful text processing decisions during their reading of science text.

CONCLUDING THOUGHTS

Considerable research, as we noted earlier, has suggested that considerate texts aid children's comprehension, but as Martins (2002) suggests and as our examples show, today's and tomorrow's science learners will be faced with many other types of texts. We realize that much work remains to be done not only to improve the ways readers process these visual environments but also to improve the ways science content is delivered. Our work in this chapter has called attention to the challenges and complexities of accessing the scientific content of today's new texts. We believe that drawing attention to these challenges is an important first step in improving text-based, science classroom instruction.

References

Alvermann, D.E. & Boothby, P.R.
(1983). A preliminary investigation of the differences in children's retention of "inconsiderate" text. *Reading Psychology, 4,* 237–246.

Armbruster, B. & Anderson, T.
(1981). *Content area textbooks.* (Reading Education Report No. 23). Urbana: University of Illinois, Center for the Study of Reading.

Armbruster, B. & Anderson, T.
(1984). *Producing "considerate" expository text: or easy reading is damned hard writing.* (Reading Education Report No. 46). Urbana: University of Illinois, Center for the Study of Reading.

Barber, J., Berger, L., Hosoume, K., Kopp, J., Sneider, & Willard, C.
(1993). *Once upon a GEMS guide: Connecting young people's literature to great explorations in math and science.* Berkeley, CA: Lawrence Hall of Science, University of California at Berkeley.

Barlow, D.
(1991). Children, books, and biology. *BioScience, 41* (3), 166–169.

Barman, C., DiSepzio, M., Guthrie, V., Leyden, M.B., & Ostlund, K.
(1992). *Science* (2nd ed.). Menlo Park, CA: Addison-Wesley.

Baumann, J.F.
(1986). Effect of rewritten content textbook passages on middle grade students' comprehension of main ideas: Making the inconsiderate considerate. *Journal of Reading Behavior, 18* (1), 1–21.

Beck, I.L., McKeown, M.G., Hamilton, R.L., & Kucan, L.
(1997). *Questioning the author: An approach for enhancing student engagement with text.* Newark, DE: International Reading Association.

Britton, B.K., Gulgoz, S., & Glynn, S.
(1993). Impact of good and poor writing on learners: Research and theory. In B.K. Britton, A. Woodward & M. Binkley (Eds.), *Learning from textbooks: Theory and practice* (pp. 1–46). Hillsdale, NJ: Erlbaum.

Brummet, D.C., Lind, K.K., Barman, C.R., DiSpezio, M.A., & Ostlund, K.L.
(1995). *Destinations in science-dance center.* Menlo Park, CA: Addison-Wesley.

Butzow, C. & Butzow, J.
(1988). Facts from fiction. *Science and Children, 25* (6), 27–29.

Camp, D.
(2000). It takes two: teaching with twin texts of fact and fiction. *The Reading Teacher, 53,* 400–408.

Crook, P.R. & Lehman, B.A.
(1991). Themes for two voices: children's fiction and nonfiction as "whole literature". *Language Arts, 68,* 34–41.

Cole.
(1987). *The magic school bus inside the earth.* New York: Scholastic.

Czerniak, C.M. & Lumpe, A.T.
(1996). Relationship between teacher beliefs and science education reform. *Journal of Science Teacher Education, 7,* 247–266.

Donovan, C.A. & Smolkin, L.B.
(2001). Genre and other factors influencing teachers' book selections for science instruction. *Reading Research Quarterly, 36,* 412–440.

Donovan, C.A. & Smolkin, L.B.
(2002). Considering genre, content, and visual features in the selection of trade books for science instruction. *Reading Teacher, 55,* 502–520.

Gibbons, G.
(1995). *Planet earth/Inside out.* New York: Mulberry.

Harlen, W.
(1997). Primary teachers' understanding in science and its impact in the classroom. *Research in Science Education, 27* (3), 323–337.

Holliday, W.G.
(2002). Selecting a science textbook. *Science Scope, 25* (4), 16–18, 20.

Hunter, B., Crismore, A., & Pearson, P.D.
(1987). Visual displays in basal readers and social studies texts. In D.M. Willows & H.A. Houghton (Eds.), *The psychology of illustration: Vol. 1. Basic research* (pp. 116–135). New York: Springer-Verlag.

Kirk, M., Matthews, C.E., & Kurtts, S.
(2001). The trouble with textbooks. *Science Teacher, 68* (9), 42–45.

James, S.
(1991). *Dear Mr. Blueberry.* New York: Margaret K. McElderry Books.

Kintsch, W.
(1994). The role of knowledge in discourse processing: A construction-integration model. In R.B. Ruddell, M.R. Ruddell & H. Singer (Eds.), *Theoretical models and processes of reading* (pp. 951–995). Newark, DE: International Reading Association.

Martins, I.
(2002). Visual imagery in school science texts. In J. Otero, J.A. Leon, & A.C. Graesser (Eds.), *The psychology of science text comprehension* (pp. 73–90). Mahwah, NJ: Lawrence Erlbaum.

Mayer, D.
(1995). How can we best use literature in teaching. *Science and Children, 32,* 16–19.

McClure, A.A. & Zitlow, C.S.
(1991). Not just the facts: Aesthetic response in elementary content area studies. *Language Arts, 68,* 27–33.

Miller, H.F. & Davis, S.F.
(1993). Recall of boxed material in textbooks. *Bulletin of the Psychonomic Society, 31,* 31–32.

Norton, D.E., Norton, S.E., & McClure, A.
(2003). *Through the eyes of a child: An introduction to children's literature* (6th ed.). Columbus, OH: Merrill Prentice Hall.

Pappas, C.C., Kiefer, B.Z., & Levstik, L.S.
(1999). *An integrated language perspective in the elementary school* (3rd ed). New York: Longman.

RAND Reading Study Group.
(2002). Reading for understanding: Toward an R&D program in reading comprehension. Santa Monica, CA: RAND.

Rice, D. & Rainsford, A.
(April, 1996). *Using children's trade books to teach science: Boon or boondoggle?* Paper presented at the annual meeting of the National Association for Research in Science Teaching, St. Louis, MO. (ERIC Document Reproduction Service ED No. 393 700).

Smardo, A.
(1982). Using children's literature to clarify science concepts in early childhood programs. *Reading Teacher, 36*, 267–273.

Skurzynski, G.
(1992). Up for discussion: Blended books. *School Library Journal, 38* (10), 46–47.

Smolkin, L.B. & Donovan, C.A.
(2001). The contexts of comprehension: The information book read aloud, comprehension acquisition, and comprehension instruction in a first grade-classroom. *Elementary School Journal, 102,* 77–122.

Smolkin, L.B. & Donovan, C.A.
(2002). How not to get lost on *The Magic School Bus*: What makes high science content read alouds? To appear in W. Saul (Ed.).

Tilgner, P.J.
(1990). Avoiding science in the elementary school. *Science & Education, 74*, 421–431.

Vardell, S.M. & Copeland, K.A.
(1992). Reading aloud and responding to nonfiction: Let's talk about it. In E.B. Freedman & D.G. Person (Eds.), *Using nonfiction trade books in the elementary classroom: From ants to zeppelins* (pp. 76–85). Urbana, IL: National Council of Teachers of English.

Walpole, S.
(1999). Changing texts, changing thinking: Comprehension demands of new science textbooks. *The Reading Teacher, 52*, 358–369.

Zack, J.E. & Osako, G.N.
(1986). Inconsiderate text and the second-grade reader. *National Reading Conference Yearbook, 35,* 339–343.

15

What Changes Need to be Implemented in Teacher Education Programs so that Teachers can Use Text Materials Effectively?

Alan Peacock and Katrina Miller

This chapter starts from the assumption, outlined in the introductory chapter, that effective use of any text material is influenced by all three dimensions of the Teacher–Learner–Text (TLT) triangle. This leads us to three distinct kinds of concerns regarding what teachers need to know, as follows.

1. The first type of concern relates to the range of types of published text material, the pedagogical styles implicit in them, access to materials and teachers understanding of what texts are intended for (*the teacher–text dimension*).
2. Second, there are concerns about the teachers' repertoire of teaching strategies and how these relate to the cultural contexts in which they operate, in terms of curriculum, location, school size, resourcing and social composition of their classes (*the teacher–learner dimension*).
3. The third type of concern has to do with the demands that different texts make on pupils, in terms of concepts, language, visual literacy, structure, format and message (*the learner–text dimension*).

RESEARCH FINDINGS RELATING TO WHAT TEACHERS NEED TO KNOW

Much of the research relating to these concerns has been discussed in detail in earlier sections. The important findings that relate to what teachers need to know are thus summarized here.

First, many kinds of text material for school pupils exist (textbooks, schemes, packs, worksheets, video, CD-ROM, websites, magazines) and a wide range of these is available to teachers in many countries. Yet even where this is the case, text material intended for pupils is rarely used, or inappropriately used, by the learners themselves (Peacock, 1995). In addition, most text material is linguistically too complex for its intended audience and makes high cognitive demands on learners (Sweller, 1994). Children also have problems with the visual imagery in many texts, yet visual literacy is not widely taught in relation to text use (Gyselinck & Tardieu, 1994; Kress and van Leeuwen, 1996); most analysis of nonfiction text tends to focus on linguistic aspects (Nuffield Foundation, 1998; Unsworth, 1991).

Second, teacher training programs often de-emphasize the use of commercially available text material, in favor of the creation by teachers of customized materials for their pupils (Ball & Feiman-Nemser, 1988). Newly qualified teachers have often had little experience of text use in Science (Peacock & Gates, 2000). In addition, the learning strategies implicit in instructional text often differ widely from those used in classrooms by teachers (Peacock, 1997), and the structure of nonfiction text is often very different from that of the narrative text used by pupils when learning to read (Van Rooyen, 1990). However, some text formats (e.g., comic strip) present no problems for most pupils (Peacock & Perold, 1995). Most nonfiction texts for pupils do not set out to teach the meta-cognitive skills required for their use (Ryf & Cleghorn, 1997).

Study of Novice Primary Teachers in the United Kingdom

Research accounts of attempts to systematically identify patterns and problems in the classroom use of nonfiction text are relatively few. Hence our study of 23 novice primary teachers in the United Kingdom set out to establish exactly how they saw the use of text in science, how they chose materials and how they used them in practice. There was a high degree of consensus amongst these teachers, despite the fact that they worked in 18 different schools and had been trained in 10 different institutions, with a variety of specialist backgrounds. The perceptions revealed by the study fell into four main categories.

(1) Nonfiction text was seen as peripheral to the direct learning of science ideas by pupils.

(2) Teachers felt that commercially published materials usually needed to be adapted in order to be of use.

(3) Science text was thought to have only a limited number of specific purposes in the science classroom.

(4) Selection or rejection of science text material was based on surface features rather than appropriateness of content or teaching approach (Peacock & Gates, 2000).

It could of course be argued that choosing not to use published text material is a perfectly legitimate option for teachers. Such a choice however has to be placed in the context of evidence that most schools worldwide still purchase (or expect the purchase of) textbooks, and expect them to be used; most primary teachers have relatively inadequate subject knowledge of science in particular; the text is often the teacher's only reliable source of science knowledge; and by creating and using their own text material for use by pupils, teachers often unwittingly create more problems for pupils than if they used published material. All this suggests that teachers would be best served by being helped to use text more effectively; in particular, it would help if teachers widened their range of strategies by which learners could use text effectively themselves.

The research quoted earlier reveals various things about teachers' training needs, if they are to use nonfiction text more effectively. Teachers in general, in all sociocultural contexts, would benefit from developing a wide range of text-related skills. In terms of the TLT triangle, these needs can be broken down as illustrated below.

The teacher–text dimension	Ways to analyze text demand How to select appropriate texts, where a choice is available
The teacher–learner dimension	How to identify a wider range of ways in which text might be used in the classroom Matching their teaching styles with those of the text being used
The learner–text dimension	How to "write" or adapt text material that does not make inappropriate or excessive demands on their pupils Giving more emphasis to nonfiction text in language and literacy learning Developing children's visual literacy Teaching text-related meta-cognitive skills; how to "read" a page of text.

The implications for training programs in different cultural contexts will be discussed in the following section.

TRAINING TEACHERS TO ANALYZE AND SELECT NONFICTION TEXT

The Teacher—Text Dimension

Two situations need considering here: (1) where teachers may not have a choice of text to be used by pupils in their classrooms, but instead are required to use a mandated text; and (2) where teachers are able to select from a range of text material available for pupils' use.

Using a Mandated Text Effectively

There are three training issues to be addressed: (1) analyzing the demands made by the text, (2) planning text use into lessons and schemes, and (3) supporting pupils when using text. Our evidence (Peacock & Gates, 2000) suggests that none of these are currently dealt with effectively in teacher education programs. Analyzing text demand will be dealt with in detail later, in relation to text choice.

Planning text use into a scheme of work involves first being clear about the objectives of each lesson or part of the scheme. A text can be used to provide background knowledge, to ask questions about the knowledge provided (e.g., in a diagram or illustration) or to give instructions for an investigation. Comparison of what the pupil's book offers with what the scheme demands will then reveal areas where there is a match: for example, the illustration on page 81 requires children to carry out an investigation into the evaporation of water, and so one lesson plan could require pupils to read the page and carry out the investigation. Trainees need to be required to build text use into their planning, not in general terms but by demonstrating which specific pages will be used by pupils, and how, in specific lessons.

Mediating text use is essential, and the discussion of children's difficulties with the example cited earlier illustrated this well. Hence teachers need training to address possible misunderstandings before beginning the activity, by asking questions such as, *"what are you going to do first? Where will you do it? What will you do next? What do you need? What will you write down?"* This approach, sometimes referred to as "Teaching the Page," has been dealt with in more detail by Walpole and Smolkin in chapter 14 in this volume.

Selecting and Using Nonfiction Text

Text appropriateness is very context-specific, in terms of the teacher, school and pupils. We noted earlier however that teachers tend to select text according to surface features, such as length, color, proportion of words to pictures, use of bold type. This may lead to teachers choosing texts that are inappropriate to the aims of the teacher's own science scheme, in terms of conceptual demand, teaching approach and visual literacy.

We have thus developed an *Index of Text Demand (ITD)* with primary teachers in mind, to help select text that will be more appropriate to their own pupils. This index uses simple criteria to focus on exactly those aspects of nonfiction text that have been shown to create problems for learners, in a range of contexts. Applying the ITD to any text is quick and simple, and provides a rough guide to the demand that it will make on the teacher's own pupils. The ITD is set out in table 15.1.

Table 15.1. Index of Text Demand (ITD)

You should first select a page or double-page spread of non-fiction text, and *considering your own pupils*, answer the following questions:

Conceptual demand
1. Are any of the ideas on the page *new* to them?
2. Are any of the concepts *abstract*?
3. Does the page contain *several concepts to be understood in order to progress*?

Language demand
4. Do the words occupy *more than 50% of the page*?
5. Does the page contain *new vocabulary*?
6. Are sentence structures *long and complex*?

Visual demand
7. Does the page contain *pictures/photographs*?
8. Does it contain a *table, chart or graph*?
9. Does it contain a *cross-sectional diagram*?
10. Does it use *symbols such as arrows or icons*?
11. Does it use illustrations which need to be *linked sequentially*, such as a cartoon, or stages in a process?

Format
12. Is the format *unfamiliar* to your pupils?
13. Do the words and sentences cut *across the page*, rather than following on down the page, as in narrative text?
14. Are words and visuals *not explicitly linked*?

Table 15.1. (Continued)

Message
15. Are *instructions ambiguous* and in need of teacher mediation?
16. Are there *practical obstacles to doing the prescribed activities* in the classroom?
17. Are the instructions *inconsistent* with your teaching style?
18. Is the text written or published in *another country or culture*?

To estimate Text Demand: count number of "yes" responses.

0–6 Low demand
7–11 Average demand
12+ High demand

Training programs should incorporate practice with the ITD across a range of nonfiction text types, in subjects such as Science, Technology, Mathematics, Geography and Citizenship. Experience of using the ITD will enable trainees to adapt and modify the index to their own needs, as well as establish the habit of assessing text demand before use. In the classroom library, nonfiction text could even be marked with the ITD score (Low, Average, High) to help pupils choose text appropriately.

There are also text types that tend not to create problems for pupils, such as comic-strip and magazine formats. These formats are more and more often used in web-based materials for pupils, and could be analyzed and used more often by trainees. A constraint on this is still pupils' access to the Internet in their classrooms: in such cases, trainees can be encouraged to download appropriate materials for use in hard copy format. Trainees must of course constantly be alert to representations of cultural hegemony in such Internet images and cultural specificity in Internet text. A critical eye here is crucial.

TEXT USE AND TEACHING STYLES

The Teacher—Learner Dimension

The training needs identified here are: (1) how to identify a wider range of ways in which text might be used in the classroom, and (2) how to match teaching styles to those of the text being used.

It has been observed in many classroom contexts that teachers employ a narrow repertoire of text use strategies, where nonfiction text is concerned. Training programs need therefore to extend this repertoire. This could be achieved in a number of ways. First, language and literacy trainers could bring subject-based text into their training programs more often, and more effectively. Science or mathematics text could well be used in training students how to teach "reading" in the wider sense. Second, time should be made for trainees to become familiar with different types of text and the pedagogical strategies (exposition, investigation, comprehension of visuals, etc.) implicit in them. This needs time spent on text analysis during training. Third, visual literacy should figure as part of all teacher education. Trainees need to be able not only to interpret diagrams and illustrations, but also to understand the kinds of visual comprehension problems their pupils encounter, and how to help them use visuals effectively. Fourth, trainees need particular help with appropriate strategies for use of text with EAL children. Selecting and using nonfiction subject-based text, and mediating its use with such pupils, is rarely given priority in training programs at present. And finally, trainees need to spend time comparing material used in language teaching with that used in nonfiction text. In particular, they need to analyze narrative and expository text for differences in use of vocabulary, syntax, format and other aspects that might need teaching.

Matching teaching styles to those of the text being used is partly a matter of text choice. But where a text is mandatory, more effective use could be made if teachers were trained to follow the pedagogical style of the text, rather than (as often happens) working against it and thus weakening its value as an earning tool. Text analysis during training is an essential precursor to this. But trainees also need encouragement and experience in the following ways.

> Making sure they themselves understand the concepts involved and the purpose of the activity required by the text
> Establishing an ethos of enquiry and activity in their classroom, rather than one of passivity, copying and recitation
> Planning their work around the text, by choosing activities that the text suggests or requires
> Making time for text-related activities to be carried out by pupils (and where necessary, plan these at appropriate times of the day or year)
> Resourcing their classroom in advance to enable pupils to fulfil text demands

This may seem a long and demanding list of tasks for trainees. Some will object that it is beyond their control, in a school pervaded by deep-rooted and inappropriate teaching styles. The justification for such a dimension in training is quite simply that without it, little improvement is likely from the low-level use of text described in chapter 9 in this volume by Murila. Cost-effectiveness of text purchase then becomes a major issue for heads, managers and administrators.

Developing Trainees' Text Mediation Skills

The Learner—Text Dimension

Research mentioned earlier indicates that trainees have difficulty in writing or adapting text material in such a way that it does not make ambiguous, inappropriate or excessive demands on their pupils. Trainees should certainly be encouraged to develop their own print materials for use by pupils; but there must be more time spent on critique and analysis of the appropriateness of materials developed, for the context in which they are to be used. Collecting and sharing a "bank" of appropriate, analyzed and trialled materials is good practice amongst groups of trainees. Where these can be stored electronically, they can subsequently be used and adapted for training with other cohorts of trainees.

Training programs could also give more emphasis to nonfiction text in language and literacy learning. A major weakness already alluded to is the lack of emphasis, in literacy programs, on developing children's visual literacy. Many nonfiction texts are constructed predominantly of visual images: "Teaching the Page" techniques need to be a part of all training programs, in order that trainees in all cultures are able to identify the purpose and content of visuals. The unnatural division between learning to teach literacy on the one hand, and learning to teach subjects on the other, would benefit from being less emphasized. It is commonplace to say that "all teachers are teachers of language" but this is rarely interpreted constructively in practice. Most science teachers do not teach their pupils to "read" science books.

This highlights the need for teaching text-related meta-cognitive skills; not only how to "read" a page of text, but also how to choose an appropriate book or section of a book, how to "fillet" (i.e., to analyze or deconstruct) it to get at the relevant parts, how to use reading and note-taking time effectively. The increased emphasis on content-testing in some cultures has had the effect of decreasing learners' awareness of the importance of such skills; memorizing the "chunks" selected for them carefully by teachers takes greater prominence, now evidenced even amongst trainees beginning their higher education.

It would be of great value if authors and illustrators of nonfiction text could build into their materials sections that address the pupil in order to teach the skills needed to use the book effectively. Introductory sections on "How to use this book" do figure in some texts, and increasingly on websites. They could however do more to help pupils manage their own learning from text, in order to minimize demands on the teacher. The goal is independent, effective use by learners.

THE CONSTRAINTS OF COMMERCIALLY PUBLISHED TEXT

Effective use of text material is still handicapped by the structure and format of the material itself, which in turn are a consequence of publishing imperatives. As Hardy explained earlier in chapter eleven, most nonfiction texts are put together by an author first being commissioned to write the words, and to provide art-work briefs. A quite separate illustrator (whom the author rarely if ever meets, and who may not have a strong grasp of the subject matter or context for use) is commissioned to draw or provide the visuals. Designers and print production personnel then work on the final layout and "look" of the text, without necessarily paying attention to what is known about learners' difficulties.

With this in mind, trainees could profitably write introductory sections for existing text material, to help them address the meta-cognitive demand. They could also cut and paste pages of text to make them more accessible to learners, perhaps by the addition of captions, icons or other instructions to readers. Taking account of Mikkila and Olkinuora's (1994) study of the benefits of "refutational" text, trainees could also be profitably engaged in adding sentences that take account of pupils' likely misconceptions ("*you may think that . . .; however . . .*"). Such exercises will help trainees to be far more likely to use text in their classrooms, and more likely to anticipate and deal with pupils' difficulties.

SUMMARY

Three kinds of learning about text are a prerequisite for trainees being able to use nonfiction text effectively, namely *analyzing* the demands made by the text, *planning* text use into lessons and schemes and *supporting* pupils when using text. The ITD has been developed to help teachers select text which will be more appropriate to their own pupils. Training programs should incorporate practice with this instrument across a range of nonfiction text types.

Familiar comic-strip and magazine formats are more and more often used in web-based materials for pupils, and could be analyzed and used more often by trainees. Language and literacy trainers could use this kind of analysis to bring subject-based text into their training programs more often, and time should be made for trainees to become familiar with the pedagogical strategies (exposition, investigation, comprehension of visuals, etc.) implicit in different examples of text. Trainees need to be able not only to interpret diagrams and illustrations, but also to understand the kinds of visual comprehension problems their pupils encounter, and how to help them use visuals effectively.

Trainees need particular help with appropriate strategies for use of text with EAL children. They need to analyze narrative and expository text for differences in use of vocabulary, syntax, format and other aspects that might need teaching. "Teaching the Page" techniques need to be a part of all training programs, in order that trainees in all cultures are able to identify the purpose and content of everything on the page. The practical nature of science makes it an excellent medium for language development, and text can play an important role in this. The need for trainees to be able to teach text-related meta-cognitive skills is therefore paramount. To help develop such skills, trainees could profitably write introductory sections for existing text material, to address the meta-cognitive demand. They could also carry out exercises involving changing pages of text to make them more accessible to learners, to take account of pupils' likely misconceptions.

Finally, trainees should not only be encouraged to develop their own print materials for use by pupils. They should also spend time on critique and analysis of the appropriateness of materials developed, for the context in which they are to be used.

THE IMPLICATIONS FOR MANAGERS OF TEACHER TRAINING PROGRAMS

The main skills required of teachers in relation to nonfiction text use relate to the three areas of *analyzing* text, *planning* for text use and *supporting* pupils whilst using text. Our experience internationally indicates that of these, only planning is dealt with extensively in most teacher education programs, regardless of culture or specialism. Literacy specialists will no doubt object that a good deal of support for text use goes on during trainees work in classrooms; but much of this, we suggest, relates to narrative text, and generally ignores all but the linguistic aspects of text use in other subjects. Training tends to focus on the subject matter knowledge of trainees and/or their generic pedagogical skills, often in relation to some national set of standards or criteria for qualification. Most such standards documents, however, make little or no mention of such aspects as nonfiction text use or visual literacy, however detailed the standards specifications are (Peacock, 2001). Attempts to train teachers in the use of specific materials (e.g., the "*Spider's Place*" materials in South Africa) have only emphasized the deficiencies in initial teacher training, where text use is concerned (Peacock & Perold, 1995).

Managers of training programs need therefore to take on board the need for attention to the issues of text analysis, planning and support for text use, with the following recommendations in mind.

> There will need to be greater collaboration between literacy trainers and subject-specific trainers, in order to focus more on the text analysis and text use issues identified here for the specific nonfiction texts used in local schools.

> Practical activities in subjects such as science and art can be related more closely to training in the use of text with EAL children. Analysis of text demand needs to be an important dimension of this collaboration.

> Visual literacy should be taught specifically by trainers in all subjects, taking account of the context in which visuals are used in their texts. Assessment should reflect this emphasis.

> Partnerships with schools need to be based on discussion and common understanding of how best to use text and to support trainees in practising such strategies during their school placements.

> Text use should be demonstrated and encouraged (rather than discouraged or ignored) by tutors involved in initial training. More use must be made of such valuable resources, especially in resource-starved contexts.

> Trainers should encourage the creation of "Resource Banks" of appropriate, analyzed and trialled materials, generated, evaluated and indexed by trainees and available for all to consult and use.

> Attention needs to be paid to the training of trainers themselves, who in many contexts may not have the repertoire of skills required to develop effective text use in their trainees.

References

Ball, D.L. & Feiman-Nemser, S.
(1988). Using textbooks and teachers' guides: a dilemma for beginning teachers and teacher educators. *Curriculum Inquiry, 18* (4), 401–423.

Gyselinck, V. & Tardieu, H.
(1994). The role of text illustrations in the construction of non-spatial mental models. In De Jong & van Hout-Wolters, *Process-oriented instruction and learning from text.* Amsterdam: VU University Press.

Kress, G. & Van Leeuwen, T.
(1996). *Reading Images: the Grammar of Visual Design.* London: Routledge.

Mikkila, M. & Olkinuora, E.
(1994). Problems of current textbooks and workbooks: Do they promote high-quality learning? In De Jong & van Hout-Wolters (Eds.), *Process-oriented instruction and learning from text.* Amsterdam: VU University Press.

Nuffield Foundation.
(1998). *Science and literacy: A guide for primary teachers.* London: Nuffield Foundation/Collins Educational.

Peacock, A.
(1995b). An agenda for research on text material in primary science for second language learners of English in developing countries. *Journal of Multilingual and Multicultural Development, 16* (5), 389–401.

Peacock, A.
(1997). The role of text material in representing science knowledge to second language learners in primary schools. *Proceedings of the Annual Meeting of the Southern African Association for Research in Mathematics and Science Education* (SAARMSE) Johannesburg, January.

Peacock, A.
(2001) The potential impact of the "Literacy Hour" on the teaching of science from text material. *Journal of Curriculum Studies, 33* (1), 25–42.

Peacock, A. & Gates, S.M.G.
(2000). Newly-qualified teachers' perceptions of the role of text material in teaching science. *Research in Science and Technological Education, 18* (2), 155–171.

Peacock, A. & Perold, H.
(1995). Helping primary teachers develop new approaches to science teaching: a strategy for the evaluation of "*Spider's Place*". *Proceedings of Annual Meeting of the Southern African Association for Research in Mathematics and Science* (SAARMSE), Cape Town.

Ryf, A., & Cleghorn, A.
(1997). The language of science: text talk and teacher talk in second language settings. *Proceedings of the Annual Meeting of the Southern African Association for Research in Mathematics and Science Education* (SAARMSE), Johannesburg.

Sweller, J.
(1994). Cognitive Load theory, learning difficulty and instructional design. *Learning and Instruction, 4*, 295–312.

Unsworth, L.
(2001) *Teaching multiliteracies across the curriculum: changing contexts of text and image in classroom practice.* Buckingham: Open University Press.

Van Rooyen, H.
(1990). *The Disparity between English as a subject and English as the medium of learning*, A Final Report of the Threshold Project. Pretoria: Human Sciences Research Council.

16

Visual Literacy in Science and Its Importance to Pupils and Teachers

Simon Gates

Ours is a visual age. We are bombarded with pictures from morning till night.

(Gombrich, 1982)

Visual literacy has been of interest to many who work in different fields, so that definitions and descriptions are legion (e.g., Hortin, 1994; Seels, 1994). Avgerinou and Ericson (1997) provide a recent review of the concept. Bearing in mind the problem of over-definition, this chapter will take as its starting point the definition cited by Pettersson (1993, p. 135):

> Visual literacy is the learned ability to interpret visual messages accurately and to create such messages, [along with the need to] translate visual images into verbal language and vice versa. (International Visual Literacy Association (IVLA), 1989)

In education there are two paths for visual literacy teaching to take: teaching generic skills, and teaching with well-designed and constructed visual materials in specific curriculum contexts. Appropriate visual materials, used by visually literate teachers, help in the construction of knowledge, its retention, recall and application. These are facets of making and using meanings with which all classroom teachers need to engage.

Children starting school are already picture users and makers. They arrive with their own visual language, and then spend years learning to become literate in reading and writing. Yet, how many are taught to get beyond the stage of "making a pretty picture of anything you like"; to learn how pictures can and do have meanings appropriate to the social culture of their school or wider community? Education has almost exclusively focused on verbal literacy, but, in spite of its many champions, visual literacy continues to be ignored wherever (as in most contexts) it is left out of the curriculum. This is strange in view of the changing position of visual images in curriculum support materials; as Unsworth (2001) makes clear, in the 1980s and 1990s, it is conspicuously the case that images have come to assume more prominence relative to print in school texts as well as in popular culture.

What kinds of experiences should teachers give pupils then, to help them interact effectively with pictures? Teachers need to judge what pupils see and understand, in their minds' eyes, from the pictures they need to use and on which they may be tested (Gates, 2001, p. 2). To do that, teachers need to be visually literate and perspicacious: they need to be able to interpret multimedia images, yet getting the right media mix is "scantily supported by research, but guided by expert experience and common-sense decisions" (Schramm, 1977, p. 34).

Seeking Out What to See

Each of us accumulates visual experiences day-by-day. These are collected through eyes that are programmed to discriminate: they actively seek out what to look for, what to inspect. The primary data are then modified centrally, so we build our own, individual visual languages. For every sighted person this is unique, personal, private and subjective.

This finding has come to light again and again. It was emphasized by Blakemore in the Reith Lectures for 1967, later published as *Mechanics of the Mind*.

> When physiologists turned their recording microelectrodes on these visual neurons, the results were a revelation. For each cell seemed not to be passively signalling the brightness or darkness of the retina . . . but to be searching for meaningful combinations of features, for the boundaries and shapes in the image that define the edge of objects (Blakemore, 1967).

Young (1978, p. 117) elaborated on this.

> We are proposing . . . that higher animals, at least, go round actively searching for things to "see" and that they "see" mainly those things that were expected because the program includes hypotheses and rules for testing them.

Hence, it is likely that children will "see" (respond to) pictures and diagrams differently, or that they will "see" what they are taught to see.

Visual Thinking

In *Visual Thinking* Arnheim (1970, p. 37) draws the same conclusion from the vantage point of a psychologist. Thinking is not divorced from perception, and visual perception is, therefore, intelligent.

> Visual perception . . . is not a passive recording of stimulus material, but an active concern of mind. The sense of sight operates selectively. The perception of shape consists in the application of form categories, which can be called visual concepts because of their simplicity and generality. Perception involves problem solving.

Arnheim (1970, p. 307) also puts in front of us the universal relevance of visual thinking, mediated through visual literacy.

> The discipline of intelligent vision cannot be confined to the art studio; it can succeed only if the visual sense is not blunted and confused in other areas of the curriculum. To try to establish an island of visual literacy in an ocean of blindness is ultimately

self-defeating. Visual thinking is indivisible. The lack of visual training in the sciences and technology on the one hand and the artist's neglect of, or even contempt for, the beautiful and vital task of making the world of facts visible to the enquiring mind, strikes me as a . . . serious ailment of our civilization . . .

No teacher can therefore afford to ignore these features of visual perception. To be of any reliable use in the classroom, pupils' and teachers' visual languages have to be used for communication, which means sharing information via dialogue in the language of pictures. We must convert our private languages into a public visual language. Visual literacy is the vocabulary and the means of using it—the visual syntax used to make pictures. In a postmodern world, pictures that have an educational function need to be discussed until their meanings are negotiated and agreed and understood by both pupils and teachers. Once literate, fluency depends on practice until we all arrive at a standard of competency in using pictures appropriate to the level of education we aim to achieve.

The semiotics of visual images, together with the visual signals sent by each of us when we engage with each other in the form of gestures and facial expressions, form essential components of communication between people. Our research shows clearly that teachers value the affective features of visual images such as brightness, simplicity, accessibility. However, there is also evidence that many cognitive features of these same images (i.e., the way in which visual images communicate science concepts) are largely ignored by teachers, as well as by those who train them (Peacock & Gates, 2000).

INFORMED VISUAL LITERACY AND DESIGN

If training in verbal skills is expected to improve thought process, assuming that one uses verbal mediation (e.g., Bruner, 1966), training teachers in the use of visual media may do the same, "given that one also uses visual thinking" (Saloman, 1972, p. 418). But until teachers know what they are doing when they use textbooks with pictures, their strategies for helping pupils to develop will be limited. We need pictures, not merely for decoration, but as functional classroom equipment. We blunder about with pictures at our peril. Lowe (1996, p. 378) draws our attention to this gap in research.

> Until quite recently, there has been comparatively little detailed study of the way individuals interact with illustrations in their own right. However, there is increasing awareness that the successful interpretation ("reading") of some of the types of illustrations used for instructional purposes may be a more demanding processing task than has been previously realised (Blystone & Dettling, 1990; Gillespie, 1993). This is particularly likely to be the case with highly abstract and specialised illustrations such as diagrams. (Constable, Campbell & Brown, 1988; Lowe, 1988)

Hartley (1978, p. 45) takes this further, to include the need to explain picture conventions.

> Little seems to be known about how children learn to interpret pictures. The emphasis placed on learning to read has not been matched with a parallel emphasis on explaining

the conventions of illustrations. This suggests that illustrations in textbooks, particularly in developing countries, are likely to be misunderstood by a large proportion of the children for whom they are intended.

Note the date of this publication, and its message, which is still largely ignored. For example, the Nuffield Foundation, in its Teachers' Guide on "Science and Literacy" (Nuffield Foundation, 1998, p. 47) provides an example of how to analyze a double-page spread of science text that completely ignores the illustrations on the pages.

Astute use of visuals in active learning moves a class toward the goals of active, independent learning. Schramm (1977, p. 102) suggests pictures have uses throughout the curriculum, as they are:

> . . . effective in attracting attention; in recalling previously stored elements of a learning process; in presenting the main stimulus material, particularly when that requires something that an individual learner or a classroom teacher would find difficult to present; and in encouraging transfer of learned skills and knowledge to new problems. But they may also be useful in other ways—for example, in guiding a learner through an exercise in learning.

Lowe's work also suggests that particular attention should be given, by teachers, to the interpretation of diagrams, because they are used in specialized contexts, and Dondis (1973) explains that visual literacy and visual design must therefore work together to create suitable products for teachers to use. In *Reading Images: the Grammar of Visual Design*, Kress and van Leeuwen (1996) focus on design for successful communication, rather than decisions about specific content. Where attempts to communicate content through effective design succeed, visual literacy turns viewers into users of meaningful pictures.

ACTIVE USE OF SUPPORTED IMAGES

Whatever the nature of the learning processes may be, assisting the active generation of effective mental images is most important when making and using visual images in teaching and learning. Hence teachers have to engage their pupils in active use of visual images in texts, with teacher as "scaffolder" or knowledgeable guide. Each of us brings our "beholder's share" to the task, so we start from different viewpoints (Gombrich, 1982). When we look at a visual image, we can only see what the programs we have detect, and the experience to recognize, gained from data previously input to our programs—this is the stuff we use in our negotiations about making meanings when we use pictures. These are exactly the skills that teachers need to teach their pupils, as well as giving them the opportunity to practise.

Still photographs of different kinds are used in teaching, and it may seem that these require little interpretation. However, photographs are often linked by drawings or symbols, and often shift from the naturalistic to the more general "cartoon" images, created by selective inclusion, exclusion and emphasis (McCloud, 1993). The line between the "real" photo and the computer-generated image becomes less and less clear, as software and technology develops: recent films such as Lord of the Rings are a testament to this. There is therefore no escape from the need for informed decision-making by educators. Images are constructed from parts put together using rules and conventions to make composites such as diagrams, models, graphs and charts. Subject-specific rules create labeled, titled, numbered and annotated images from symbols, together with the conventions and notations of mathematics and written language. All these rules and conventions may need teaching to pupils, if they are to make best use of visual material.

Linking Words and Images

Visual images in school books are usually supported by words. Our dependence on words to inform and operate our visual literacies has been emphasized by Gombrich (1999). Yet recent studies in primary classrooms in the United Kingdom suggest that pupils find it very difficult to link visual material to written text without help, and that strategies taught during literacy lessons are not often transferred to the use of text-books during science lessons (Peacock & Weedon, 2002). The teaching of such skills therefore needs to be situated in the specific context of a subject, and often in the specific context of a text being used.

For example, research on carbon cycle diagrams explored with secondary science teachers in England suggested that their visual literacy was more apparent than real, since the removal of word clues made it difficult for them to talk their way round a diagram (Gates, 2001). Wileman (1993) illustrates the varying levels of support that may be found in visuals, and thus the degree of visualization needed, which has a bearing on the ease with which some of us may interpret—or misinterpret—a visual image (see figure 16.1).

FROM NOVICE TO EXPERT

Peacock and Gates (2000) investigated perceptions of the role of text material in teaching science among newly qualified teachers in primary schools—schools for 5–11-year-olds in Southern England. Of the 23 teachers who took part, only four had trained in science, but all taught the subject since, in England, at this level primary school teachers are usually expected to teach all subjects to one class. For whole-class teaching with younger children, most of the teachers chose "Big Books," that is, large-format picture books or posters, as "triggers" for discussion. The absence of print was seen by the teachers as a bonus, and allowed them and their children to generate and introduce vocabulary associated with science, rather than grapple with unfamiliar words.

For older classes these teachers added books with more text and their own work-sheets. As part of the study, these teachers were invited to examine a wide range of pupils' science text. They used a "flick-through" appraisal, and focused on the more accessible child-centered issues to do with color, format, thickness and attractiveness; but significantly, they took the factual content on trust, since they did not feel they had enough science subject knowledge to be discerning about it. This limited their ability to construct suitable narratives around the text and visual images. They made clear that they had encountered some picture types during training, but none could remember a course dedicated to training in either visual literacy, or the context in which different picture types might help them construct knowledge with pupils, let alone reinforce, learn and apply it.

This raises two subject-knowledge issues for teachers. First, strategies for interpretation available to novices, along with their level of science knowledge, limits them to a

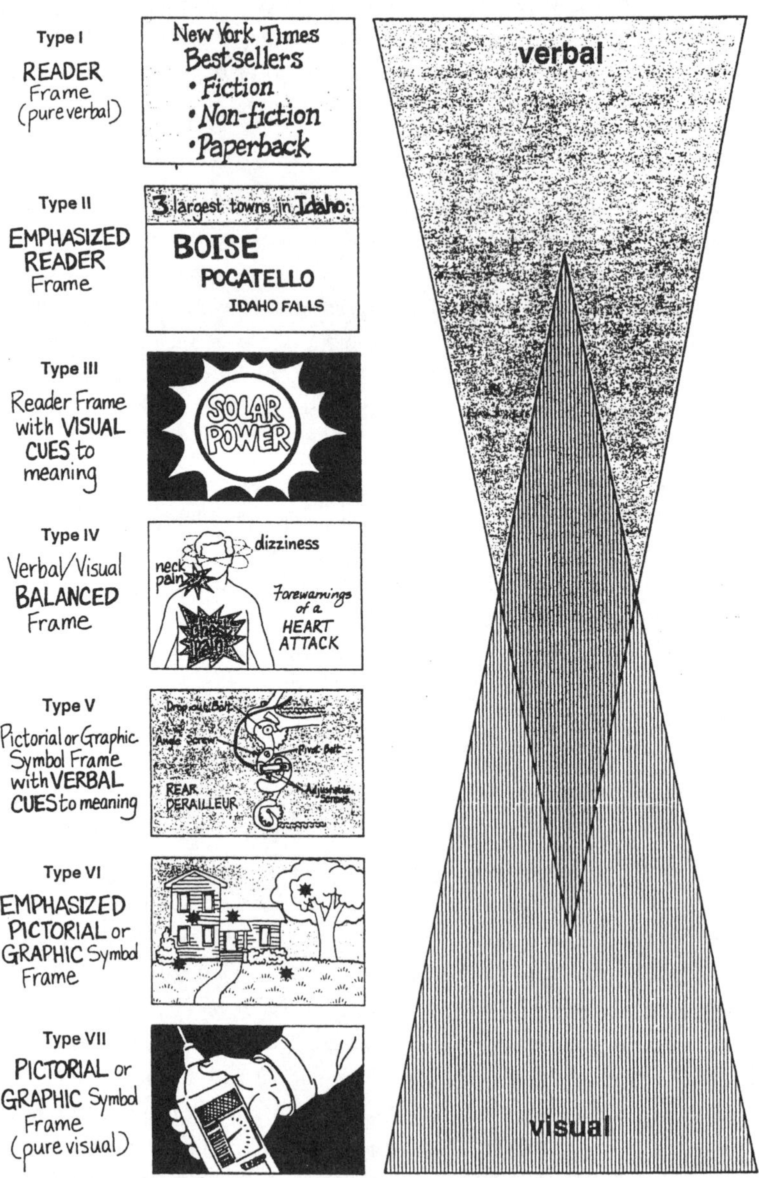

Figure 16.1. Wileman's typology: How visual is your visual aid?

superficial use of pictures for teaching. Second, the use of a variety of diagrams is advocated, because they re-present an object or a theory in a manageable form, a purposeful abstraction to aid explanation. For teacher to do either, Bennett and Carré (1993, p. 18) cite Anderson's (1991) argument that content knowledge is of central importance in teaching science. They report research that indicated that primary teachers in training changed their positions so little that some understood what they were about less than able 11-year-olds.

Lowe (1996) has also highlighted the need for content knowledge, since novices and experts review diagrams in specialist fields with different levels of insight. He uses the example of weather maps to demonstrate that, where teachers are also novices they lack domain-specific, situational content knowledge. So they, like their pupils, only bring the general visual skills of domain-general and visuo-spatial understandings to the problem. Hence teachers must not only acquire visual literacy skills but also sufficient subject matter knowledge of the content, if they are to use visual elements effectively in their teaching.

EFFECTIVE REPRESENTATIONS

The choice and use of effective visual representations has been seen as crucial to learning by much research into teacher development. To move from novice to expert therefore involves widening the repertoire of representational skills available for use.

Bruner (1966, p. 28) introduces the three parallel representational emphases that children develop, for processing information and for representing it—*enactive*: "through manipulation, and action"; *iconic*: "through perceptual organization and imagery"; *symbolic*: "through symbolic apparatus." These are not stages, they are emphases, each added to the one before, and by the time pupils change to "senior" schools at the start of their "teen" years, most should be capable of deploying all three to acquire new concepts, learn new narratives, solve novel problems. Teachers may not know how children achieve these transitions, but reflective practice offers some successful classroom strategies for those with visual insights.

To be able to modify children's various frameworks of science concepts, then, teachers must have "grown beyond them" themselves. It is difficult to see how teachers can use pictures purposefully with a class if they themselves cannot see into them and thus have no strategies for getting beyond their use as decorative illustrations.

TAKING A LOOK AT DIAGRAMS IN PARTICULAR

Published collections of visual images provide the user with plenty of experiences of ways of presenting information visually (Lockwood, 1969; Tufte, 1997). Time spent with such publications helps to train the teacher's eye in visually literate output. Lockwood (1969, p. 6) states:

> There is a real need for the presentation at all levels of statistical and explanatory information in a way which is clear, and attractive. By looking through the illustrations, it is apparent which do this, and which are not so successful. . . . Diagrams are not things which happen. They need to be as carefully considered as any other aspect of design. My hope is to get designers to produce better solutions and new approaches to the older problem of communicating clearly and with interest.

Petterrson (1993, p. 209) describes diagrams as,

> illustrations that systematically show the relationship between various factors. There are many kinds of diagrams. It is far too easy to make diagrams confusing, difficult to understand, and/or misleading. Diagrams need to be correct and simple.

Diagrams allow information to be located, so that any number of elements may be clustered in selected positions on the page (Larkin & Simon, 1987). This has advantages over linear sequencing in speech or writing, for exploring some kinds of problems, provided the diagrams are constructed effectively. However, pupils brought up largely on a diet of narrative text may find it difficult to "navigate" their way around such diagrams, indicating the need for teaching the conventions inherent in diagrams such as the use of arrows.

Lowe (1993) suggests that instructional diagrams should limit their information content to a small (less than 10) number of pieces whilst Bruner (1966, p. 12) sees this in terms of mental information handling.

> We may be limited in our attention span, but the semantic squeeze is enormous. This may not be appropriate for pictures—maybe they have their own system for squeezing information and compacting it, so they are not cluttered as soon as we think. Compacting or condensing is important. Let me only suggest here that compacting or condensing is the means whereby we fill our seven slots with gold rather than dross.

There is a distinction to be made here, however, between diagrams we use, and those we have had a hand in creating. Bruner's reference to the possibility that pictures may "not be as cluttered as we think" may apply to those that we ourselves construct. Evidence for this comes from Kinchin's work with schoolchildren making concept maps. In his experience they can handle concept maps with 20–30 component entities (Kinchin, 2000). It may be that making such relational diagrams for yourself makes all the difference to the ease with which you can make and hold their meanings in your head.

Another paradox to be faced is that some diagrams have a simple appearance because they are abstract. Adding iconic and digital components (Schramm, 1977) makes them more concrete, more supported by words and other digital codes, but, at first sight, more complicated. There are, however, "attention-saving skills in perception that are imparted and then become the basis for understanding the icons we construct for representing things by drawing, diagram, and design" (Bruner, 1966, p. 26). Once learnt, these may provide a way forward.

VISUAL NARRATIVES IN SCIENCE——MULTIMODAL AND MULTI-GENRE LITERACY

Lemke (1998, p. 87) states,

> Science is not done, is not communicated, through verbal language alone. It *cannot* be. The "concepts" of science are not solely verbal concepts, though they have verbal components. They are semiotic *hybrids*, simultaneously and essentially verbal, mathematical, visual-graphical, and actional-operational. The . . . textual genres of science are historically and presently, fundamentally and irreducibly, *multimedia genres*.

The recent initiative in England for "literacy in science" seems, once again, to have eclipsed all except verbal literacies. Yet, science teachers need to use images on two levels: (a) to guide and practice the class in visual literacy—to make meanings transparent;

(b) to ensure their content-related meanings are appropriate. Unsworth (1997, p. 35) writes about "reading images: the visual construction of meaning" in science.

> ...the use of images in science involves selective deployment of visual resources necessary for pictorial constructions of specialized knowledge.

And, according to Kress and Van Leeuwen (1996, pp. 168–171), "young learners . . . need to be gradually and critically apprenticed to this visual scientific coding orientation." We can facilitate this by drawing on knowledge about the "grammar" of images in using science texts and in generating learning experiences to help students bridge from more familiar visual coding orientations to those of science and technology. An example of this might be teaching pupils the many uses of arrows in science diagrams, for example the science-specific employment of arrows to indicate both the direction and size of a force. Nor does teaching the uses of arrows simply mean learning to interpret them: it also means learning to employ them appropriately. Pupils need to play different "games" in the three sciences, each of which deploys some subject-specific representations (Shayer & Adey, 1981). These games may help them learn the grammar or conventions of the visual image types used in science texts.

Perhaps the greatest range of image types, and even pedagogic dependency on visual representations, is in Biology (AQA, 2000). Teaching some visual literacy skills in Biology is long established in England, since national test questions used to require candidates to construct "pictures" and label diagrams in their answers. Questions such as: "Make a large, fully labeled diagram to illustrate the *carbon cycle*" provided opportunities for the construction of annotated diagrams, seen by some teachers and their pupils as efficient point-scoring answer formats. However, the skills needed to make and interpret such diagrams (rather than copy them) are unlikely to be taught to pupils below secondary school level, even though such biological diagrams proliferate in primary school texts.

Carbon Cycle Diagrams: A Case Study

Not only has the landscape of pictures in secondary biology texts changed: in England, the landscape of exam papers has reversed. These papers now contain many and varied visual representations, fed by a sustained demand for novel images to supply "unseen" questions in future test papers, to try to ensure that each next test is fair. Consequently, neither teachers nor their pupils can afford to ignore the range of external representations used in biology.

In Biology, the carbon cycle is a descriptive narrative; it relates to the "report" genre given in Unsworth (2001, p. 23). This topic consists of a sequence of facts, selected to tell the story at a level appropriate for secondary science education. An "appropriate" account would meet the needs of the age group and ability range in the class being considered. Concrete and more abstract concepts allow progression from the familiar, to general conclusions and links with other topics. Work on the carbon cycle with pupils is unlikely to be linear. Side issues will appear in the story that unfolds in a classroom. With experience, swift decisions will be made by a teacher during the lesson to admit issues raised by pupils or to close down their exploration. Description and explanation interweave in a nonlinear fashion as the teacher sees fit.

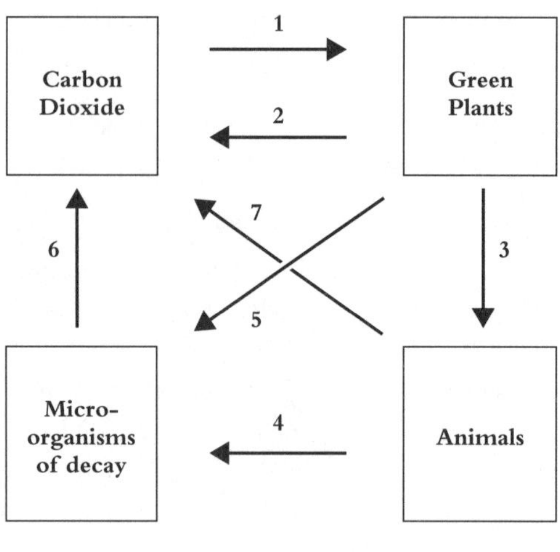

Figure 16.2. Carbon cycle verbal diagram

The carbon cycle features in the mandatory Revised National Curriculum (DfEE, 2000), implemented via Exam Board syllabuses in England. Two versions of the carbon cycle are presented here: one verbal, and one visual. The verbal version has appeared, unaltered, in exam syllabuses over several years, and will be tested at least until 2003. It is shown in figure 16.2.

The constant cycling of carbon is called the carbon cycle.
In the carbon cycle:

➢ Carbon dioxide is removed from the environment by green plants for photosynthesis; the carbon from the carbon dioxide is used to make carbohydrates, fats and proteins which make up the body of plants;
➢ Some of the carbon dioxide is returned to the atmosphere when green plants respire;
➢ When green plants are eaten by animals and these animals are eaten by other animals, some of the carbon then becomes part of the fats and proteins which make up their bodies;
➢ When animals respire some of this carbon becomes carbon dioxide and is released into the atmosphere;
➢ When plants and animals die, some animals and microbes feed on their bodies; carbon is released into the atmosphere as carbon dioxide when these organisms respire. . . .

By the time microbes and detritus feeders have broken down the waste products and dead bodies of organisms in ecosystems and cycled the materials as plant nutrients, all the energy originally captured by green plants has been transferred.
(NEAB GCSE Science: Biology (1161) 1998:33–34, and AQA GCSE Biology (3411) 2000.

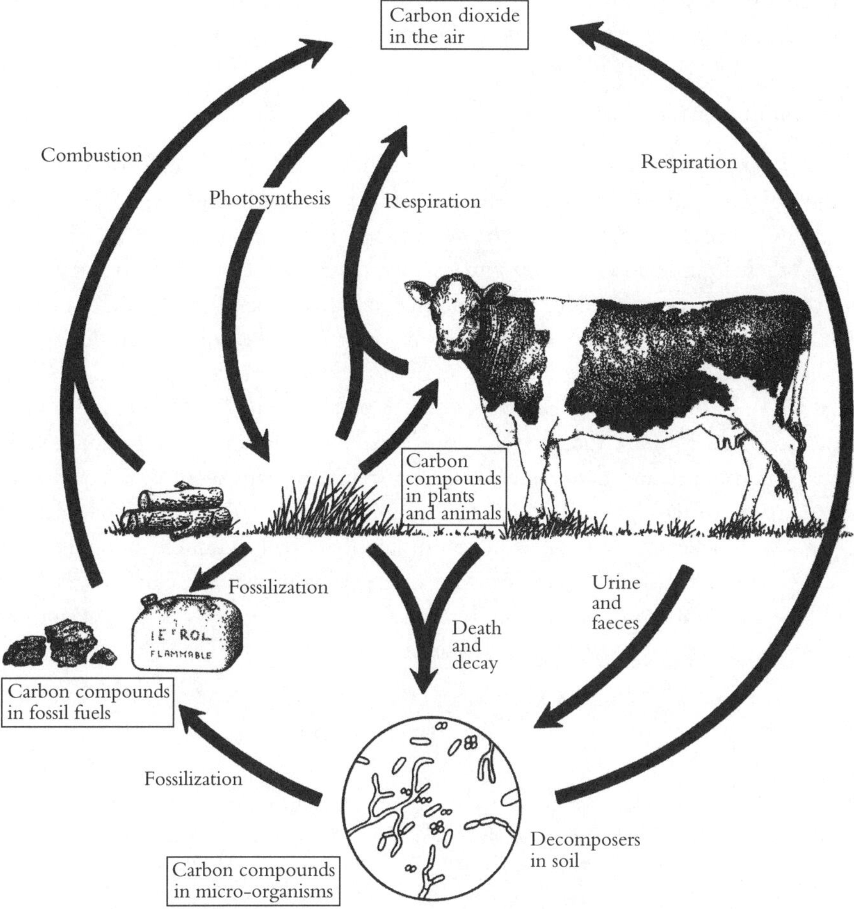

Figure 16.3. The carbon cycle

There are endless possible versions of this story, but to be complete and unadorned, they must all contain an irreducible number of component entities and processes. There are four components, linked to seven processes. Put together, these form a fixed, repeating sequence, where the end becomes the beginning. Written or spoken as linear sequences, they can be drawn as circles, or cycles. A visual version is shown in figure 16.3. However, the diagram, though simple, only makes sense once the key has been digested. Few such diagrams in either textbooks or exam papers have keys. This leaves the teacher with the task of revealing the meanings of the conventions used in it, and assumes the scientific knowledge and willingness to do so. Recent research has shown that some teachers may not be able to do this without specific training (Gates, 2002) particularly in developing countries where teachers have usually had much less training (see Murila, chapter 9).

The above diagram is abstract and lacks pupil appeal. Textbooks have more iconic, naturalistic hybrids, designed to get and hold attention. One such diagram, appreciated by teachers interviewed in a study about external representations of the carbon cycle, is shown as figure 16.2. Teachers found this diagram more effective, despite it still being difficult to interpret, on the grounds that they could identify processes with visual representations of the elements involved in the process.

In Conclusion

Visual literacy is a powerful teaching skill, enabling the use of purpose-made pictures in the dialogues, or conversations, between pupils and with their teachers. Visual images are an essential element of the form and content of conversations about science and many other things. Those who are visually literate can translate visual language in and out of speech and writing. The visual and the verbal complement each other's virtues. Pictures cannot assert, cannot provide closure. Precise spoken or written descriptions can be turgid, whereas diagrams can demonstrate relationships at a glance. These processes of creating pictures and translating them allow pupils and teachers to negotiate useful meanings within subject domains across the whole curriculum. Multimodal, multi-genre dialogues reveal where concepts are transparent or opaque, where they are right or wrong. Such penetrating insights facilitate attainment of syllabus content goals, enhance the self-esteem and promote the individual fulfillment of pupils and teachers. They contribute to inclusive and successful educational communities. Hence the importance of incorporating the teaching and learning of visual literacy into the curriculum, from the beginning of education.

References

Anderson, C.
(1991). Policy implications of research on science teaching and teachers' knowledge. In M. Kennedy (Ed.), *Teaching academic subjects to diverse learners*. New York: Teachers College Press.

Arnheim, R.
(1970). *Visual thinking*. London: Faber and Faber.

Assessment and Qualifications Alliance (AQA).
(2000). *General Certificate of Secondary Education (GCSE) Biology (3411)*, 42–43.

Avgerinou, M. & Ericson, J.
(1997). A review of the concept of visual literacy. *British Journal of Educational Technology*. 280–291.

Bennett, N. & Carré, C. (Eds.).
(1993). *Learning to teach*. London: Routledge.

Blakemore, C.
(1967). *Mechanics of the mind*. The Reith Lectures, broadcast by the British Broadcasting Corporation (BBC), London.

Blystone R. V. & Dettling, B. C.
(1990). Visual literacy in science text books. In M. Rowe (Ed.), *What research says to the science teacher: The process of knowing* (pp. 19–40). National Science Teachers Association.

Bruner, J.S.
(1966). *Toward a theory of instruction*. Harvard: University Press, Cambridge, Massachusetts.

Constable, H., Campbell, R., & Brown, R.
(1988). Sectional drawings from science books: An experimental investigation into pupils' understanding. *British Journal of Educational Psychology, 58*, 89–102.

Department for Education and Employment.
(2000). *Science: The National Curriculum for England: Key Stages 1–4.*

Dondis, D.A.
(1973). *A primer of visual literacy.* Cambridge, Massachusetts: MIT Press.

Gates, S.
(2001). Using the language of pictures for A-level biology teaching. *Salters-Nuffield Advanced Biology Newsletter, 4*, 2–3.

Gillespe, C.S.
(1993). Reading graphic displays: What teachers should know. *Journal of reading, 36*, 350–354.

Gombrich, E.H.
(1982). *The image and the eye: Further studies in the psychology of pictorial representation.* London: Phaidon.

Gombrich, E.H.
(1999). *The uses of images.* London: Phaidon.

Hartley, J.
(1978). *Designing instructional text.* London: Kogan Page.

Horton, J.A.
(1994). Theoretical foundations of visual learning. In D. Moore and F.M. Dwyer (Eds.), *Visual literacy: A spectrum of visual learning.* Englewood Cliffs: Educational Technology.

International Visual literacy Association (IVLA).
(1989). Untitled leaflet.

Kinchin, I.M.
(2000). Concept mapping in biology. *Journal of Biological Education, 34* (2), 61–68.

Kress, G. & van Leeuwen, T.
(1996). *Reading Images: The grammar of visual design.* London: Routledge.

Larkin, J.H. & Simon, H.A.
(1987). Why a diagram is (sometimes) worth ten thousand words. *Cognitive Science, 11*, 65–99.

Lemke, J.
(1998). Multiplying meaning: visual and verbal semiotics in scientific text. In J.R. Martin and R. Veel, *Reading science: critical and functional perspectives on discourses of science.* London: Routledge.

Lockwood, A.
(1969). *Diagrams: A visual survey of graphs, maps, charts and diagrams for the graphic designer.* London: Studio Vista.

Lowe, R.K.
(1988). "Reading" scientific diagrams: Characterising components of skilled performance. *Research in Science Education, 18* (1), 12–122.

Lowe, R.K.
(1993). *Successful instructional diagram*. London: Kogan Page.

Lowe, R.K.
(1996). Background knowledge and the construction of a situational representation from a diagram. *European Journal of Psychology of Education, 11* (4), 377–397.

McCloud, S.
(1993). *Understanding comics: The invisible art*. New York: Harper Collins.

Moore, D.M. & Dwyer, F.M. (Eds.).
(1994). *Visual literacy: A spectrum of visual learning*. Englewood Cliffs: Educational Technology Publications.

Northern Examinations and Assessment Board (NEAB).
(1998). *GCSE Science: Biology (1161) pp. 33–34*.

Nuffield Foundation.
(1998). *Teachers' guide on science and literacy*. Nuffield.

Peacock, A. & Gates, S.
(2000). Newly qualified primary teachers' perceptions of the role of text material in teaching science. *Research in Science and Technological Education, 18* (2), 155–171.

Peacock, A. & Weedon, H.
(2002). Children working with text in science: disparities with "Literacy Hour" practice. *Research in Science and Technological Education, 20* (2), 185–197.

Pettersson, R.
(1993). *Visual information*. Englewood Cliffs: Educational Technology Publications.

Saloman, G.
(1972). Can we affect cognitive skills through visual media? An hypothesis and initial findings. *Audio-Visual Communications Review, 20* (4), 401–422.

Seels, B.A.
(1994). Visual literacy: The definition problem. In D.M. Moore and F.M. Dwyer (Eds.), *Visual literacy: a spectrum of visual learning*. Englewood Cliffs: Educational Technology Publications.

Schramm, W.
(1977). *Big media, little media: Tools and technologies for instruction*. London: Sage

Shayer, M. & Adey, P.
(1981). *Towards a science of science teaching: Cognitive development and curriculum demand*. London: Heinemann.

Tufte, E.R.
(1997). *Visual explanations, images and quantities: Evidence and narrative*. Cheshire, Connecticut: Graphics Press.

Unsworth, L.
(1997). Scaffolding reading of science explanations: accessing the grammatical and visual forms of specialized knowledge. Reading: Klewer.

Unsworth, L.
(2001). *Teaching multi-literacies across the curriculum: Changing contexts of text and image in classroom practice*. Buckingham: Open University Press.

Wileman, R.
(1993). *Visual communicating*. Englewood Cliffs: Educational Technology Publications.

Young, J.Z.
(1978). *Programs of the brain*. Oxford: Oxford University Press.

17

Friendly Web Pages: Their Development and Use

Robertta H. Barba

eb pages, including science websites, are often packed with facts and concepts and filled with inaccurate, poorly organized, and uninteresting information (Blankenhorn, 2002; Herring, 2001). In spite of this, surveys show teachers spend a large amount of on-line time encouraging students to visit websites and to use websites as an authority source in the science classroom (Christian, 1997; McNulty, 2002). Difficulties students encounter in comprehending information found at websites, may be more attributable to their being reader "unfriendly" rather than their being too difficult for the targeted age group (Dreher & Singer, 1989). Low-verbal learners, students with limited English proficiency, and students from culturally diverse backgrounds often find the textual content of science websites difficult to understand even when those students have a basic mastery of the English language. Friendly websites are those that have been constructed and developed with a consideration for the attributes of considerate prose, page layout and design, user interactivity and/or navigation, and instructional devices.

CONSIDERATE PROSE OR FRIENDLY TEXT

Considerate prose or friendly text helps the learner recall background information, perceive relationships among ideas, make inferences, and draw conclusions. Textual passages in websites should assist students in constructing declarative knowledge of science facts, concepts, and rules and principles. Many websites are not friendly in that they do not assist learners in structuring new knowledge. Text-friendly websites are those that incorporate a consideration for organization, cohesion, conceptual density, meta-discourse, and readability of prose.

Text Organization

Text organization not only includes the purpose and arrangement of textual materials in a website, but also the choice of rhetorical patterns used to show the relationship among ideas. The five commonly used rhetorical patterns found in textual passages are:

(1) the question and answer format (response pattern),
(2) the cause and effect relationship (covariance pattern),
(3) the sequencing of events in chronological order (temporal pattern),
(4) the comparison and contrasting of characteristics (adversative patterns), and
(5) the listing of characteristics to define concepts and ideas (attribution patterns).

The most commonly used text organization patterns for science websites are question and answer (Frequently Asked Questions or FAQs), compare and contrast, and cause and effect patterns. Many science students, especially elementary-aged children have difficulty constructing meaning from textual materials that use the adversative and covariance patterns of text organization. Websites, which use the response, temporal, and attribution rhetorical patterns, have been shown to increase student comprehension and, thus, are reader friendly (Berninger, Whitaker, & Ferg, 1996; Klusewitz & Lorch, 2000; Tyree, Fiore, & Cook, 1994).

Cohesion

Cohesion refers to how website authors tie information together from sentence to sentence, paragraph to paragraph, and web page to web page. Cataphora is a cohesion pattern used when cited elements point to a later referent in the text or to a secondary page at a website. Anaphora, on the other hand, is used when text passages point to a prior referent or to a higher-level web page. Five cohesive patterns are commonly used in textual passages:

(1) constructing sentences or phrases such that word's meaning depends on a previous word (reference),
(2) repetition of words or the use of synonyms (lexical cohesion),
(3) deletion of previously stated words or ideas (ellipsis),
(4) substitution, and
(5) conjunction.

Research has shown that the relative lack of cohesion makes science text passages boring, slows the reading rate of students, lowers reading comprehension rates, and reduces student recall (Bavin, 2000; Blankenhorn, 2002; Leahy, 1995; Lewin, 1998). Friendly websites employ all types of cohesive devices to tie together sentences, paragraphs, and web pages. Cohesion increases student comprehension of the written material. Writers of science websites need particularly to include reference, lexical, and ellipsis patterns of cohesion to benefit students who have difficulty comprehending verbal materials. Additionally, the use of hyperlinking or connecting students to on-line glossaries can improve cohesion in websites (Ojala, 2000).

Explication

Writers use explication when they state facts, ideas, and their relationships directly instead of requiring readers to infer, organize, or construct the relationships themselves.

Websites, especially science websites, tend not to explicate information systematically. Explication devices include:

> vocabulary (defining new terms using language familiar to the student),
> background knowledge (relating new ideas to students' prior knowledge), and
> organizing ideas with real-world applications.

Friendly science text passages activate students' prior knowledge, use common analogies or analogies that are part of the student's milieu, and present readers with real-world applications of new knowledge (Mioduser, Nachmias, Lahav, & Oren, 2000; Lewin, 1999). The use of real-world knowledge, culturally familiar or culturally syntonic examples, and everyday vocabulary is especially important for students using science websites. Often, readers are unfamiliar with the concepts and thus need cognitive hooks to understand what is being said.

Conceptual Density

Conceptual density refers to the number of new ideas and vocabulary words contained in a textual passage. Websites are often conceptually dense; that is, they introduce many concepts in a very short textual passage. Research shows that friendly text passages use wordier text, while controlling the introduction of new concepts. Explication helps students bridge the gap between their own knowledge and experience and new knowledge contained in the website (Kumpf, 2000; Lewin, 1999). Web textual passages should be of sufficient length so that concepts are explained in detail, so that readers can bring prior knowledge to their understanding of the content material.

Meta-Discourse

Meta-discourse is like a conversation between the author and the reader. It occurs when the author of a textual passage talks directly to the reader about the information in the website. Meta-discourse may include statements of textual goals, such as "You will learn . . ." Meta-discourse may assist the learner in previewing or recalling prior knowledge: "You recall that you have learned . . ." or "When you were a child . . ." Stressing the importance of an idea to the reader ("You realize that this is important . . .") is a form of meta-discourse. Finally, stressing an attitude toward a fact or an idea ("Your attitude toward . . .") is a use of meta-discourse.

Research indicates that readers prefer textual materials that use this interaction between the author and the reader, that is, materials that help them to negotiate and personalize meaning (Delahunty, 2001). Previous research studies have shown that the use of meta-discourse improves a reader's comprehension of information that the author is attempting to convey (Cheng & Steffensen, 1996; Kumpf, 2000; Kramarski & Feldman, 2000). Finally, research indicates that meta-discourse increases students' declarative learning (Cheng & Steffensen, 1996; Kumpf, 2000).

Readability

Are science students able to "read" science websites? In an effort to determine an answer to this question, a survey of websites was undertaken for this chapter. Thirty-one websites, recommended by the National Science Teachers Association as being appropriate for children, were surveyed (see table 17.1). Using a sample size of approximately 1,000 words from each site, it was determined that the average science website had a grade equivalent of approximately 6.46. The Flesch-Kincaid Grade Levels of the surveyed websites ranged from 2.6 to 12, with a standard deviation of 2.58.[1]

The Reading Easescore for the same science websites was computed to be 61.16. The Reading Ease scale ranges from 0 to 100. The higher the reading ease score, the easier the passage is to read. Conversely, the lower the reading ease score, the more difficult the textual passage. In the case of the surveyed websites, the Reading Ease scores ranged from 14.4 to 84 with a standard deviation of 19.01 points.

When dealing with readability, questions such as, "are sentences long enough to explicate adequately cause/effect relationships?" "are sentences long enough to define new terms?" and "are sentences long enough to compare and contrast ideas?" become salient. Two-hundred-twenty common words (e.g., a, the, and, some, but, to, from) make up 75 percent of the material found in the average textual passage. Including these common words in readability formulae do not give an accurate picture of the level of difficulty of textual materials.

In writing of readability and websites MacColl and White (1998) point out that, the focus in website design should be on the audience. According to these authors, website designers should (1) simplify their language, (2) create simple tabular material when using large amounts of data, (3) incorporate inviting graphics, (4) enlist the aid of journalists and other communicators to facilitate the development of friendly text, and (5) make certain that data supports the conclusions.

Friendly science web pages are those that incorporate the elements of considerate text. They meet the educational needs of learners by including a consideration for organization, cohesion, conceptual density, meta-discourse, and readability of prose.

Page Layout and Design

In addition to including considerate prose, designers of friendly web pages should incorporate "good" page layout and design in their work. Williams and Tollett (2000) point out that anyone can make an ugly web page and lots of people do. They go on to state "the only reason so many people make bad web pages is that they don't understand basic principles of page layout and design" (Williams & Tollett, 2000). They also note that alignment, proximity, repetition, and contrast are principles that underlie every printed piece whether on screen or elsewhere.

Alignment

Alignment simply means that items on the web page are lined up with each other. The lack of alignment has been identified as the single most prevalent problem on web pages (Williams & Tollett, 2000). As a rule, nothing should be placed on a web page at random. Everything (banners, bars, buttons, text, navigation aids, and graphics) should have a reason for being where it is. Alignment doesn't mean that everything is aligned along the same edge; it means that everything is either aligned left, or aligned right, or center aligned. Alignment includes both vertical and horizontal alignment.

Table 17.1. Readability of Science Websites

Name of site	URL	Flesch Reading Ease	Flesch–Kincaid Grade Level
Operation RubyThroat★	http://www.rubythroat.org	14.4	12.0
Academic Resources.Net	http://www.academicresources.net	28.2	11.6
The Science of Energy WebSite	http://www.nsta.org/Energy/	77.3	3.9
All About GPS: Sherlock Holmes' Guide	http://www.allgps.com	65.8	5.9
Annenberg/CPE: Journey North★	http://www.learner.org	47.0	9.0
Athro, Limited	http://www.athro.com	40.4	8.9
Beyond Books	http://www.beyondbooks.com	78.0	3.5
Bottomquark	http://www.bottomquark.com	58.6	6.4
Bugscope	http://bugscope.beckman.uiuc.edu	35.3	9.7
CIESE	http://www.k12science.org	54.1	8.0
Concepts for Chemistry Class	http://members.home.net/jdenuno/chemconcepts.htm	53.8	8.6
Crystal Ball Science★	http://www.crystalballscience.com	65.5	6.3
CuteScience.com	http://www.cutescience.com	84.0	2.6
Dr. Chordate Sings Songs of Science	http://www.tranquility.net/~scimusic	75.8	5.0
Education World★	http://www.educationworld.com	59.8	6.6
The Flying Turtle	http://www.ftexploring.com	67.7	4.8
For Kids, Teens & Educators★	http://vm.cfsan.fda.gov/~dms/educate.html	74.9	4.4
GIS in K–12 Schools★	http://www.esri.com/industries/k-12/index.html	34.8	9.9
HOT Science	http://www.myschoolonline.com	61.7	6.8
Kids page★	http://www.delta-education.com/kids	83.3	2.9
SEED★	http://www.slb.com/seed	54.1	6.8
SCI + Mate	http://science-math-technology.com	8.8	4.1
Science Fair and Project Ideas★	http://members.ozemail.com.au/~macinnis/scifun	83.7	4.9
Discrepant Event Demonstrations★	http://www.scienceinquiry.com/demo3-38.htm	80.6	5.0
Science PlayWiths★	http://members.ozemail.com.au/~macinnis/scifun	81.6	4.0
Science@NASA★	http://science.nasa.gov	73.7	4.2
Sciencemaster★	http://www.sciencemaster.com	28.0	10.2
Seeing Our World in Different Light	http://sirtf.caltech.edu/Education/IRapp/benefits.html	60.6	6.0
Time for Kids.com★	http://www.timeforkids.com/TFK	73.0	4.3
Think Quest: Women in Science★	http://www.thinkquest.org	60.4	7.4
Wood Collection	http://www.woodcollection.com	60.9	6.4

★ Particularly good examples.

Figure 17.1. A firmly aligned web page (Operation Tropical Fish)

Firmly aligned web pages speed user interactivity. Firm alignment is not just aesthetically pleasing; it also leads to clearer communication of ideas and concepts. When science web pages are firmly aligned, the pages not only look better; but also they communicate better. Figure 17.1 illustrates a firmly aligned web page.

In this illustration, the graphics and text are firmly aligned on the left side and along the horizontal baseline.

Proximity

Proximity is the second element of web page construction. Proximity aids in the development of friendly or considerate text because items that are conceptually related are placed together physically on the page. When items that belong together are grouped close together, information is much more organized and easier to read. Visual space creates a hierarchy of information (Peek, 1998; Williams & Tollett, 2000).

When titles and subtitles are closely connected to their paragraphs or subsections, the page is visually tidier and communication is clear (Quinn, 1995). Space is often used to delineate sections of a web page, to organize information to speed reader interactivity and to facilitate communication with the user, as in figure 17.2.

Figure 17.2 illustrates the use of space and contrasting fonts (different color and bolding) as a way to visually connect subtitles and the text body. Proximity can improve a web page's readability.

Repetition

Websites should be unified, thematic wholes. On a website, repetition of colors, fonts, illustrations, format, alignment, typography, and graphic elements (buttons, bars, and

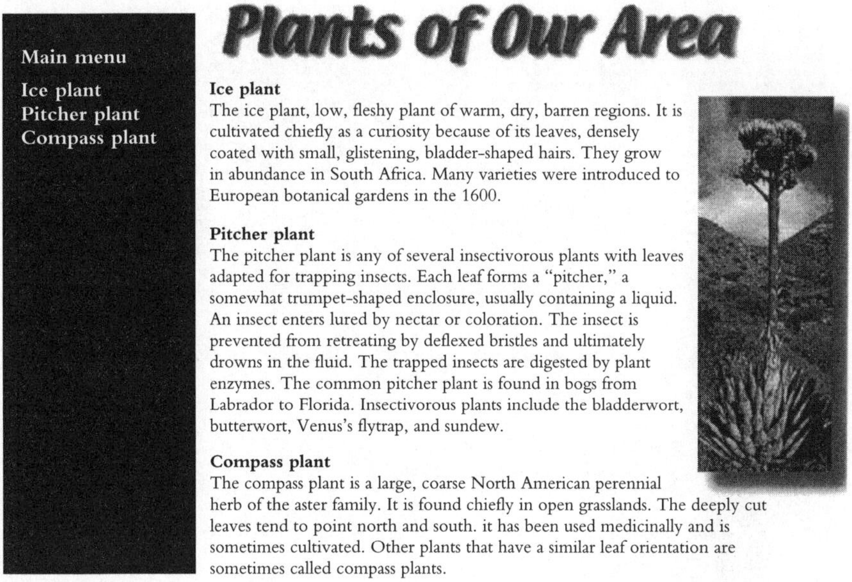

Plants of Our Area

Main menu

Ice plant
Pitcher plant
Compass plant

Ice plant
The ice plant, low, fleshy plant of warm, dry, barren regions. It is cultivated chiefly as a curiosity because of its leaves, densely coated with small, glistening, bladder-shaped hairs. They grow in abundance in South Africa. Many varieties were introduced to European botanical gardens in the 1600.

Pitcher plant
The pitcher plant is any of several insectivorous plants with leaves adapted for trapping insects. Each leaf forms a "pitcher," a somewhat trumpet-shaped enclosure, usually containing a liquid. An insect enters lured by nectar or coloration. The insect is prevented from retreating by deflexed bristles and ultimately drowns in the fluid. The trapped insects are digested by plant enzymes. The common pitcher plant is found in bogs from Labrador to Florida. Insectivorous plants include the bladderwort, butterwort, Venus's flytrap, and sundew.

Compass plant
The compass plant is a large, coarse North American perennial herb of the aster family. It is found chiefly in open grasslands. The deeply cut leaves tend to point north and south. it has been used medicinally and is sometimes cultivated. Other plants that have a similar leaf orientation are sometimes called compass plants.

Figure 17.2. Use of space and contrasting fonts (Plants of Our Area)

banners) unifies the site. Primary and secondary pages ought to look as though they belong together. Repetition makes this happen.

When web page designers repeat elements—backgrounds, typeface, links, buttons, and colors they are improving the unity of the website (Ackerman & Hartman, 2000; Peek, 1998). Repetition makes websites cohesive and facilitates communication with the user or learner (Luck & Hunter, 1997). Figure 17.3 illustrates a Thematic Website.

In figure 17.3, the home page and the secondary pages all have the same background color, font color, font style, and spacing. The site becomes visually thematic and conveys the message to the user that the site is thematically unified.

Contrast

Contrast is the design element that draws the users eye to the web page. Contrast guides the eye around the page. It allows the user to skim through the information and select critical information. When all the type on a web page is the same, there is no hierarchy of importance for information. The user has trouble picking out the essential elements because every element is given the same level or priority. If everything is equally important, then nothing has priority. Contrast helps the user define what is important and what is supporting information.

Contrast includes design features such as bold fonts, different colors of fonts, graphic markers or cues, space around objects and so forth. To be effective, contrast must be strong. Williams and Tollett state that if two elements such as type, rules, graphics, color, texture, and so forth are not the same, then the web page designer should make them very different (2000, p. 118). Illustrations have not been included here as it is difficult to convey the above in black and white.

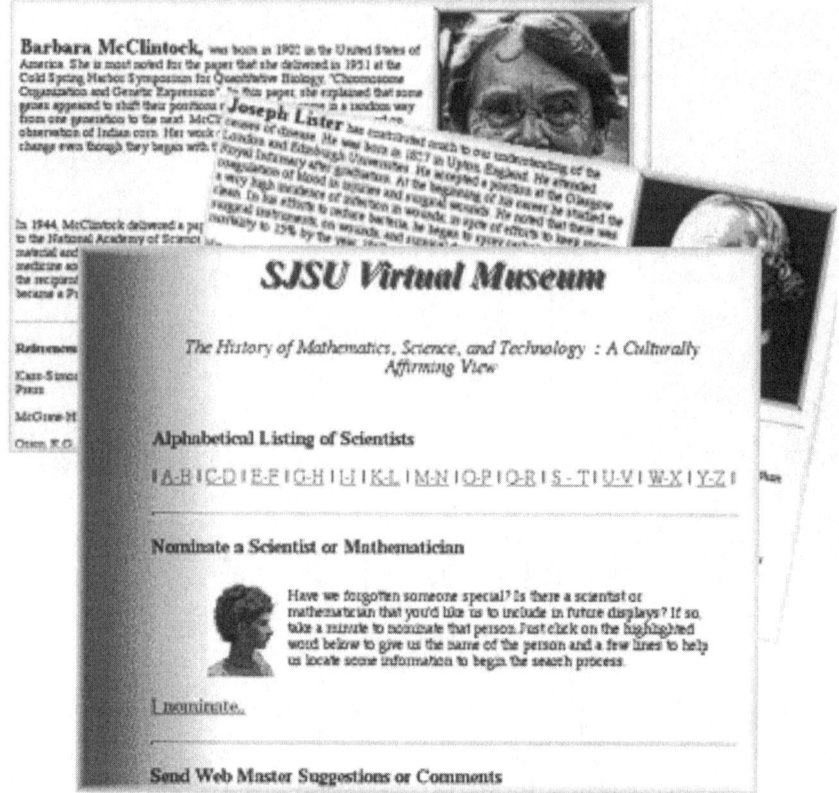

Figure 17.3. A thematic website (Virtual Museum)

User Interactivity and/or Navigation

Friendly science web pages are those that consider page layout and design as well as being concerned with the elements of considerate prose. Friendly web pages are those that make use of "best practice" in page layout and design and facilitate the users visual interaction with the content material.

User interactivity and/or navigation are a concern for the way that a website works and how the viewer interacts with the pages. User interactivity can also be a concern for students with disabilities and the way(s) that students access information contained at the website.

Links and Navigation Devices

Hyperlinks, buttons, and menus are commonly used navigational aids. Some aspects of interactivity and/or navigation are predetermined. Specifically, hyperlinks are normally blue in color and are underlined. Hyperlinks are familiar to most website users. Web pages constructed using cascading style sheets typically have bolded hyperlinks of a different color from the rest of the text. Hyperlinks allow the user to move from one place to another within a document or from one page to another on the website.

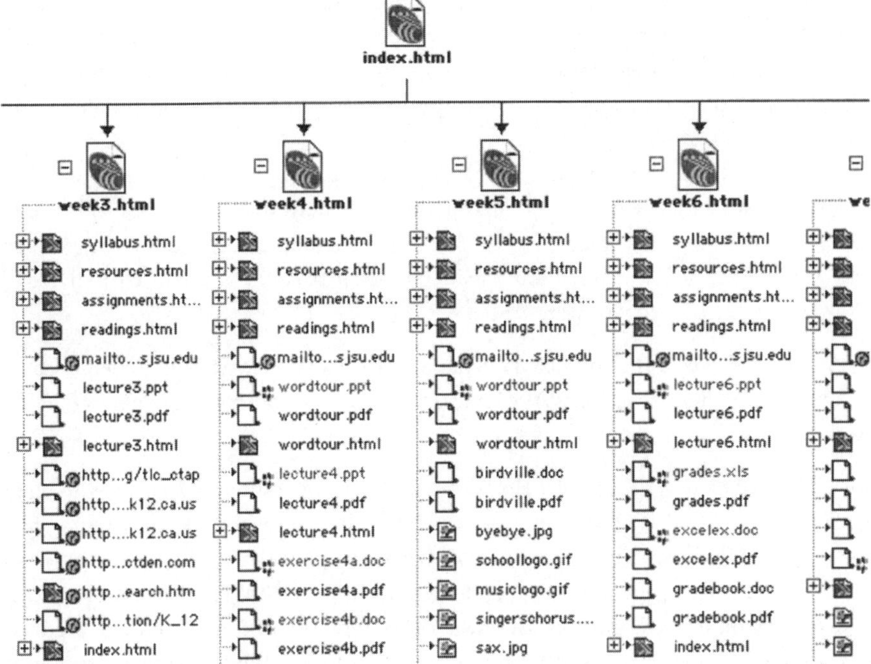

Figure 17.4. A sample site map

In addition to hyperlinks, users may move from one place to another via buttons, menus, or search functions. Menus (whether in text form or displayed as graphic buttons) at the top, side, or bottom of a web page are commonly used navigation devices. More recently website designers have incorporated localized search engines where the user enters a term or phase into a text field to facilitate user navigation. Finally, site maps (such as the one shown in figure 17.4) can be used as navigational aids.

Figure 17.4 shows a site map generated using the Macromedia DreamWeaver product. Site maps can serve as navigational tools to facilitate user interactivity.

When users can easily find their way around a website and back to the home page, the site is well designed from a navigation viewpoint. On the other hand, if a user has difficulty moving from one location to another or if the organization of content is not readily apparent, the user tends to get lost at the website. Friendly web pages are those that facilitate the users' movement from one location to another.

Consideration for Students with Disabilities

Consideration for the needs of students with disabilities ought to be of prime concern for all web page developers, including those who develop science web pages. Berlis, Kraus, and Stoddard (1996) point out that three things are vital in developing accessible web pages: layout and design, accessibility by adaptive technologies, and user interface.

For many students, the web is yet another roadblock, an inhospitable, highly visual medium, not designed with their needs in mind. Science website designers have access to information; as such they should use their resources, particularly information technologies to make information more accessible for those with disabilities. The needs of these users vary and require a variety of solutions. While some users will require text enlargement, others may require voice output software or scanners and Braille output devices (Valenza, 2000).

Several pieces of software exist, which assess web pages in terms of their accessibility for students with disabilities. *Bobby* is perhaps the best-known piece of software in this category. *Bobby* was created by CAST (http://www.cast.org/bobby) in 1996 to help web page authors identify and repair significant barriers to access by individuals with disabilities. *Bobby* is software that:

> - analyzes sites using the U.S. Federal Government's Section 508 guidelines, and
> - analyzes sites using the WAI Conformance A, AA, and AAA guidelines (CAST, 2002).

Bobby WorldWide (CAST, 2002) helps web page developers identify changes to their pages so users with disabilities can more easily use their websites. For example, a blind user will be aided by adding a sound track to a movie, and a written transcript of a sound file on a web page will aid a hard-of-hearing user. *Bobby* will recommend that these be added if they do not already exist. *Bobby* grew out of CAST's underlying mission, which is to expand opportunities for people with disabilities through innovative uses of computer technology.

Designing a well-organized website helps visitors navigate through the information presented. In designing science websites so that they are accessible by students with disabilities, the authors and editors of WAVE (2000) and DO-IT (2002) recommend that designers:

> - maintain a simple, consistent page layout throughout the site,
> - keep backgrounds simple,
> - make sure there is enough visual contrast between background and foreground objects and/or text,
> - use standard HTML coding,
> - design large buttons,
> - caption video and transcribe audio segments,
> - make hyperlinks descriptive so that they are understood out of context,
> - include appropriate ALT tags to describe each and every graphic element (pictures, bars, banners, and buttons),
> - include menu alternatives for image maps to ensure that the embedded links are accessible; that is, use redundant menus,
> - include descriptive captions for pictures and transcriptions of manuscript images,
> - use tables and frames sparingly and consider alternatives, and
> - provide alternatives for forms and databases.

Well-designed science websites are accessible to students with disabilities as well as the general population.

Instructional Devices

Instructional devices are those reading strategies that help the reader to focus attention to shifts in topic, the relative importance of ideas, and the relationship among elements. Conventions such as headings and subheadings, glossaries, and visualization strategies (e.g., diagrams, tables, graphics, and flow charts) are commonly used instructional devices. Research has shown that embedding instructional devices or strategies within the text supports the learning of all students and proportionally benefits bilingual/bidialectic students (Atkinson, Derry, & Renkl, 2000; Meira, 1998). Photographs, diagrams, charts, and tables of data that illustrate textual at a website material increase the learning of students, especially low-verbal students and students for whom English is a second language. There is a strong aptitude-by-treatment interaction favoring low-verbal learners that supports the enhancement of textual materials with visual and graphic displays (Lewin, 1998).

Summaries of textual information embedded in written materials, including the textual passages at websites, benefit all categories of learners; that is, low-, average-, and high-verbal learners. Since transferring knowledge from one situation to another is a major purpose in learning, friendly text passages written in considerate prose facilitate this objective by providing suggestions for the application of information to new situations. No matter how "friendly" the website, the use of the website is even more vital in the learning of students. Science websites are being used more often as the primary source of science information in many classrooms. While the quality of those websites could be greatly improved through the addition of elements of friendly text or friendly prose, the use of these websites is the vital concern in reading and comprehending information.

Summary

Friendly science web pages are those that are designed and developed with a consideration for the elements of friendly text, exhibit "best practice" in terms of page layout and design, have carefully developed user interfaces and/or navigational devices, and contain instructional devices that enhance learning. It should be pointed out that even the "best" science website could be misused or ineffectively utilized in science instruction. Likewise, a "poorly" designed science website can, in the hands of a competent teacher, become a powerful learning tool.

Note

1. The Reading Ease score, developed by Rudolf Flesch, is computed by multiplying the average sentence length by 1.015, then multiplying the number of syllables per 100 words by .846, adding them, and subtracting the sum from 206.835. The result is the Reading Ease Score. The scale ranges from 0 to 100. The higher the score, the easier it is to read.

   The reading grade level is based on the Fog index. This is calculated by determining the average sentence length plus the percentage of long words with all of this multiplied by 0.4. A long word is one with more than two syllables. The reading grade level score is designed to indicate what level of education, on average, would be required to comprehend the document.

The sites were accessed from the NSTA website (http://www.nsta.org) by using their "Children" hyperlink. A list of 38 websites is generated through this search procedure.

References

Ackerman, E. & Hartman, K.
(March, 2000). Designing a web page. *eTechNotes*. Retrieved from http://fbeedle.com/technote/01-00/01-00.html.

Atkinson, R.K., Derry, S.J., & Renkl, A.
(2000). Learning from examples: instructional principles from the worked examples research. *Review of Educational Research, 70* (2), 181–214.

Bavin, E.L.
(2000). Ellipsis in Walpiri children's narratives: an analysis of frog stories. *Linguistics, 38* (3), 569–589.

Berlis, J., Kraus, L., & Stoddard, S.
(1996). *Design of accessible web pages.* Retrieved March 6, 2002 from http://www.infouse.com disabilitydata/guidelines96.html.

Berninger, V.W., Whitaker, D., & Feng, Y.
(1996). Assessment of planning, translating, and revising in junior high writers. *Journal of School Psychology, 34,* 23–52.

Blankenhorn, D.
(2002). Site usability standards still the same. *B to B, 87* (1), 16.

CAST.
(2002). *About Bobby.* Retrieved March 6, 2002 from http://www.cast.org/Bobby/About-Bobby313.cfm.

Cheng, X. & Steffensen, M.S.
(1996). Metadiscourse: a technique for improving student writing. *Research in the Teaching of English, 30,* 149–81.

Christian, S.
(1997). *Exchanging lives: middle school writers online.* Urbana, IL: NCTE.

Delahunty, G.P.
(2001). Discourse functions of inferential sentences. *Linguistics, 39* (3), 517–545.

Disabilities, Opportunities, Internetworking & Technology (DO-IT).
(2002). *Information on accessible web page design.* Retrieved March 6, 2002 from http://www.washington.edu/doit/ Resources/web-design.html.

Dreher, M.J. & Singer, H.
(1989). Friendly texts and text-friendly teachers. *Theory into practice, 28,* 98–104.

Flesch, R.
(1949). *The art of readable writing.* New York: Harper & Row.

Herring, M.Y.
(2001). 10 reasons why the internet is no substitute for a library. *American Libraries, 32* (4), 76–78.

Klusewitz, M.A. & Lorch, R.F.
(2000). Effects of headings and familiarity with a text on strategies for searching a text. *Memory and Cognition, 28* (4), 667–76.

Kramarski, B. & Feldman, Y.
(2000). Internet in the classroom: Effects on reading comprehension. *Educational Media International, 37* (3), 149–155.

Kumpf, E.P.
(2000). Visual metadiscourse: Designing the considerate text. *Technical Communication Quarterly, 9* (4), 401–424.

Leahy, R.
(1995). Style matters. *College Teaching, 43,* 7–12.

Lewin, L.
(1998). Taming the web: Reading for comprehension. *Multimedia Schools, 5* (4), 50–52.

Lewin, L.
(1999). "Site Reading" the world wide web. *Educational Leadership, 56* (5), 16–20.

Luck, D.D. & Hunter, J.M.
(1997). Visual design principles applied to world wide web construction. In *Vision Quest: Journeys toward Visual Literacy.* Selected Readings from the Annual Conference of the International Visual Literacy Association. Cheyenne, Wyoming.

MacColl, G.S. & White, K.D.
(1998). *Communicating educational research data to general, nonresearcher audiences.* College Park, MD: ERIC/AE Digest. (ERIC Document Reproduction Service No. ED422406.)

McNulty, K.T.
(2002). Fostering the student-centered classroom online. *T.H.E. Journal, 29* (7), 16–22.

Meira, L.
(1998). Making sense of instructional devices: the emergence of transparency in mathematical activity. *Journal for Research in Mathematics Education, 29* (2), 121–142.

Mioduser, D., Nachmias, R., Lahav, O., & Oren, A.
(2000). Web-based learning environments: Current pedagogical and technological state. *Journal of Research on Computing in Education, 33* (1), 55–76.

Ojala, M.
(2000). Online reading as a nonlinear activity. *Econtent, 23* (5), 6.

Peek, R.
(1998). Web page design standards. *Information Today, 15* (9), 45–46.

Quinn, C.A.
(1995). From grass roots to corporate image—The maturation of the web. *Cause/Effect, 18* (3), 49–51.

Tyree, R.B., Fiore, T.A., & Cook, R.
(1994). Instructional materials for diverse learners: features and considerations for textbook design. *Remedial and Special Education, 15,* 363–377.

Valenza, J.K.
(2000). Surfing blind. *School Library Journal Supplement*, 34–36.

WAVE.
(2000). *Techniques for accessibility evaluation andrRepair tools W3C Working draft*, April 26, 2000. Retrieved on March 6, 2002 from http://www.w3.org/WAI/ER/IG/ert/.

Williams, R. & Tollett, J.
(2000). *The non-designer's web book.* Berkeley, CA: Peachpit Press.

18

A Phenomenological Anthropology of Texts and Literacy

Wolff-Michael Roth

Wolff-Michael Roth

TEXTS AND LIVED EXPERIENCE: THREE CASES

Case One

About five years ago, I started gardening and developed it to the point that I now produce all the vegetables my family eats throughout the year. As I am writing this chapter, it is winter and I am supposed to prune several trees and bushes that we planted. Never having pruned before, my wife and I had bought a book entirely dedicated to pruning, containing many photos and diagrams of partially pruned pushes, where to cut and what to leave. Over the past several weeks, I had repeatedly taken up the book, tried to read and make sense of it, and subsequently laid it aside, completely frustrated by the fact that I did not know where to start cutting my own trees and bushes. Last week, we read that there was a free workshop on in a tree nursery and fruit farm. During the weekend, we attended it. The 25-year pruning veteran who ran the workshop started to talk and after 15 minutes, I turned around to my wife and said, "no better than the book." But once he started pruning and talking about why he was cutting the branch he was about to cut, and why he was leaving another one nearby, and when he pointed to a pruned tree that he wanted his tree to look like, things became better. As he went on, I started predicting which branches he would cut. Taking his actual cutting or not cutting as feedback, my predictions became increasingly better. Two hours later, I returned home and began pruning a few bushes and small trees. Inside, I took another look at the book and now, everything was clear. I realized that the book was telling me exactly what I had to do, and it did so in a very clear way.

Case Two

One of my research projects concerns the reading of graphs by scientists. For this purpose, my graduate students and I had culled graphs that were prevalent in introductory ecology courses and associated textbooks, including a simple line graph showing a linear death rate intersecting at two points with an inverse parabolic birthrate. Over the years, we have asked about 50 scientists (half from ecology the other half from physics) to read the graph. Astonishingly, almost none of the nonuniversity ecologists with masters and Ph.D. degrees and between 6 and 25 years of research experience in the field could provide a standard reading of the graph; similarly, many physicists provided nonstandard interpretations. At the same time, my ethnographic work in various workplaces shows that even individuals without scientific training become highly competent users of graphs that are part of their familiar, everyday job setting.

Case Three

Recently, I conducted several multiyear ethnographic studies of scientists and their graduate students. Some of the actions that biologists and ecologists engage in during fieldwork concern the identification of plants and animals, for which they also draw on field guides. Over the past half-dozen years, my research assistants and I have recorded numerous situations where scientists or their graduate students attempt to classify some entity but, even though both field guide and entity were present in the situation, they had great difficulty in making the match between descriptions and representations on the page (photographs, diagrams) and the worldly things they supposedly describe.

Six Problematic Issues in the Consideration of Text and Visual Representations

The preceding chapters in this section are about designing better textbooks and about teaching with or training for teaching with textbooks in primary science classes. None of my three cases have anything to do with primary science and yet they teach us much about how or how not to approach texts for young students. When science educators reflect on children and their learning, particularly about difficult moments, they often use deficit approaches. There is something wrong with primary children and even their teachers when they do not make sense of science texts or texts that make reference to and describe scientific objects and events. Yet the three episodes show that even highly trained and successful individuals may have difficulty making sense of scientific texts and diagrams that are not directly from and about their familiar world.

In the first case, I was struggling to come to grips with what turned out to be an excellent book about pruning. I have hardly ever seen a book with instructions apparently so clear. There was not a word that was unfamiliar. There were many drawings and photographs of particular trees and bushes. Furthermore, I have these kinds of trees and bushes in my garden. Yet when I went into the garden with the book, standing right next to a currant bush, making the book and my garden a reality come together seemed impossible. Similarly, the scientists who unsuccessfully attempted to read graphs or identify specimens with the field guide in their hands had problems in bringing together the texts and images, on the one hand, and the reality of their field experiences on the other. These failures by individuals who have proven many times over that they are intelligent, studious, and experienced scientists tell us that there are some problematic issues in current conceptions about learning through reading text.

The first issue (in the previous chapters and elsewhere in our science education community) pertains to the notion of reading for *information* (e.g., chapter 17, in this volume). In his seminal work on information theory, Claude Shannon (1948) showed that the notion of information required that sender and receiver be tuned and operate in reverse; that is, a message is information only when sender and receiver code and decode some sign in the same way. But this is not given in the case of schoolchildren reading science texts; it was also not given in the three cases mentioned here. Although the pruning book contained only familiar words, the graph was from an introductory book on the scientists' own field, and the field guides contained familiar words and images, what the respective authors might have wanted to say was evidently not understood by the individuals involved. But the technicians in my various ethnographic studies used words that were much more technical and scientific and read graphs much more complex than those in the texts and representations presented to the scientists. So when words and graphs are an integral part of familiar, everyday practice they are no longer difficult although much less demanding words and images remain impenetrable. All of this suggests that we need to think about texts and visual representations differently. I do so in terms of practice (Bourdieu, 1990): If texts and representations are part of familiar practices, we know how to employ them, what they imply, when not to use them, or how to talk *about* them. When words and representations are not part of everyday practice, they are unfamiliar, and they do not by themselves suggest how to be employed, used, what they imply, and so on.

The second issue, related to the first, is the idea that some words and visual representations are supposedly *abstract* versus others that are *concrete* (e.g., in chapter 16, in this volume about simple but *abstract* images). Take the situation of texts and representations in the three cases mentioned here. When texts or images do not fit into what is familiar background to us, we talk about them as *abstract*, or, as "jargon." Taking one look at science textbooks shows us that there are many new terms, sometimes 25 or more bold-faced and therefore "important" words in a single chapter. Yet, even as science educators reject jargon, many science educators also expect students to learn science from texts that often consist of linear compilations of a few statements that contain the new words. My own pruning experience showed that the change over from abstract to concrete can happen rather quickly. In the course of an afternoon with a pruning expert, the textbook on pruning had become very concrete, clear, and concise. We learn from this that *abstract* and *concrete* are relational rather than ontological terms (Roth, 1995). That is, a text appears abstract when we are unfamiliar with it and its relation to concrete situations; it appears concrete when it transparently expresses something in my familiar world. *Abstract* literally means, "taken out of context" (Lat. *abs-* away, and *trahere*, pull, take). It therefore means that we experience text and representations as abstract when they or the things they are about are not part of our own familiar world but dropped into it from a different world.

The third issue pertains to learning from text. Coming to know *about* something means that we understand observation sentences and observation categoricals, the constituents of theory (Quine, 1995). To science educators *reading for content* is when students come to understand unfamiliar observation sentences and observation categoricals. In reading, students encounter unfamiliar (abstract) words and representations about unfamiliar objects and events. Yet scholars have suggested that we can theorize and understand theory only in relation to those situations that we are already familiar with (Heidegger, 1977). This puts readers into a double bind. They can only learn what they already understand in an existential way because to interpret text they already need to understand it: but to enhance their understanding they need to engage in analysis of what they already understand (Ricœur, 1991). We come to grips with any text or any visual representation that we encounter by drawing on our existential understanding of what the world is like and how it works. This understanding precedes any thinking and reflecting, it is part of our constitution—or in the words of phenomenological philosophers, this understanding is an existential of our being.

The fourth issue concerns the ways of thinking about language and about concepts that are current in science education. The general presuppositions that appear to be made are (a) concepts exist independent of language, which is merely used to communicate the contents of our minds and (b) language has representational function. To begin with the latter point, it is true that we use language to talk *about* objects and events. But more importantly, and at the very root of any language and communicative behavior, we use language as a way to get around the world. When my wife calls out, "Watch it!," and I duck and thereby avoid being hit on the head by a low tree branch, I do not represent, decode, and then process a message to reflect upon its meaning. I simply duck in the same way as my feet find their way on a rocky beach without thinking about how to place them. That is, there is no difference between knowing a language and knowing one's way around the world more generally (Davidson, 1986). But when I tell a story about not having been hit by the branch or about avoiding some water hole or garbage on the beach, my language has the character of being about something. I use it for representational purposes.

When children use language in school, they first and foremost explore a part of the world, attempting to find structure. It is only after they have done a lot of talking that they can find useful patterns in this language. Therefore, in the beginning of exploring some new domain, we might expect their language to be more like the language that characterized science during the Middle Age, when after one hundred years of inconclusive muddle, people all of a sudden found themselves talking in a way that took the interlocked theses of Copernicus for granted (Rorty, 1989). That is, students' language can become language about something only after they have explored that something, or, in fact, created this something to be talked about subsequently. In talking, students lay a garden path, and it is only after completing their walk that they can find useful or beautiful patterns in it.

The other point pertains to the relationship between concepts and language. Here, I agree with Wittgenstein (1958) who suggested that words have no meaning other than taking particular places in different language *games*. Thus, rather than talking about the *concept* of atom, we are better off talking about the places and situation where we allow the word atom to occur and not to occur. There are no concepts apart from the way we talk about particular things, which themselves are available only through textual mediation. Derrida (1967) wrote, "Il n'y a pas de hors-texte" (there is no outside [of] text), where text refers to phrases, gestures, tones, situations and other sorts of marks (Derrida, 1995). That which is purely language in language is inextricably interwoven with other parts of experience, forming a cloth—the etymological root of "text" is the Latin *texere*, to weave (Derrida, 1982). That is, there are no concepts independent of language and there is no language independent and extractable from the cloth of life. Therefore, rather than attempting to get concepts into children's minds or having children construct concepts in their heads, we ought to set up opportunities where they can participate in particular life forms, characterized by their language games and experiences. This then leads us back to the preceding paragraph and the statement that knowing language and knowing one's way around the world are indistinguishable.

The fifth issue has to do with our understanding of the reading process. Reading is often taken as unproblematic and, if students do not understand, we blame them or their mental make up. A different tack is taken by a phenomenological hermeneutic of the reading act (Ricœur, 1985). Accordingly, there are three dialectical features in reading. First, any text that teaches something new to readers must frustrate the expectation of an immediately intelligible textual configuration and thereby places on them the burden of configuring the text (including representations). That is, while reading, readers actually have to develop a method for reading the particular text (Livingston, 1995). In reading compound texts including figures, captions, and sidebar texts, readers have to search the material ground for organizing their reading. Reading therefore is also a search for coherence, whereby the text brings both words and a textual world, and readers bring their embodied understanding of how the world works, a world in which effective action unfolds. It is only in the praxis of reading, then, that the two worlds are configured allowing the intersection to occur.

The first dialectic is associated with a second one, the contradiction embodied in the fact that reading reveals not only a lack of textual determinacy but also an excess of meaning. Thus, my pruning book seemed to lack both clear instructions of how to prune my current bushes and at the same time there were many different ways in which I could understand particular text-image assemblies. Every text, even the most fragmentary ones, allow multiple readings and the same readers, even when using academic texts, will find themselves understanding certain passages differently over time, as they come back and back again to the same (physically at least) text. Every text, therefore, both lacks and has excess of something with respect to reading.

The third dialectic emerges from the search for coherence between an intelligible configuration of the text and a corresponding configuration of the lived world of everyday action. When this search is too successful, in fact, when there is no search at all and readers immediately feel projected into the world described, they lose themselves in it. The scientists and technicians I researched did not look *at* their graphs but looked *through* them to a world beyond; they no longer searched for coherence but "lost themselves" in their familiar world. On the other hand, when the search for coherence fails, the text and representations remain foreign with respect to the reader's familiar world; readers then fail to assimilate the textual world to their own. When I initially turned away from the pruning book, I experienced this failure to assimilate the text and its images to the world of my garden, despite the apparent equivalence of the textual world and my own worlds, and despite the equivalence of the drawings and photographs with the bushes that were actually in front of me.

The sixth issue relates to the relation between spoken text, often referred to as discourse, and written text. Much of educational practice does not distinguish the two. For example, there are many who set up classroom environments that allow students to talk science and then test the same students using written evaluations. Others propose writing as a way of learning science, without clarifying what the relationship is, for example, between laboratory talk and the written reports students subsequently produce. Yet there are ontological differences between written and oral language (Ricœur, 1991), or, in other words, orality and literacy are associated with different forms of consciousness (Ong, 1982). Discourse refers and is tied to the situation of speaking. In oral discourse, reference is ostensive, pertaining to and relying on local contingencies to achieve its purpose. That is, in oral discourse we take a place and orient to our immediate lifeworld.

Writing, on the other hand, no longer addresses itself to a specific listener co-present in the situation; written text no longer contains the ostensive references of the dialogue but projects into a world created by the non-ostensive references of all texts (Ricœur, 1991). At the same time, this world can only be understood through the concrete realizations of particular experiences by the individual reader. Thus, although the pruning book showed generalized drawings about where and how to cut, and although the text described in general how, when, and where to cut, I faced the problem of knowing where and how to cut *this* bush in *this* place here, at *this* time, and with its contingently shaped and placed branches. I understood the generalized descriptions only after I had come to successfully predict where and what to cut in the concretely realized praxis of pruning my bushes.

Teaching with Text as Mediated Activity

In the forgoing section, I articulated communication, language, and reading from the phenomenological perspective of a person using language in discourse and writing, and coming face to face with language in reading texts. This perspective is quite different from that normally taken in science education. But I concur with the chapter authors that textbooks and teachers have special functions in school science. Here, I take my cues from activity theorists who view teaching with and about texts as mediated practice (Cole & Engeström, 1993). Activity theory is particularly suited to the epistemology both explicit and implicit in this chapter because it makes us theorize reading as a practice. Reading is not explained by something that goes on in the head, but by an examination of reading as when it actually occurs.

The mediational nature of teaching literacy is expressed in figure 18.1. Thus, teachers already mediate their access to an aspect of the world (e.g., volcanoes, atoms) via text; or, conversely, they have worldly experiences that they can bring to encounters with text (e.g., about volcanoes, atoms). Students, on the other hand, may be unfamiliar with both

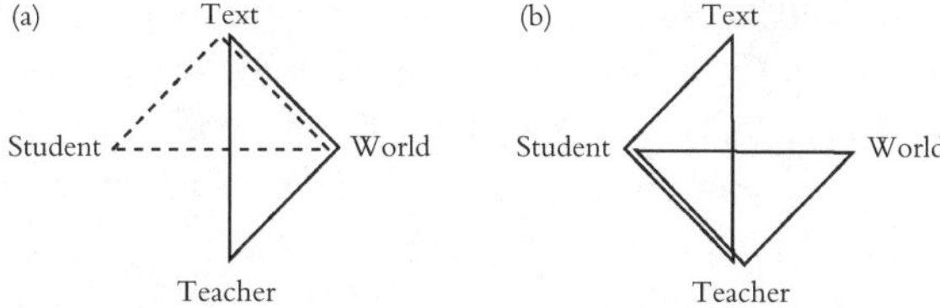

Figure 18.1. Learning to read is the outcome of a double mediation. (a) Teachers mediate their access to the world via text and also have experiences in the world that mediate their access to the text. Students on the other hand have neither form of mediated access. (b) In teaching, the teacher mediates both between student and text and between student and world, and thereby sets a context for the students mediated access to world and text

textual resources for mediating their access to the world and worldly experiences to access the text (figure 18.1a, broken line). Thus, it does not surprise me that British eighth grade students had difficulties reading graphs, which were said to represent the relationship of shrimp frequency and oxygen levels in a river as a function of distance from a factory (Preece & Janvier, 1992). Here, the students had neither experiences with oxygen levels nor with shrimps or shrimp frequencies to mediate their access to the graph; and they were not familiar with graphs as a way to access experiences with shrimp frequencies and oxygen levels.

In primary schools, pupils often gain worldly experiences by engaging in hands-on investigations that teachers set up and take pupils through; and students gain textual experiences when teachers read with them and talk about the texts they read (figure 18.1b). When the texts are about the aspects of the world that students have had opportunities to engage with, the two mediational practices overlap to help pupils build their own mediated access to world and text. To strengthen the relation between text and associated world, students not only read texts about aspects of the world but also engage first in talking and later in writing about experienced aspects of this world. I am suggesting talking first, because in discourse, students still have all the means of ostensive reference by means of words, gesture, and presence of the talked-about entities themselves (Roth & Lawless, 2002). Once they have developed more elaborate discourse, that is, discourse that relies less on visual and gestural means of representation, they have sufficient verbal resources to begin writing about the events. Being familiar with the double mediation of text and world, pupils have developed literary practices.

Reflections on the Previous Chapters

The previous chapters provide valuable studies and analyses of a variety of issues concerning students, texts and images, and teachers. There simply is not enough space to do a full analysis of every point I noted during my reading. In this section, I therefore take up some salient points made in individual or multiple chapters in the light of my own perspectives on language, text, and reading.

In chapter 13, the authors direct their readers' attention to the important teacher–learner–text relationship while highlighting several issues such as culture, relationship between instructional language and mother-tongue, and sociolinguistic context (see also chapter 15, in this volume). My framing of the issue not only added a fourth component, world, but also quadrupled the number of mediated relations. Rather than considering teacher–student–text relations (one of the two triangles in figure 18.1b above), we have to consider four triadic relations (the four triangles in figure 18.1). Viewing these relations in terms of mediation also makes clear the nature of the language required on the part of the teacher, and the kinds of efforts that have to be undertaken to assist students, who may start with a very different language-world relation, to read and analyze the target text. If, for example, a students' root language is different from the middle-class language that characterizes textbooks and teacher–student interactions in most schools, then we can expect significant problems to arise. Students will not only fail to understand a particular text and a particular course, but in their production of failure will also reproduce another generation of future parents whose children face the same contradiction between root and instructional language.

The authors of chapter 13 also point out that some teachers at the primary level have little training in the selection and use of science texts, as well as difficulties mastering the linguistic repertoires themselves. It is evident that the worlds and access to texts that they mediate for their students (figure 18.1) will be very different from those of another teacher who might have the required competencies. It is not surprising then that a teacher who does not feel confident in scientific discourse will draw on the textbook as a resource to structure their being in the classroom, as the authors of chapter 14 point out. By simply reading the text, they no longer have to produce their own texts or "acquire content knowledge" (chapter 16, in this volume).

What can science educators do about this? My view of scientific knowledge and language as a world that we learn to navigate suggests that it might help traveling with such teachers for a while, showing them around in the world and how to guide others. Thus, rather than bemoaning the situation when some primary teachers said they could not teach science, I began about ten years ago to teach *with* them. We now call this model co-teaching, designed not to cut up the work so that we only get to do what we are good at, but to learn from one another while teaching (Roth, 2002). In a way, co-teaching allows tacit learning to occur while doing our job—teaching children science in an interesting way.

Finally, talking about language as being indistinguishable from being in and finding one's way around the world is very different from saying that students, or teachers for that matter, have correct conceptions or misconceptions. It is not even appropriate to say that these students have not yet mastered scientific language. "To say that one's previous language was inappropriate for dealing with some segment of the world (for example, the starry heavens above, or the raging passions within) is just to say that one is now, having learned a new language, able to handle that segment more easily" (Rorty, 1989, p. 14). It should be clear by now, however, that without the preceding talk, however incorrect, there would not have been any linguistic material that could have been ordered into a language.

The authors of chapter 14 articulate some interesting issues that can be found in the other chapters, too. Thus, they point out differences between reading trade books versus reading science textbooks and introduce the notion of the (in-)considerate text.

In the context of my framework, it is immediately evident that students' use of trade books would require less mediational work than their use of science textbooks. Trade books develop worlds not unlike those that even young students know and are familiar with. Embedded in these narratives are statements about objects and events that also feature in science textbooks. But they do so in a very different way. Science texts consist of factual statements chained into long strings of text. During a recent stay in one of my research sites (a fish hatchery), a participant talked about taking an on-line course in genetics. Whereas she is a highly competent fish culturist, she failed to establish any coherence between the texts and her understanding of how the world works. As a consequence, she said that every sentence seemed important so that she wanted to highlight the entire text rather than the most relevant parts. This immediately leads us into the second issue, the (in-)considerate text (or (un-)friendly web page (chapter 17)). Was the fish culturists' (web-based) course text inconsiderate?

In my view, texts are not considerate or inconsiderate. Texts only come to life in the act of reading, which is to say in a lived praxis that establishes a reader–text–world relationship. I disagree with the authors of this and other chapters that blame texts (or their authors) thereby making an ontological attribution. Recall my experience with the pruning book. Initially, I had a very hard time. I did not manage to begin pruning on the basis of my reading of the text and the drawings. Yet some time later, after spending an afternoon with a pruning expert, I found that the book was actually excellent, accurate, and very well done. Really at issue here are changing (mediated) relations: it is only by considering the larger context that we can make statements about why or why not a particular text allowed learning to occur.

In my reading, chapter 15 draws our attention to numerous (some problematic) issues of teaching and learning via texts. These issues include the divergence in type and quality of texts, efforts in teacher training to de-emphasize the use of commercially available books, problems in learning from images, the divergence in textbook-implicit learning strategies and those implicit in teachers' pedagogy, and the absence of meta-cognitive strategies in textbooks that would allow readers to reflect on their progress. Two aspects struck me in reading this chapter more than anything else because they seem to me symptomatic of science education: (a) the discourses about knowing, learning, textbooks, and so forth do not relate to one another so that it is difficult to understand how they are useful in understanding the phenomenon of a classroom; and (b) the rationalization of activities that we normally engage in as a matter of course, without reflecting or even having the time to reflect upon in ongoing praxis.

First, we can read about visual literacy, cognitive demands, teaching skills, pedagogical content knowledge, learning strategies, language, discourse, and science concepts. Rather than coming together and synergistically allowing better understandings of teaching and learning that I experience in *this* classroom, on *this* day, and concerning *these* children, all of these terms and theories can amount in the ears of teachers to a cacophony that they cannot related to their experience. These terms also reduce teaching and learning to variables that individual teachers cannot relate to their experience, because the terms classify attributes rather than lived experience. If we were to adopt a discourse of living and learning as being and becoming in particular settings, with language simply constituting an indistinguishable part of this—because the distinction between knowing a language and knowing one's way around the world has been erased—then we might be able not only to pull our discourses together but also allow teachers to make sense of them. For example, in *Being and Becoming in the Classroom* (Roth, 2002), I describe teaching not only as a way of being but also as a continuous becoming; as we teach, we extend our room to maneuver, which is equivalent to saying that we have become more competent practitioners. I describe how a new teacher was continuously becoming in the process of teaching with me, and how I was becoming (a better teacher) by teaching with her, despite my 20-year teaching experience.

Similarly, as we work with children, we assist children in extending their room to maneuver, and therefore foster their becoming in the world. The term *extending* was chosen deliberately, because it implies quite different actions if I work with a White middle-class student or with a recent immigrant child who is in the process of learning to navigate our (Anglo-American) world. Many textbooks may not be appropriate, because they are inappropriate in the system of quadruple relations that I articulated above (figure 18.1) for extending the world of those students that are supposed to work with it.

Second, teachers often do not understand what university researchers are talking about, and they often discredit university research and teaching because it has little to do with their teaching praxis (lived experience of teaching). What then do we experience when we teach, in the heat of the moment, when there is no time out to think about the next move? We simply teach, doing what appears as the sensible next move or moves, in the same way that we walk instead of placing feet (Roth, 2002). As teachers, we do not plan what to do next, we do not implement a program in the way artificial intelligence and cognitive science models work, but we act in a world that is so intimately ours that we are wedded to it. Training programs of the type that the authors of chapter 15 are writing about would have to account for this. How do you assist someone to expand her room to maneuver *in* practice rather than their discourse *about* practice? How do you allow a (new) teacher to *become* better in mediating the relationship between students, their (personal) life-world and experiences, and our shared world of the text? That is, science teacher educators have to confront the contradiction that one learns a practice by practicing it but future science teachers are to learn to teach by hearing about teaching. I recommend accepting future teachers as new teachers to the profession and integrating them into the everyday affairs of a working place (i.e., a school), as we have done with science teacher training at the University of Pennsylvania (Roth & Tobin, 2002). Similarly, if we want students to read and appreciate refutational texts, then we need to provide them with opportunities to read and write refutational texts, and test them on their competencies in doing that rather than doing something else (like defining concepts).

Chapter 16 addresses an issue that is particularly close to my interests, for I have conducted research into the use of visual representations by students, technicians, and scientists. In the attempt to understand, for example, scientists' readings of graphs, and particularly graphs that they were not familiar with (e.g., case 2 mentioned earlier), I have had to squarely face the question, "What does it mean to interpret a graph, text, photograph, data table, and so on?" I have come to realize that interpretation does not mean to uncover something that is implied by but not directly available *in* the visual representation; rather, whenever a visual representation is unfamiliar to a person, it becomes an occasion for the individual to elaborate existing understanding *in front of* the representation. If we look at the reader-visual representation-world interaction, there is no such thing as "misinterpreting a visual image". The person was simply occasioned to articulate an aspect of her world that differs from what some other person (teacher, textbook author) may have wanted to be articulated. Rather than attempting to fix the students and their deficits, we ought to view the possibility of alternate readings as the norm. This then would focus our (teacher) attention on the problem of how to bring these alternative readings out into the open so that they can be discussed, weighed, and discarded on rational grounds rather than because a teacher says so.

Earlier, I articulated phenomenological hermeneutic and anthropological approaches to reading, which focused on the dialectic that emerges from the search for coherence between an intelligible configuration of the text and an intelligible configuration of the experienced (and taken-for-granted) world. We found the scientists and others engaged in elaborating configurations of the world they know rather than in making inferences about a world they did not yet know. There is no more meaning to pictures than there is to language: Visual literacy, from my perspective, simply means that we have expanded the world that we understand to include visual images of different sorts. Visual literacy is not something that is in your or the children's heads. As any other literacy, scientific and visual literacies are to me forms of lived praxis, and as such something we do with others in relevant situations. Becoming visually literate then simply means to participate in an emergent feature of collective human practice (Roth, 2003).

These points also raise the question about meaning. Chapter 16 and others articulate meaning as if it was an attribute of text and visual representations; constructivist theory portrays people facing unfamiliar texts and visual representations as *making meaning* of them. But the perspective outlined here suggests that when readers establish coherence, texts and visual representations accrue to already and inherently intelligible worlds, worlds of which we have an existential understanding from the beginning. It is not that new meaning is constructed, created, or found but that unfamiliar entities (words, discourse, representations) become integrated in worlds already *shot through* with meaning.

The idea of "friendly" web pages promulgated in chapter 17 immediately struck me as a curious idea. As I read and reread the text, I was thinking about young people and the complex worlds they navigate in music videos and video games or in the production of web pages and graffiti. I was also thinking about my neighbors' children who attend to multiple chat channels at the same time as they are working on their homework, which itself might involve surfing the Internet for resources. Thus, rather than requiring less complex displays, they seem to be happy with and actively create more complex displays and interactions. Perhaps our unquestioned assumption about textual and visual organization arises in part from the ideology of information transfer. Therefore, if students "don't get" what they are supposed to get, we blame either text (web page) or student when the issue we need to look at lies in the mediated relation of person–text–world (figure 18.1). The issue appears to be one of allowing developments in person and world so that texts become recognized as useful mediating tools for accessing salient parts of the world.

Let me give an example. For a long time, I simply could not stand to listen to twentieth-century classical music, a form of "text" that I appeared to be unable and unwilling to access. Then, less than ten years ago, I was invited to a concert by the Symphonic Orchestra of Berlin, which played, among other pieces, *Les Ameriques* by Edgar Varese. As I sat there listening, I began to experience soundscapes, auditory pillars, carvings, and deserts. I not only began to listen increasingly to modern classical music but I also began to hear the music I used to like so much in a new and different light and with a renewed pleasure. I now listen predominantly to this type of music. Somehow my listening capabilities were transformed in this first experience, which itself was possible only because of my extended experience in other forms of music.

Is twentieth-century music impenetrable and unfriendly? Clearly not! I was *becoming* an amateur of this kind of music. The music itself is not unfriendly. Was I deficient? Clearly not! I have *become* a lover of classical music without training on my own. I must have had the potential to become an amateur of classical music. I infer that we (students, teachers) need more than anything else opportunities to become familiar with different kinds of media so that we not only become competent in navigating them but also in making judgments about strengths and weaknesses with respect to our culture's predilections.

Conclusion

In this chapter, I have developed a view of text, language, literacy, teaching, and learning that is nonreductionist and places emphasis on our lived experience in a world that includes texts and visual representations. It is through this view that I have read the chapters in this section of the book. This view does not begin by thinking about children and their primary teachers in deficit terms, but by thinking about them as navigating worlds that differ from the worlds of scientists and science educators. These worlds *are* texts, with language and lived experience as warp and weft. The question for me is not how we can fix children, texts, or teachers, but how we can support the efforts of human beings in expanding their worlds so that they have greater room for maneuvering, more possibilities for acting, and ever-expanding opportunities for continuously becoming, whatever they choose to be. I am much more concerned about how we develop identities as integral and constitutive members of collectives, and how we can contribute to making (scientific, literacy, textual) literacy emerge as a feature of collective praxis. I am much more concerned to see people participating in human endeavors and changing their participation in the process than in seeing them regurgitate some irrelevant verbal tokens under exam conditions. It is more important that people actually participate in contentious issues that also involve scientists and science even if they do not know the Krebs cycle or the number of protons and neutrons in a model of the Beryllium atom. At the collective level, we already practice such a division of labor—physicists do not have to build the buildings that house their labs nor do they have to be competent in anything else other than their specialty. But we ask students and teachers to be competent in reading every text or understanding every discourse that someone else decided that they ought to be competent in. In closing, therefore, I would like to see students and teachers involved in choosing and rejecting their language, textbooks, representations, and web pages in the same way that I advocated their involvement in epistemological discussions so that they want to interrogate knowledge claims whoever made them (Désautels & Roth, 1999). What we need is a better world, and students and teachers who use and produce language and texts ought to be an integral part of making and remaking the world that we really want.

References

Bourdieu, P.
(1980). *Le sens pratique*. Paris: Les Editions de Minuit.

Cole, M. & Engeström, Y.
(1993). A cultural historical approach to distributed cognition. In G. Salomon (Ed.), *Distributed cognitions: Psychological and educational considerations* (pp. 1–46). Cambridge: Cambridge University Press.

Davidson, D.
(1986). A nice derangement of epitaphs. In E. Lepore (Ed.), *Truth and interpretation* (pp. 433–446). Oxford: Blackwell.

Derrida, J.
(1967). *De la grammatologie*. Paris: Editions de Minuit.

Derrida, J.
(1982). *Margins of philosophy*. Chicago: University of Chicago Press.

Derrida, J.
(1995). *Pointsinterviews, 1974–1994*. Stanford, CA: Stanford University Press.

Désautels, J. & Roth, W.-M.
(1999). Demystifying epistemology. *Cybernetics & Human Knowing, 6* (1), 33–45.

Heidegger, M.
(1977). *Sein und Zeit*. Tübingen, Germany: Max Niemeyer.

Livingston, E.
(1995). *An anthropology of reading*. Bloomington: Indiana University Press.

Ong, W. J.
(1982). *Orality and literacy: The technologizing of the word*. London: Routledge.

Preece, J. & Janvier, C.
(1992). A study of the interpretation of trends in multiple curve graphs of ecological situations. *School Science and Mathematics, 92,* 299–306.

Quine, W. V.
(1995). *From stimulus to science*. Cambridge, MA: Harvard University Press.

Ricœur, P.
(1985). *Time and narrative* (vol. 3). Chicago: University of Chicago Press.

Ricœur, P.
(1991). *From text to action: Essays in hermeneutics, II*. Evanston, IL: Northwestern University Press.

Rorty, R.
(1989). *Contingency, irony, and solidarity.* Cambridge: Cambridge University Press.

Roth, W-M.
(1995). *Authentic school science: Knowing and learning in open-inquiry science laboratories.* Dordrecht, The Netherlands: Kluwer Academic Publishers.

Roth, W-M.
(2002). *Being and becoming in the classroom.* Westport, CT: Greenwood.

Roth, W-M.
(2003). Scientific literacy as an emergent feature of human practice. *Journal of Curriculum Studies, 35,* 9–24.

Roth, W-M. & Lawless, D.
(2002). Signs, deixis, and the emergence of scientific explanations. *Semiotica, 138,* 95–130.

Roth, W-M. & Tobin, K.
(2002). *At the elbow of another: Learning to teach by coteaching.* New York: Peter Lang.

Shannon, C.
(1948). A mathematical theory of communication. *The Bell Systems Technical Journal, 27,* 379–423, 623–656.

Wittgenstein, L.
(1958). *Philosophical investigations,* 3rd ed. (G.E.M. Anscombe trans.). New York: MacMillan.

Author Index

Subject Index